D0849706

The period 1660–1780 saw major changes in the relationship between religion and ethics in English thought. In this first part of an important two-volume study, Isabel Rivers examines the rise of Anglican moral religion and the reactions against it expressed in nonconformity, dissent and methodism. Her study investigates the writings which grew out of these movements, combining a history of the ideas of individual thinkers (including both prominent figures such as Bunyan and Wesley and a range of lesser writers) with analysis of their characteristic terminology, techniques of persuasion, literary forms, and styles. The intellectual and social milieu of each movement is explored, together with the assumed audiences for whom the texts were written. The book provides an accessible, wide-ranging and authoritative new interpretation of a crucial period in the development of early modern religious and moral thought.

The Poetry of Conservatism 1600–1745: A Study of Poets and Public Affairs from Jonson to Pope (Cambridge: Rivers Press, 1973).

Classical and Christian Ideas in English Renaissance Poetry: A Students' Guide (London: Allen & Unwin, 1979).

Books and their Readers in Eighteenth-Century England (editor) (Leicester: Leicester University Press, 1982).

CAMBRIDGE STUDIES IN EIGHTEENTH-CENTURY
ENGLISH LITERATURE AND THOUGHT 8

Reason, Grace, and Sentiment, I

CAMBRIDGE STUDIES IN EIGHTEENTH-CENTURY ENGLISH LITERATURE AND THOUGHT

General Editors: Dr HOWARD ERSKINE-HILL, Litt.D., FBA, *Pembroke College, Cambridge*
and Professor JOHN RICHETTI, *University of Pennsylvania*

Editorial Board: Morris Brownell, *University of Nevada*
Leopold Damrosch, *Harvard University*
J. Paul Hunter, *University of Chicago*
Isobel Grundy, *University of Alberta*
Lawrence Lipking, *Northwestern University*
Harold Love, *Monash University*
Claude Rawson, *Yale University*
Pat Rogers, *University of South Florida*
James Sambrook, *University of Southampton*

The growth in recent years of eighteenth-century studies has prompted the establishment of this series of books devoted to the period. The series is designed to accommodate monographs and critical studies on authors, works, genres and other aspects of literary culture from the later part of the seventeenth century to the end of the eighteenth. Since academic engagement with this field has become an increasingly interdisciplinary enterprise, books will be especially encouraged which in some way stress the cultural context of the literature, or examine it in relation to contemporary art, music, philosophy, historiography, religion, politics, social affairs, and so on.

Titles published

Reason, Grace, and Sentiment

A Study of the Language of Religion and Ethics
in England, 1660–1780

VOLUME I
WHICHCOTE TO WESLEY

ISABEL RIVERS

Fellow of St Hugh's College, Oxford

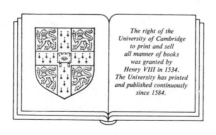

The right of the
University of Cambridge
to print and sell
all manner of books
was granted by
Henry VIII in 1534.
The University has printed
and published continuously
since 1584.

CAMBRIDGE UNIVERSITY PRESS

Cambridge

New York   Port Chester   Melbourne   Sydney

Published by the Press Syndicate of the University of Cambridge
The Pitt Building, Trumpington Street, Cambridge CB2 1RP
40 West 20th Street, New York, NY 10011, USA
10 Stamford Road, Oakleigh, Melbourne 3166, Australia

First published 1991

Printed in Great Britain at the University Press, Cambridge

British Library cataloguing in publication data
Rivers, Isabel
Reason, grace, and sentiment: a study of the language of
religion and ethics in England, 1660–1780.
Vol.1, Whichcote to Wesley
1. England. Religious movements, history
I. Title
291.0942

Library of Congress cataloguing in publication data
Rivers, Isabel.
Reason, grace, and sentiment: a study of the language of religion
and ethics in England, 1660–1780 / Isabel Rivers.
p.   cm. – (Cambridge studies in eighteenth-century English
literature and thought ; 8–)
Includes bibliographical references and index.
Contents: v. 1. Whichcote to Wesley.
ISBN 0–521–38340–4 (v. 1)
1. Religious thought – England – 17th century. 2. Religious
thought – England – 18th century. 3. England – Church history – 17th
century. 4. England – Church history – 18th century. 5. Christian
ethics – England – History – 17th century. 6. Christian ethics-
England – History – 18th century. 7. England – Intellectual
life – 17th century. 8. England – Intellectual life – 18th century.
I. Title. II. Series: Cambridge studies in eighteenth-century
English literature and thought: 8, etc.
BR756.R58 1991
209′.42′09032–dc20   90–35459 CIP

ISBN 0 521 38340 4

In memory of my father
Anthony Haigh
1907–1989

Contents

Preface

I have been working on this study since the early 1970s, though my love of the English moralists dates back at least to 1964–5, when I took the paper of that name in Part 2 of the Cambridge English Tripos. I am grateful to the Mistress and Fellows of Girton College for electing me to the Ottilie Hancock Research Fellowship, 1970–3, thus enabling me to begin my work, and also for allowing me to stay in college during periods of leave in 1979 and 1983. I should also like to thank the University of Leicester for granting me those periods of leave, and its Research Board for financial support while I stayed in Cambridge. The Principal and Fellows of St Hugh's College kindly granted me further periods of leave in 1987 and 1989, thereby enabling me to complete Volume I. My reading was largely done in the Cambridge University Library, Leicester University Library, the London Library, Dr Williams's Library, and the Bodleian. I am grateful to all these institutions, particularly the London Library and Dr Williams's, in which it is always such a pleasure to work. The generous lending policy of the London Library has made my task much easier.

I have been unbelievably lucky in the critical interest shown in my work by the three scholars who have read and commented on the book in detail: Dr J. D. Walsh, of Jesus College, Oxford (especially Chapter 5), the Rev. Dr G. F. Nuttall (especially Chapters 3 and 4) and Dr N. H. Keeble, of the University of Stirling (the whole volume). They have proved an ideal audience. Where I have disagreed with them, I have thought carefully about my reasons for doing so. I should also like to thank Dr John Spurr and Dr Roger Fallon for making me rethink aspects of Chapter 2.

The first version of Chapter 5 appeared in *Prose Studies*, IV (1981), and material from the Introduction in M. Coyle *et al.*, eds., *Encyclopaedia of Literature and Criticism* (1990), from Chapters 2 and 3 in N. H. Keeble, ed., *John Bunyan: Conventicle and Parnassus* (1988), and from Chapters 4 and 5 in I. Rivers, ed., *Books and their Readers in Eighteenth-Century England* (1982). I tried out some of my ideas in an undergraduate seminar I ran with the late Ian Hilson at the University of Leicester from 1975 to 1980, and also in papers I gave at conferences at Newcastle upon Tyne Polytechnic in 1983 and 1986.

In its original form this study would have appeared at half its projected length. I am grateful to Dr Howard Erskine-Hill and the Cambridge

University Press for agreeing to publish it in two volumes, thus giving me the opportunity of attempting to do justice to a very complex subject.

Successive tutors' secretaries at St Hugh's, Laura Marsland and Ria Audley-Miller, have wordprocessed my mixture of typescript and manuscript with great efficiency. Deborah Quare, Librarian of St Hugh's, very helpfully suggested the jacket illustration.

During the long stages of reading and writing Tom Rivers has cheerfully urged me to press on. I much regret that I did not finish in time for Anthony Haigh to read 'The Three Graces'.

Abbreviations

All titles in the notes are given in shortened form; full titles (except for journals) will be found in the Bibliography. Titles reduced to initials are given below.

ATR	*Anglican Theological Review*
BQ	*Baptist Quarterly*
DNB	*The Dictionary of National Biography*
EHR	*English Historical Review*
ES	*English Studies*
HJ	*Historical Journal*
HLQ	*Huntington Library Quarterly*
JEH	*Journal of Ecclesiastical History*
JHI	*Journal of the History of Ideas*
JHP	*Journal of the History of Philosophy*
JURCHS	*Journal of the United Reformed Church History Society*
LH	*Literature and History*
LQHR	*The London Quarterly and Holborn Review*
MLQ	*Modern Language Quarterly*
MP	*Modern Philology*
NQ	*Notes and Queries*
PS	*Prose Studies*
PWHS	*Proceedings of the Wesley Historical Society*
RB	Richard Baxter, *Reliquiae Baxterianae* (1696)
TCHS	*Transactions of the Congregational Historical Society*

Introduction

This book is the first of two volumes dealing with the changes in the ways in which the relationship between religion and ethics was perceived in the period from the mid-seventeenth to the later eighteenth centuries by different religious and secular movements, denominations, and individuals, and the kinds of language in which these changes were expressed. Broadly speaking, two crucial shifts in ideas took place in this period. The first is an emphasis in Anglican thought on the capacity of human reason and free will to co-operate with divine grace in order to achieve the holy and happy life. This optimistic portrait of human nature represents a rejection of the orthodox Reformation tradition, which stresses the depravity of human nature and God's arbitrary exercise of his free grace in electing the few to salvation. The second is the attempt to divorce ethics from religion, and to find the springs of human action not in the co-operation of human nature and divine grace but in the constitution of human nature alone. The first shift comes to represent a new orthodoxy, and its effects in the period are very wide-reaching; the second shift, which in part arises from the first, remains heterodox in the period under consideration but its long-term influences are incalculable. Volume I deals with the rise in the second half of the seventeenth century of Anglican moral religion and the reaction against it of movements which attempted in different ways to continue or return to the Reformation protestant tradition in response to what was seen to be its betrayal by the Church of England. This volume essentially explores the tension between the languages of reason and grace. Volume II will deal with movements which took up ideas implicit in Anglican moral religion and developed them in the direction of naturalism, scepticism, and sentimental ethics, to which Anglican thinkers were necessarily hostile although they had to some extent prepared the ground which made these developments possible. It will essentially explore the tension between the languages of reason and sentiment.

Although 1660 and 1780 are the limiting dates of this study I have inevitably looked before and after. The re-establishment of the Church of England at the Restoration in effect guaranteed the dominance of moral, rational religion and the defeat of Reformation orthodoxy, but the struggle between competing versions of protestant thought goes back as far as the

1

mid-sixteenth century, and the underlying tensions are as old as Christianity. In the first chapter of Volume I I summarise the central disputes of the mid century and the principal religious and ethical traditions on which English thinkers drew, and I explore briefly some religious works of the 1640s and 1650s which are significant because they epitomise the main conflicting positions and continue to be widely read and influential for the next hundred years. I have not dealt with writers of the 1640s and 1650s who, for whatever reason, were no longer read and disappeared from view in the later seventeenth and eighteenth centuries. The second chapter concentrates on the period 1660–1700 and the work of the group within the Church of England sometimes pejoratively termed latitude-men, especially Whichcote, Wilkins, Barrow, Tillotson, Fowler, Patrick, and Glanvill, who were largely responsible for defining and popularising the changes of emphasis in Anglican thought. The rest of the book is concerned with different kinds of response to the new orthodoxy. Chapter 3 explores nonconformist thought from the 1660s to the 1690s and its origins in the 1640s and 1650s, and contrasts the views of Baxter and Bunyan, who were the major representatives of different types of nonconformity and who reacted in very different ways to changes in the Church of England, though their religious views overlap more than might be expected. Chapter 4 is concerned with the development of dissent in the first half of the eighteenth century, and the ways in which Watts and Doddridge, its most influential writers, tried to reconcile different tendencies in dissenting thought and yet remain true to the protestant tradition. The final chapter looks at the thought of John Wesley from the 1730s to the 1780s, and his attempt, drawing on many different traditions, to reform the Church of England from within and to create a new synthesis of the competing elements his predecessors had juggled with. Volume II will conclude with an account of the later eighteenth century, and will look forward to the developments, as the first chapter of Volume I looks back to the antecedents, of the religious and ethical conflicts explored in the two books.

I have chosen to analyse these particular writers in detail in Chapters 2 to 5 of this volume for two reasons: because in terms of the nature of their arguments and the extent of their influence they seem to me to be undeniably the most important, and because I have found them the most interesting. They are all, despite their different approaches, aware of the complexity of the terms and ideas they deal with and careful to treat them with subtlety, and I have tried to do each of them justice. My detailed concentration on their work has resulted in the exclusion of representatives of several other traditions who have a place in the story: the reader will find no prolonged attention to Roman Catholics, non-jurors, high-church Anglicans, or Quakers. However, I am confident that my account does not misrepresent the central developments in the period.

My subject is the language of religious and moral prose, and my methods are those of the literary historian of ideas.[1] I have concentrated on language because I am interested in the history of religious and moral thought for its own sake, not in relation to another subject, such as science or politics, and because I believe that it is only through the careful study of language that meaning can be ascertained. I take 'language' in a broad sense to include terms and phrases, style, and rhetoric; I am thus concerned not only with the definition of certain ideas by a specific writer, but with the techniques of persuasion and the literary forms he employs. The development of ideas and languages from conflict between denominations or movements is particularly striking in this period. A good deal of the religious and ethical writing is polemical in character; members of particular movements tend to define their own positions in relation to what they see as the erroneous views and deceptive languages of their opponents, and are concerned to persuade their readers of the truth of their own ideas and the appropriateness of the manner in which they are expressed. In reading a given writer I have therefore asked the following questions: what form does the author employ (for example philosophical or theological treatise, popular handbook, essay, sermon, dialogue)? What are the implications of this choice of form? What is his purpose in writing? What does he take the function of books to be? What are his characteristic terms and arguments? Who else is using them in the same or different ways? What are his attitudes to language? Are they consistent with his practice? What is the intended audience of the work? Is there more than one (for example his intimates, his allies, those who already share his views, those whom he regards as dangerous, those whose views he intends to refute rationally or demolish polemically)? How does he treat his audiences? Do his ideas, arguments, terms, or style differ depending on the form he chooses or the audience he addresses? How does he respond to works addressed to him? Who are the authorities to whom he defers, or whom he recommends? Who are the rival authorities whom he attempts to dislodge? With what group does he identify himself? What label does he attach to himself? What is the origin of the label (his opponents, his allies, himself)? What use does he make of literary sources of different kinds? Is the language he uses peculiar to himself, that of a group to which he belongs, or the transmutation of the language of another group?

Each chapter (excluding the first chapter of Volume I and the last of Volume II) is divided into three parts: the first part provides an account of the social and intellectual milieu of the movement or thinker under discussion, taking account of ecclesiastical and political developments where relevant, with some biographical information; the second investigates kinds of book, circumstances of publication, intended audiences, literary assumptions, and style; the third (the most important) analyses ideas and their expression. This

[1] For a fuller statement see my 'Literature and the History of Ideas', in M. Coyle, *et al.*, eds., *Encyclopaedia of Literature and Criticism* (1990).

structure is designed to be as useful as possible to the reader. I have not taken the reader's knowledge of the period for granted, and I have not engaged in debate with recent historians of ideas. I hope this method of presentation will make the book accessible to undergraduates as well as scholars. Students of history, theology, and literature will probably find different kinds of material of interest to them, though my aim has been to cross twentieth-century disciplinary boundaries and to encourage my readers to do the same.

I have not tried to argue for the truth or falsehood of the views I have explored; I have not taken the side of dissenter against churchman, or of Arminian against Calvinist, or (in Volume II) of freethinker against Christian. But I have tried within my limitations as a twentieth-century secular reader to give a truthful account of what those views were and how they developed as they did. In this attempt I am attaching myself to the tradition inaugurated by Mark Pattison in his essay 'Tendencies of Religious Thought in England 1688–1750' (*Essays and Reviews*, 1860), which he describes in his *Memoirs* as the first 'scientific history of the self-development of opinion' to be published in this country. The hostility with which it was received – the reviewers 'were all busily occupied in finding or making contradictions between the writer's words and the thirty-nine articles' – led Pattison to abandon the study of religious thought,[2] but this essay was the starting point for Leslie Stephen's magisterial *History of English Thought in the Eighteenth Century* (1876), as Stephen acknowledges in the Preface. No serious student of the relationship between religious and moral thought in the eighteenth century can afford to neglect Stephen's account. Since their day there has been a wealth of historical investigation of the kind Pattison called for, some of the best of it by representatives of particular denominations, notably Frank Baker, G. R. Cragg, H. R. McAdoo, and G. F. Nuttall. I have drawn widely on the work of these and other historians of seventeenth- and eighteenth-century thought, as the notes and bibliography show, but I hope that in my concentration on language I have succeeded in giving the subject a new interest and emphasis.

[2] Pattison, *Memoirs* (1969, first published 1885), 314–15.

1

The conflict of languages in the mid-seventeenth century

certain it is that words, as a Tartar's bow, do shoot back upon the understanding of the wisest, and mightily entangle and pervert the judgement. So as it is almost necessary, in all controversies and disputations, to imitate the wisdom of the mathematicians, in setting down in the very beginning the definitions of our words and terms, that others may know how we accept and understand them, and whether they concur with us or no. For it cometh to pass, for want of this, that we are sure to end there where we ought to have begun, which is, in questions and differences about words.

Bacon, *The Advancement of Learning* (1605)[1]

the *Contentions* of the Clergie have done far more hurt to the Christian World, than the most bloody Wars of Princes ... those few that at great cost and labour come to the bottom of the differences do perceive, that the *Proud Opinionators* have striven partly about *unrevealed* or *unnecessary* things, but chiefly about *meer ambiguous words* and *arbitrary humane notions*; and multitudes condemn and revile each other, while they mean the same things, and do not know it.

Baxter, *Catholick Theologie* (1675)[2]

The modern reader of religious and moral writing in the mid-seventeenth century rapidly becomes aware of paradox: the extraordinary range and diversity of appeals to religious and moral authority in the period is combined with widespread confidence that apparent conflict can be resolved if only language is employed as it should be. The sources of authority, human and divine, are variously defined as reason, the light of nature, common notions, conscience, grace, Scripture, the Spirit, tradition, and human learning. For some, the more original and untypical of seventeenth-century moralists and controversialists, whose work provoked hostility at the time but which has proved of most interest to modern readers, these authorities are necessarily incompatible, and only a few of them can be authentic. Thus at one extreme of

---

[1] Ed. Johnston (1974), 128.
[2] 'The Preface, against Clergie Mens Contentions, and Church-distracting controversies', a3ᵛ, c5.

the spectrum the reason and common notions shared by all men may be held up as the only universal moral authority in opposition to the corruptions of tradition and the written word, as they are by the so-called first deist, Lord Herbert;[3] or at the other extreme the Spirit speaking in all men, the light within, may be set not only against carnal human reason and learning but also above Scripture, as it is by the Quaker George Fox.[4] Writers of diametrically opposed views are certain that their linguistic methods will resolve religious and moral disputes and settle the foundations of religion and ethics. If only men will begin as in mathematics with the definition of names and give up the authority of 'an *Aristotle*, a *Cicero*, or a *Thomas* [Aquinas]', as the materialist philosopher Thomas Hobbes argues,[5] following Bacon, or if only they will speak the language of Canaan and the Holy Ghost, and reject the vanity of school theology and metaphysics, as the sectarian John Webster urges,[6] then the truth will be established. It is obvious to the modern reader that the differences between the extreme positions are real and insoluble, and not merely verbal. The differences in the centre of the spectrum are more subtle. For the majority of moralists and divines, all the sources of authority listed above are valid to varying degrees. Their problem is to establish the hierarchy of these authorities and to balance their respective claims. Thus the authority of Scripture is paramount, but Scripture must be interpreted with the aid both of the Spirit and of human reason and learning; grace regenerates the human faculties and makes all man's endeavours after good possible, but the faculties or powers of the soul – reason, understanding, conscience, will, affections – are themselves divine implantations. Emphasis on the operation of the Spirit may, but need not, be accompanied by distrust of human learning. Interest in classical ethics may, but need not, imply an optimistic view of human nature. For some there is tension and indeed conflict between the different sources of authority, whereas for others they exist in a dependent relationship. For the modern reader the problem is to determine the significance of these differences in emphasis and the implications of the language and rhetoric of individual writers for their religious and moral positions.

The forms this writing took and the audiences to whom it was addressed provide very important indicators of a writer's meanings, intentions, and influence. It might be primarily speculative or doctrinal, concerned with establishing the truth of specific ethical or religious positions, and take the form of a philosophical or theological treatise, perhaps written in Latin for an international educated audience. In some cases important works were subsequently translated into English to reach a wider readership, for example the puritan William Ames's *Medulla Sacrae Theologiae* (1627), translated after his death and published by parliamentary order as *The Marrow of Sacred*

---

[3] *De Veritate* (1624); *De Religione Laici* (1645).
[4] *Journal* (1694), ed. Nickalls (1975), 17, referring to the year 1647.
[5] *Leviathan* (1651), ed. Macpherson (1968), 105–6.   [6] *Academiarum Examen* (1654), 8, 10.

Divinity (1642). It might take the form of a public creed or confession compiled by many hands, such as the *Confession of Faith* and *Larger and Shorter Catechisms* (1647) produced by the Westminster Assembly of Divines to replace the Thirty-Nine Articles of the Church of England. Or such writing might be primarily controversial, designed to refute the views of opponents or persuade a particular group of readers of the truth of a particular position. Some works might be both doctrinal and controversial in form, for example the Anglican William Chillingworth's *The Religion of Protestants a Safe Way to Salvation* (1638), which develops a very important theory of the rational interpretation of revelation in the extremely unpalatable (for the modern reader) but common form of a point by point refutation, in this case of a Jesuit work. One danger of controversial literature, of which the modern reader should be constantly aware, is that controversialists tend to simplify their opponents' views; such accounts should not be accepted at face value unless corroborated by the statements of those under attack. The rhetoric of controversy sometimes has the effect of pushing apart positions which are closer than they appear to be. Finally, religious and moral writing might be primarily practical, concerned to teach the reader how to practise the Christian life, and designed for many different kinds of audience, both learned and popular.[7] Such writing almost always has a significant doctrinal content. It might take the form of a popular devotional and doctrinal handbook, such as Lewis Bayly's much reprinted and influential *The Practice of Pietie* (c. 1612). The religious best-sellers of the later seventeenth century were largely of this kind.[8] Or it might take the form of the printed sermon, perhaps the most important medium for the dissemination of religious and moral thought to the general reader. Although there were crucial differences between adherents of the puritan–nonconformist tradition and of the prelatical wing of the Church of England as to the centrality or otherwise of the sermon in divine service – the *Directory for the Publique Worship of God*, published by parliamentary order in 1644 to replace the Elizabethan Book of Common Prayer and its prescribed liturgy, calls the preaching of the word 'the power of God unto Salvation [Romans 1:16], and one of the greatest and most excellent Works belonging to the Ministry of the Gospel'[9] – clergy, ministers and lay preachers of all persuasions used the printed sermon to propagate their interpretation of the problematic relationship between religion and ethics, or, to use the biblical and contemporary phrase, faith and works. The modern reader should give careful attention to tone and emphasis, to what is stressed and what omitted, in order to establish not only the argument but the tendency of the work in hand: in particular the reader needs to be aware of what is taken for granted, the unstated moral and theological assumptions to

[7] See Baxter's classification of his own books into doctrinal, practical, and controversies (with subheadings) in *Compassionate Counsel to all Young Men* (1681), Keeble, *Baxter* (1982), 157.

[8] See Sommerville, *Popular Religion* (1977), Chapter 3.   [9] *Directory* (1644), 27.

which the preacher appeals, even the unacknowledged quotations from authors it might not be appropriate to name.

The central dispute about the sources of moral and religious authority and the appropriate language for expressing them is very conveniently summarised in a fascinating series of letters that passed in 1651 between two Cambridge divines, Anthony Tuckney (1599–1670) and Benjamin Whichcote (1609–83).[10] Tuckney, Presbyterian, Calvinist, one-time member of the Westminster Assembly and co-author of the *Larger and Shorter Catechisms*, and now Master of Emmanuel College, wrote to Whichcote, his former pupil and now Provost of King's and Vice-Chancellor of the university, to complain of the unorthodox implications of his weekly lectures (i.e. sermons) and their dangerous consequences for the students: 'we fear, the truth of Christ, much dearer than dearest friends, hath bin and may be prejudiced; and so young ones in the universitie tainted, and others greeved, by a vein of doctrine; which runnes up and down in manie of Your discourses'. Tuckney criticises Whichcote for his favourite terms and phrases – ingenuous, nature, reason, *recta ratio*, for his supposed reliance on philosophy, metaphysics, and the writings of rational Anglicans such as Hooker, Chillingworth, and Hammond, for his sympathy for the virtuous heathen, for his apparent misuse of Scripture, and above all for his slighting of grace and the doctrine of justification by faith. These views and habits have led some to charge Whichcote with following in the footsteps of Socinians and Arminians – 'those very things, which You hint, They dilate'. Whichcote deftly sidesteps Tuckney's criticisms about influences and labels, but he confronts the central issue about the nature of man and the relationship between religion and ethics unhesitatingly. Where Tuckney wishes that preachers would choose texts that treat 'of the advancing of Faith above Reason, and of the Impotencie and Weakness of Nature; rather than the Power of itt', Whichcote insists, 'I count itt true sacriledge, to take from God; to give to the Creature: yett I look att itt, as a dishonouring God, to nullify and make base his workes; and to think Hee made a sorrie worthless peece, fitt for no use; when hee made man.'[11]

This correspondence is important because it refers to many (though not all) of the principal intellectual traditions and religious positions available to an educated English protestant in the mid century, and it makes clear just what the issues at stake were felt to be. The principal traditions on which such a reader and thinker might draw were classical ethics, especially Plato, Aristotle, Cicero, and Seneca; the church fathers, especially Augustine; medieval scholasticism, especially Aquinas, and its continuation in the

---

[10] First published by Salter as Whichcote, *Eight Letters* (1753); see further discussion in Chapter 2 below, also in Culverwell, *Light of Nature*, ed. Greene and MacCallum (1971), Introduction, xlii; Greene, 'Whichcote' (1981); Powicke, *Cambridge Platonists* (1926), Chapter 2; Roberts, *Puritanism to Platonism* (1968), Chapter 2; Tulloch, *Rational Theology* (1872), II, Chapter 2.

[11] *Eight Letters*, 18, 27, 37–8, 80, 97, 112–13.

sixteenth and seventeenth centuries by Roman Catholic thinkers such as
Suarez; the humanist tradition, especially Erasmus; continental Reformation
theology, especially Calvin and Beza; English puritanism, especially Perkins
and Ames; modifications of the Calvinist tradition by the French Huguenot
Amyraut (Amyraldus) and the school of Saumur; repudiations of aspects of
Calvinism by the Dutch Arminius and his followers the Remonstrants,
especially Grotius, and by opponents of puritanism in the Church of England,
especially Hooker, Chillingworth, and Hammond; Polish Socinianism
(named after Socinus), a heretical form of Christian rationalism and antitrini-
tarianism; and English antinomianism, an extreme and widely criticised form
of Calvinism, whose adherents were alleged to believe that Christians are free
from the moral law.[12] In controversial writing contemporaries freely and often
inaccurately bandied about the labels Pelagian, Socinian, papist, and Arminian on the one side, for those who emphasised reason, free will, capacity for
moral choice, and conditions for justification, and Calvinist and antinomian
on the other side, for those who emphasised human depravity, predestination,
free grace, and justification by faith alone. Those on the Calvinist wing warned
of a slippery slope leading from Arminianism, Socinianism and Pelagianism to
infidelity and atheism; conversely, those on the Arminian wing saw a different
but equally dangerous slope leading from Calvinism and antinomianism to
irrationality, enthusiasm, libertinism, and atheism. But it is important to
remember that these labels are almost always pejorative, and that individual
writers rarely use them of themselves. The only one of these labels of which
polemicists do not seem to have been ashamed is Calvinist, as Tuckney makes
clear; he agrees with Whichcote in preferring to be called a Christian, 'yett,
when diversities of judgements have unhappilie begotten diversities of
denominations; I had rather, by reason of my adhaering to the truth, that
CALVINE maintained; men shoulde call mee a Calvinist; than by reason of
eyther an indifferencie, or by a propending to somthing that Socinians or
Arminians hold; men, though unjustlie and sinfullie, shoulde besmeare me
with their appellation'.[13] The diversities of judgement were complex, and it is
more useful at this stage to consider briefly the central concepts that were at
issue than to attempt to define and differentiate a series of denominational
positions.

The disputes, which are essentially about the nature of the relationship
between man and God, centre on the respective parts played by reason and
faith as the basis of knowledge of God, and by faith and works as the basis of

[12] Useful studies of some of these traditions include: Fiering, *Moral Philosophy* (1981); Kendall,
English Calvinism (1979), Miller, *New England Mind* (1939), and Wallace, *Puritans and
Predestination* (1982); Armstrong, *Calvinism and the Amyraut Heresy* (1969); McAdoo, *Spirit of
Anglicanism* (1965), Trevor-Roper, *Catholics, Anglicans, and Puritans* (1989), Chapters 2 and 4,
and Tulloch, *Rational Theology* (1872); Harrison, *Beginnings of Arminianism* (1926) and *Armi-
nianism* (1937); McLachlan, *Socinianism* (1951) and Wilbur, *Unitarianism* (1946 and 1952).

[13] *Eight Letters*, 79.

the Christian life. Related disputes concern the extent of human passivity or activity in relation to divine action, and the subordinate or central status of ethics in religion. The orthodox Reformation account (usually called Calvinism) can be summarised as follows.[14] The first man, Adam, created by God in his own image, was possessed of perfectly integrated faculties and was capable of perfect obedience to the law of God. Adam's original sin, his freely chosen disobedience, has burdened the human race with calamitous consequences. Human nature is now corrupt: the faculties are so depraved that man is incapable of obedience to the law and can only choose to sin. For this continuing disobedience, this inability to act with righteousness, God has justly condemned the human race to a double death, the mortality of the body and the eternal damnation of the soul. However, through his mercy God grants a measure of undeserved freedom from this punishment. The majority of mankind, the reprobate, are justly condemned for sin, but the elect few are predestined for salvation, not for any merit that God foresees in them, but by his own free grace. This is achieved through the process of redemption by God's greatest gift to man, his Son. Through his death and his perfect obedience Christ takes on man's sin and pays the penalty for it, though he is inherently sinless, and imputes to man his righteousness, though man is inherently unrighteous. God accepts Christ's imputed righteousness or merits as man's, and thus grants man salvation. Man is thus saved not by his own efforts but by God's grace; he is justified, i.e. accepted by God as righteous despite his unrighteousness, by faith alone, by trust that God will fulfil the promises of the gospel made to his elect. The elect man is now regenerate, freed from the consequences of his corrupt nature, though many traces of that nature remain. He is granted perseverance so that he can continue in a state of grace. As a consequence of his justified state he performs good works and lives a sanctified life, and hence has evidence that he is of the elect, but his works contribute nothing to his justification: they are its fruit, not its cause. Within the limits of his nature he obeys the moral law, not slavishly through fear but freely through love. In this life he is not fully sanctified, i.e. morally perfect, he is still liable to occasional sin, and he may not always have full assurance of his election, but despite doubts and backslidings he does not fall from the state of grace.

From the point of view of the modifiers and opponents of this tradition, the Calvinist account of religion and ethics exaggerates the gap between God and man, the opposition between grace and nature, the weakness of the fallen human faculties, and the passivity of man in the process of salvation, removes the freedom of the will and human responsibility for action, elevates justification above sanctification, feeling above practice, and faith above holiness, and makes God, in his arbitrary election of the few and reprobation of the rest,

---

[14] Adapted from Rivers, *Classical and Christian Ideas* (1979), Chapter 8.

the author of sin. Conversely, in the account loosely called Arminian, man is free to work out his own salvation in co-operation with grace.[15] Christ died for all, not simply for the elect; grace is offered to all, and the elect are those who God foresees will accept grace and have faith. Faith is not granted freely, without regard to human action, but is conditional on repentance; it consists not only in trust, but also in obedience. Justification and sanctification are therefore closely allied; works are not simply the consequence of faith, but a necessary part of it. In both accounts faith and holiness are inseparably connected, but in the Calvinist account the stress is on faith, with holiness as the fruit, whereas in the Arminian account the stress is on holiness, with faith as the forerunner. The human faculties, although impaired by the fall, are not wholly vitiated; right reason, which is as much a gift of God as faith, can enable man to know God and discern the good, although he cannot follow the good without the help of grace. Christ stands in relationship to man not only as redeemer but also as example of perfect faith and obedience for him to imitate. The process of salvation involves constant human effort and choice, and it is always possible for man to fall from grace through his own fault. From the Calvinist point of view, this account overvalues the creature at the expense of the creator: it places too much emphasis on human reason, choice, and action, and not enough on God's inexplicable mercy to sinners who are utterly undeserving of his grace.

These summaries of the central disputes inevitably simplify very complex arguments, and overemphasise the differences between the positions. To some extent this is an accurate reflection of the effect that the extraordinary political and ecclesiastical changes of the 1640s and 1650s had on religious and moral thought. Indeed from the 1620s through to the 1660s there is a constant pendulum from one account to the other. In the 1620s the official position of the English Church, despite the occasional surfacing of contrary views, was Calvinist; it was hostile to the Dutch Arminians, the Remonstrants, whose doctrines were condemned at the Synod of Dort in 1619.[16] In the 1630s Charles I and Archbishop Laud provoked doctrinal controversy by their support for Arminian views together with an exalted conception of episcopacy; in the early 1640s, with the execution of Laud and the defeat of his programme for the Church, Calvinist views dominated again and were codified in the Westminster *Confession*. In the late 1640s and 1650s, during the period of religious experimentation that was encouraged by the victory of the Independents in the Civil War and the relative tolerance intermittently exercised by the Cromwellian regime, Calvinism was challenged by three distinct groups: the sequestrated Church of England clergy, who would not

[15] Studies which usefully contrast aspects of these accounts are Allison, *Rise of Moralism* (1966); McGee, *Godly Man* (1976); New, *Anglican and Puritan* (1964).

[16] See Tyacke, *Anti-Calvinists* (1987). The best study of the shifts in position in the mid century is Wallace, Chapters 3 and 4.

accept the abolition of the liturgy and who attacked the doctrine as well as the ecclesiastical discipline of their opponents; the radical sects, who would not accept the authority of the Calvinist clergy and who developed aspects of the doctrine of grace in some very unexpected directions; and some of the younger generation of clergy, who conformed to the new church discipline but who turned away from Calvinist doctrine with distaste. In the 1660s, with the re-establishment of the Church of England, Calvinism came to be perceived very largely as nonconformist and Arminianism as conformist doctrine, despite the exceptions on each side. It is to be expected that these ecclesiastical and political differences would have the effect of exacerbating theological and ethical differences and concealing common ground.

Both the divergences and the contiguities can be seen from a brief comparison of certain key texts from each side in the dispute. The examples are chosen not from controversial literature but from practical works influential at the time which continued to hold their own, in some cases well into the eighteenth century, and which were almost all valued in different ways by the writers with whom this book is principally concerned. They are, on the puritan/Calvinist side, Lewis Bayly's handbook *The Practice of Pietie* (c. 1612), the Westminster *Confession of Faith* and *Larger Catechism* (1647), and two sermon collections, Thomas Goodwin's *A Child of Light Walking in Darknesse* (1636) and Edmund Calamy's *The Godly Mans Ark* (1657). On the Anglican/Arminian side, they are Henry Hammond's *A Practical Catechisme* (1644) and two handbooks, Jeremy Taylor's *Holy Living* (1650) and the anonymous *Practice of Christian Graces* (1658), better known by its subtitle *The Whole Duty of Man* and usually attributed to Richard Allestree.[17] From their different perspectives these works confront the central problem of the relationship between religion and ethics.

The earliest of these works, *The Practice of Pietie*, is designed to provide a compendium of doctrine and a detailed guide to the conduct of daily life, 'directing a Christian how he may walk all the day with God',[18] to meditation and prayer, and to preparation for death. Many of the subjects and emphases later found in the principal nonconformist and dissenting guides, Baxter's *Christian Directory* (1673) and Doddridge's *Rise and Progress of Religion in the Soul* (1745), have their origin in *The Practice of Pietie*. It was a basic book in puritan households. Baxter recommends it to families in Part II, Chapter 21 of *A Christian Directory* among other puritan books 'which direct you in a course of daily communion with God, and ordering all your conversations' (i.e.

---

[17] *The Practice of Pietie, The Godly Mans Ark, Holy Living*, and *The Whole Duty of Man* figure in Sommerville, Chapter 3, 'The Religious Best Sellers of Restoration England'. See also Sommerville, Chapter 6, for an effective comparison of the two traditions. For Allestree's authorship see *DNB*, s.v. Dorothy, Lady Pakington; Elmen, 'Allestree' (1951).

[18] *Practice of Pietie* (1643 edn), 222. See Stranks, *Anglican Devotion* (1961), Chapter 2; Wakefield, *Puritan Devotion* (1957), Chapter 6.

behaviour).[19] It was one of two godly books Bunyan's first wife brought him on their marriage in about 1649, having inherited them from her father.[20] By the end of the century its style and theology had long been out of date for Anglican readers; Simon Patrick (two years older than Bunyan) describes rather condescendingly in his autobiography (written in the first decade of the eighteenth century) how his mother was 'bred up by the rules of the Practice of Piety, a book of great note in those days'.[21] Bayly is anxious to clarify the connection between predestinarian theology and the necessity for works. Doctrine and practice cannot be separated. In an interesting section on 'the hinderances which keep back a sinner from the practice of piety', Bayly lists a series of ways in which 'the grounds of religion' may be mistaken. These include thinking that good works are unnecessary and concluding from the doctrine of predestination that works of piety are in vain. Bayly insists that 'good works are the true fruits of a true faith', and that God has predestinated the means as well as the end (a recurrent argument in puritan works): 'If therefore upon thy calling thou conformest thy selfe to the *Word* and *example* of *Christ* thy master, and obeyest the good motions of the *holy Spirit*, in leaving sin, and living a godly life: then assure thy selfe that thou art one of those, who are *infallibly* predestinated to everlasting salvation.' Further on, in a section dealing with extraordinary practices of piety such as fasting, Bayly stresses that there is no merit in good works, but that the elect must do them to glorify God, to show themselves thankful for their redemption, to make sure their election, and to win others to Christian profession.[22] Thus works are necessary but subordinate. Without them there is no evidence of the operation of grace; they illustrate the truth of doctrine but have no intrinsic value.

This problem of balancing the doctrine of grace with practice, of giving due weight to the latter while not allowing it to derogate from the former, is manifest in the Westminster *Confession* and *Larger Catechism*.[23] The exposition of the relationship in these works was extremely important in shaping the thinking of generations of puritans, nonconformists, and dissenters. It should not be assumed, because the Long Parliament and the Westminster Assembly failed to establish a Presbyterian system of church government in the 1640s and because the Book of Common Prayer and Thirty-Nine Articles of the Church of England were reinstated in 1661–2, that the *Confession* and *Catechisms* disappeared from view. The *Confession* was adopted by the Congregational churches with modifications in the Savoy *Declaration of Faith and Order* of 1658, but, more important, the *Catechisms* played a central part in nonconformist and dissenting education. In an epistle to the reader prefacing

---

[19] Baxter, *Practical Works*, ed. Orme (1830), IV, 269. See also the recommendation in *The Poor Man's Family Book, Works*, XIX, 509.

[20] Bunyan, *Grace Abounding*, ed. Sharrock (1962), 8.   [21] Patrick, *Auto-biography* (1839), 3.

[22] *Practice of Pietie*, 146–9, 401–2.

[23] See Kendall, *English Calvinism*, Chapter 14 for the argument (perhaps overstated) that the Westminster doctrines of predestination and faith do not cohere.

the edition of 1658, the Presbyterian Thomas Manton quotes at length from a private letter (from Richard Baxter) recommending that families should proceed from the *Shorter* to the *Larger Catechisms* and thence to the *Confession*, and concluding: 'if they once understand these grounds of religion, they will be able to read other books more understandingly, and hear sermons more profitably, and confer more judiciously, and hold fast the doctrine of Christ more firmly, than ever you are like to do by any other course'.[24] The veneration in which the *Catechisms* were held is illustrated by Samuel Palmer's striking reply to the complaint made at the beginning of the eighteenth century by Samuel Wesley, high churchman, former nonconformist, and father of John Wesley, that the dissenting academies had produced no important works of philosophy and divinity: 'Our Catechism is a most compleat *System* of morality'.[25]

The grounds of religion are established in both the *Confession* and *Catechisms* by the accounts of God's unchangeable decrees and his free grace in predestinating, calling, justifying, adopting, sanctifying, and saving the elect.[26] Human faith and works are seen as a necessary link in a chain forged by God. Man is passive until called and quickened by the Spirit.[27] The account of faith stresses both that it is a free gift and that it involves human action. 'Faith, thus receiving and resting on Christ and his righteousnesse, is the alone instrument of Iustification; yet is it not alone in the person justified, but is ever accompanied with all other saving graces, and is no dead faith, but worketh by Love [James 2:20; Galatians 5:6].' (The phrase 'receiving and resting on Christ' is repeated several times to emphasise both the divine gift and the human response to it.)[28] The justified do good works for precisely the reasons adduced by Bayly: 'by them believers manifest their thankfulnesse, strengthen their assurance, edifie their Brethren, adorn the profession of the Gospel, stop the mouths of the adversaries, and glorifie God'.[29] The elect are sanctified, cannot fall from grace, will persevere to the end, and have assurance of their election; yet because of the remaining corruption of human nature sanctification is imperfect, the saints may fall into grievous sins, and assurance may be very hard to obtain:

True beleevers may have the assurance of their salvation divers wayes shaken, diminished, and intermitted, as, by negligence in preserving of it, by falling into some

---

[24] *Confession of Faith* (1855 edn), 9–10; see *RB*, Part I, 122 (I owe this identification to G. F. Nuttall). Cf. Baxter's recommendation that 'to methodise knowledge' families should proceed from the shorter to the larger catechism and thence to a body of divinity such as Ames's *Marrow*; *Christian Directory*, Part II, Chapter 21, *Practical Works*, ed. Orme, IV, 269. For editions and adaptations see Carruthers, *Westminster Shorter Catechism* (1957). John Wesley's edition in *A Christian Library*, XXXI (1753) and ed. Jackson, XIV (1822) deletes the predestinarian elements; see the edition by Macdonald (1906).

[25] S. Wesley, *Defence of a Letter* (1704), 2–3; Palmer, *Vindication* (1705), 93.

[26] *Confession*, Chapter 3; *Catechism*, qns 12–13. The questions are not numbered in early editions.

[27] *Confession*, Chapter 10; *Catechism*, qn 67.

[28] *Confession*, Chapter 11 (1650 edn), 26, Chapter 14; *Catechism*, qn 72.

[29] *Confession*, Chapter 16 (1650 edn), 32.

speciall sin, which woundeth the conscience, and grieveth the spirit: by, some sudden, or vehement temptation, by Gods withdrawing the light of his countenance, and suffering even such as fear him to walk in darknesse, and to have no light: yet are they never utterly destitute of that seed of God, and life of faith, that love of Christ and the brethren, that sincerity of heart, and conscience of duty, out of which, by the operation of the Spirit, this assurance may, in due time, be revived: and by the which, in the mean time, they are supported from utter despair.[30]

Though God's decrees are absolute and election is certain, the life of the elect is one of struggle, self-questioning, and uncertainty. Works must be performed as signs of election – yet the unregenerate may also perform good works, which in their case are sinful and unacceptable to God.[31] Nothing which has its origin in fallen human nature is of any value to salvation. The doctrine of grace thus has complex consequences for the status of ethics. On the one hand the source of all good is grace. Any moral system that posits a human origin for good action is fundamentally wrong. On the other hand grace manifests itself in works. Any interpretation of the doctrine of grace that slights human action or frees the regenerate from the obligations of the moral law is also fundamentally wrong. These are the poles of legalism and antinomianism that orthodox Calvinism is always struggling to avoid. Further, since works are only one of the means by which the regenerate can be sure of their election, feeling is potentially as important as practice. The doctrine of assurance encourages the examination of mental states as much as the practice of good works for evidence that the believer is in a state of grace. Assessing the relative importance of feeling and practice was to remain a considerable problem for the inheritors of the Calvinist tradition.

Some of these characteristic concerns can be briefly illustrated from the sermons of Edmund Calamy (1600–66) and Thomas Goodwin (1600–80), two of the principal spokesmen for the Presbyterians and Congregationalists respectively. Both Calamy and Goodwin were educated at Cambridge in the second decade of the century, a time when the dominance of Calvinist doctrine was beginning to be challenged, but both were resistant to Arminianism. Goodwin left a detailed autobiographical account (published posthumously by his son) of his experience of conversion under puritan teaching, in which he explained that though the Arminian doctrine of the freedom of the will to turn towards or away from God suited his experience in his unconverted state, it was not consonant with his observation that the godly held constantly to their religious principles and practices without falling away.[32] In the 1620s and 1630s both were preachers and lecturers, Goodwin, unlike Calamy, becoming a separatist and spending a brief period in exile in

---

[30] *Confession*, Chapters 13, 17, 18 (1650 edn), 27–8; *Catechism*, qns 78–81.
[31] *Confession*, Chapter 16.
[32] Goodwin, *Works*, V (1704), 'The Life of Dr. Thomas Goodwin', vi, x. See Haller, *Rise of Puritanism* (1957), 75–9, 94–6; Watkins, *Puritan Experience* (1972), 83–8.

Holland. By 1640 both were ministers of London churches. Both rose to prominence at this time, though they followed rather different paths. Calamy was one of the group calling themselves Smectymnuus (the vehement corporate pamphleteer against the bishops – his are the second two initials), and a member of the Westminster Assembly. He remained a conservative Presbyterian in his sympathies, opposed Cromwell, welcomed the return of Charles II, and refused the offer of a bishopric at the Restoration. His eldest son and grandson (named after him) were nonconformists, the latter famous as the eighteenth-century historian of nonconformity; two other sons were Church of England clergy.[33] Calamy is a significant representative of the group who attacked Laudian episcopacy with fury and were then shocked at the rise of the sects. Goodwin, also a member of the Westminster Assembly, was leader of the small but influential group of 'dissenting brethren' who opposed the Presbyterian system of church government. His importance grew with the triumph of Cromwell and the Independents. Whereas Calamy remained a London minister throughout the 1650s, Goodwin was President of Magdalen College, Oxford (where he ministered in his own house to a gathered church) and one of the chief proponents of the Savoy *Declaration*. At the Restoration he lost his Oxford post and returned with his church to London.

What characterises the chosen sermon collections of Goodwin and Calamy is a concentration on the exposition of the doctrine of grace through the details of the experience of individual believers, warning them against the temptations of false doctrines (legalism and antinomianism), and comforting and supporting them in their afflictions and doubts as to their status as children of God. This concern with the varied predicaments of individuals and the minister's responsibility to address himself to them was to remain a peculiar feature of the nonconformist and dissenting traditions. *The Directory for the Publique Worship of God* advises that before the sermon the minister should pray '*that hee may divide the Word of God aright, to every one his portion*' and its recommendations for preaching include the following: 'In applying Comfort, whether generall against all tentations, or particular against some speciall troubles or terrours, he is carefully to answer such objections, as a troubled heart and afflicted spirit may suggest to the contrary.'[34] Goodwin's *Child of Light Walking in Darknesse*, first published in 1636 but based on sermons preached eight years earlier, was reprinted several times in the 1640s, and continued to be read in the mid-eighteenth century; Doddridge in his *Lectures on Preaching* to his academy students recommends it as 'very useful for afflicted consciences'.[35] Goodwin sets out to show how, in what cases and

---

[33] Calamy (the third), *My Own Life* (1829), I, 56 ff.   [34] *Directory*, 26, 32–3.
[35] Doddridge, *Works*, ed. Williams and Parsons (1802–5), V, 431. Doddridge included *Child of Light* in the reading list he compiled for Wesley. See *Arminian Magazine*, I (1778), 421, and Doddridge, *Correspondence*, ed. Humphreys (1829–31) IV, 487. Wesley's abridgement appeared in *A Christian Library*, XI (1752) and ed. Jackson, VI (1820).

for what ends, God 'leaves his children to distresse of conscience'. Throughout, a crucial distinction is drawn between the gracious state of the true believer who is allowed by God to walk for a time in darkness but who will ultimately be assured of his salvation, and the false security of the unregenerate man who walks in the light of his own legal righteousness but will ultimately be punished for his mistake (Goodwin's text, Isaiah 50:10–11, contrasts the servant of the Lord who walks in darkness with those who walk in the light of the fire they have themselves kindled). Darkness essentially means '*distresse of conscience, and desertion in the want of assurance of justification*'; it is caused in different ways by the Spirit, by Satan, and by our own hearts. Under the last heading, Goodwin is particularly anxious to warn of the strength and danger of 'carnall and corrupt reason in men'. 'Carnal reason is the most desperate enemy to faith of all other principles in man. For untill faith be wrought, it is the most supreme principle; but then faith deposeth and subjecteth it, and afterwards doth often contradict it, yea excludes it, as unskilfull in its matters, from being of its counsell.' Paradoxically, reason is a danger in different ways both to the unregenerate and the regenerate: 'So that as in men whilest unregenerate, carnall reason endeavours by false reasonings to preserve a good opinion of their estates in them: In like manner the very same principle of carnall reason continuing its opposition to faith, doth as much persuade to a bad opinion of their estates when they are once regenerated.' Goodwin deals harshly and abruptly in the final section with the unregenerate man walking in the light of his own fire, his own reason, ingenuity, honesty, sobriety, and natural righteousness. The bulk of his analysis is devoted to comforting the afflicted believer with considerable sympathy and subtlety and to showing him how to recover the light.[36]

Calamy writes in the same tradition but with some interesting differences of emphasis. He is as strong a supporter of the doctrine of grace as Goodwin, but the intervening period of revolution and religious experimentation has made him wary of what he sees as its abuses. *The Godly Mans Ark*, first published in 1657 and reprinted many times up to the end of the century, is a collection based on a funeral sermon for one of Calamy's parishioners, '*whom God did pick out to make an example of great affliction, and great patience*'. It is designed to comfort those labouring under great tribulations and afflicted consciences by teaching them a 'real, right, and particular Application of the Promises'. In the dedication to his parishioners at St Mary's Aldermanbury Calamy provides them with rules and directions '*for the right ordering of your lives and conversations in these dangerous and divided times*'; the dedication is in effect a doctrinal and devotional handbook in miniature. Calamy stresses that doctrine must be lived as well as learnt. A true Christian should diffuse the grace God has given him. He is not merely a passive recipient of grace, but the

---

[36] Goodwin, *Child of Light*, in *Certaine Select Cases Resolved* (1647), 2, 4, 22, 25–6, 158–60.

active means whereby others receive it: '*A true Christian is like a* Needle touched with the Loadstone. *A* Needle *(truly touched) draweth another, and that will draw another, and that, another*: *Whosoever hath his* heart truly touched by effectual grace, will labour to convert others, and they, others.' He should labour to effect this chain of conversion in three ways: '*by* seasonable *and* religious admonitions, *and* exhortations; *by* communicating of experiences, *and especially by the* shining pattern of a holy life and conversation'. Calamy lays considerable emphasis on practice, but practice is not possible without right understanding. His parishioners must avoid as poison doctrines '*Which lift up* corrupt nature, *and exalt* unsanctified reason' (the temptation of Arminianism and Socinianism) and those '*which preach* free-grace, *to the utter ruine* of good works' (the temptation of antinomianism and libertinism). They must take heed of a threefold apostasy; in their judgements, from faith; in their affections, from love to the ordinances of the church; and in their conversations, '*from that humble and exact walking with God in all good duties, both towards God, and man, which was the credit, and honour of the good old Puritan in former daies*'. Doctrine, discipline, and practice are inseparable.[37]

For the beleaguered supporters of the episcopalian Church of England in the 1640s and 1650s, Calvinist doctrine, far from providing the grounds of religion from which practical holiness inseparably followed, was itself destructive of practice. Their central texts, Hammond's *Practical Catechisme*, Taylor's *Holy Living*, and *The Whole Duty of Man*, represent a very important shift in doctrine, argument, emphasis, and vocabulary, and the production of such texts was a deliberate attempt on the part of this group of Anglicans to undermine the assumptions of puritanism and transform popular religious opinion. Henry Hammond (1605–60), Jeremy Taylor (1613–67), and Richard Allestree (1619–81), the likely author of *The Whole Duty*, were prominent among a small number of clergy who were firm royalists, who were sequestered from their livings or expelled from their college fellowships (in some cases both) in the 1640s, who refused to compromise in any way with the Cromwellian Church in the 1650s, who were officially debarred in 1655 from preaching, teaching, and using the Book of Common Prayer (though in practice they had a certain amount of freedom), and who found protection as chaplains in royalist households which they used as centres for the defence of their religious position.[38] (Unlike these, the majority of the clergy accepted the changes in church organisation and retained their livings and posts even though some of them were out of sympathy with the prevailing doctrine.) Hammond was originally named a member of the Westminster Assembly, but like the other episcopalians nominated he refused to sit. He and Allestree were at Christ Church, Oxford, in the 1640s and expelled in 1648; he and Taylor served at different stages as chaplains to Charles I. He spent the decade of the

---

[37] Calamy, *Godly Mans Ark* (1658 edn), A2^v–A3^v, A4, b3, b3^v, b5–6^v.
[38] See Bosher, *Restoration Settlement* (1951), Chapter 1.

1650s at Westwood in Worcestershire, the house of Sir John Pakington, where he propagated his view of the church partly by his writings (scholarly, controversial, and practical) and partly, as his friend John Fell recounted in his biography, by providing the gentry with chaplains and schoolmasters and by giving financial support to selected university students and to the sequestered and exiled clergy.[39] Taylor spent the late 1640s and early 1650s at Golden Grove, Carmarthenshire, the house of the Earl of Carbery, where he wrote many of his doctrinal and practical works, including *Holy Living*; he was imprisoned briefly in the mid 1650s, spent some time in London, and in 1658 went to Ireland at the invitation of his new patron, Viscount Conway.[40] Allestree, about whom much less is known, lived privately in Oxford and in a gentry household near Banbury in the 1650s; in the same period he travelled abroad as a royalist agent, on one occasion being briefly imprisoned on his return.[41] Hammond, whom Charles II intended to make Bishop of Worcester, did not live to see the king's return, but after the Restoration Taylor became Bishop of Down and Allestree (who inherited Hammond's library) Regius Professor of Divinity at Oxford. Though Hammond had a very high view of episcopacy, his death was mourned as 'an unspeakable loss' by those, such as Gilbert Burnet and Baxter, who sympathised with his doctrinal but not his ecclesiastical views; both agreed that, as Baxter put it, 'his Piety and Wisdom would sure have hindred much of the violence which after followed'.[42]

Hammond published his *Practical Catechisme* anonymously in 1644; surprisingly, in view of his subsequent prolific output, he had originally intended it for private circulation and had to be persuaded to let it appear publicly.[43] Despite the fact that it is a much more intellectually demanding work than the popular *Holy Living* and *Whole Duty*, it was extremely influential. Burnet, recommending it to divinity students at the end of the century, observes that 'Dr. *Hammond's Practical Catechism*, is a Book of great Use; but not to be begun with, as too many do: It does require a good deal of previous Study, before the Force of his Reasonings is apprehended; but when one is ready for it, it is a rare Book, and States the Grounds of Morality, and of our Duty, upon true Principles.'[44] The grounds it states are emphatically not those of the puritan doctrinal compendium, Ames's *Marrow of Sacred Divinity* (1642), which it may have been intended to replace, nor of the forthcoming Westminster *Confession*. Simon Patrick found himself labelled an Arminian for using it to instruct his Cambridge pupils in the 1650s.[45] The ethical orientation of the *Catechisme* is clear from Hammond's statement about Christ's function in his 'Epistle to the

---

[39] Fell, *Life of Hammond* (1661), 74–7, 92, 142. See also Packer, *Transformation of Anglicanism* (1969), and Trevor-Roper, 215–27.

[40] See Stranks, *Taylor*, (1952).   [41] Allestree, *Forty Sermons* (1684), Preface [by Fell].

[42] Burnet, *History*, I (1724), 177; *RB*, II, 208.

[43] Fell, *Life of Hammond*, 32; Hammond, *Practical Catechisme* (1648 edn), A3ᵛ.

[44] Burnet, *Pastoral Care* (3rd edn, 1713), 150.

[45] *Auto-biography*, 26.

Reader'. The end of Christ's incarnation, death and resurrection was to redeem men from iniquity, and the design of his sermons when on earth was to make their righteousness exceed that of the Pharisees, '*in effect, the reformation of lives, & heightning of* Christian practice to the most elevated pitch, being the *one only design of all our* christianity'. Hammond unfairly accuses his opponents of seeing religion as a matter of speculation, not practice, '*so, that he that* knows *most, that* believes *most, is the onely* sanctified *person*'.[46] (Ames stresses that 'Divinity is practicall, and not a speculative discipline.')[47] In Book I Hammond is therefore concerned to redefine the nature of faith and the relationship between justification and sanctification. The Scholar explains to the Catechist that God's promises to man are conditional on his living well. Justifying faith 'is a cordiall sincere giving up your selfe unto God, particularly to Christ, firmly to rely on all his promises, and faithfully to obey all his commands delivered in the Gospel'. Hammond sees sanctification as divided into two parts. The first part, the beginning of a new life, precedes justification: '*i.e.* I must first believe, repent, and return ... before God will pardon'. The second part, the sanctified state or holy life, follows it. Hammond objects to the view that justification precedes repentance in part because 'this is apt to have an ill influence on practice, and therefore I thought fit to prevent it'. He describes the process of salvation as follows: by means of the Spirit and the word God calls a sinner to repentance. If he answers the call and resolves on a new life God justifies him and pardons his sins, then gives him more grace and 'assists him to *doe*, (as before he enabled to *will*) to perform his good resolutions'. If he continues in that state and those performances till death, he is rewarded with life. In Book IV section iii, entitled 'of Profession of Christianity without action', Hammond makes clear his hostility to what he sees as the tendency of puritan emphasis on experience: '*Hearing of Sermons*, and *professing of love* to, and *zeal* for *Christ*, may passe for piety a while, but in the end it will not be so. 'Tis *true Christian practice*, that will hold out in time of triall ... This doctrine of Christian duty and obedience is such that can never deceive any man that is content to build upon it.'[48]

Unsurprisingly, Hammond was attacked by a group of London ministers for his '*infamous and pernicious errours*' (including his belief that Christ died for all and his account of faith). He countered that he held nothing contrary to the Church of England.[49] But Hammond not only stated the grounds of religion and ethics very differently from the way in which they were understood in the Calvinist tradition, he also moved the emphasis of religious writing away from

[46] *Practical Catechisme*, A2, A3.
[47] Ames, *Marrow* (1642), 3; cf. Hammond's title page: '*Theologia est Scientia Affectiva, non Speculativa.*'
[48] *Practical Catechisme*, 7–9, 29, 67–71, 224.
[49] Hammond, *A Brief Vindication of Three Passages in the Practical Catechism from the Censures affixt on them by the Ministers of London* (1648, appended to *Practical Catechisme*), 2, 5, 9.

grace, justification by faith, regeneration, and the delineation of the experience of the godly.[50] In his doctrine the problem of assurance, which frequently
caused great pain and heart-searching to puritans, does not arise. His
characteristic terms – condition, repentance, duty, obedience, and performance – are central to the enormously popular and influential Anglican
handbooks of the 1650s, *Holy Living* (1650) and *The Whole Duty of Man*
(1658).[51] Though these works are concerned not with establishing the
grounds of religion but with guiding devotion and conduct, they take
Hammond's doctrine for granted. Taylor in his dedicatory epistle to the Earl
of Carbery insists that in describing religion 'I have neither served nor
disserved the interest of any party of Christians as they are divided by
uncharitable names from the rest of their brethren; and no Man will have
reason to be angry with me for refusing to mingle in his unnecessary or vitious
quarrels'. Yet Taylor's view of religion would have been utterly unacceptable
to a Calvinist. His opening chapter bypasses the question of human depravity
and lifts up corrupt nature in the way that Calamy warns against: 'It is
necessary that every Man should consider, that since God hath given him an
excellent nature, wisdom and choice, an understanding soul, and an immortal
spirit, having made him Lord over the Beasts, and but a little lower then the
Angels; he hath also appointed for him a work and a service great enough to
imploy those abilities'. For Taylor holy living is largely in the individual's own
hands. The general instruments of holy living are care of time, purity of
intention, and devotion. Following Paul's injunction to live 'soberly, righteously, and godly, in this present world' (Titus 2:11–12, a text that is also
central to *The Whole Duty*), Taylor divides Christian ethics – which 'is nothing
else but the Law of Nature and great Reason' – into three parts, sobriety,
justice, and religion, concerned respectively with 'all our deportment in our
personal and private capacities', 'our duty in all relations to our Neighbour',
and 'the offices of direct Religion, and entercourse with God'. Under the
heading of sobriety he attaches great importance to contentedness, 'the sum of
all the old moral Philosophy, and a great duty in Christianity', to which we
are bound 'by Reason and Religion, by duty and interest, by necessity and
conveniency, by example, and by the proposition of excellent rewards, no
lesse then peace and felicity'. Under the heading of religion he discusses faith,
hope, and charity, which 'make our duty to God and obedience to his
Commandments to be *chosen, reasonable,* and *delightful*', and repentance.[52]
Although it is no part of Taylor's plan to set out the essentials of the Christian
creed, the order and manner in which he treats these subjects is significant. In
Calvinist works the moral law and man's duty to God and his neighbour are

---

[50] This shift is deplored by Allison.
[51] They are analysed by Stranks, *Anglican Devotion*, Chapters 3–4, McAdoo, *Caroline Moral
Theology* (1949), Chapter 6, and Spurr, 'Anglican Apologetic' (1985), 190–2.
[52] *Holy Living* (1650) ¶7, 1, 61, 129, 228.

treated *after* God's acts towards man. Thus Ames's *Marrow* is divided into two books, the first dealing with faith, the second with observance; the *Larger Catechism* makes a clear transition at Question 91 from what the Scriptures teach concerning God to what they require as the duty of man. Taylor's account of faith in Chapter 4, section i is in its brevity and emphases deliberately controversial. He dismisses predestination, ignores justification, and defines faith in effect as a moral disposition: 'true faith is full of ingenuity, and hearty simplicity, free from suspicion, wise and confident, trusting upon generals without watching and prying into unnecessary or undiscernable particulars'. (Wesley in his edition of *Holy Living* comments: 'The reader will observe, this section is not clear, nor full.')[53] Repentance assumes far more importance in Taylor's scheme than in the Calvinist one (where it does of course play an important part): it 'containes in it all the parts of a holy life, from the time of return to the day of our death inclusively'.[54] It thus replaces regeneration, the shift in terms putting the emphasis firmly not on divine but human action.

The Whole Duty of Man was published anonymously in 1658 with a letter from Hammond, who appears to have been sent the sheets by the bookseller for endorsement, recommending it as equally fitted to 'the meanest capacities' and 'the best proficients' (Taylor aimed at the same double audience); the proficients would of course have recognised its underlying doctrinal assumptions. It was thus identified at the outset as an anti-Calvinist, anti-puritan work, and was evidently closely associated with Hammond's *Catechisme* at the time: the early eighteenth-century Arian William Whiston was told by his father 'that after the Restoration, almost all Profession of Seriousness in Religion would have been laughed out of countenance, under Pretence of the Hypocrisy of the former Times, had not two very excellent and serious books, written by eminent Royalists put some stop to it: I mean *The Whole Duty of Man* and Dr. Hammond's *Practical Catechism*'.[55] *The Whole Duty* had a huge readership in the later seventeenth and eighteenth centuries, and was widely distributed by organisations such as the Society for Promoting Christian Knowledge, but it had, understandably, a mixed reception from evangelicals.[56] It takes its subtitle from Ecclesiastes 12:13: 'Fear God, and keep his

---

[53] *Holy Living*, 229, 235; Wesley, *Christian Library*, ed. Jackson, IX (1820), 194. For Wesley's abridgement, first published in *Christian Library*, XVI (1752), see Rivers, ed., *Books and their Readers* (1982), 155.

[54] *Holy Living*, 333.

[55] Whiston, *Memoirs* (1729), 10; cited Packer, *Transformation of Anglicanism*, 27.

[56] George Whitefield objected in 1740 that he could not find 'the word Regeneration so much as once mentioned', Tyerman, *Life of Whitefield* (1876), I, 363; Henry Venn tried to supplant it with *The Complete Duty of Man* (1763). The anonymous *New Whole Duty of Man* (1741) was designed to contain *The Faith as well as Practice of a Christian* and supply *The Credenda of the Christian Religion, which are wanting in that Book tho' Essentially necessary to Salvation*. For Wesley's abridgement of and comments on the original version in *A Christian Library* see Chapter 5 below, p. 252.

commandments: for this is the whole duty of man.' This would have seemed a deliberately legalist choice, as is evident from Ames's comment on this text in *The Marrow of Sacred Divinity*: 'In the old Testament (fitly for that legall and servile estate) Divinity seemes sometime to be divided into the feare of God and observing of his Commandements'. Ames goes on to argue that 'by a metonymie faith is included in the former part', so that this text is used to support his position that faith and obedience are always joined together, but that faith holds the first place.[57] Allestree's main title, *The Practice of Christian Graces*, shows that his emphasis is firmly on the second part, obedience. Like Hammond, he states that no one can expect benefit from the scriptural promises unless he performs the condition attached, and that 'God hath given these *Promises*, to no other *end*, but to *invite* us to *holiness* of life'. The first partition establishes the basis of duty by the light of nature and Scripture (especially the Ten Commandments, the Sermon on the Mount, and Titus 2:11–12); the remaining partitions guide the reader through specific duties and virtues, showing him how to live a good life and thus fulfil the main purpose of Christ's coming into the world. Towards the end of the book Allestree stresses the pleasure that is to be derived from the practice of Christian graces, implicitly attacking the Calvinist concern with spiritual darkness and afflicted consciences, and striking the note that is to dominate in Anglican religious literature after 1660:

'Tis a special pollicy of *Satans*, to do as the *spies* did, *Num.* 23.28. [properly 13:32] bring up an ill report upon this good land, this *state of Christian life*, thereby to discourage us from entering into it, to fright us, with I know not what Gyants we shall meet with; but let us not thus be cheated, let us but take the courage to try, and we shall indeed finde it a *Canaan*, a *land flowing with milk and honey*: God is not in this respect to his people a *wilderness, a land of darkness, Jer.* 2.31. His service does not bereave men of any true joy, but helps them to a great deal: *Christs yoke is an easy*, nay a *pleasant yoke*, his *burden a light*, *yea a gracious burden* [Matthew 11:30]. There is in the practise of Christian duties a great deal of present pleasure . . .[58]

These two groups of texts, Calvinist and anti-Calvinist, are among the most popular of the religious works of the mid century that continued to be read for a considerable time thereafter and that helped in different ways to shape the Anglican, nonconformist, dissenting, and Methodist traditions. Four of the authors discussed in detail in the following pages, Wilkins, Baxter, Doddridge, and Wesley, were concerned not only with disseminating their own religious views but with keeping alive the traditions of seventeenth-century religious literature, by recommending, teaching, editing, and publishing the principal texts. Wilkins in *Ecclesiastes* (1646, revised in 1669), Baxter in *A Christian Directory* (1673), Doddridge in *Lectures on Preaching* (delivered in the 1730s and 1740s, but not published till 1804), and Wesley in his many publishing ventures from the 1730s onwards, including *A Christian Library*

[57] Ames, *Marrow*, 5.   [58] *Whole Duty* (1659 edn), 1, 3–4, 8, 382–3.

(1749–55), all publicised the religious writers of the mid-seventeenth century, sometimes distinguishing differences of doctrine or style, sometimes deliberately linking writers of contrary views.[59] The central puritan and Anglican traditions epitomised in this chapter see ethics as essential to religion – faith is not divorced from practice. Both have an equally demanding view of the holy life. Contrary to what their opponents allege, writers in the Arminian tradition do not disparage grace, and those in the Calvinist tradition do not ignore works. The differences are more complex than this: they involve emphasis, style, and language. Critics on each side are often afraid not so much of the actual assumptions of the group they oppose as of what they perceive to be the tendencies of these assumptions. The puritan/ nonconformist tradition emphasises God's acts and man's passivity, and hence tends to concentrate on how individuals respond in different ways to the operations of grace. The study of the human affections, how they function, how they can be aroused and directed in the service of God, becomes of central importance. The danger is that signs of grace, experiences, or 'frames' of feeling may take priority over good action. The Anglican tradition emphasises man's active relationship with God, his responsibility for the holy life, and hence tends to concentrate on human rationality and capacity to choose the good. The danger is that an ideally free, reasonable, and benign human type may be posited, and human weakness and difference underestimated. The chapters that follow explore the ways in which these traditions developed and these dangers were confronted in the next hundred and twenty years.

[59] For example, Wilkins lists among English divines eminent for sermons and practical divinity Thomas Goodwin, Hammond and Taylor in *Ecclesiastes* (1675 edn), 82; Baxter includes in his list of 'affectionate practical English writers' for students of divinity *The Practice of Pietie*, *The Whole Duty*, and the *Practical Catechism* in *Christian Directory*, Part III, qn 174, *Practical Works*, ed. Orme, V, 587; Doddridge, though recommending his students to read puritans, nonconformists, dissenters, and writers of the Established Church, does not include mid-century Anglicans in *Lectures on Preaching*, *Works*, ed. Williams and Parsons, V, Lectures 2–4; Wesley attempts to reconcile the differences between all the writers he includes in *A Christian Library*. These lists are compared (not always accurately) in Monk, *Wesley* (1966), Appendix I.

2

The religion of reason:
the latitude-men

none have with more strength of reason demonstrated, that the grand designe of the Gospel is to make men good: not to intoxicate their brains with notions, or furnish their heads with a systeme of opinions; but to reform mens lives, and purifie their natures.

Fowler, *The Principles and Practices, of Certain Moderate Divines* (1670)[1]

Surely nothing is more likely to prevail with wise and considerate Men to become Religious, than to be throughly convinced, that *Religion* and *Happiness*, our *Duty* and our *Interest*, are really but one and the same thing considered under several Notions.

Tillotson, Preface to Wilkins, *Of the Principles and Duties of Natural Religion* (1675)[2]

the great design of the christian religion is to restore and reinforce the practice of the natural law, or which is all one, of moral duties.

Tillotson, Sermon 103, 'Instituted Religion not Intended to Undermine Natural'[3]

Religion produceth a sweet and gracious Temper of *Mind*; *calm* in its self, and *loving to Men*. It causeth a *Universal Benevolence* and *Kindness* to Mankind. For, these are the Things of which it doth consist; *Love, Candour, Ingenuity, Clemency, Patience, Mildness, Gentleness*, and all other instances of *GOOD-NATURE*.

Whichcote, *Select Sermons* (1698)[4]

1 The origins of latitude

The terms 'latitude-men' and 'latitudinarian' were first used pejoratively in the 1650s and early 1660s to describe an influential group of men who in terms of doctrine wanted to reduce the Christian religion to a few plain essentially moral fundamentals, easily to be apprehended and put into practice by the ordinary rational man, and in terms of discipline were

---

[1] Part I, 18.   [2] 6th edn (1710), A6.   [3] *Works*, ed. Barker (1742–3), VI, 1688.
[4] Part II, Sermon 6, 431.

prepared to accommodate themselves to the church government of the day.[5]
They found no difficulty in both holding office during the Interregnum, when
the Church of England was under attack, and conforming to the Church in
1662, when its position was secured and defined by Act of Parliament.[6] They
saw questions of ecclesiastical organisation and ceremony as secondary,
'things indifferent' – not things of no importance, but things that are not
prescribed in Scripture and that the state has the right to determine. To some
extent they sympathised with the nonconformists who for reasons of conscience could not bring themselves within the pale of the Church of England,
but they regarded their stand as unnecessary and their sufferings as partly
self-inflicted. In the 1660s the number of the latitude-men was relatively small
and their influence restricted, though increasing; by the 1690s the latitudinarians (the name that became standard) were the dominant, though not the
majority, party in the Church of England. Initially for very different reasons
they were regarded with suspicion both by the nonconformists, who saw them
as time-servers and heathen moralists, and by the group who had been loyal
to the Church of England in the 1650s and were to become known as high
churchmen, who thought that they were betraying the Church from within.
Later, because of their involvement in schemes for the comprehension of some
of the nonconformists within the Church, and, when these failed, their
support for the toleration of protestant dissenters guaranteed by the Act of
1689, they secured the friendship of dissenters but increased the enmity of
high churchmen. By the end of the century their definition of Christianity as a
largely moral religion based on reason had become commonplace. To its
supporters it was a position that was simple, obvious, and self-evidently true;
to its opponents it was subversive, dangerous, and opened the way to
Socinianism, deism and atheism. The latitudinarian came to be seen by his
high church opponent as one who was indifferent (in the pejorative sense) not
only to the institutions and forms of religion but to its content as well. The
nonjuror Charles Leslie maliciously characterised the views of Archbishop
Tillotson as follows in *The Charge of Socinianism against Dr. Tillotson Considered*
(published in 1695 after Tillotson's death): 'His politics are Leviathan, and
his religion is Latitudinarian, which is none; that is, nothing that is *positive*,
but against every thing that is positive in other religions.'[7] This definition is

[5] The most useful accounts of Restoration Anglicanism and the position of latitude are Cragg,
From Puritanism to the Age of Reason (1950); Griffin, 'Latitudinarianism' (1962); McAdoo, *Spirit of
Anglicanism* (1965); Simon, *Three Restoration Divines*, I (1967); Spurr, 'Anglican Apologetic'
(1985); Sykes, *From Sheldon to Secker* (1959), Chapter 5. Spurr, 'Latitudinarianism' (1988),
overstates the case against modern historians' use of the label. Jacob, *Newtonians* (1976),
Chapter 1, sees latitudinarianism in social rather than religious terms.

[6] On the restoration of the Church see Bosher, *Making of the Restoration Settlement* (1951); Green,
Re-Establishment (1978); R. A. Beddard, 'The Restoration Church', in Jones, *Restored Monarchy*
(1979); A. Whiteman, 'The Restoration of the Church of England', in Nuttall and Chadwick,
eds., *From Uniformity to Unity* (1962).

[7] Quoted in Birch, *Tillotson* (1753), 297.

put more succinctly but hardly more fairly in the mid-eighteenth century by John Wesley; speculative latitudinarianism is 'an indifference to all opinions ... the spawn of hell';[8] a latitudinarian is 'one that fancies all religions are saving'.[9]

These hostile definitions imply that latitudinarianism is essentially amorphous. However, the stance of the latitude-men was originally adopted in response to the intellectual and theological climate prevailing during the Interregnum, especially at Cambridge. Early defenders of the latitudinarian position were at pains to make this point clear: latitude was a reaction against both Calvinist doctrine and the restrictions on the Church of England in the Cromwellian period by those who, unlike the group associated with Hammond, were nevertheless willing to work within the Cromwellian establishment. Three very illuminating apologies were published in the 1660s and 1670s which explain the circumstances in which the latitudinarian label had its origin: *A Brief Account of the New Sect of Latitude-Men* (1662), by S. P. (usually attributed to Simon Patrick);[10] *The Principles and Practices, of Certain Moderate Divines of the Church of England* (1670), by Edward Fowler (*Abusively called Latitudinarians* is added to the title of the second edition of 1671); 'Antifanatical Religion, and Free Philosophy', Essay VII of *Essays on Several Important Subjects in Philosophy and Religion* (1676), by Joseph Glanvill (an abbreviated version of an unpublished manuscript entitled 'Bensalem being A Description of A Catholick & Free Spirit both in Religion & Learning. In a Continuation of the story of the Lord Bacon's New Atlantis').[11] In addition Gilbert Burnet gave a sympathetic account of the origins of the movement in the first volume of his *History of his Own Time* (published posthumously in 1724). There is some difference in emphasis in the three following definitions of the term, but the general agreement is clear. The first is by Patrick:

[They] were so far from being sowred with the Leaven of the times they lived in, that they were always looked upon with an evil eye by the successive usurping powers, and the general out-cry was, that the whole University was over-run with *Arminianisme*, and was full of men of a Prelatical Spirit, that apostatized to the Onions and Garlick of *Egypt*, because they were generally ordained by Bishops; and in opposition to that hide-bound, strait-lac'd spirit that did then prevail, they were called *Latitude-men*; for that was the first original of the name, whatever sense hath since been put upon it.[12]

The second is by Glanvill, in a passage from 'Bensalem' which did not appear in 'Anti-fanatical Religion':

---

[8] *Works*, ed. Baker (1975, in progress): Volumes I–IV, *Sermons*, ed. Outler (1984–7), II, 92, No. 39, 'Catholic Spirit' (1755). See Chapter 5 below, p. 226.
[9] *Complete English Dictionary* (1777, first published 1753).
[10] The case for Patrick's authorship is put in *Brief Account*, ed. Birrell (1963), Introduction.
[11] The greater part was first published by Cope in '"The Cupri-Cosmits"' (1954).
[12] *Brief Account*, 5.

One of the most Common names given them was Latitudinarian from a word that signifies compass or largeness, because of their opposition to the narrow stingy Temper then called Orthodoxness; and their opinion of the lawfulness of Compliance with the Rites and Ceremonies of the Church of Bensalem [i.e. England], which had been cast out with so much detestation as Anti-Christian and Abominable. These were the first occasions of that name, which was very hatefull to them, because it signified a Fundamental Contrariety to their Spirits and Opinions. But afterward among them that knew not those persons, it came to be taken in a worse sense, and Latitudinarian went for one of a large Conscience and Practice ... When they came to be better understood, they were called Cupri-Cosmits, which word hath its derivation from the place of their Rise [i.e. Cambridge], and the disposition of their Spirits, which was Catholic and general, not Topical or confined to opinions and Sects.[13]

Glanvill's definition is more restricted than that of Burnet, which dates from a later period (Burnet probably began writing his history in the 1680s) and takes account of high church hostility to latitudinarian sympathy for non-conformists:

All these, and those who were formed under them, studied to examine farther into the nature of things than had been done formerly. They declared against superstition on the one hand, and enthusiasm on the other. They loved the constitution of the Church, and the Liturgy, and could well live under them: But they did not think it unlawful to live under another form. They wished that things might have been carried with more moderation. And they continued to keep a good correspondence with those who had differed from them in opinion, and allowed a great freedom both in philosophy and in divinity: From whence they were called men of Latitude. And upon this men of narrower thoughts and fiercer tempers fastened upon them the name of Latitudinarians.[14]

Patrick, Glanvill and Burnet are describing the position of two generations of latitude-men. The first were students at Cambridge before the Civil War and fellows and heads of colleges during the Interregnum; the second were students during the late 1640s and the 1650s predominantly at Cambridge, though some were educated at Oxford, and were strongly influenced by the first. The first generation of latitude-men – in particular Whichcote, More, Smith, and Cudworth – have customarily been labelled 'the Cambridge Platonists' since the nineteenth century.[15] There are several difficulties involved in the use of this label: it is not one that contemporaries used; it draws attention to one particular facet of their interests at the expense of others; it excludes one very important member, Wilkins, who exceptionally was not educated at Cambridge; it also obscures the continuity of interest between the first and second generations. The network of relationships and

---

13 Cope, '"The Cupri-Cosmits"', 271.   14 *History*, I, 188. For the dating see I, Preface, 1.
15 See Tulloch, *Rational Theology* (1872), II: *The Cambridge Platonists*, Powicke, *The Cambridge Platonists* (1926), and more recently the anthologies by Cragg (1968) and Patrides (1969). The last provides a very useful bibliography. For a reversion to the original term see Nicolson, 'Christ's College and the Latitude-Men' (1929–30).

influence between the two generations was extensive, and a sketch of these is given to indicate how latitudinarian ideas were transmitted and became the dominant intellectual force in late seventeenth-century England.

Benjamin Whichcote (1609–83) and John Wilkins (1614–72) are in many ways the key figures of the first generation.[16] Whichcote was a student and subsequently a fellow of Emmanuel College, Cambridge, a vital centre of puritan thought in the late sixteenth and early seventeenth centuries. Here he tutored John Smith (1616–52) and John Worthington (1618–71). Ralph Cudworth (1617–88) and Nathaniel Culverwell (1619–51) were also students at Emmanuel while Whichcote was teaching there, and themselves subsequently became fellows.[17] In 1644 Whichcote moved to King's College as Provost; at approximately the same time Smith became a fellow of Queens' and Cudworth Master of Clare Hall. During the Interregnum the latitudemen held important posts in Cambridge: Whichcote at King's, Cudworth as Master of Christ's, where Henry More (1614–87) had been a student and was a fellow, Worthington as Master of Jesus. Whichcote's main influence over the students and fellows was achieved through his Sunday afternoon lectureship at Trinity Church, where he preached for almost twenty years. As shown in the previous chapter, this influence was seen as dangerous by Whichcote's one-time tutor, Anthony Tuckney, Master of Emmanuel and later of St John's, but Whichcote's adherents saw it very differently. Tillotson claims in his funeral sermon for Whichcote that 'in those wild and unsettled times [he] contributed more to the forming of the students of that university to a sober sense of religion than any man in that age.'[18] Glanvill gives a corroborating account of Whichcote in his portrait gallery of the 'Cupri-Cosmits': 'He was a Famed Preacher in the University of Cupri, and season'd the youth there with good principles, and Rules, in Times when they were scarce. He did in this way very much propagate the Primitive Christian Spirit, and greatly contribute to the overthrow of the Phanatical Genius of that Age.'[19]

The influence of Wilkins was of a rather different kind. He was educated at Magdalen Hall, Oxford, and became Warden of Wadham in 1648. In London in the 1640s he developed his lifelong interest in science, and during the Interregnum Wadham under his Wardenship became an important centre for scientific thought and experiment. Wilkins maintained good relations with both puritans and royalists – he married Cromwell's sister, yet Cavaliers sent their sons to Wadham, and he was a close friend of the royalist John Evelyn. His half-brother Walter Pope commented in 1697 that he 'had nothing of Bigottry, Unmannerliness, or Censoriousness, which were then in the *Zenith*,

---

[16] For Whichcote see Roberts, *From Puritanism to Platonism* (1968); for Wilkins see Shapiro, *John Wilkins* (1969). *DNB* gives details of all the latitude-men named.

[17] For Cudworth see T. Birch, 'An Account of the Life and Writings of Ralph Cudworth', in Cudworth, *True Intellectual System*, ed. Birch (1743), and Passmore, *Cudworth* (1951); for Culverwell, see *Light of Nature*, ed. Greene and MacCallum (1971), Introduction.

[18] Tillotson, Sermon 24 (1683), *Works*, II, 154.   [19] Cope, '"The Cupri-Cosmits"', 275.

amongst some of the Heads, and Fellows of Colleges in *Oxford*.[20] Tillotson claimed (on information supplied by others) that '*in the late times of confusion, almost all that was preserved and kept up of Ingenuity and Learning, of good Order and Government in the* University *of* Oxford, *was chiefly owing to his prudent conduct and encouragement*'.[21] In 1659 Wilkins moved to Cambridge for a brief period as Master of Trinity, where, according to Burnet, 'he joined with those who studied to propagate better thoughts, to take men off from being in parties, or from narrow notions, from superstitious conceits, and a fierceness about opinions'.[22]

Of the second generation who were 'formed under' the Cambridge latitude-men, the most important are Simon Patrick (1626–1707) and especially John Tillotson (1630–94).[23] Patrick was a student at Queens' while Smith was a fellow, and he testifies in his autobiography how Smith turned him from Calvinism and brought him to believe 'that God would really have all men to be saved'.[24] In 1652 Patrick preached Smith's funeral sermon, included by Worthington in his edition of Smith's *Select Discourses* (1660). Tillotson was brought up in a Calvinist family, and tutored at Clare Hall by a Congregationalist;[25] like Patrick, he turned against the theology of his youth. His reaction from Calvinism is attributed by Burnet not to the personal influence of one particular latitude-man but to his reading of Chillingworth's *Religion of Protestants*, 'which gave his mind the ply that it held ever after, and put him on a true scent'. Burnet continues, 'As he got into a true method of study, so he entred into friendships with some great men, which contributed not a little to the perfecting his own mind . . . But that which gave him his last finishing, was his close and long Friendship with Bishop *Wilkins*.'[26] This friendship, however, dates from immediately after the Restoration – Tillotson left Cambridge before Wilkins went to Trinity. Two other important members of the second generation at Cambridge were Isaac Barrow (1630–77) and Edward Stillingfleet (1635–99).[27] Barrow, one of Hammond's protégés and later admired by both Whichcote and Wilkins, was a known royalist, but this did not prevent him holding a fellowship at Trinity. His early fame was as a mathematician. In 1655 he failed to be appointed Regius Professor of Greek because of his Arminianism, and as a result travelled abroad, returning in 1659 during Wilkins's Mastership. Stillingfleet, briefly a fellow of St John's,

20 Pope, *Life of Seth* [Ward], ed. Bamborough (1961), 29.
21 Wilkins, *Sermons*, ed. Tillotson (1682), Preface, A4.
22 *History*, I, 187.   23 For Tillotson see Birch, *Tillotson*.
24 *Auto-biography*, 18. Patrick's title is 'A Brief Account of my Life, with a Thankful Remembrance of God's Mercies to Me'.
25 David Clarkson, Tillotson's tutor, after the Restoration was assistant and successor to the Congregational leader John Owen at his London church.
26 *Sermon Preached at the Funeral of* [Tillotson] (1694), 11–12.
27 For Barrow see A. Hill, 'Some Account of the Life of Dr. Isaac Barrow', in Barrow, *Theological Works* (1830), I; Osmond, *Barrow* (1944); Pope, *Life of Seth*, Chapters 19–22. For Stillingfleet see [Bentley], *Life and Character of . . . Stillingfleet* (1710); Carroll, *Common-sense Philosophy* (1975).

published his first book, *Irenicum*, in 1659, attempting to find common ground between the Church of England and its opponents, though he later regretted some of his arguments. In addition, some latitudinarians were educated at Oxford: Edward Fowler (1632–1714) and Joseph Glanvill (1636–80) both had puritan connections (Glanvill greatly admired Baxter) but their defences of the latitudinarian position testify to the influence of the first generation. Theophilus, one of the speakers in Fowler's *Principles and Practices*, says that he was taught 'by a most *judicious*, as well as *pious* Divine', who kept him from 'false notions', and later he gives a detailed account of how he gave up his belief in the absolute decrees of the Calvinist God.[28] The narrator in Glanvill's 'Anti-fanatical Religion' describes how he was a student at university when the 'divines of Bensalem' began their opposition to the theology and methods of the 'Ataxites' or puritans.[29] Among the Cambridge latitude-men Glanvill particularly venerated More, whose friend and correspondent he later became.

After the Restoration London became the focal point of latitudinarian influence. For various reasons some members of the group retained their college fellowships and headships while others were ejected: Cudworth and More remained at Christ's and Barrow at Trinity (he became Master in 1672), but Whichcote and Wilkins among others lost their Cambridge posts. Whatever their treatment as a result of the Restoration, however, all the latitude-men conformed to the Church of England in 1662, and within the next few years many of them, including Stillingfleet, Patrick, and Fowler, obtained livings in the City of London. The most important pulpit was that of St Lawrence Jewry, with which the principal latitude-men were associated: Tillotson was Tuesday Lecturer there from 1661 (and shortly afterwards also Preacher at Lincoln's Inn); Wilkins was Vicar from 1662 until the Great Fire of 1666 when the church was burnt down, and on one occasion employed Barrow as guest preacher; when Wilkins became Bishop of Chester in 1668 he suggested that Whichcote should succeed him as Vicar, and Whichcote remained until his death in 1683 (he was obliged to use the Guildhall chapel for seven years until St Lawrence was rebuilt). The city pulpits thus became the main source of latitudinarian ideas in the reign of Charles II, just as Cambridge colleges had been in the Interregnum.

Wilkins was the dominant figure among the latitude-men until his death in 1672, and his interest in science came to the fore during this period. He was the moving spirit behind the Royal Society and its first secretary, and many latitude-men became fellows in the early days of the society, for example More, Cudworth, Barrow, Glanvill, and Tillotson, some of them on Wilkins's

---

[28] *Principles and Practices*, Part I, 158, Part II, 233–6.
[29] *Essays*, 7, 7ff. See Cope, *Glanvill* (1956).

recommendation.[30] With Wilkins's help Barrow was made Professor of Geometry at Gresham College, shortly afterwards becoming Lucasian Professor of Mathematics at Cambridge. In the 1660s the latitude-men were thus closely linked by education, intellectual interest, academic and ecclesiastical posts, friendship, even by marriage (Tillotson married Wilkins's step-daughter).

Their most significant common attitude was to the Church. They had found conformity on the terms of the Act of Uniformity (1662) an easy and obvious step to take (the main provisions being episcopal ordination and 'assent and consent' to the Book of Common Prayer) but several of them maintained their friendships with moderate nonconformists (which largely meant Presbyterians), and they were willing to consider broadening the base of the Church of England so that it might include those who wanted to conform but who found the requirements for conformity too stringent, an attitude that made them unpopular among stricter churchmen.[31] John Beard-more (who was Tillotson's pupil at Cambridge in 1651, and who wrote a biographical sketch of him in 1694) notes Wilkins's 'great moderation in the points agitated betwixt the Conformists and Nonconformists, about liturgy, ceremonies, &c. which made him become the object of odium and envy to a very great party'.[32] Edmund Calamy, the early eighteenth-century historian of nonconformity, reports a conversation between Wilkins and the Presbyterian John Howe: Wilkins asked Howe why someone of his latitude had not conformed; Howe replied 'That that *Latitude* of his, which he was pleas'd to take notice of, was so far from inducing him to Conformity, that it was the very thing that made and kept him a Non-conformist.' Calamy further reports that when Wilkins was made Bishop of Chester he told the Bishop of Durham, John Cosin, that he was a better friend to the Church through his moderation than Cosin through his rigour: 'For while you my Lord, said he, are for setting the Top on the piqued end downwards, you won't be able to keep it up, any longer than you continue whipping and scourging: Whereas I, says he, am for setting the broad end downward, and so 'twill stand of it self.'[33] The latitudinarians recognised that persecution was a cruel and hopeless way of bringing nonconformists into the Church, and tried to reconcile them to it through rational persuasion; according to Burnet, they to some extent succeeded through the use they made of their pulpits: Tillotson 'brought several over to the Church, by the force of reason, and the softness of perswasion and good usage; but was a declared enemy to violence and severities on those heads'.[34]

[30] On the relations between science and religion see the different approaches of Hunter, *Science and Society* (1981), Jacob, *Newtonians*, and Westfall, *Science and Religion* (1958).
[31] For nonconformist objections to the Act of Uniformity of 1662 see Chapter 3.
[32] 'Some Memorials of . . . Tillotson', in Birch, *Tillotson*, 390.
[33] Calamy, *Life of Howe* (1724), 31–4.
[34] Burnet, *History*, II, 76; cf. I, 191, and Beardmore's similar comment, 'Memorials of . . . Tillotson', in Birch, *Tillotson*, 400.

There were in principle two legal means whereby nonconformists who were not prepared to join the Church of England on the terms of the Act of Uniformity might be accommodated: comprehension, which would entail changes in discipline and ceremony and which was aimed at moderate nonconformists, largely Presbyterians, who were unhappy with their new separatist status; and indulgence, or toleration, which would allow freedom of worship to those nonconformists, largely Congregationalists and sectaries, who had no wish to be comprehended within the Church of England.[35] The latitudinarians differed about the desirability of establishing legal means as opposed to assisting individual nonconformists. Wilkins and Tillotson were promoters of comprehension, whereas Patrick and Stillingfleet were far more critical of nonconformity and did not firmly support comprehension until the reign of James II. They were all opposed to the Declarations of Indulgence issued by Charles II and James II which granted toleration to protestants and Roman Catholics alike. Ultimately because of high church opposition the movement for comprehension failed, and the Toleration Act of 1689 gave protestant dissenters limited indulgence.

In the reign of William III the latitudinarians became the most powerful group in the Church. William soon gave important posts to prominent members: in 1689 Burnet became Bishop of Salisbury, Stillingfleet Bishop of Worcester, Patrick Bishop of Chichester, and Tillotson Dean of St Paul's (in succession to Stillingfleet). The expulsion of the nonjurors (who would not take the oath of allegiance to William and Mary) left many vacancies in the Church, including several bishoprics and the Archbishopric of Canterbury. With some reluctance, the latitudinarians took these posts: in 1691 Tillotson became Archbishop of Canterbury, Patrick was appointed to Ely, Fowler to Gloucester, and like-minded men to other sees. Gilbert Burnet (1643–1715), the youngest of the group, assumes a particular importance as the historian of the origins of latitude in the Interregnum, its development under Charles II and James II, its dominance under William III and the increasing high church opposition to it under Queen Anne. Burnet, a Scot educated at Aberdeen who was unsympathetic to the Presbyterians, was early much influenced by his reading of Plato, Hooker, John Smith, and More, and his friendship with Robert Leighton (1611–84), Archbishop of Glasgow, himself a great admirer of the Cambridge men; Burnet wrote of Leighton in his autobiography that 'He raised in me a just sense of the great end of religion as a divine life in the soul that carried a man farre above forms or opinions.'[36] In 1662–3 Burnet visited London, Oxford, and Cambridge for the first time and

---

[35] See Spurr, 'Church of England' (1989), and R. Thomas, 'Comprehension and Indulgence', in Nuttall and Chadwick, eds., *From Uniformity to Unity*. Spurr, 943–4, argues that Anglican support for comprehension was very rare.

[36] *Supplement to Burnet's History*, ed. Foxcroft (1902), 460–2. For Leighton see Henderson, *Religious Life in Seventeenth-Century Scotland* (1937), Chapter 6, and Knox, *Leighton* (1930). Doddridge, who admired Leighton enormously, published an edition of his works in 1748.

met Tillotson, Stillingfleet, Whichcote, Wilkins, More, and Cudworth. His predisposition was confirmed: 'I easily went into the notions of the Latitudinarians.'[37] He subsequently became a friend and admirer of Tillotson, 'the man of the truest judgement, and best temper, I had ever known', he wrote after Tillotson's death in 1694.[38] For several years Burnet was an adviser to William and Mary. He sums up the influence of the latitudinarian bishops in the 1690s and the high church opposition to them as follows:

It was visible to the whole Nation, that there was another face of strictness, of humility and charity among them, than had been ordinarily observed before: They visited their Dioceses more; They confirmed and preached oftner, than any who had in our memory gone before them; They took more care in examining those whom they Ordained, and in looking into the behaviour of their Clergy, than had been formerly practised; But they were faithful to the Government, and zealous for it; They were gentle to the Dissenters, and did not rail at them, nor seem uneasy at the Toleration. This was thought such a heinous matter, that all their other diligence was despised; And they were represented as men, who designed to undermine the Church and to betray it.[39]

Over a period of sixty years latitude developed from the characteristic of a minority movement at Cambridge to the position linking the chief office-holders in the Church. Inevitably aspects of latitudinarian thought changed during this period: the attitudes of a man like More, for example, who refused promotion and spent his working life at Christ's, are bound to differ from those of Tillotson, whose responsibilities became increasingly public. However, it is possible to define the underlying assumptions and the intellectual antecedents of latitude. The latitude-men were united in their opposition to what they regarded as atheism, enthusiasm, and superstition, which they believed to be mutually supporting intellectual evils undermining rational religion. By atheism they meant a number of things, including libertinism, Epicurean atomism, determinism, and especially the works and influence of Hobbes; by enthusiasm they meant any manifestations of puritanism that divorced faith from reason or stressed faith at the expense of works; by superstition they meant the Roman Catholic Church, because allegiance to it seemed to imply abdication of individual reason in favour of arbitrarily imposed judgement. They repeatedly argued the logical connection between these positions; enthusiasm undermined respect for religion and its ministers and led to atheism – '*the Hypocrisie of one Age makes way for the Atheism of the next*' claimed Stillingfleet[40] – and this in turn led to superstition. All three in different ways abused or denied reason. Tillotson, according to Burnet, saw the discrediting of reason as a Catholic conspiracy: 'the Design seemed to be laid, to make us first Atheists, that we might be the more easily

---

[37] *Supplement*, 463.   [38] *History*, II, 135.   [39] *History*, II, 126.
[40] *Origines Sacrae* (1662), 'Epistle Dedicatory', a4.

made Papists'.[41] Burnet himself perceived the transition from one mode of irrational or anti-rational thought to another as part of a historical cycle:

There is a Circulation observed in the general Corruptions of Nations: Sometimes Ignorance and Brutality over-runs the World, that makes way for Superstition and Idolatry: When Mankind is disgusted with these, then fantastical and Enthusiastical Principles, and under these hypocritical Practices have their Course; these being seen through, give great Occasions to profaneness, and with that, *Atheism*, and a Disbelief of all Religion, at least of all Revealed Religion, is nourished . . .[42]

The latitudinarians' weapon against all these tendencies was to define and propagate their view of the essentially rational basis of religion.

A number of philosophical and religious traditions contributed to the formation of this view: classical philosophy, especially Platonism; the early fathers of the church, especially the Greeks; the scholastic tradition of natural law; the defenders of the Church of England against the puritans and Catholics; the Dutch Remonstrants; the new philosophy. Different aspects of this eclectic grouping were emphasised by different latitude-men, but they shared a hostility to predestinarian theology (several of them record their early revulsion from the doctrine of reprobation)[43] and a habit of reading the Bible alongside and in the light of classical ethics. Glanvill gives a summary of the studies of the divines of Bensalem in 'Anti-fanatical Religion', and there are full listings of recommended authors in the enlarged editions of Wilkins's *Ecclesiastes*, sections iii and iv, and in Burnet's *Discourse of the Pastoral Care*, Chapter 7. The principal names cited by the latitude-men are those of Plato, Aristotle, Cicero, Seneca, Plutarch, Epictetus, Marcus Aurelius, Plotinus, and Hierocles among the ancients; Origen, Basil, and Chrysostom among the fathers; Aquinas;[44] and Episcopius, Grotius, Chillingworth, Taylor, and Hammond among the moderns. These names are invoked for a consistent purpose: the authors praised are those who define man as a free, rational, and social being, capable of imitating God. In this context Burnet explains Whichcote's motivation as a teacher:

being disgusted with the dry systematical way of those times, he studied to raise those who conversed with him to a nobler set of thoughts, and to consider religion as a seed of a deiform nature, (to use one of his own phrases.) In order to this, he set young students much on reading the ancient Philosophers, chiefly *Plato, Tully* [i.e. Cicero], and *Plotin*, and on considering the Christian religion as a doctrine sent from God, both to elevate and sweeten humane nature, in which he was a great example, as well as a wise and kind instructer.[45]

[41] *Sermon Preached at the Funeral of* [Tillotson], 15.
[42] *Pastoral Care* (3rd edn, 1713), Preface, xv.
[43] More gave up the doctrine of predestination when he was a boy at Eton (Ward, *Life of More*, ed. Howard (1911), 59–60); Patrick was shocked by a sermon on reprobation as a child (*Auto-biography*, 5); Cudworth told the Remonstrant Limborch how he abandoned Calvinism when he went to Cambridge (Powicke, *Cambridge Platonists*, 111). See also notes 24, 28.
[44] McAdoo, *Spirit of Anglicanism*, emphasises the importance of Aquinas.   [45] *History*, I, 187.

It is a recurrent motif of the latitude-men (as it was of the sixteenth-century humanist Erasmus) that the heathen moralists put Christians to shame: Whichcote comments that Cicero 'is a better *Divine* than some who pretend to be Christians; and yet seem to deny Reason'.[46] In answer to Tuckney's rebukes, Whichcote defends the value of such reading: 'The time I have spent in Philosophers, I have no cause to repent-of; and the use I have made of them, I dare not disowne . . . it makes me secrettlie blush before God, when I find eyther my heart head or life challenged by them'.[47] Tillotson, in his earliest surviving sermon preached in 1661 'at the Morning-Exercise at Cripple-gate' to the congregation of the puritan Samuel Annesley, makes a similarly Erasmian point:

When I read the heathen writers, especially TULLY and SENECA, and take notice, what precepts of morality and laws of kindness are every where in their writings, I am ready to fall in love with them. How should it make our blood rise in many of our faces, who are Christians, to hear with what strictness TULLY determines cases of conscience, and how generously he speaks of equity and justice towards all men?[48]

The works of the classical philosophers and of later writers who acknowledged their influence, more immediately the seventeenth-century Arminian theologians, both Dutch and English, seemed to the latitude-men to provide a liberation from the intellectual restrictions, the false zeal, the combativeness of the Calvinist theology in which they had been brought up. This sense of liberation is captured in Glanvill's fable: missionaries returning from foreign parts bring back the works of Hammond, Taylor, and Grotius to Bensalem, stimulating the development of 'anti-fanatical religion'.[49] In their efforts to define and propagate this religion, the latitude-men emphasise practice as much as ideas, laying particular stress on social demeanour, temper, language, the tone of religious discourse. The terms they repeatedly use to characterise their position are moderation and sobriety, and it is these characteristics that the apologists for latitude urge their readers to adopt. 'It is high time to be reconciled to *Moderation* and *Sobriety*,' urges Fowler, '. . . *Divine Truth* is far more unlikely to be found among men of violent and boisterous Passions, than among those that are *soberly* and *sedately considerative*.' He explains that he wants the Church of England to 'be so inlarged, as to take in all that are of any Reason, Sobriety and Moderation'.[50] According to Patrick, the latitude-men are 'so far from being any ways dangerous to the Church . . . they seem to be the very Chariots and Horsemen thereof; for by their sober and unblameable conversation, they conciliate respect and honour to her; by

---

[46] *Select Sermons*, Part I, Sermon 3, 104. See Erasmus's colloquy 'The Godly Feast' (*Convivium religiosum*) (1522), in *Colloquies*, trans. Thompson (1965).

[47] *Eight Letters*, 60.

[48] Birch, *Tillotson*, 465. Annesley, an associate of Baxter, became a nonconformist in 1662. His daughter Susanna married Samuel Wesley and was the mother of John Wesley.

[49] *Essays*, No. 7, 6.   [50] *Principles and Practices*, 'To the Reader', x–xi; Part III, 334.

their Learning and industry they defend her; by their moderation they are most likely to win upon the minds of dissenters'.[51] A favourite biblical quotation in this connection is Philippians 4:5: 'Let your moderation be known unto all men.' Fowler prints it on the title page of *Principles and Practices*; Beardmore associates it with Tillotson;[52] Wilkins's Sermon 13 on this text is a detailed analysis of the intellectual, political, and social benefits of moderation (it was republished in abbreviated form in 1710 as *A Moderate Church-man the best Christian and Subject* and addressed to the latitudinarian Benjamin Hoadly as a low-church answer to high-church hysteria). In the preface to Wilkins's *Sermons Preached upon Several Occasions* (1682) in which this sermon appears Tillotson praises '*the admirable candour and moderation of* [Wilkins's] *temper in matters of difference and dispute*', and continues: '*I am still of the old Opinion that* moderation *is a* Virtue, *and one of the peculiar ornaments and advantages of the excellent constitution of our Church, and must at last be the temper of her Members, especially the* Clergy, *if ever we seriously intend the firm establishment of this Church.*'[53]

In this accommodating temper (illustrated for example by Tillotson in his friendships with the Socinian Thomas Firmin, the nonconformist Richard Baxter, and the high churchman Robert Nelson), the latitudinarians propagated their often-repeated views that religion is reasonable and natural to man, that the essence of religion is morality, that the practice of its precepts is profitable and pleasant and in man's best interest, that holiness and happiness are identical, and that to be religious is the truest wisdom. The objection to this account of religion made at the time was that it was in Tuckney's words 'a kinde of a Moral Divinitie';[54] puritans and nonconformists labelled the latitude-men 'by way of *contempt*' as 'The *Rational Preachers*', '*Moral Preachers*', '*meer Moral Men, without the Power of Godliness*'.[55] The modern reader cannot arrive at a fair assessment of the position of the latitude-men without taking into account their deliberate attempt to win their audiences away from the puritan inheritance from which they had freed themselves.

2 The polemics and preaching of the latitude-men

The latitude-men cannot profitably be read in isolation from each other. Although there are important differences in emphasis and method especially among the first generation (More being the most prolific, idiosyncratic, and unreadable member, and Cudworth the most original), from the 1660s there is a marked tendency towards a group vocabulary and a group style which is not restricted to the younger generation. The difference between the schol-

---

[51] *Brief Account*, 12. [52] Birch, *Tillotson*, 398.
[53] *Sermons*, ed. Tillotson (1682), 'The Publisher to the Reader', A2ᵛ–A3.
[54] *Eight Letters*, 39.
[55] Fowler, *Principles and Practices*, 103, 117; Pope, *Life of Seth*, 46. See also Patrick, *Auto-biography*, 60, and Beardmore in Birch, *Tillotson*, 407.

arly, ornate, individual styles of Smith, More, and Cudworth and the popular, plain, collective style of Wilkins and Tillotson can partly be attributed to environment and the expectations of certain audiences: the first group clearly have in mind a leisured, erudite, university audience with the inclination to pursue quotations in Latin, Greek, and Hebrew; the latter aim with clear and unadorned argument to capture the judgement of city congregations. But this is not an entirely satisfactory explanation: Whichcote and Barrow (who also address university audiences) have far more in common with Wilkins and Tillotson than with More and Cudworth. It is perhaps fair to say that insofar as they were not interested in popularising their thought, More and Cudworth remained out of step with what was to become an essential characteristic of latitudinarian writing. The group in which Tillotson was the central figure and which included members of both generations not only shared certain views about the nature and function of religion but also believed that those views should be made evident through plain and rational exposition. The result was a certain anonymity of expression which makes it difficult and indeed pointless to try to establish which member of the group originated a particular argument. It is more important to establish the significant links which existed between the latitude-men as authors and editors and to concentrate on the characteristic features of latitudinarian writings; what emerges is the development of a collective language and rhetorical method which by the end of the century had largely succeeded in ousting the rival language of nonconformity and establishing itself, despite high church denunciation and deist exploitation, as the standard for rational public discourse.

The personal links between and the publishing history of Whichcote, Wilkins, Barrow, and Tillotson clearly illustrate this collective language. Paradoxically the works of Whichcote, the eldest member of the group, were the last to appear in print (mostly at the beginning of the eighteenth century), and so they will be considered after the others; there are special, perhaps insoluble problems connected with them. Wilkins published a number of popular scientific and religious works from the late 1630s to the early 1650s, the most important from the point of view of the development of latitude being *Ecclesiastes*, a handbook for preachers first published in 1646. This was an extremely popular work which was reprinted many times in the course of the century and at the beginning of the next, and revised three times; the nature of the revisions tells us a good deal about the growing importance of the latitudinarian position. *Ecclesiastes* began essentially as a list of recommended authorities on biblical study, doctrine, ecclesiastical controversy, ethics etc, together with brief instructions to the preacher on the method of arranging sermons and the choice of appropriate style. In 1669 Wilkins revised and enlarged the book (the fifth impression but the first revised edition), dividing the previously continuous text into sections – 'Concerning Method', 'Concerning Matter', 'Concerning a Regular Scheme of the chief Heads in Divinity', 'Concerning Expression', extending the book lists, and, most important, distinguishing between natural and revealed religion and providing clear statements on the role of reason, the appeal of religion to interest, and the pursuit of happiness. Central latitudinarian principles were thereby made available in a simple and convenient form. In the early 1690s, twenty years after Wilkins's death, Tillotson (who was now Archbishop of Canterbury), recognising the continuing influence and importance of the book, asked John Williams (later Bishop of Chichester) to revise it and bring it up to date. In this new revised edition of 1693 (in fact the seventh edition), Williams – as he explained in the 'Advertisement to the Reader' – retained Wilkins's revised text but, acting on the advice of colleagues, considerably expanded his book lists, adding the names of over a thousand authors, and indicating his alterations with 'crotchets' (square brackets). In 1704 another expanded text appeared (the eighth edition), incorporating the additions of 1693 and with further additions marked with a dagger; the 'Advertisement' explains that 'the principal design was to shew the particular places, where the Chief Subjects of Religion were treated of by Authors of the greatest eminency and esteem for their Piety, Learning, and Judgment, in our own Nation, whose works are easie to be had'. As a result the seventh and especially the eighth editions of *Ecclesiastes* list the major works of latitudinarian authors published in the previous thirty years. The names of Barrow, Stillingfleet, Tillotson, Patrick, Fowler, More, and Wilkins himself recur repeatedly. In the 1704 edition John Locke's *Essay concerning Human Understanding* (first published in 1690) and *Reasonableness of Christianity* (1695) are listed, and the up-to-dateness of the work is evidenced by the inclusion of the recently published *Discourses* of Whichcote (Volumes I–III, 1701–3). The publishing and editing history of *Ecclesiastes* from the late 1640s to the early 1700s can thus be seen to illustrate the systematic attempt by latitude-men to propagate their views and shape the education of the clergy, and it would certainly repay study in this light.[56]

Tillotson's initiative in arranging the second revision of *Ecclesiastes* was the conclusion of a long association with Wilkins's work. At Oxford during the 1650s and in London in the years immediately following the Restoration Wilkins was engaged on his most elaborate scientific undertaking, an attempt to create a universal language and a system of classification for 'things and notions', which was finally published in 1668 under the auspices of the Royal Society as *An Essay towards a Real Character and a Philosophical Language*. *The History of the Royal Society*, written by Thomas Sprat under Wilkins's direction

---

[56] Copies of *Ecclesiastes* were sometimes interleaved with blank pages for the owner to add notes on his own reading. I owe this point to Mary Clapinson, Keeper of Western Manuscripts, Bodleian Library. For Isaac Watts's annotated copy of the 1693 edition in Dr Williams's Library, see Stephenson, 'Watts and ... *Ecclesiastes*' (1966).

and published the year before the *Real Character*, publicised Wilkins's influential views on language in a more accessible way.[57] Wilkins had several
assistants in his work, including Tillotson. The friendship and professional
association between the two was close, and on his death in 1672 Wilkins left
Tillotson his papers. In 1675 Tillotson edited and published Wilkins's *Of the
Principles and Duties of Natural Religion*, of which slightly less than half had been
left ready for the press. To judge from the number of editions the book went
through until the 1730s this was the most popular and influential of his works.
Burnet tells the candidate for orders that 'by reason of that Pest of Atheism,
that spreads so much among us, the Foundations of Religion must be well
laid: Bishop *Wilkins*'s Book of *Natural Religion*, will lead one in the first Steps
through the Principles that he has laid together in a plain and natural
Method'.[58] (Its importance for this purpose was recognised by David Hume,
who paid Wilkins the compliment in *Dialogues concerning Natural Religion*
(1779) of not only rebutting his arguments but parodying one of his passages.)[59] In 1682 Tillotson also published a small collection of Wilkins's
Sermons (which is, however, much more substantial than the edition of 1677,
with which he does not seem to have been connected), with a preface (already
cited) praising the strength of Wilkins's style and the moderation of his
temper.

Tillotson was also responsible for editing Barrow's works. In the 1660s
Barrow concentrated on his mathematical studies, publishing his lectures in
1669–70. However, he resigned his chair in mathematics to his pupil Isaac
Newton in 1669 and concentrated for the remaining few years of his life on
divinity, preparing his large body of sermons and his anti-Catholic *Treatise of
the Pope's Supremacy*. At his death in 1677 he had only published the sermon on
'The Duty and Reward of Bounty to the Poor' (1671), with another in the
press. According to Tillotson, Barrow on his deathbed gave him particular
permission to publish the book, which duly appeared in 1680.[60] Tillotson also
took on the task of editing Barrow's sermons, which must have been much
more onerous than his work on Wilkins. Over a period of ten years Tillotson
brought out several collections of the sermons, culminating in the handsome
four-volume folio edition of the *Works* (1683–7). There was a continuing
demand for this edition in the first half of the eighteenth century, with four
more editions appearing by 1751 (Henry Fielding, who gave Barrow's *Works*
the crucial role of converting the infidel hero of his final novel *Amelia*, owned a

[57] *History of the Royal Society*, Part I, section xx, 'A proposal for erecting an English Academy', Part
II, section xx, 'Their manner of Discourse'.
[58] *Pastoral Care*, 149.
[59] Wilkins, *Natural Religion* (6th edn, 1710), Book I, Chapter 6, argument 3, 'From the admirable
contrivance of Natural Things', 81; Hume, *Dialogues*, ed. Price (1976), Part XII, 245–6, ll.
22ff. This parody is not noted by the editor.
[60] *A Treatise of the Pope's Supremacy*, 'The Publisher to the Reader', A3, in Barrow, *Works*, ed.
Tillotson, I (1683).

set of the fifth edition of 1741).[61] Barrow's nineteenth-century editor, Alexander Napier, alleged that Tillotson took unwarranted liberties with Barrow's text. However, Irène Simon, after a thorough comparison of Barrow's manuscripts with Tillotson's edition, has concluded that Tillotson's revisions were responsible ones, mostly involving some grammatical and syntactical alterations and the division of some long texts.[62] We may infer from this analysis that his methods were similar in the case of Wilkins: that is to say, he did not significantly rewrite the texts he edited, but made alterations in the interests of clarity and accessibility.

It can of course be argued that Tillotson, far from seeking to put his own stamp on the writings of Wilkins and Barrow, was heavily influenced by them and that his own work is derivative. Doddridge, who made a thorough study of the divines of the established church, pointed out in his *Lectures on Preaching* that Tillotson made great use of Wilkins and Barrow, going on to claim that 'Many of TILLOTSON's finest sermons were a kind of translation from' Barrow, and that Tillotson's 'The Wisdom of Being Religious' 'is taken in a great measure' from Wilkins.[63] (Doddridge also noted that Tillotson made great use of the *'Fratres Poloni'* (i.e. the Socinians) without mentioning them.) It is worth stressing that Doddridge was a firm admirer of Tillotson. Thomas Birch, Tillotson's eighteenth-century biographer, was anxious to rebut the charge of Tillotson borrowing from Barrow, pointing out that Tillotson's first collection of sermons appeared in 1671.[64] Given the close connection between the three men, it seems pointless to make an issue of who got into print first. On these grounds it might be argued that Tillotson's anti-Catholic polemic, *The Rule of Faith* (1666), influenced Wilkins's *Natural Religion*, which uses some of the same arguments. It seems safer to assume a convergence of opinion and a process of mutual influence.

Tillotson's first important publication was the sermon 'The Wisdom of Being Religious' (1664). By the time of his death in 1694 fifty-four sermons had appeared, but this was far from being the bulk of his work. Two hundred sermons were edited by Ralph Barker from 1695 to 1704 and dedicated to William III by Tillotson's widow; in a postscript 'To the Reader' Barker claims that he has followed Tillotson's own editorial methods, sometimes joining sermons together (in fact Tillotson's practice with Barrow was to divide long sermons) and leaving out repetitions, but never altering the words or the sense.[65] To judge from the £2,500 paid by the printer to his widow for the manuscripts, substantial sales must have been envisaged. In the first half

---

[61] Fielding, *Amelia*, ed. Battestin (1983), 511.
[62] Simon, 'Note on the Text of Barrow's Sermons', in *Three Restoration Divines*, I; 'Tillotson's Barrow' (1964).
[63] Doddridge, *Works*, ed. Williams and Parsons, V, Lecture 4, 435, 437.
[64] Birch, *Tillotson*, 101.
[65] Tillotson, *Works*, XI, 5501. See Simon, 'Note on the Text of Tillotson's Sermons', in *Three Restoration Divines*, II (1976).

of the eighteenth century there were many editions of the *Works* containing 254 sermons and *The Rule of Faith*; in 1752 Thomas Birch in his new edition increased the number to 255 by including the 1661 Cripplegate sermon. In his lifetime and long after Tillotson's popularity as an author was astonishing.

It is unfortunate that Tillotson did not undertake the editing of Whichcote's manuscripts. Whichcote had published nothing by the time of his death in 1683; his far-reaching influence on his contemporaries, to which Tillotson testifies in his funeral sermon, was achieved through the pulpit. Tillotson's own association with Whichcote at St Lawrence Jewry and his experience as editor of Wilkins and Barrow would have made him the best qualified person for the task. However, unlike Wilkins and Barrow, Whichcote evidently did not intend his sermons for publication. So far as can be learned from the editors of his works, Shaftesbury, Jeffery, and Salter, the manuscripts of Whichcote's sermons survived in two forms, Whichcote's own notes (he did not preach from a full text) and shorthand transcripts made by different members of his audience.[66] In 1698 the third Earl of Shaftesbury anonymously published an edition of twelve *Select Sermons*, chosen from two manuscript volumes dating from 1678 to 1680.[67] This was Shaftesbury's first publication. It seems reasonable to assume that he selected those sermons that were most in agreement with his own opinions, especially on the subject of sympathy. In the Preface he explains that his text is based on transcripts compared with Whichcote's notes, complains about Whichcote's style – he was '*more used to School-Learning, and the Language of an University, than to the Conversation of the fashionable World*', but assures the reader that he has been sparing in his editorial alterations.[68] This edition was reprinted twice in the eighteenth century. The next, and most useful, editor was John Jeffery. Jeffery was Vicar of St Peter Mancroft, Norwich, and a friend of Sir Thomas Browne (and in 1716 was to publish the first edition of Browne's *Christian Morals*). According to Birch, Jeffery was a protégé of Tillotson and often preached for him at Lincoln's Inn, and it was probably Tillotson who introduced Jeffery to Whichcote; Tillotson was also responsible for Jeffery's promotion to Archdeacon of Norwich in 1694.[69] Jeffery edited three volumes of Whichcote's *Several Discourses* (1701–03); there was evidently enough demand for a second edition of the first volume to appear in 1702 before the first edition was complete. This is the fullest collection of Whichcote's works. Jeffery received Whichcote's papers from his nephew and executor, also named Benjamin Whichcote, and

---

66 The first volume to appear under Whichcote's name was *Some Select Notions … Faithfully Collected from him by a Pupil and particular Friend of his* (1685). Its authenticity is doubted by Roberts, 'A Critical Examination of Whichcote's Writings', *Puritanism to Platonism*, 273.

67 See Voitle, *Shaftesbury* (1984), 111: the ms volumes, one of them signed by the unitarian Thomas Firmin, are in the Public Record Office.

68 *Select Sermons*, A8ᵛ–A9ᵛ. Shaftesbury adds that Whichcote's '*best Friends disown*' the work recently published in Whichcote's name, i.e. *Select Notions*.

69 Birch, *Tillotson*, 299–300.

in the 'Epistle Dedicatory' to the first volume explained that he had compared copies and corrected them by Whichcote's notes. In an advertisement to the second volume he asked those having any of Whichcote's notes in their custody to deliver them to his executor, for use in the preparation of further discourses for the press (i.e. Volume III).[70] In 1707 a fourth volume of *Discourses* was edited by Samuel Clarke (anonymously), based on transcripts, not on Whichcote's notes, and apparently (according to Salter)[71] without Jeffery's approval. The four volumes were reprinted in 1751.

Jeffery took the interesting step at the same time as he was editing the *Discourses* of reducing the large collections of published and unpublished sermons, Whichcote's notes and his hearers' transcripts, to about 5,000 aphorisms of which he published 1,000 in a small volume in 1703, without identifying Whichcote or himself.[72] In 1753 Samuel Salter, Jeffery's grandson, published a revised and much enlarged edition of 1,200 *Moral and Religious Aphorisms*, based on Jeffery's collection (by this time the original manuscripts had disappeared). This form was to prove the most effective in making Whichcote's work known. It is possible to see how Jeffery and Salter worked by comparing the aphorisms with passages with which they coincide (not always entirely) in the *Select Sermons* and *Discourses*. Salter's long preface to the new edition is an extremely useful account of the previous editorial history of Whichcote's works. Salter further included in this edition for the first time the invaluable correspondence that had passed between Whichcote and Tuckney in 1651 on the subject of Whichcote's supposedly damaging influence in Cambridge. The copy text Salter used was Jeffery's brother's transcript of Whichcote's manuscripts, and though Salter assured the reader that he had copied his copy faithfully, he suspected 'that Dr. WHICHCOTE might not always *write* exactly; nor Mr. JEFFERY always *read* exactly'.[73]

The publishing history of Whichcote's works has been given at length partly because of its inherent complexity and partly because it illustrates the problems of reading the works of the group of latitudinarians under discussion. The frequent overlapping of argument and vocabulary in works by different authors can easily be accounted for when we consider the close relationship between them and the importance of the oral medium of the sermon through which their ideas were diffused. However, there are occasions when this convergence results in the incorporation of identical passages in works by different authors. For example, in Book I, Chapter 14 of *Natural Religion* Wilkins distinguishes between natural principles and moral duties, arguing that acts of the first category are necessary, whereas we have a liberty of acting as regards the second. He continues: 'So that Self-love, and the proposing of Happiness as our chief end, though it be the foundation of duty,

---

[70] *Several Discourses*, ed. Jeffery, I (2nd edn, 1702), A4; II (1702), facing p. 1.
[71] *Moral and Religious Aphorisms*, ed. Salter (1753), 'Preface to this New Edition', xviii.
[72] 'Preface to this New Edition', xix. [73] *Eight Letters*, Preface, xxxviii.

that *basis* or *substratum* upon which the Law is founded, yet it is not properly a moral Duty, about which men have a liberty of acting.'[74] This is an important distinction in Wilkins's thought, and it is repeated in the first sermon of the 1682 volume.[75] What is the reader to make of the fact that not only the same argument but the same passage appears in Part I, Sermon 6 of Whichcote's *Select Sermons*?[76] After the distinction between natural principles and moral duties has been established, Whichcote's sermon develops along different lines, and indeed parts of the sermon are recognisable in Aphorism no. 546 and in Discourse 14.[77] It would therefore seem that the sermon was Whichcote's. What is the relationship between Wilkins's texts of 1675 and 1682 (edited by Tillotson) and Whichcote's text of 1698 (edited by Shaftesbury)? Were the transcripts of Whichcote's sermons sometimes confused with the transcripts of sermons by other preachers? Or did Wilkins and Whichcote deliberately borrow from each other? Was the concept of individual authorship unimportant to them? It is unlikely that these questions can now be answered, but textual similarities such as this would certainly be worth investigating further. This example demonstrates (as do Doddridge's observations on Tillotson) the need to regard latitudinarian writing as a largely collective enterprise and the danger of concentrating exclusively on an individual author.

The latitude-men wrote many kinds of books – Patrick, for example, was read throughout the eighteenth century as a biblical commentator, and Burnet is now remembered as a historian – but for our purposes three broad categories are important: controversial works and treatises; handbooks; and sermons. These categories are not hard and fast, since some sermons (for example Tillotson's against Catholicism) are controversial in intent, but they indicate the latitudinarians' chief objectives as authors: to define their religious position and refute that of their opponents; to prepare the clergy for their function; and to persuade their audiences of the benefits of the religious life. As controversialists the latitudinarians had three main sets of opponents: atheists, puritans and nonconformists, and Catholics. The atheists, unlike the nonconformists and Catholics, are curiously amorphous; no atheist undertook to reply to the barrage of polemical literature aimed at demonstrating 'the evil and unreasonableness of infidelity' (the title of the first of Barrow's *Sermons on the Creed*).[78] No seventeenth-century English writer identifies himself explicitly as an atheist; indeed the libertine Earl of Rochester told Burnet 'That he had never known an entire *Atheist*, who fully believed there was no God'.[79] However, the latitude-men had no doubt of the dangerous increase in atheist,

---

[74] *Natural Religion*, 213–14.   [75] *Sermons*, 11–12.   [76] *Select Sermons*, 214–16.
[77] *Several Discourses*, I, 358.
[78] Barrow, *Theological Works*, IV.
[79] Burnet, *Rochester* (1680), 22. See Allen, *Doubt's Boundless Sea* (1964), Chapter 6.

infidel, materialist, Epicurean, and libertine views, stimulated by the influence of Hobbes. Burnet gives the following account of *Leviathan* and its reception in the 1650s:

His main principles were, that all men acted under an absolute necessity, in which he seemed protected by the then received doctrine of absolute decrees. He seemed to think that the universe was God, and that souls were material, Thought being only subtil and unperceptible motion. He thought interest and fear were the chief principles of society: And he put all morality in the following that which was our own private will or advantage. He thought religion had no other foundation than the laws of the land. And he put all the law in the will of the Prince, or of the people: For he writ his book at first in favour of absolute monarchy, but turned it afterwards to gratify the republican party. These were his true principles, tho' he had disguised them, for deceiving unwary readers. And this set of notions came to spread much. The novelty and boldness of them set many on reading them. The impiety of them was acceptable to men of corrupt minds, which were but too much prepared to receive them by the extravagancies of the late times.[80]

The latitude-men set themselves to combat these views in a number of works, ranging from treatises and sermons to Burnet's exemplary biography. These include John Smith's 'Short Discourse of Atheism', the third of the *Select Discourses* (published in 1660 but preached between 1650 and 1652, and directed against the 'atheists' of antiquity, Epicurus and Lucretius);[81] More's tortuous *Antidote against Atheism* (1652, with several subsequent enlarged editions); Stillingfleet's extremely thorough *Origines Sacrae, or a Rational Account of the Grounds of Christian Faith* (1662);[82] Tillotson's 'Wisdom of Being Religious' (1664); Wilkins's *Natural Religion* (1675); Glanvill's 'The Usefulness of Real Philosophy to Religion', the fourth of his *Essays* (1676); Cudworth's massive *True Intellectual System of the Universe* (1678); Burnet's *Rochester* (1680). Easily the most readable of this group are the works by Tillotson, Wilkins, and Burnet. This tradition was continued in the Boyle lectures set up in 1691 by the will of the scientist Robert Boyle to combat infidelity,[83] though towards the end of the century the enemy was more frequently defined as a freethinker or deist than an atheist (as is recognised in Stillingfleet's *Letter to a Deist* of 1677, perhaps the first English work to be directed at this category of opponent).

The latitude-men were very clear as to the need for this body of anti-atheist literature and their motives in supplying it. Their arguments are aimed partly at those who are drawn away from religion by natural philosophy into materialism, and partly at those who are too worldly and witty to be religious.

---

[80] Burnet, *History*, I, 187–8. See Mintz, *The Hunting of Leviathan* (1962).

[81] Worthington, Smith's editor, observes that Smith did not live to see atheism being 'closely and craftily insinuated', *Select Discourses*, 'To the Reader', xx.

[82] Strongly recommended by Burnet, *Pastoral Care*, 149, alongside Wilkins's *Natural Religion* and Grotius's *Truth of the Christian Religion* (the latter available in Patrick's translation).

[83] The collected series was published as *A Defence of Natural and Revealed Religion* (1739).

More writes in his *Apology*, 'I conceiv'd that there was assigned naturally to my care such a province as this, namely, *To manage the truth of our Religion in such a way as would be most gaining upon men of a more Rational and philosophical* Genius, *the Present Age abounding so much with such.*'[84] Stillingfleet informs the reader that he has published *Origines Sacrae* 'out of a just resentment of the affronts and indignities which have been cast on Religion; by such, who account it a matter of judgement to disbelieve the Scriptures, and a piece of wit to dispute themselves out of the possibility of being happy in another world'.[85] On the whole it was the second group rather than the first who engaged the attention of the latitude-men. But however much contempt they might have felt for such opponents (Whichcote makes the recurrent point that no truly rational man can be an atheist),[86] it was on their behalf that they undertook a series of systematic expositions of the rational grounds of religion and especially of the importance of natural as distinct from revealed religion.

Whereas atheism in its various manifestations was a perennial threat, latitudinarian attacks on enthusiasm and on the separation of the non-conformists were understandably restricted to the period from the 1650s to the 1680s. Some works, for example More's *Enthusiasmus Triumphatus* (1656) and *Explanation of the Grand Mystery of Godliness* (1660), were directed at what were regarded as the extreme manifestations of sectarian enthusiasm. Some, notably Patrick's *Friendly Debate betwixt . . . a Conformist* [and] *a Non-Conformist* (1669), Fowler's *Principles and Practices* (1670) and *The Design of Christianity* (1671), and Glanvill's 'Anti-fanatical Religion', the seventh of his *Essays* (1676), compared the language, method, and doctrine of latitude-men and nonconformists in a range of tones varying from hostility to a somewhat deceptive friendliness. There was no shortage of replies to these criticisms. As a result Patrick wrote two further parts and an appendix to the *Friendly Debate* and Fowler became embroiled in an unpleasant controversy with Bunyan.[87] Stillingfleet's *Unreasonableness of Separation* (1681), written in response to nonconformist attacks on his sermon on *The Mischief of Separation* (1680), takes an unfavourable view of the historical basis of nonconformity and the prospects for indulgence, and contains a bitter attack on Baxter.[88] The broader significance of these controversies with the nonconformists is that they allowed the latitude-men to clarify their ideas as to the need for a simple religious vocabulary and a basically moral interpretation of the gospel. On the whole there is a tendency in latitudinarian writing to ignore or limit those issues that were of especial interest to nonconformists. This tendency is noticeable in Tillotson, who avoided entering into controversy with non-

---

[84] *The Apology of Dr. Henry More . . . Wherein is contained . . . A more General Account . . . of his Writings*, appended to *The Mystery of Iniquity* (1664), 482.
[85] *Origines Sacrae* (1662), 'The Preface to the Reader', b2.
[86] See e.g. *Select Sermons*, Part I, Sermon 1, 44; Sermon 3, 103–4.
[87] See Chapter 3 below.   [88] *Unreasonableness of Separation*, Preface, xxxvi–ix, lxxxv–viii.

conformists and disapproved of pulpit attacks on them, but who was consistently dismissive of their characteristic doctrines, even after 1689: see, for example, his sermons 15, 'The Distinguishing Character of a Good and a Bad Man' (1676), and 202, 'The Fruits of the Spirit, the Same with Moral Virtues' (1690), which are critical of the nonconformist concern for the individual's spiritual condition and the signs of assurance, and 106–10, 'Of the Nature of Regeneration', and 227, 'Of Justifying Faith', which attempt to eliminate the need for controversy by collapsing together terms which the nonconformists and their forebears had carefully distinguished.[89]

One of the objections the latitude-men had to nonconformity was that separation weakened protestant resistance to the spread of Catholicism.[90] They were united in their antipathy to popery; for obvious political reasons, Rome came to seem a much more powerful and immediate enemy than atheism, and therefore was made the object of concerted attack. Burnet describes how in the reign of the Catholic James II Tillotson, Stillingfleet, Patrick, and Thomas Tenison organised anti-Catholic sermons and the publication of a 'great variety of small books, that were easily purchased and soon read. They examined all the points of Popery with a solidity of judgement, a clearness of arguing, a depth of learning, and a vivacity of writing, far beyond any thing that had before that time appeared in our language.'[91] In part, the anti-Catholic writings of the Restoration period were a continuation of similar disputes of the 1630s, Chillingworth's *Religion of Protestants* (1638) considerably influencing the arguments employed by Stillingfleet and Tillotson.[92] The importance attached to Chillingworth's book is indicated by the fact that four editions were published between 1664 and 1687, the last being an abridged version made by Patrick, who added a useful analysis of the contents. The principal anti-Catholic treatises are Stillingfleet's *Rational Account of the Grounds of Protestant Religion* (1665), which begins as a reply to a Catholic attack on Archbishop Laud, Tillotson's *The Rule of Faith* (1666), a reply to a Catholic attack on Stillingfleet, and Barrow's *Treatise of the Pope's Supremacy* (1680), a historical examination of the early papacy. In addition Tillotson preached many anti-Catholic sermons, including 11, 'The Hazard of Being Saved in the Church of Rome' (1673), 21, 'Of the Trial of the Spirits' (1679), and 26, 'A Discourse against Transubstantiation' (1684), in which the arguments of the treatises are set forward more simply.[93] These anti-Catholic writings are of great importance philosophically and in relation to the development of freethinking in the 1690s, since they seek to define the

---

[89] In *Works*, I, X, VI, XI. See below, p. 56.
[90] See e.g. Tillotson's Sermon 20, 'At the Yorkshire Feast' (1679), *Works*, II, 21 ff; Stillingfleet, *Unreasonableness of Separation*, Preface, ii, iv, xxix.
[91] *History*, I, 673; according to Patrick, *Auto-biography*, 122, James II complained to Archbishop Sancroft about the anti-Catholic preaching of himself, Stillingfleet, and Tillotson.
[92] See Van Leeuwen, *The Problem of Certainty* (1963).   [93] In *Works*, I and II.

relation between reason and faith and the grounds of assent to Christian doctrine.

A fourth, numerically insignificant set of opponents were the Socinians, more usually known from the end of the century as unitarians, who denied the divinity of Christ and stressed his moral, exemplary function, and in general attached great importance to reason and toleration in religious matters.[94] Chillingworth had been charged with Socinianism by both Catholic and Presbyterian opponents, 'an imputation', his eighteenth-century biographer Pierre Des Maizeaux noted, 'which seems to have been the lot of Men distinguish'd by the excellency of their parts; and more particularly, of those who have endeavour'd to free Religion from Enthusiasm and Fanaticism, and to establish it upon its true rational grounds and foundations'.[95] Des Maizeaux concludes his biography with a quotation from Tillotson's Sermon 224 on 'The Efficacy, Usefulness and Reasonableness of Divine Faith', which praises Chillingworth and continues: 'But if this be *Socinianism*, for a Man to enquire into the Grounds and Reasons of Christian Religion, and to endeavour to give a satisfactory account why he believes it, I know no way but that all considerate inquisitive men, that are above Fancy and Enthusiasm, must be either *Socinians* or *Atheists*.'[96] Tillotson and Stillingfleet were both anxious to differentiate their rational defences of Christianity from Socinianism, and to stress their adherence to the doctrine of the Trinity and their acceptance of religious mysteries above reason. In 1693 Tillotson published a collection of sermons on the divinity of Christ (sermons 43–6, first preached 1679–80), partly for the benefit of his friend the unitarian Thomas Firmin.[97] Stillingfleet, who had written against the Socinians earlier, became an active participant in the Trinitarian controversy in the 1690s, and in his *Discourse in Vindication of the Doctrine of the Trinity* (1697) implicated Locke's *Essay concerning Human Understanding* (1690) in the Socinian attack on mysteries, thereby initiating an important exchange of letters.[98] Tillotson was a great admirer of the reasonable temper of the Socinians – in Sermon 44 he says that 'they are a pattern of the fair way of disputing, and of debating matters of religion without heat and unseemly reflections upon their adversaries' – but he was sure that truth was not on their side.[99] This stand is important in indicating the self-imposed limits to the rationalism of the latitude-men, a rationalism that was so much in evidence in the controversies with atheists and Catholics.

[94] See McLachlan, *Socinianism*.
[95] Des Maizeaux, *Chillingworth* (1725), 370–2. See also Trevor-Roper, *Catholics, Anglicans and Puritans*, 186–92.
[96] Des Maizeaux, *Chillingworth*, 372; Tillotson, *Works*, XI, 4966.
[97] Tillotson, *Works*, III; Birch, *Tillotson*, 292 ff.
[98] [Bentley], *Stillingfleet*, 78 ff. For Locke's religious views see *Reason, Grace and Sentiment*, Volume II.
[99] *Works*, III, 254–5.

Though the latitude-men were tireless controversialists, they saw themselves first as preachers and pastors. From the 1660s particularly in London a remarkable change in preaching style and method was effected whereby the elaborate witty preaching of earlier Anglicans and what was regarded as the speculative and enthusiastic preaching of the puritans gave way to a new plainer, more simple kind of sermon.[100] Wilkins through his theories and Tillotson through his practice were largely responsible for this change. Burnet summed up Tillotson's influence as follows:

His notions of Morality were fine and sublime; His thread of Reasoning, was easy, clear, and solid; He was not only the best Preacher of the age, but seemed to have brought Preaching to perfection; His sermons were so well heard and liked, and so much read, that all the Nation proposed him as a Pattern, and studied to copy after him.[101]

This change, which seemed natural and inevitable at the end of the century, was achieved as the result of a concerted programme in the period after the Restoration. The revised 1669 version of Wilkins's *Ecclesiastes* contains clear instructions as to the aims and methods of the new style. The conflict between puritan modes of preaching and that of the latitude-men, and the anticipated success of the latitude-men in bringing audiences round to their way, is described by the apologists for the new style, Patrick, Fowler, and Glanvill.[102] A good deal of discussion was stimulated by John Eachard's anonymously published and provocative letter on *The Grounds and Occasions of the Contempt of the Clergy* (1670). Eachard saw two main grounds for contempt, the clergy's ignorance and their poverty; under the first heading he attacked abuses in preaching, drawing freely on Patrick's *Friendly Debate* for his illustrations.[103] Taking up Eachard's criticisms, James Arderne drew up a set of brief and practical *Directions concerning the Matter and Stile of Sermons* (1671), expanding some of the points Wilkins had made in *Ecclesiastes*. In turn, Glanvill drew on Arderne in *An Essay concerning Preaching and A Seasonable Defence of Preaching* (1678).[104]

Some of the most interesting observations on the new style are to be found in a book written long after the battle had been won, Burnet's *Discourse of the Pastoral Care* (1692; reprinted with additions 1713). This book, which was

---

[100] Useful studies of this change are Cope, *Glanvill*, Chapter 7; Jones, 'The Attack on Pulpit Eloquence in the Restoration', in *The Seventeenth Century* (1951); Lessenich, *Elements of Pulpit Oratory* (1972); Mitchell, *English Pulpit Oratory* (1932), Chapters 8–9; Simon, *Three Restoration Divines*, I, Chapter 1; Williamson, 'The Restoration Revolt against Enthusiasm', in *Seventeenth Century Contexts* (1960). Glanvill's revisions of his own style provide one indicator of this change.

[101] *History*, II, 135; see also *Sermon Preached at the Funeral of* [Tillotson], 13–14.

[102] *Friendly Debate, passim*; *Principles and Practices*, 104 ff, and *Design of Christianity*, 261; *Essays*, No. 7, 41–6.

[103] *Contempt of the Clergy*, 57–61.

[104] Arderne, *Directions*, ed. Mackay (1952), Introduction, viii–ix, xiii.

Burnet's own favourite, was written at the suggestion of Tillotson and Queen Mary; Tillotson read it in manuscript and commented, 'The work is as perfect in its kind, as I hope to see anything.'[105] The general object of the book is to provide rules for improving the standard of education and practical pastoral work among the Anglican clergy, which Burnet compares unfavourably with that of the clergy of the Church of Rome.[106] The most interesting chapters are numbers 7, 'Of the due Preparation of such as may and ought to be put in Orders', 8, 'Of the Functions and Labours of Clergymen', and 9, 'Concerning Preaching'. In the last of these Burnet makes some interesting comments on the change in preaching style effected in the fourth-century eastern Church by Basil and Chrysostom, who 'brought Preaching from the dry Pursuing of *Allegories* that had vitiated *Origen*, and from the excessive Affectation of Figures and Rhetorick that appears in *Nazianzen*, to a due Simplicity; a native Force and Beauty, having joined to the Plainness of a clear but noble Stile, the Strength of Reason, and the Softness of Persuasion'.[107] It is worth noting that, according to Burnet, Tillotson prepared himself for writing sermons by studying the Scriptures, the classical moralists, and of the fathers chiefly Basil and Chrysostom,[108] and that according to Hill, Barrow much preferred Chrysostom to any of the other fathers and during his stay in Constantinople from 1658 to 1659 read all his works.[109] Burnet continues in Chapter 9 of *Pastoral Care*:

But without flattering the present Age, or any persons now alive, too much, it must be confessed, that [preaching] is brought of late to a much greater Perfection than it was ever before at among us. It is certainly brought nearer the Pattern that St. *Chrysostom* has set, or perhaps carried beyond it. Our language is much refined, and we have returned to the plain Notions of simple and genuine Rhetorick.[110]

What were the principal characteristics of the latitudinarian sermon? Although advice on preaching was directed at the ordinary parish priest (Eachard, for example, in *The Contempt of the Clergy* points out the absurdity of learned preaching for country people, and Burnet concludes that 'a *Preacher* is to fancy himself, as in the Room of the most unlearned Man in his whole Parish'),[111] in contrast the sermons of the chief latitude-men were addressed to learned, wealthy, and politically important audiences. Thus Whichcote, apart from brief periods in country livings in Somerset in the early 1640s and Cambridgeshire in the 1660s, preached either in Cambridge or in city churches: St Anne's Blackfriars, the Guildhall Chapel, and St Lawrence

105 Burnet, *History*, II, 637, *Pastoral Care*, 224; Birch, *Tillotson*, 264–6.

106 *Pastoral Care*, Preface, vii–viii.

107 *Pastoral Care*, 191.   108 *Sermon Preached at the Funeral of* [Tillotson], 13.

109 'Life of Barrow', Barrow, *Theological Works* I, xv. For Barrow's repeated citation of Chrysostom, see e.g. Sermon 28, 'Motives and Arguments to Charity', *Works*, II. Non-conformists, on the other hand, would be much more likely to read Tertullian and Augustine (I owe this point to N. H. Keeble).

110 *Pastoral Care*, 192.   111 *Contempt of the Clergy*, 39; *Pastoral Care*, 199.

Jewry, in the last of which, according to Tillotson in his funeral sermon, he had 'a very considerable and judicious auditory, though not very numerous by reason of the weakness of his voice in his declining age'.[112] Indeed the diarist John Evelyn complained on 28 May 1682 that the minister at St Lawrence, unidentified but presumably Whichcote, 'spake so very low, & was so feeble an old man, that I could by no meanes hear what he saied'.[113] The majority of Barrow's sermons were preached in Cambridge, though a few were preached in city churches and at Whitehall before Charles II. Tillotson had a brief period in the early 1660s in country livings in Hertfordshire and Suffolk, but according to Birch his attempt to introduce the new style of preaching to his Suffolk congregation, who were accustomed to the puritan way of doing things, was very unpopular: they 'universally complain'd, that Jesus Christ had not been preach'd amongst them, since Mr. TILLOTSON had been settled in the parish'. His city sermons, on the other hand, were very popular, especially among the clergy; Beardmore remarked that 'many, that heard him on *Sunday* at *Lincoln's Inn*, went joyfully to St *Laurence* on Tuesday, hoping they might hear the same sermon again'.[114] Tillotson's published sermons were mostly preached in the city, though many were preached at Whitehall before successive monarchs; these sermons necessarily had a public, official standing.

Latitudinarian sermons were far from being simply moral essays, as nonconformists and dissenters alleged, but the rational, expository element was of great importance. Wilkins comments in the preface to the revised *Ecclesiastes*, evidently with his eye on puritan methods:

The great End of Preaching, being either to inform *or* perswade; *This may be most effectually done by such rational ways of* Explication *and* Confirmation, *as are most fit and proper to satisfie mens judgments and consciences. And this will in all times be accounted good sense, as being suitable to the Reason of Mankind; whereas all other ways are, at the best, but particular fashions, which though at one time they may obtain, yet will presently vanish, and grow into disesteem.*[115]

In the second section, 'Concerning Method', Wilkins divides the sermon into three parts, explication, confirmation, and application. Reason plays a particularly important role in the second part, confirmation or 'proofs'. It is significant that in the first edition of *Ecclesiastes* confirmation is dealt with cursorily; there is a reference to 'carnal reason', a favourite puritan phrase which is deleted from the revised edition and which Wilkins would certainly have come to regard as enthusiastic cant.[116] In the revised edition Wilkins recommends that 'The Arguments from Reason, should be rendered so plain and so cogent, as may be sufficient to satisfie any teachable man, concerning the truth, or fitness, or necessity of what we would persuade to.'[117]

---

[112] Tillotson, *Works*, II, 154.   [113] Evelyn, *Diary*, ed. de Beer (1955), IV, 282.
[114] Birch, *Tillotson*, 28, 408.
[115] *Ecclesiastes* (1675 edn), 'To the Reader', A5. This preface is not in the first edition (1646).
[116] *Ecclesiastes* (1646), 14.   [117] *Ecclesiastes* (1675), 27.

These rational, carefully structured discourses were either read from full scripts or delivered from written notes, unlike puritan and nonconformist sermons, which were usually delivered from memory.[118] Evelyn, whose *Diary* records his reactions to the changes in preaching from the Interregnum to the end of the century, comments of a preacher who was forced to break off his sermon because it was too dark that he used written notes, 'as they now generaly did all over England & not as formerly, (& [as] yet in all other Countrys) they preach'd Memoriter, which whether so well, I leave to others to Judge: Reading much hindring Action, which we in English pulpits are defective in: In the meane time written sermons being more studyed & methodical, have likewise greate advantages'.[119]

In this emphasis on methodical structure and on convincing the hearer's understanding through rational proof lies one of the chief differences between the latitudinarian tradition of preaching and that of the puritans and their nonconformist and dissenting heirs. Only extreme nonconformists scorned reason, and the latitudinarians did not neglect the affections, but the emphasis is different. The dissenters were later to regard their ability to move the affections as one of the great strengths of their tradition. In *Ecclesiastes*, in two passages present in the first edition and retained in subsequent ones, Wilkins does give the affections their due. The application, the final part of the sermon, is especially concerned with the affections, and Wilkins concludes his account in section ii thus; 'as the *milder affections*, τὰ 'ἤθη, do best suit with the *Introduction*, which insinuate into the love and attention of the hearers; so τὰ πάθη, the more *eager* and *vehement affections* will best become the Conclusion, as supposing then that we have won the cause we did contend for, convinced and perswaded the Auditory beyond all opposition'. (Note that moving the affections follows after persuading the reason.) In section v, 'Concerning Expression', he comments, using puritan phraseology that Baxter was to make peculiarly his own (though the first edition of *Ecclesiastes* antedates any of Baxter's publications): 'It must be *affectionate* and cordial, as proceeding from the heart, and an experimental acquaintance with those truths which we deliver'.[120] Similarly Arderne distinguishes the main body of the sermon which deals with the judgement from the exhortation which addresses the affections. He advises the preacher to change his manner and tone in the exhortation, in terms which are again reminiscent of Baxter: 'the design is to inflame and kindle the affections, and if you be but luke-warm, they may be benummed: here you must give yourself that liberty and boldness of speech, which resembles *ex tempore* talk upon the warmth of a sudden and present thought'.[121]

[118] Mitchell, *English Pulpit Oratory*, 20 ff. Birch, 416–17, notes that Tillotson originally learnt his sermons by heart and then gave up the practice.
[119] Evelyn, *Diary*, V, 555, 1 January 1704.   [120] *Ecclesiastes* (1675), 38, 201.
[121] *Directions*, 16.

However, though the importance of moving the affections in the concluding application of the sermon was recognised, contemporaries were in no doubt that the fundamental emphasis of the latitudinarian sermon was on the persuasion of the reason. William Lloyd, in his funeral sermon for Wilkins in 1672, stressed his talent for rational exposition as a preacher: 'He express'd all things in their true and natural Colours ... His Plainness was best for the Instruction of the simple ... He applied himself rather to their Understanding than Affections'.[122] Beardmore makes similar points about Tillotson's method:

his endeavour was to make all things clear, to bring truth into open light; and his arguments of persuasion were strong and nervous, and tended to *gain the affections by the understanding*: and those, that heard him with attention, must either be persuaded to become good, or else they must do violence to their best faculties, and notoriously act contrary to their own reason.[123]

Patrick explicitly compares the two traditions of preaching in relation to the function of reason and the affections. There are two ways of moving the affections, argues Conformist, by the senses and imagination or the reason and judgement:

I believe your affections are moved in the first way very often, by melting tones, pretty similitudes, running sentences, kind and loving smiles, and sometimes dismally sad looks ... and the truth is, you are like to be moved very seldom in our churches by these means ... For one may be affected, whether he will or no, by objects of sense: but reason convinces and moves us by sober consideration ...[124]

In spite of Patrick's sneering tone, an important distinction is being made.

The other central characteristic of latitudinarian preaching is a concern with the careful use of language. There are religious, political, intellectual, and social reasons underlying the latitudinarian attempt to simplify and clarify the language of religious discourse, but three are especially important: opposition to puritanism, the influence of the new science, and the latitude-men's appraisal of the self-interest of their audience. Language was recognised at the outset as a dividing point between the latitude-men and the puritans. Several of Tuckney's complaints to Whichcote centre on Whichcote's alleged reluctance to use biblical language, and his introduction of philosophical language in his sermons. Whichcote's favourite terms are castigated: 'I doe not fancy,' says Tuckney, 'as some others, this affected word *Ingenuous*; and I wish, the thing it self were not idolized; to the prejudice of *Saving Grace*.' He objects to 'the big words, sometimes of "divinest reason", and sometimes of "more than mathematical demonstration"'. He complains

---

[122] *Sermon Preach'd at the Funeral of ... Wilkins*, appended to Wilkins, *Natural Religion* (1710 edn), 26.

[123] Birch, *Tillotson*, 409 (my italics).

[124] *Friendly Debate*, in *Works*, ed. Taylor (1858), V, 278.

that Whichcote's reading of philosophy has made his ministry less edifying, 'as partlie not being well understood, by very manie of your auditours; and less affecting the heart, when so buisying the head to understand both words and things'. He begs Whichcote: 'affect not to speak in schoole-language; nor to runne-out in schoole-notions: it is farre different from the scripture, both style and matter: it was begot in the depth of anti-christian darkeness'.[125] Tuckney and Whichcote are truly at cross-purposes. Tuckney regards Whichcote's use of the classical and scholastic language of reason and natural law as confusing: it obscures the plain words of the gospel. Whichcote, by contrast, sees his task as to clarify meaning, to enlighten the understanding, to reach the things behind words. He defends his rationalist position:

Sir, I oppose not rational to spiritual; for spiritual is most rational: But I contradis-tinguish rational to conceited, impotent, affected CANTING: (as I may call it; when the Ear receeves wordes, which offer no matter to the Understanding; make no impression on the inward sense.) And I think, where the demonstration of the spirit is, there is the highest purest reason; so as to satisfie, convince, command, the minde: things are most thorowlie seen-into, most cleerlie understood; the minde not so much amused with forms of Wordes, as made acquainted with the inwards of things; the reason of them and the necessarie connexion of termes cleerlie layde-open to the mind and discovered.[126]

This emphasis on not being deluded by attractive-sounding terms but on seeing through words to things is central to the latitudinarian view of language. It is a recurrent complaint of the early latitude-men, as of the sequestered Anglicans, that the puritans are obsessed by notions and specu-lations, and that this obsession with defining the terms of specific doctrines has nothing to do with real religion. This is the burden of Cudworth's celebrated *Sermon Preached before the House of Commons* (1647).[127] Tuckney warns of the tendency of such complaints: 'that there is a God and a Christ, will thus come to bee but a notion and speculation'.[128] By 'notions and speculations', which could well be termed a latitudinarian cant phrase, the latitude-men seem to mean two different things: either subjects which cannot fruitfully be discussed because they are not open to rational exposition or solution, or subjects which are the creation of a specialist cant language and have no basis in reality, which are in effect terms without meaning. In the first category come the favourite Calvinist topic of predestination and the interpretation of biblical mysteries. In 1662 Charles II issued a directive to the Archbishops forbidding preaching on such topics as free will and reprobation. This is reflected in Arderne's *Directions*: 'We ought not ... to chuse obscure passages

---

[125] *Eight Letters*, 2, 37.   [126] *Eight Letters*, 108.
[127] *Cambridge Platonists*, ed. Patrides, 96–9; cf. Hammond, *Practical Catechisme*, 'Epistle to the Reader', A3 (quoted above, p. 20), and Evelyn's complaint that 'all devotion [is] now plac'd in hearing Sermons and discourses of Speculative & notional things', *Diary*, III, 160, 21 October 1655, also III, 184, 2 November 1656.
[128] *Eight Letters*, 39.

[of Scripture], or sublime controversies, or nice speculations to be propoun-
ded to any in publick, much less to the uncapable multitude.' Subjects to be
avoided include 'How . . . Free-will and Gods foreknowledge of its action can
be reconciled?' The preacher should not 'set up for a Mystery-man' by
attempting, for example, to interpret the Book of Daniel.[129] But being a
'mystery man' can mean not only the impudent attempt to penetrate real
mysteries but also the creation of mysteries where none are intended in the
text. Thus Fowler includes as the chief offenders in a list of unholy ministers
who affect high-flown language those 'that seek to approve themselves to their
Auditors to be men of Mysteries, and endeavour to make the plain and easie
Doctrines of the Gospel as intricate and obscure as ever they are able'.[130]

The latitude-men repeatedly accuse the puritans of deluding their audito-
ries, obscuring the gospel, and inhibiting the practice of real religion by their
use of terms and phrases. Wilkins makes this criticism at an early stage: ''tis a
dangerous fault, when men cannot content themselves with *the wholesome form
of sound words*, but do altogether affect new light, and new language, which
may in time destroy practical Godliness'.[131] Patrick claims that he wrote *A
Friendly Debate* in part 'to preserve [the nonconformists] from being abused by
phrases'. Looking back at the 1650s, Conformist says that the nation was
overrun with folly because of men 'inventing strange language'; sectaries
easily took advantage of the people because they were 'so much in love with
new-minted words'. In contrast conformist ministers 'do not seek to please
their itching ears, and gratify the longings of their fancies with new-found
words, affected expressions, and odd phrases; but tell us those things that
concern our Saviour and his holy life in plain and proper language'.[132]
Glanvill gives a similar account in 'Anti-fanatical Religion' of the language of
the Ataxites: 'All fill'd their Discourses with the words of *Light, Faith, Grace,
the Spirit*; and all talk'd in set *Phrases*, phancifully and ignorantly about them.'
The divines of Bensalem set out to purge religion 'from sensless *phrases*,
conceited *mysteries*, and unnecessary words of *Art*'. Glanvill lists their programme for plain preaching: they avoided speculation, needless words, subtle
distinctions, mysteries, '*canting Fanatick Phrases*', and held it as a rule 'that
unwonted words were *never* to be us'd, either in Pulpits, or elsewhere, when
common ones would as fitly represent their meaning'.[133]

Tillotson above all put this linguistic programme into practice. Beardmore
comments:

His composures were no jargon, or cant; did not consist of phrases or forms of words
suited to any sect, or party of men, or that had little real matter in them. It was one
thing, that he disliked in the Nonconformists, that they used divers distinctive phrases

---

[129] *Directions*, 3–4. For the directive see Cope, *Glanvill*, 155.   [130] *Design*, 261.
[131] *Ecclesiastes* (1675), 201; in the first and subsequent editions.
[132] *Friendly Debate, Works*, V, Preface to the Sixth Edition (1683), 255; 291, 293, 303.
[133] *Essays*, No. 7, 6, 31, 42–3.

and expressions, that seemed to have some sublime meaning; when, if search'd to the bottom, they were scarce sense, or however might be better expressed in more plain and intelligible words.[134]

Beardmore may have in mind Tillotson's sermon 52 'Of the Education of Children' (one of four on family religion preached at St Lawrence Jewry in 1662 but not published till 1694), in which Tillotson criticises parents who 'take great care to plant little and ill-grounded opinions in the minds of their children, and so fashion them to a party by infusing into them the particular notions and phrases of a sect, which when they come to be examined have no substance, nor perhaps sense in them'.[135] A particularly interesting example of a sermon in which false speculation, cant terms and phrases, and obscuring the meaning of the gospel are all associated is 'Of Justifying Faith' (227, one of a group on this topic), in which Tillotson blames the antinomian tendencies of some accounts of justifying faith on the misuse of metaphor. For Tillotson (as for all latitudinarians and almost all Anglicans) active repentance and obedience are conditions of justification: the use of popular non-scriptural metaphors such as 'resting, and relying, and leaning upon CHRIST, appre-hending, *and* laying hold, and applying of CHRIST' encourages moral passivity. (The language of the *Westminster Confession* as well as popular puritan preaching is glanced at here.) Tillotson believes that the whole problem could be averted if language were used more carefully:

he that would teach men what faith is, he must first acquaint men with the thing, and describe it in as proper and simple words as can be, and not by figurative and metaphorical phrases. Indeed after a man hath delivered the simple notion of a thing in proper words, he may afterwards illustrate it by metaphors: but then these are not to be insisted upon, and strained to the utmost extent of the metaphor, beyond what the true notion of the thing will bear.

When the minister is dealing with Scripture metaphors, his task is not 'to darken his discourse by them, but to explain them, and make them intelligi-ble, to translate them into english, and instead of them to use such phrases as people are more familiarly acquainted with, and are used in our own language'.[136]

Tillotson's breathtakingly confident conviction that doctrinal disagreement can be made to disappear if language is simplified owes much to Wilkins's scientific study of language. Burnet is clear about the importance of this influence: 'His joining with Bishop *Wilkins* in pursuing the Scheme of an Universal Character, led him to consider exactly the Truth of Language and Stile, in which no Man was happier, and knew better the Art of preserving the Majesty of things under a Simplicity of Words'.[137] One of the main objects of Wilkins's *Essay towards a Real Character and a Philosophical Language* (1668) was

---

[134] Birch, *Tillotson*, 406.   [135] *Works*, IV, 486.   [136] *Works*, XI, 5007, 5018, 5020–1.
[137] *Sermon Preached at the Funeral of* [Tillotson], 13.

to preserve 'the Majesty of things under a Simplicity of Words': Wilkins had no expectation that his new symbolic language, the 'real character', would be adopted, but he was sure that his 'philosophical language', i.e. the tabular classification of '*all things and notions that fall under discourse*' of which the bulk of the book consists, would be conducive to real knowledge and beneficial to religion and society: '*this design will . . . contribute much to the clearing of some of our Modern differences in* Religion, *by unmasking many wild errors, that shelter themselves under the disguise of affected phrases; which being Philosophically unfolded, and rendered according to the genuine and natural importance of Words, will appear to be inconsistencies and contradictions*'. An important feature of 'philosophical language' is the elimination of ambiguity through avoiding variety of phrases and verbal ornaments, partly because 'they prejudice the native simplicity of [speech], and contribute to the disguising of it with false appearances', and partly because 'they are very changeable, every generation producing new ones'. Such ornamented, various, ambiguous language is actually destructive of knowledge, argues Wilkins: 'witness the present Age, especially the late times, wherein this grand imposture of Phrases hath almost eaten out solid Knowledge in all professions'.[138] Interestingly, the resulting hostility of the scientific movement to the use of metaphor in discursive prose, which is treated in Sprat's *History of the Royal Society* and reflected in Tillotson's sermon discussed above, is modified by Arderne, who argues that metaphors cannot be rejected entirely because 'the poverty of conceptions, or the scarcity of words constrains, that in every sentence almost the adjectives & epithetes are in strictness metaphorical'. Arderne goes on to give cautious and limiting rules for the use of metaphors: they must be clearly expressed, well known, appropriate to the matter to which they are applied, and 'to say all in a word . . . fashionable [presumably in the sense of useful], and such, which the best custom of speech hath allowed.'[139] It is fair to say that in religious writing it is the cautious advice of Arderne with regard to metaphor and ornaments rather than the drastic advice of Wilkins which is followed in practice.

The latitude-men show no awareness that their own language is in any way idiosyncratic or sectarian, despite the strictures of their puritan or non-conformist opponents in the 1650s and 1660s: what to their critics is the specialised language of the schools or the heathen moralists, to the latitude-men is a language that is philosophically based, rational, clear, and of universal validity. However, to some extent their language can be seen as a response to the needs and assumptions of their politically and socially important audiences in the court and city. Thus Burnet stresses the influence

138 *Essay towards a Real Character*, Dedication, a^v–b, Part I, 18; cf. Glanvill, 'The Usefulness of Real Philosophy to Religion', *Essays*, No. 4, 26. See Christensen, 'Wilkins' (1946); Jones, 'Science and English Prose Style in the Third Quarter of the Seventeenth Century', in *The Seventeenth Century*; Salmon, '"Philosophical" Grammar in John Wilkins' *Essay*' and 'Language-Planning in Seventeenth-Century England', in *Study of Language* (1979).
139 *Directions*, 24–5.

of Charles II's taste in establishing the popularity of latitudinarian preaching: 'this help'd to raise the value of these men, when the King approved of the style their discourses generally ran in; which was clear, plain and short'.[140] On some occasions the latitude-men deliberately take note of the material interests of their city audiences by applying mercantile language to religion. Thus in *Natural Religion* Wilkins illustrates his argument that '*A Present Good may reasonably be parted with, upon a probable expectation of a future Good which is more excellent*' with the example of merchants venturing their stocks in foreign countries; if wise men were to assure us that there was an undiscovered country where we could increase our gain a thousand times by venturing everything, then it would be a rational act for us to do so.[141] This illustration, which can partly be seen as an updating of the parables of the Kingdom (e.g. Matthew 13:45–6), is used again in Wilkins's Sermon 10 on liberality ('the most gainful way of Trading'), preached at the Spital on Easter Wednesday 1663,[142] and is developed at length in Barrow's Sermon 31, 'The Duty and Reward of Bounty to the Poor', preached in the same place on the same occasion in 1671:

Liberality is the most beneficial traffick that can be; it is bringing our wares to the best market; it is letting out our money into the best hands; we thereby lend our money to God, who repays with vast usury; an hundred to one is the rate he allows at present, and above a hundred millions to one he will render hereafter; so that if you will be merchants this way, you shall be sure to thrive, you cannot fail to grow rich most easily and speedily.[143]

But there is more at issue here than the adoption of an appropriate, 'fashionable' metaphor for the persuasion of a particular audience. Mercantile language is used in this sermon because it is the immediate application of a general principle, the need to appeal to the hearer's interest (there is surely an underlying pun on interest as financial return on invested capital and interest as the individual's advantage). It is a fundamental assumption of the latitude-men that religion is fitted to man in his worldly state, that it teaches him to differentiate his immediate from his best interests, and that his pursuit of the latter also achieves the former – religion is of temporal as well as spiritual and eternal benefit. In a key passage in *Ecclesiastes* concerning the confirmation of the sermon, Wilkins explains that rational arguments for the necessity of a course of action are made on two grounds, duty or interest. Duty is based on notions of true and false, right and wrong, and therefore the judgement must be convinced; interest, 'or the advantage accruing to our selves by it', is based on the consideration of good and evil, and 'doth therefore belong to the exciting of the *Will* and *Affections*, and may more properly be styled *Motives*. And because those Affections which do chiefly influence the

---

[140] *History*, I, 191.   [141] *Natural Religion*, 14–16.   [142] *Sermons*, ed. Tillotson, 313.
[143] *Theological Works*, II, 243. Of this sermon Tillotson said '*perhaps there is nothing extant in* Divinity *more perfect in its kind*', Barrow, *Works*, ed. Tillotson, I, A4.

Inclinations and Actions of Men, are Love and Hatred, Hope and Fear; therefore one proper way of *perswasion* or *disswasion*, is by representing a thing as being *for* or *against* a man's Interest upon either of these Accounts.'[144] Arderne advises, summarising or anticipating countless latitudinarian sermons, that the preacher should show how the performance of religious duties brings honour and reputation, pleasure and delight, and is safe and prudent; men are to be reduced (i.e. brought back) to holiness and virtue by the demonstration that religion 'is a way of pleasantness' [cf. Proverbs 3:17]: 'These are the motives of the greatest reach'.[145] The latitudinarian sermon thus posits a hearer who is felt to be representative of ordinary humanity, whatever his particular needs: he is a being who is rational and self-interested, and who will respond both to the demonstration that religion is true and to the persuasion that its practice will make him happy.

3 The design of religion

In the following account of the principles of latitudinarian religion no attempt is made either to trace the evolution of the ideas of a particular latitude-man or to investigate in detail points of disagreement between individuals; rather the object is to clarify and illustrate the central features of their thought, to indicate some inconsistencies between different aspects and the steps the latitude-men took to reconcile them, and to look forward to some of the ways in which these ideas were developed in the next century. This summary is based largely but not exclusively on the following works: the sermons of Whichcote, Barrow and Tillotson; Fowler's *Principles and Practices* and *The Design of Christianity*; Wilkins's *Natural Religion*; Glanvill's *Essays*; and Burnet's *Exposition of the Thirty-Nine Articles* (1699).[146] On the whole illustrations are taken from works published after 1660, but there are two exceptions, ornate and metaphorical works written well before the reformation of style had begun to take effect: Culverwell's *An Elegant and Learned Discourse of the Light of Nature* (delivered in Emmanuel College and published posthumously in 1652 with a dedication to Tuckney) and Smith's *Select Discourses* (published posthumously in 1660). Latitudinarian ideas are considered under three main headings: common notions and the role of reason; the relationship between natural and revealed religion; and the nature and end of man.

Common notions and the role of reason

The latitudinarians held man to have been created and to remain, despite the effects of sin, a rational being endowed with innate knowledge of God, good

---

[144] *Ecclesiastes* (1675), 27–8; not in 1st edn.   [145] *Directions*, 15.
[146] The work of More, Cudworth, and Locke is treated in *Reason, Grace, and Sentiment*, Volume II, and is hardly touched on here.

and evil, and moral duties.[147] Two favourite biblical metaphors are
repeatedly invoked to express this knowledge and its operation: light, from
Proverbs 20:27, 'The spirit of man is the candle of the Lord, searching all the
inward parts of the belly' ('spirit' is translated 'understanding' in the subtitle
to Culverwell's *Discourse*, chapter 1), and inscription, from Romans 2:14–15,
'For when the Gentiles, which have not the law, do by nature the things contained in the law, these, having not the law, are a law unto themselves: Which
shew the work of the law written in their hearts.' Whichcote told Tuckney that
'these phrases of the Apostle [from Romans 1 and 2], concerning men not
under a gospel dispensation ... have forced upon me all those notions I do
entertain, or have publiquely delivered; concerning natural light, or the use of
reason'. Tuckney replied crustily that Whichcote's auditors 'conceeve, that
that saying of "the candle of the Lord, etc." so over-frequently quoted, makes
nothing to that purpose; and those instances out of Rom. I and II as little'.[148]

The ideas expressed in these metaphors are by no means exclusively biblical: though their biblical credentials are stressed, they are amalgamated by
the latitude-men with similar ideas drawn from classical and scholastic philosophy. Several key terms are used, sometimes virtually synonymously or in
close conjunction (though they are not necessarily all compatible with each
other), to denote the innate knowledge shared by all mankind of the nature of
God, the independent existence of good and evil, and the obligations owed to
God and other men, knowledge which is separate from and antecedent to
knowledge received by means of biblical revelation. These terms are common
notions (a translation of the Greek κοιναὶ ᾽έννοιαι and the Latin *communes
notitiae*) or innate, connate, connatural or self-evident notions; truths of first or
natural inscription; first principles; natural law, natural light, light of nature,
or natural sense; right reason (Greek ᾽ορθὸς λόγος and Latin *recta ratio*); and
conscience. Passages from classical, early Christian, scholastic, and modern
authors (notably Aristotle, Cicero, Arrian, Origen, Aquinas, and Grotius)
which illustrate or explain these terms are often translated, cited, or paraphrased. Thus Smith comments, '*Arrianus* hath well observed, That the
Common Notions of *God* and *Vertue* imprest upon the Souls of men, are more clear
and perspicuous then any else; and that if they have not more *certainty*, yet have
they more *evidence*, and display themselves with less difficulty to our *Reflexive*
Faculty then any Geometrical Demonstrations'.[149] Fowler quotes Origen: '*See
whether or no the agreeableness of the precepts of our Faith with the common notions of
humane nature, be not that which hath caused them to be so readily entertained, by the
ingenuous hearers of them.*'[150] Culverwell appeals to Aquinas; 'as *Aquinas* does

---

147 Yolton, *Locke and the Way of Ideas* (1956), Chapter 2, distinguishes not very convincingly
    between the 'naive' and 'modified' forms of this theory.
148 *Eight Letters*, 9, 20.
149 *Select Discourses*, 1, 'The true Way or Method of attaining to Divine Knowledge', 14.
150 *Principles and Practices*, 49, from Origen, *Against Celsus*, III, 40.

very well tell us, the Law of *Nature* is nothing but *participatio Legis aeternae in Rationali creatura*, the copying out of the eternal Law, and the imprinting of it upon the breast of a Rational being'.[151] Culverwell also frequently quotes Cicero, including an elaborate free translation (too long to give in full) of the celebrated passage on right reason in *De Republica*: 'This Law never paints its face, it never changes its colour, it does not put on one Aspect at *Athens* and another face at *Rome*, but looks upon all Nations & persons with an impartial eye, it shines upon all ages and times, and conditions, with a perpetual light, *it is yesterday and today, the same for ever* [Hebrews 13:8]' (note that Culverwell explicitly associates right reason with Christ, the logos).[152] Interestingly, in view of the later hostility of Christian apologists such as Baxter, Culverwell quotes Lord Herbert's *De Veritate* with approval: '*Tota fere Ethica est Notitia communis*: All Morality is nothing but a collection and bundling up of natural Precepts'.[153] Culverwell explicitly identifies the unwritten moral law of Aristotle and Cicero with the Pauline law written in the heart;[154] similarly in a useful summary Wilkins identifies Cicero's innate law with the Pauline law: 'Such kind of Notions as are *general* to mankind, and not confined to any particular Sect or Nation, or Time, are usually stiled κοιναὶ ᾽εννοιαι, Common Notions, λόγοι σπερματικοὶ, Seminal Principles; and *Lex Nata*, by the *Roman Orator*, an innate Law, in opposition to Lex scripta, and in the Apostles phrase, the *Law written in our hearts*.'[155]

The appeals to these central figures and the harmonising of their thought and expression with the key statements from Proverbs and St Paul are designed to demonstrate the antiquity, universality, and truth of the theory of common notions. Similarly the widespread use of the biblical metaphors, particularly that of the law written in the heart, is designed to reinforce the view that these notions are obvious and indelible. Frequent variations on the metaphor of inscription are those of printing, stamping, impressing, engraving, and sealing. The following are some examples chosen from a wide range. Culverwell paraphrases a quotation by Grotius from Philo:

right Reason (saies he) is that fixt and unshaken Law, not writ in perishing paper by the hand or pen of a creature, nor graven like a dead letter upon livelesse and decaying Pillars, but written with the point of a Diamond, nay with the finger of God himself in the heart of man: a Deity gave it an *Imprimatur*; and an eternal Spirit grav'd it in an immortal minde.[156]

Chapter 7 of Culverwell's *Light of Nature* contains a series of images for the

---

[151] *Light of Nature*, 34. The editors usefully identify Culverwell's citations. Cf. Smith, *Select Discourses*, no. 5, 'Of the Existence and Nature of God', 156.

[152] *Light of Nature*, 48–9, from *De Republica*, III, xxii.

[153] *Light of Nature*, 55. Baxter attacked *De Veritate* in an appendix to *More Reasons for the Christian Religion* (1672), in *Practical Works*, ed. Orme, XXI.

[154] *Light of Nature*, 48, referring to Aristotle, *Politics*, III, xi; *Nicomachean Ethics*, X, ix; Cicero, *Pro Milone*, IV, 10.

[155] *Natural Religion*, 55.   [156] *Light of Nature*, 46; cf. 37, 45.

operation of the law of nature, including water, seeds, the growth of plants, the hatching of eggs, as well as the more usual one of writing: 'There are stampt and printed upon the being of man, some cleare and undelible principles, some first and Alphabetical Notions; by putting together of which it can spell out the Law of Nature.'[157] Smith states, 'if we would know what the *Impresse* of Souls is, it is nothing but God himself, who could not write his own name so as that it might be read but onely in Rationall Natures'; 'God hath stamp'd a Copy of his own Archetypal Loveliness upon the Soul.'[158] Fowler's Philalethes (lover of truth) says, 'I am clearly sensible, that nothing reveled by God can possibly contradict those principles that are impressed in (as I think) *indelible* characters upon the souls of men'.[159] Barrow argues that the ways of truth 'are in very legible characters graven by the finger of God upon our hearts and consciences, so that by any considerate reflection inwards we may easily read them'.[160] Beardmore attributes Tillotson's success as a 'rational preacher' to his appeal to this engraved law: 'there was something in the hearts and consciences of men not debauch'd, that mov'd them to give assent and consent to what he spoke, as being agreeable, and connatural, as I may say, to the common reason and faculties of mankind, to that νόμος 'ἔγϱαπτος, that law of GOD written and engraven upon man's heart'.[161]

Although this vocabulary of inscription is very widely used, it is not necessarily to be understood literally, i.e. as a reference to immediate, intuitive perceptions rather than to truths potentially discoverable by the faculty of reasoning. Culverwell, who much enjoys playing with metaphors, makes it clear that by common notions he does not mean something akin to Platonic ideas; he prefers the view of Aristotle and Aquinas that 'the true rise of knowledge is from the observing and comparing of objects, and from thence extracting the quintessence of some such principles as are worthy of all acceptation ... These are the true and genuine ϰοιναί 'ἔννοιαι [common notions].'[162] Fowler talks of 'the Divine *Moral* Laws: That is, Those which are of an Indispensable and Eternal obligation, which were first written in mens hearts, and Originally Dictates of Humane Nature, or necessary Conclusions and Deductions from them'.[163] Speaking of the universal consent of mankind that God exists, Tillotson says, 'no one and constant reason of this can be given, but from the nature of man's mind and understanding, which hath this notion of a deity born with it and stamped upon it; or which is all one, is of

---

[157] *Light of Nature*, 54.
[158] *Select Discourses*, no. 5, 124; 9, 'Of the Excellency and Nobleness of True Religion', 382.
[159] *Principles and Practices*, 220.
[160] Sermon 5, 'Upright Walking Sure Walking', *Theological Works*, I, 116.
[161] Birch, *Tillotson*, 406.   [162] *Light of Nature*, 81–2.   [163] *Design*, 8.

such a frame that in the free use and exercise of itself it will find out GOD'.[164] Stillingfleet argues with more clarity that there is no connate idea of God in the soul, but there is a faculty in the soul whereby it can form the notion of God.[165] This faculty seems to be equivalent to what other writers mean by the metaphor of inscription. The emphasis in these examples is not so much on the human mind or heart as a passive recipient of God's writing, as on the active process of ratiocination and deduction whereby the mind discovers God and the moral law.

There seems little doubt that one reason for the great popularity of the metaphor of inscription was that it reinforced the theory that the moral law is not the positive or arbitrary command of a mysterious God, as Calvinism might seem to suggest, nor the result of human imposition, as Hobbes stated, but self-evident and indisputable. (Conversely, Locke's attack on the theory of innate ideas and common notions in Book I of *An Essay concerning Human Understanding* was thought by some to undermine the moral law.) Fowler's Theophilus (lover of God) states this central principle of the latitudinarians:

That Moral good and evil are not onely such because God commands the one, and forbids the other; but because the things themselves are so essentially and unalterably. That there is an eternal Reason, why that which is good should be so and required, and why that which is evil should be so and forbidden; which depends not so much on the divine will as the divine nature.[166]

This is the law of 'eternal and immutable morality' (the title of Cudworth's ethical treatise, not published till 1731): it is clear, unchanging, and evident to the rational human mind, and hence radically different from God's 'eternal and immutable purpose' as described in the *Westminster Confession*, which is secret and not open to human investigation.[167] Hence it is a favourite maxim of the latitudinarians that there are self-evident first principles in morality just as in mathematics.[168]

The use of the metaphors of light and inscription is closely associated with the way in which reason is defined.[169] There are essentially two views of reason: as a divine implantation, and as a faculty of ratiocination. These views are not contradictory or mutually exclusive, but there is a definite shift in the period away from right reason towards reasoning as the primary meaning. Whichcote frequently uses the term in the first sense, for example: 'This is the Rule in all things, That a Man act according to *Reason*, which is the *Candle of*

---

[164] Sermon 1, 'The Wisdom of Being Religious', *Works*, I, 33.
[165] *Origines Sacrae*, Book III, Chapter 1, 'Of the Being of God', 369.
[166] *Principles and Practices*, 12–13.
[167] *Confession* (1855 edn), Chapter 3, 29; cf. *Larger Catechism*, qn 13.
[168] E.g. Whichcote, *Aphorisms*, no. 298; *Select Sermons*, Part II, Sermon 6, 452; *Eight Letters*, 2; Fowler, *Design*, 8.
[169] For accounts of reason see Harth, *Swift and Anglican Rationalism* (1961), Chapter 2; Simon, *Three Restoration Divines*, I, Chapter 2; Spurr, 'Rational Religion' (1988).

the Lord set up in him; and by this he should be directed, and see his way before him. For even the Grace of God doth adjoyn it self only to our Higher Principles.'[170] Culverwell seems to imply both meanings in his use of the metaphors. This is his explication of 'the candle of the Lord': 'God hath breathed into all the sons of men Reasonable souls which may serve as so many Candles to enlighten and direct them in the searching out their Creatour, in the discovering of other inferiour beings, and themselves also.' He defines reason by means of the inscription metaphor: '*Reason* is the Pen by which *Nature* writes this Law of her own composing; This Law 'tis publisht by Authority from heaven, and Reason is the Printer.'[171] As the faculty whereby the law of nature is interpreted and man's moral conduct guided, reason is closely associated with conscience. Thus Whichcote defines reason as 'man's natural Perfection, his *Home-informer*, and *Monitor* within his Breast', and urges 'Let us approve our selves to our *Home-God*' (which may mean either reason or conscience).[172] In his Sermon 38, 'A Conscience Void of Offence towards God and Men' (1691), Tillotson defines conscience as 'a principle or faculty whereby we judge of moral good and evil, and do accordingly direct and govern our actions', and also as 'a domestick judge, and a kind of familiar GOD'.[173] It seems fair to assume that as reason shifts its meaning from right reason to reasoning, so conscience takes its place in the moral vocabulary.

In its second meaning reason may still have moral connotations. Fowler defines reason as '*that power, whereby men are enabled to draw clear Inferences from evident Principles*' – and goes on to show how the precepts of the gospel are inferred to be our duty by this means.[174] Wilkins defines it as 'that faculty whereby we apprehend, compare, and judg of Moral things'.[175] The most helpful attempt to distinguish between the meanings of reason is made by Glanvill in 'The Agreement of Reason and Religion': reason firstly means principles – 'those imbred *Fundamental Notices*, that God hath implanted in our souls', 'That which he hath written upon our Minds and Hearts' – and secondly the faculty of understanding. Though reason in the second sense has been impaired by the fall, the principles of truth written on the soul (reason in the first sense) 'are the same that they ever were, though we discern them not so clearly as the Innocent State did'.[176] This has some resemblance to Whichcote's favourite distinction between the reason of things (i.e. principles) and the reason of our minds (i.e. judgement): 'The *Rule* of Right is, the Reason of Things; the *Judgment* of Right is, the Reason of our minds, perceiving the Reason of things.'[177]

The latitude-men frequently state that religion is rational or reasonable –

[170] *Several Discourses*, I, no. 11, 294.   [171] *Light of Nature*, 20, 65.
[172] *Select Sermons*, Part I, Sermon 4, 159; *Several Discourses*, I, no. 3, 62.
[173] *Works*, III, 86, 102.   [174] *Principles and Practices*, 70.
[175] *Ecclesiastes* (1675), 124–5, not in 1st edn.
[176] *Essays*, no. 5, 5, 17, 20.
[177] *Aphorisms*, no. 33; cf. no. 523, from *Several Discourses*, I, no. 13, 322.

Whichcote claims that 'There is nothing so intrinsically Rational, as Religion is' – but the emphasis of these statements varies.[178] The earlier writers are much concerned with puritan attacks on carnal reason and the unnecessary divorce between reason and faith. Culverwell devotes the first chapter of the *Light of Nature* to making a case for reason against its detractors, though in his last chapter he insists on the limits of reason. Similarly Smith states: 'It's a fond imagination that Religion should extinguish Reason; whenas Religion makes it more illustrious and vigorous; and they that live most in the exercise of *Religion*, shall find their *Reason* most enlarged.'[179] It is against these fond imaginers that Glanvill argues 'The Agreement of Reason and Religion'; the argument of that essay is summarised as the teaching of the divines of Bensalem on reason in 'Anti-fanatical Religion':

That *Reason* is a Branch and Beam of the Divine Wisdom; *That Light* which he hath put into our Minds, and *that Law* which he hath writ upon our Hearts: That the Revelations of God in Scripture, do not *contradict* what he hath engraven upon our Natures: That *Faith* it self, is an *Act of Reason*, and is built upon these two Reasonable Principles, *That there is a God*; and, That *what he saith is true* ... That God never disparageth Reason, in Scripture ... That *Carnal* Reason is the Reason of *Appetite* and *Passion*; and not the Dictates of our Minds ... That to decry, and disgrace *Reason*, is to strike up *Religion* by the Roots, and to prepare the World for *Atheism*.[180]

This passage is a very useful indication of why and in what ways reason is regarded as an essential support of religion. There are two important points here. The first, that reason is both the divine moral law and the means of interpreting it and guiding men to follow it, has already been considered. Looked at in this way, reason is an active moral force: when the principles of religion are fully apprehended by the reason men cannot help but put them into practice. Thus Whichcote argues: 'When the Principles of our Religion become the *Temper* of our Spirits, then we are truly religious; and the only way to make them become so, is, to reason ourselves into an Approbation of them: for nothing, which is the Reason of Things, can be refused by the Reason of Man; when understood.'[181]

The second point, the apparent paradox that faith is an act of reason, needs further comment. It does not mean that nothing is to be believed except what can be apprehended by the reason, but that we must be convinced by our reason that we are required to believe what is beyond our reason. Faith and reason must not contradict each other, but faith can be beyond reason (this distinction was to provide the freethinkers with a lot of amusement).[182] As Whichcote put it, 'We are not to submit our Understandings to the belief of

178 *Aphorisms*, no. 457, from *Several Discourses*, I, no. 4, 106.   179 *Select Discourses*, no. 9, 388.
180 *Essays*, no. 7, 17–18.   181 *Aphorisms*, no. 28.
182 Locke develops these arguments in *Essay*, Book IV, Chapters 16–18 and modifies them in *The Reasonableness of Christianity* (1695). Contrary to Cleanthes' assertion in Hume's *Dialogues*, Part I, 156, Locke was not 'the first Christian, who ventur'd openly to assert, that *Faith* was nothing but a species of *Reason*'.

those things, that are *contrary* to our Understanding. We must have a Reason, for that which we believe *above* our Reason.'[183] Tuckney found this 'very strange divinity'.[184] In *A Rational Account of the Grounds of Protestant Religion* Stillingfleet defines faith as 'a *rational* and *discursive* act of the mind'. He continues,

> *Faith* in us, however it is wrought, being a *perswasion* of the mind, it is not conceivable how there should be any *discursive act* of the mind, without some *reason* causing the mind to assent to what is propounded to it. For without this, Faith would be an unaccountable thing, and *the spirit of revelation* would not be *the spirit of wisdom*; and *Religion* would be exposed to the contempt of all unbelievers, if we were able to give no other account of Faith, then that it is wrought in us by the *Spirit of God*.[185]

There cannot be a distinction between the grounds for accepting God's law revealed in Scripture and God's law written in the heart. Tillotson puts the same case in Sermon 56, 'The Excellency of Abraham's Faith and Obedience' (1686):

> Reason is the faculty whereby revelation is to be discerned ... Faith ... is an assent of the mind to something as revealed by GOD: now all assent must be grounded upon evidence; that is, no man can believe any thing, unless he have or thinks he hath some reason to do so ...
>
> Indeed it is reason enough for any article of our faith, that GOD hath revealed it; because this is one of the strongest and most cogent reasons for the belief of any thing. But when we say GOD hath revealed any thing, we must be ready to prove it, or else we say nothing. If we turn off reason here, we level the best religion in the world with the wildest and most absurd enthusiasms.[186]

Paradoxically, though the object of this endeavour was to unite faith and reason, religion and philosophy, revealed and natural religion, its unforeseen long-term effect was to reduce the meaning of faith to an epistemological question and to restrict the role of reason in its association with faith to the task of proving the Scriptures true and worthy of assent.

Natural and revealed religion

Wilkins states with his usual clarity: 'I call that *Natural Religion*, which men might know, and should be obliged unto, by the mere principles of *Reason*, improved by Consideration and Experience, without the help of *Revelation*.' It comprehends (1) belief in the divine nature, (2) apprehensions of his perfections, and (3) suitable affections towards him – i.e. the duties of religion.[187] Book I is concerned with expounding these points in detail. Wilkins's arguments were to be repeated and elaborated by countless writers

---

[183] *Aphorisms*, no. 771.　　[184] *Eight Letters*, 21.
[185] *Rational Account*, I, Chapter 7, 'The Protestant Way of Resolving Faith', p. 203.
[186] *Works*, IV, 830, 834.　　[187] *Natural Religion*, 39–40.

for a hundred years until Hume took them apart in *Dialogues concerning Natural Religion*.

If these principles of natural religion are easily to be perceived by a rational being, what for the latitude-men is the function of revealed religion, the gospel, the institution of Christianity? Is latitudinarian religion moral divinity 'onlie with a little tincture of Christ added', as Tuckney complained?[188] Such questions were never put in this way by the latitude-men, though they certainly were by the freethinkers at the turn of the century who pushed latitudinarian ideas to their logical extremes. The latitude-men were more interested in showing the essential congruity between natural and revealed religion and in interpreting the latter in the light of the former. Burnet said that Tillotson 'judged that the best way to put a stop to growing Impiety, was first to establish the Principles of natural Religion, and from that to advance to the Proof of the Christian Religion, and of the Scriptures: which being once solidly done, would soon setle all other things'.[189] Tillotson repeatedly asserts that revealed religion depends on natural: 'natural religion is the foundation of instituted and revealed religion; and all revealed religion does suppose, and take for granted, the clear and undoubted principles and precepts of natural religion, and builds upon them'.[190] In his strongly anti-Catholic Sermon 21, 'Of the Trial of the Spirits' (1679), Tillotson lists six points for discerning true and false revelations:

1. Reason is the faculty whereby revelations are to be discerned ... 2. All supernatural revelation supposeth the truth of the principles of natural religion ... 3. All reasonings about divine revelations must necessarily be governed by the principles of natural religion ... 4. Nothing ought to be received as a revelation from God which plainly contradicts the principles of natural religion, or overthrows the certainty of them ... 5. Nothing ought to be received as a divine doctrine and revelation, without good evidence that it is so: that is, without some argument sufficient to satisfy a prudent and considerate man ... 6. And lastly, no argument is sufficient to prove a doctrine or revelation to be from GOD, which is not clearer and stronger than the difficulties and objections against it ...[191]

Taken out of context, this argument might look extremely damaging to revealed religion, and it could be used in this way by those disposed to do so. But the latitude-men were not so disposed; this kind of argument was brought against specific doctrines of which they disapproved, such as the Catholic doctrine of transubstantiation or the Calvinist doctrines of predestination and imputed righteousness. It was against such doctrines that the congruity of natural and revealed religion was stressed. They are seen as an inevitable pairing, the truths of first inscription and of after-revelation:[192] 'the one 'tis

---

[188] *Eight Letters*, 39.   [189] *Sermon Preached at the Funeral of* [Tillotson], 30.
[190] Sermon 103, 'Instituted Religion not Intended to Undermine Natural', *Works*, VI, 1680.
[191] *Works*, II, 31–5.   [192] Whichcote, *Select Sermons*, Part I, Sermon 1, 6.

written by the pen of nature; the other by the finger of the Spirit'.[193] Hence the similarity between heathen morality and the precepts of the gospel is often stressed. Glanvill lists the three fundamental principles of religion (initially without specifying whether he means natural or revealed) as belief in (1) the being of God, (2) providence, and (3) moral good and evil, and he adds the following subsidiary principles: God will (1) pardon us if we repent, (2) assist us if we endeavour, (3) accept our imperfect services if we are sincere, and (4) reward or punish us in another world. He continues, 'These contain the Matter and Substance of the Gospel; more clearly and explicitly reveal'd to the Christian Church; but in some measure owned also by the Gentiles.'[194] It is notable that though Glanvill is here cautious about the gentiles he makes Christianity as unchristian as possible in order to bring it closer to natural religion. Fowler makes a similar claim, though with an important exception: 'I know no duties enjoyned in the Gospel, besides that of Faith in Christ, and the two Sacraments, but may be found, as to the substance of them, at least *commended* as *noble perfections*, in some one or other of the Heathenish writings.'[195]

It is not only the agreement of the heathens with the gospel that is stressed. In a very important passage in *A Brief Account* on the doctrines of the latitude-men, Patrick argues that the principles of natural religion, revelation, the interpretation of revelation by the early church, and the agreement of the Church of England with that church, are all aspects of reason and all naturally tend to the same conclusions. The interpretation of Christian doctrine by the latitude-men and their repudiation of Calvinism is given the support of revelation, antiquity, reason, and philosophy. Patrick continues:

Thus the freedom of our wills, the universal intent of Christ's death, and sufficiency of Gods Grace, the conditions of justification, and many other points of the like nature, which have been almost exploded in these latter degenerate ages of the world, do again begin to obtain, though with different persons upon different accounts; some embrace them for their evidence in Scripture, others for the concurrent testimony of the primitive Church for above four hundred years; others for the reasonableness of the things themselves, and their agreement both with the Divine Attributes and the easy suggestions of their own minds. Nor is there any point in Divinity, where that which is most ancient doth not prove the most rational, and the most rational the ancientest; for there is an eternal consanguinity between all verity; and nothing is true in Divinity, which is false in Philosophy, or the contrary.[196]

One of the chief aims of the latitude-men is to establish a view of the nature of God which is consistent with the promptings of reason, philosophy, and antiquity. Thus God must be absolutely perfect, wise, and good, and the

---

[193] Culverwell, *Light of Nature*, 139.
[194] *Essays*, no. 5, 3–4. These principles bear a strong resemblance to Herbert's five articles of religion in *De Veritate*, trans. Carré (1937), 291–302. Herbert's deism is treated in *Reason, Grace, and Sentiment*, II.
[195] *Principles and Practices*, 79–80.   [196] *Brief Account*, 10–11.

neo-Augustinian Calvinist God, whose judgements are mysterious and arbitrary, who denies man free will, who by his decrees elects only a few of mankind to salvation and reprobates the majority to damnation, and who is therefore the author of sin (though Calvinists certainly never allowed this consequence), must necessarily be false. In his *Exposition of the Thirty-Nine Articles* Burnet, writing at the end of the century after the eclipse of Calvinism, gives a fair and impartial survey of the history of the controversy between the different kinds of Calvinist and the Remonstrants (or Arminians) over predestination (Article XVII), but in the preface he states that he adheres to the doctrine of the early Greek church from which Augustine departed.[197] Fowler, writing thirty years earlier in direct response to Calvinism, is not at all impartial, insisting that the doctrine of God's absolute decrees is worse than atheism: ''tis more dishonourable to the infinitely-just and holy God, to assert that he is the author of sin, than to say that there is no God at all'. Fowler argues that any account of God that contradicts our innate notions of his nature or our natural sense of moral good and evil cannot be true, and if passages of Scripture are used to support this false account they must be interpreted in another sense.[198]

Although the latitude-men sometimes speak as if natural and revealed religion were virtually identical, they are of course well aware of the crucial differences between them, and of what is absent from the heathen moralists. Fowler's Philalethes points out that the argument that the gospel duties are to be found in heathen writings disparages the gospel and makes it 'meer Natural Religion'. Theophilus answers that the gospel consists of things to be known as well as things to be done, promises as well as precepts. He makes two points to stress the superiority of the gospel: first, all the precepts that are 'scattered here and there very thinly among much Trash and Rubbish in other books' and that are discoverable by reason are there expressed 'in a most plain and intelligible manner'; second, and this is clearly the most important consideration, 'The Gospel gives far greater helps to the performance of our duty; and enforceth its precepts with infinitely stronger, and more perswasive Motives and Arguments, than were ever before made known.' These are the sacrifice and example of Christ, God's free pardon to sinners, grace, the help of the Spirit, and the promise of heavenly reward.[199] The same argument is developed in *The Design of Christianity*, where Fowler stresses three advantages that Christians have over pagans: (1) the principles of natural light (e.g. the existence and nature of God) are further confirmed by revelation; (2) the principles that the heathens could at best conclude were very probable (e.g. the immortality of the soul, future rewards and punishments, forgiveness of sins, and the assistance of grace) are undoubtedly certain to Christians; (3) Christians have doctrines made known to them through the gospel (e.g. God's

---

[197] *Thirty-Nine Articles* (1699), vi.   [198] *Principles and Practices*, 201, 213, 217–18, 220.
[199] *Principles and Practices*, 86–9.

gift of his Son and the Holy Ghost to men, the union of Christians with Christ and the nature of their heavenly reward) 'which no man could ever without Divine Revelation in the least have *dream'd* of'.[200] Although Wilkins does not deal with specifically Christian doctrines in *Natural Religion*, he makes similar points about the limitations of the heathens in the chapter 'Of Faith', and in the final chapter, '... shewing the Excellency of the Christian Religion ...', he emphasises that though for the heathens conformity to the divine law written in the heart must be acceptable to God, 'it is not enough for us who enjoy this *Revelation*, to perform those moral Duties which are of natural Obligation, unless we also do them in Obedience to *Christ* as our Lord and Lawgiver'.[201] The latitude-men are agreed that though in theory natural religion teaches the moral duties of the gospel, only the helps and promises provided by the gospel enable them to be put into practice. Natural truth fits man in the state of innocence, revealed truth fits him in his lapsed state.[202] Burnet tried to show Rochester 'the Defects of *Philosophy*, for reforming the World', arguing that a man cannot adhere to the precepts of morality 'unless the Mind does inwardly comply with, and delight in the Dictates of Virtue. And that could not be effected, except a mans nature were internally regenerated, and changed by a higher Principle: Till that came about, corrupt Nature would be strong, and *Philosophy* but feeble.'[203]

Though Tuckney's stricture – moral divinity with a little tincture of Christ – is unfair (but perfectly understandable from the Calvinist point of view) there is no doubt that the latitudinarian interpretation of Christian doctrine was essentially moral. The latitude-men repeatedly emphasise that Christianity is plain and easy to understand, and though they accept that it contains mysteries above reason, they tend to play them down. Burnet argued with Rochester that the Christian mysteries 'are neither so unreasonable, that any other Objection lies against them, but this, that they agree not with our Common Notions' – given the importance attached to common notions, this is surely a serious objection – 'nor so unaccountable that somewhat like them, cannot be assigned to other things [i.e. in the natural world], which are believed really to be, though the manner of them cannot be apprehended'.[204] The reluctance of the latitude-men to discuss mysteries can be attributed partly to their view of language as a medium for rational communication: it is not profitable to talk about what is incomprehensible. Burnet commented disapprovingly on Convocation's censure of William Whiston for his Arian views in 1712: 'I have ever thought, that the true Interest of the Christian Religion was best consulted, when nice disputing about Mysteries was laid

---

200 *Design*, Chapter 14, 134–53.
201 *Natural Religion*, Book I, Chapter 13, 198–99; Book II, Chapter 9, 395–6.
202 Whichcote, *Select Sermons*, Part I, Sermon 1, 40.
203 Burnet, *Life and Death of ... Rochester* (1680), 36, 45.
204 *Rochester*, 105–6.

aside and forgotten.'[205] His treatment of the doctrine of the Trinity in his *Exposition of the Thirty-Nine Articles* is tellingly brief: 'if God has declared this inexplicable thing concerning himself to us; we are bound to believe it, though we cannot have any clear Idea how it truly is' (Burnet is presumably objecting here, as Stillingfleet did, to the anti-trinitarian implications of Locke's epistemology).[206] In a letter of 23 October 1694 Tillotson congratulated Burnet on his caution: 'In the article of the Trinity you have said all, that I think can be said upon so obscure and difficult an argument'.[207]

Tillotson was reluctantly drawn into the Trinitarian controversy against the Socinians in the 1690s. In Sermon 48, 'Concerning the Unity of the Divine Nature, and the Blessed Trinity' (1693), he accepts the mystery and incomprehensibility of the doctrine, yet he asserts that there is a rational basis for believing it: 'it is not repugnant to reason, to believe some things which are incomprehensible by our reason; provided that we have sufficient ground and reason for the belief of them: especially if they be concerning GOD, who is in his nature incomprehensible; and we be well assured that he hath revealed them'.[208] Interestingly, Tillotson goes on to warn that this argument does not apply to transubstantiation (the Catholic doctrine that Christ is really present, though imperceptible, in the communion bread and wine). Tillotson's favourite argument against transubstantiation is that it contradicts the evidence of our sense, whereas the evidence for miracles derives from our senses:

> if the testimony of sense be to be relied upon, then transubstantiation is false; if it be not, then no man is sure that Christianity is true. For the utmost assurance that the apostles had of the truth of Christianity was the testimony of our own senses concerning our SAVIOUR's miracles ... And we who did not see our SAVIOUR's miracles (as the apostles did) and have only a credible relation of them, but do see the sacrament, have less evidence of the truth of Christianity than of the falshood of transubstantiation.[209]

Tillotson was evidently unaware that this kind of argument about evidence could be used against all Christian mysteries, and indeed the argument in the last sentence about kinds of evidence being balanced against each other is precisely that used by Hume in his essay 'Of Miracles' to show that the Christian religion can only rest on faith because it has no basis in reasonable evidence.[210]

The favourite biblical texts of the latitude-men, frequently cited, paraphrased, or expounded in sermons, provide a clear guide as to what they took

---

[205] *History*, II, 603.   [206] *Thirty-Nine Articles*, Article I, 37.   [207] Birch, *Tillotson*, 314.
[208] *Works*, III, 376.
[209] Sermon 11, 'The Hazard of being Saved in the Church of Rome' (1673), *Works*, I, 263.
[210] Hume, *Enquiry Concerning Human Understanding* (first pub. 1748 as *Philosophical Essays Concerning Human Understanding*), ed. Selby-Bigge and Nidditch (1975), Section X.

to be the central meaning of Christianity. They are listed below with some examples of their interpretation and application:

Fear God, and keep his commandments: for this is the whole duty of man.
(Ecclesiastes 12:13)

The meaning of this text is discussed by Wilkins in *Natural Religion*, Book II, Chapter 1, 'Shewing in general how Religion conduces to our Happiness'. Wilkins points out that the word 'duty' is not in the Hebrew, and interprets the phrase 'the whole of man' as referring to 'the *Essence*, the *Happiness*, the *Business* of Man'.[211]

Her ways [those of wisdom] are ways of pleasantness, and all her paths are peace.
(Proverbs 3:17)

The text is expounded in Barrow's Sermon 1, 'The Pleasantness of Religion'.[212]

For my yoke is easy, and my burden is light.   (Matthew 11:30)

An almost hedonistic interpretation of this saying of Christ is common, for example: 'Every good man feels that Christ's yoke is not less *Pleasant* than it is *Easie*, nor his Burthen more Light than it is Delightful.'[213]

For this is the love of God, that we keep his commandments: and his commandments are not grievous.   (I John 5:3)

Tillotson's Sermon 6, 'The Precepts of Christianity not Grievous', has this laborious paraphrase: God 'hath commanded us nothing in the gospel that is either unsuitable to our reason, or prejudicial to our interest; nay, nothing that is severe and against the grain of our nature, but when either the apparent necessity of our interest does require it, or an extraordinary reward is promised to our obedience'.[214]

For the grace of God that bringeth salvation hath appeared to all men,
Teaching us that, denying ungodliness and worldly lusts, we should live soberly, righteously, and godly, in this present world.   (Titus 2:11–12)

This is perhaps the most widely cited text. Sobriety, righteousness, and godliness, which are usually taken to represent our duty to ourselves, our neighbour, and God, are frequently analysed by the latitude-men, notably by Whichcote in his sermons, 'the Moral Part of Religion reinforced by Christianity'.[215]

---

[211] *Natural Religion*, 286–7; cf. *Sermons* (1677), Sermon 2 (on this text), 40. Cf. the account of *The Whole Duty of Man*, Chapter 1 above, pp. 22–3.

[212] *Theological Works*, I; cf. Arderne, *Directions*, 15, quoted above, p. 59.

[213] Fowler, *Design*, 305; cf. *Whole Duty*, 383, quoted above, p. 23.

[214] *Works*, I, 154.

[215] *Several Discourses*, III, nos. 1–2; cf. Fowler, *Principles and Practices*, 75–8; *Whole Duty*, 4; and Taylor, *Holy Living*, 61, quoted above, p. 21.

Pure religion and undefiled before God and the Father is this, To visit the fatherless and widows in their affliction, and to keep himself unspotted from the world.

(James 1:27)

In emphasising the importance of personal righteousness Glanvill conflates this with the previous text: the apostles 'plainly tell us, That Religion was *doing Righteousness* [I John 3:7], and consisted in *visiting the Widow and Fatherless*, and *being unspotted with the World*; in *denying* all *ungodliness*, and *worldly lusts*, and living *soberly, righteously,* and *Godly*'.[216]

Wherefore, my beloved, as ye have always obeyed … work out your own salvation with fear and trembling. For it is God which worketh in you both to will and to do of his good pleasure. (Philippians 2:12–13)

Whichcote, in stressing the importance of a man's own intention towards and choice of good, provides the following paraphrase in the hope of solving some important contemporary controversies about the freedom of the will: 'Scripture doth attribute to us that which God does, and bids us do that which God doth with us: That which we do is attributed to God: and that which God doth by us, is both ascribed to God, and to us; we work, and God works; we are awakened, directed, and assisted by him.'[217]

Finally, brethren, whatsoever things are true, whatsoever things are honest, what-soever things are just, whatsoever things are pure, whatsoever things are lovely, whatsoever things are of good report; if there be any virtue, and if there be any praise, think on these things. (Philippians 4:8)

This seems to have been Whichcote's favourite biblical text: 'A weighty Scripture, a Summary and Comprehension of all Perfection'; 'this full and pregnant Scripture, that doth contract and epitomize our Religion', he says at the beginning and end of his thirteen sermons on the text.[218]

As these quotations illustrate, for the latitude-men the religious life is essentially moral, its pursuit brings pleasure and happiness in this world, and it is achieved by active human effort in co-operation with divine grace. In establishing this view of Christianity the latitude-men, like other Anglicans, put particular stress on the relationship between faith and works and the importance of conditions for salvation. They opposed the Calvinist doctrines of irresistible grace and imputed righteousness because they thought that these attribute everything to God and nothing to man, and supported the pre-Augustinian, Erasmian, and Arminian view that man's will is free, that God's grace is given to all, and that man can work with or against it as he chooses. There are exceptions to this full-scale Arminianism: Culverwell (who died in 1651) remained, however inconsistently, a Calvinist, rejecting the view that grace is universally offered, though he was obviously unhappy about

216 *Essays*, no. 7, 23–4.
217 *Several Discourses*, I, no. 4, 'The Joy which the Righteous have in God' (1668), 103–4.
218 *Several Discourses*, IV, no. 1, 1, no. 13, 272; cf. *Select Sermons*, Part II, Sermon 1, on this text.

the implications of the doctrine of the divine decrees. For example, on the vexed question of the salvation of the heathen (who are categorically damned in the *Larger Catechism*), after sidestepping the issue of whether they could be saved, he continues:

> though we say not with the Pelagians, that the emprovements of nature can make men happy, nor yet with the Semi-Pelagians, that natural preparations and predispositions do bespeak & procure Grace; nor yet with the Papists and Arminians, that works flowing from Grace do contribute to more Grace & Glory, yet this we say, that upon the improvement of any present strength, God out of his free goodnesse, may if he please give more.[219]

Fowler, mindful of scriptural inconsistency on the subject of human co-operation with divine grace – 'The truth is, the Scripture seems one while to give all to *God* in the work of Regeneration and Conversion; and another while to make it wholly mens own act' – preferred the 'middle way' between Arminianism and Calvinism, the theory that some are absolutely elected by God but that others can co-operate with or refuse grace.[220] This theory, sometimes known as Baxterianism after Richard Baxter, was to become increasingly associated with nonconformity and dissent, and is not typical of latitude. Thus when Calamy objected to Burnet that he had omitted the middle way from his account of Article XVII in his *Exposition of the Thirty-Nine Articles*, Burnet replied 'that the true reason of that was, because he could not see how that called the middle way differed from one of the extremes'.[221] Whichcote makes clear the objection to Calvinist doctrine: 'some Men put all upon God, and say when He please to come, with Irresistable Grace, the Work will be done; and the Man shall be Converted; for *who hath resisted his Will?* [Romans 9:19] And till then, the Work will not be done, for they can do nothing.' Against this he insists that 'Conversion is a mutual act, and so is Faith'.[222]

For the latitude-men grace contains the idea of virtue, just as faith contains the idea of works. The importance of grace is never denied – Tillotson reported that Whichcote on his deathbed 'disclaimed all merit in himself; and declared that whatever he was, he was through the grace and goodness of GOD in JESUS CHRIST'.[223] But the source of moral activity is not really distinguished from the activity itself, so that grace and virtue are seen to be the

---

[219] *Light of Nature*, 165–6; *Larger Catechism*, qn 60. It was not entirely inappropriate that Culverwell's editor, William Dillingham, dedicated the book to Tuckney.

[220] *Principles and Practices*, 174–5, 228ff.

[221] Calamy, *My Own Life*, I, 470–1. In Sermon 108 Tillotson sets out contemporary views on grace: the two extreme views, irresistible grace given only to the elect or sufficient grace offered to all, and the two middle views, irresistible grace to the elect, sufficient grace to the rest who reject it, or irresistible grace to the elect, sufficient grace to the rest, some of whom accept and some reject it, *Works*, VI, 1772–73. For Baxter's account of the middle way see Chapter 3 below.

[222] *Several Discourses*, I, no. 12, 314–15; II, no. 7, 137.

[223] Sermon 24, 'Preached at the Funeral of the Reverend Benjamin Whichcot', *Works*, II, 157; cf. no. 203, 'The Necessity of Supernatural Grace, in order to a Christian Life', *Works*, X.

same thing. Thus Whichcote says, '*that* that we call *Grace* or *Vertue* (for, to me, they are all one) *Goodness*, and *Righteousness, these* are that that we call *Real Holiness*'.[224] Similarly More argues, 'howbeit those three Names, which among Men so often occur, of *Virtues, Grace*, and the *Divine Life*, may seem distinct; Yet, if *rightly* ponder'd, they are all but one and the same Thing'.[225] Which term is used would seem to depend on whether the human or divine perspective is being considered; Tillotson explains that 'grace and virtue are but two names that signify the same thing. Virtue signifies the absolute nature and goodness of these things: grace denotes the cause and principle by which these virtues are wrought and produced ... namely, by the free gift of GOD'S HOLY SPIRIT to us.'[226] Whichcote concurs: '*that which is in the Subject Virtue; in respect of God, as the Author of it, is Grace*'.[227] But the tendency is for the difference in perspective to be blurred.

Similarly faith is usually defined to include works and co-operation with grace. Fowler defines justifying faith as '*such a belief of the Truth of the Gospel, as includes a sincere resolution of Obedience unto all its Precepts*; or (which is the same thing) includes *true Holiness* in the nature of it';[228] Glanvill defines saving faith as '*such a Belief as works on the Will and Affections*, and *produceth the Works of Righteousness*'.[229] Tillotson refuses to be labelled a Pelagian, on the grounds that he does not think man can act alone without grace, but at the same time he insists on co-operation with grace as a necessary condition of salvation.[230] This condition consists of assent to the truth of the gospel, trust in Christ, repentance, obedience, and holiness.[231] The latitudinarians' difficulties with some of these discriminations are evident in Burnet's account of faith and works in his *Exposition of the Thirty-Nine Articles* (Articles XI and XII). He attempts to limit the condition (presumably to avoid seeming to tie down God) by insisting that we must not imagine that the condition upon which justification is offered to us is the consideration that moves God (this can only be the death of Christ). Yet at the same time it is the condition that makes us capable of receiving redemption and grace. Burnet's exasperation with the disputes about justification (which for the latitude-men are very much disputes about terms) shows in his account of good works: all are agreed that good works are necessary to salvation; therefore it is a speculation of little consequence whether works are a condition of justification or the effect of justifying faith.[232] Those holding the second view would certainly not have agreed with him.

---

[224] *Select Sermons*, Part II, Sermon 1, 256.
[225] *Account of Virtue* (1690), 'Epistle to his Reader', A6.
[226] Sermon 202, 'The Fruits of the SPIRIT, the Same with Moral Virtues', *Works*, X, 4608.
[227] *Several Discourses*, III, no. 1, 2.   [228] *Design*, 221; cf. *Principles and Practices*, 114, 157.
[229] *Essays*, no. 7, 22.
[230] Sermon 107, 'Of the Nature of Regeneration, and its Necessity, in order to Justification', *Works*, VI, 1760. For Wesley's criticism see Chapter 5 below, n. 217.
[231] Sermon 227, 'Of Justifying Faith', *Works*, XI, 5007.
[232] *Thirty-Nine Articles*, 123, 126, 128.

A corollary of this attempt to identify works with faith is the insistence that the epistles of Paul and James on faith and works are not contradictory (e.g. Romans 2:28 and James 2:24) and that the post-Lutheran emphasis on Paul is misleading. Hammond had argued that his account of justifying faith was the clearest way of reconciling James and Paul;[233] similarly, Tillotson argues that they cannot be reconciled unless faith includes obedience.[234] In reply to Tuckney's complaints about moral divinity, Whichcote objects, 'Our Saviour insists much on Moral Divinitie (Matth. chap v.vi.vij). St. PAUL neglects itt not (Phil. iv.8). St. JAMES is whole in itt; so as to seeme less to mind Faith . . . Do not, Sir, disserve one truth; to serve another.'[235] Fowler urges, 'I think it desirable that we would cease to prefer S. *Paul's* language before S. *James* his.' If they were interpreted by each other, 'then, I dare say, this Controversie would quickly be at an end among us'.[236] Birch describes Tillotson's plans for a new book of homilies which never materialised; among other corrections to the sixteenth-century theology that now seemed wrong-headed, 'some expressions in the first book of Homilies, that seemed to carry justification by faith only, to a height that wanted some mitigation, were to be well examined', and Paul's statements on the subject were to be reconciled with those of James.[237]

The latitude-men thought the clarification of their doctrines necessary because of what they regarded as the dangerous consequences of the doctrines of their opponents, but their real interests were practical. Doctrinal disputes obfuscated the issue, which was essentially clear and simple. Whichcote claimed: 'There are but *Two* things in Religion; Morals and Institutions: Morals may be known, by the *Reason* of the Thing; Morals are owned, as soon as spoken; and they are nineteen parts in twenty, of all Religion.'[238] At the time of Tillotson's death Beardmore noted that thirty years earlier Tillotson had told him 'that Christianity, as to the practical part of it, was nothing else but the religion of nature, or pure morality, save only praying and making all our addresses to GOD in the name, and through the mediation of our Saviour, and the use of the two sacraments of Baptism and the Lord's Supper'.[239] In his final sermon before William and Mary (1694), Tillotson repeated his view of the inseparability of faith and a good life, and the essentially moral nature of religion, and went on to defend himself from the kind of criticism he had always received from his opponents:

I foresee what will be said, because I have heard it so often said in the like case; that there is not one word of JESUS CHRIST in all this. No more is there in the text [Titus 3:2]. And yet I hope that JESUS CHRIST is truly preached, whenever his will and laws, and the duties injoined by the Christian religion, are inculcated upon us.

But some men are pleased to say, that this is mere morality: I answer, that this is

---

[233] *Practical Catechisme*, 27.   [234] Sermon 227, *Works*, XI, 5013.   [235] *Eight Letters*, 63.
[236] *Principles and Practices*, 189.   [237] *Tillotson*, 367–8.   [238] *Aphorisms*, no. 586.
[239] Birch, *Tillotson*, 408.

scripture morality, and Christian morality, and who hath anything to say against that?[240]

The nature and end of man

Stated simply, the latitudinarian view of morality is as follows. Man is by nature sociable and disposed to act well; sin is an unnatural deviation from this disposition; man naturally pursues happiness, though he often miscalculates the method of attaining it; happiness is achieved through holiness, and understood properly is in fact the same thing; the religious life is the most advantageous because religion enables man to act according to his true nature and in his own best interest by choosing the path that will make him holy and therefore happy. It is the task of the religious moralist to channel man's innate desire for happiness by appealing to his prudence and self-interest and demonstrating that the rewards of the religious life easily outweigh any others. The religious man is holy and happy, prudent and wise, and rewarded here as well as hereafter.

The natural sociability of man is repeatedly emphasised, and is elaborated by means of a number of important linked terms widely used among all the latitude-men, but especially by Whichcote, Barrow and Tillotson. Thus man is seen to possess good nature, candour, and ingenuity, and his temper, complexion, inclination, disposition, constitution, and frame lead him naturally towards sympathy, benevolence, beneficence, charity, and humanity to his fellows. The naturalness of this fellow-feeling is reinforced by the use of words with co-prefixes, such as conformity, congruity, consanguinity, and connatural; the last of these is one of Whichcote's favourite adjectives, and the heaping up of such 'co-' terms is a typical device of Barrow. The following are central examples of the use of these linked words by Whichcote, Barrow and Tillotson. The first is from Whichcote:

There is in Man, a secret *Genius* to Humanity; a *Bias* that inclines him to a Regard of all of his own Kind. For, whatsoever some have said; *Man's Nature* is not such an untoward Thing (unless it be abused,) but that there is a secret *Sympathy* in Human Nature, with Vertue and Honesty; with Fairness and good Behaviour; which gives a man an Interest even in bad Men.

Part of this passage (among others) is quoted with approbation by Shaftesbury in his preface: because of this '*Defence of* Natural Goodness' Shaftesbury calls Whichcote 'the Preacher of Good-Nature'.[241] Whichcote claims that 'Man, *as Man*, is Averse to what is Evil and Wicked; for *Evil* is unnatural, and *Good* is connatural to Man'; 'The several Virtues of Religion are connatural to the *Frame* of man; they are according to his Nature, and agreeable to his

[240] Sermon 42, *Works*, III, 217.   [241] *Select Sermons*, Part II, Sermon 4, 381; Preface, A8.

Reason'.[242] Barrow, in his group of sermons on charity, insists on its inherent
naturalness:

in common language this practice is styled humanity, as best sorting with our nature,
and becoming it; and the principle whence it springeth is called good-nature: and the
contrary practice is styled inhumanity, as thwarting our natural inclinations, or
divesting us of manhood; and its source likewise is termed ill-nature, or a corruption of
our nature.[243]

Barrow further argues that the practice of charity, by analogy with eating and
drinking or sexual intercourse, has a natural pleasure annexed to it which acts
as a stimulus to performance:

The very constitution, frame, and temper of our nature directeth and inclineth us [to
the practice of charity] ... Such is the natural sympathy between men ... that we
cannot see, cannot hear of, yea, can hardly imagine the calamities of other men,
without being somewhat disturbed and afflicted ourselves. As also nature, to the acts
requisite toward preservation of our life, hath annexed a sensible pleasure, forcibly
enticing us to the performance of them: so hath she made the communication of
benefits to others to be accompanied with a very delicious relish upon the mind of him
that practises it; nothing indeed carrying with it a more pure and savoury delight than
beneficence. A man may be virtuously voluptuous, and a laudable epicure by doing
much good.[244]

Tillotson makes the same point about charity more simply:

to do good is the most pleasant employment in the world. It is natural; and whatever is
so is delightful. We do like our selves whenever we relieve the wants and distresses of
others. And therefore this virtue among all other hath peculiarly entitled itself to the
name of humanity. We answer our own nature, and obey our reason, and shew our
selves men, in shewing mercy to the miserable.[245]

Barrow reinforces this idea of man's natural instinct towards his fellows by the
repetition of the co-prefix. For example, he states that the 'duties of common
humanity' are 'grounded upon our community of nature and cognation of
blood', and argues in another sermon that 'we are obliged to these duties by a
tacit compact and fundamental constitution of mankind ... For to this
purpose do men congregate, cohabit, and combine themselves in sociable
communion, that thereby they may enjoy a delightful conversation.'[246]

   In putting forward this view of human nature the latitude-men explicitly
repudiate the Hobbesian view of the state of nature as a state of war, and

242 *Aphorisms*, nos. 42, 554.
243 Sermon 28, 'Motives and Arguments to Charity', *Theological Works*, II, 79; cf. Sermon 26, II,
    37, with very similar wording.
244 Sermon 31, 'The Duty and Reward of Bounty to the Poor', *Theological Works*, II, 224–5.
245 Sermon 18, 'The Example of Jesus in doing Good', *Works*, I, 427.
246 Sermon 25, 'Of the Love of our Neighbour', *Theological Works*, II, 8; Sermon 30, 'Of a
    peaceable Temper and Carriage', II, 144. Barrow may be imitating Cicero's use of co-prefixes
    to express the idea of harmony; see Spitzer, *Classical and Christian Ideas of World Harmony*
    (1963), 148.

associate themselves instead with the Aristotelian view of man as a being made for society. Thus Whichcote argues: 'We may detest and reject that Doctrine which saith, that God made Man *in a State of War*. Undoubtedly, Man, if he have not abused himself, is the mildest Creature under Heaven. *Man* is a sociable Creature, delights in Company and Converse'.[247] Barrow is outraged by the 'monstrous paradox' in vogue that men are naturally enemies, and cites with approval Aristotle's statement that they are naturally friends.[248] Barrow's contrast is adopted by Tillotson: 'So far is it from being true, which Mr. Hobbes asserts as the fundamental principle of his politicks, "That men are naturally in a state of war and enmity with one another," that the contrary principle, laid down by a much deeper and wiser man, I mean Aristotle, is most certainly true, "that men are naturally akin and friends to each other." '[249]

No attempt is made to substantiate these claims about human nature, though Glanvill states that the divines of Bensalem founded their moral philosophy 'upon the excellent *knowledge* of *Humane Nature* and *Passions*', and 'dislik'd nothing more then Ill-nature'.[250] Further, confusion can arise from the fact that the portrait of human nature given sometimes refers to ideal nature before the fall, and sometimes to what all men have within themselves. Thus Whichcote in the following examples expressed in the past tense is putting forward the first view: '*A Vicious Man* is a Moral Monstre. We are to declare the Nature of Man; not from what it *is*, by Defection and Apostasy; but from what God *made* it: what it *was*, and what it *should be*'; 'Natural Religion was the very Temper and Complexion of Man's Soul, in the Moment of his Creation: It was his natural Temper, and the very Disposition of his Mind: It was as con-natural to his Soul, as Health to any Man's Body.'[251] In contrast, Barrow in the following statement in the present tense specifically refers to man after the fall:

Man having received his soul from the breath of God, and being framed after the image of his most benign parent, there do yet abide in him some features resembling God, and relics of the divine original; there are in us seeds of ingenuity, of equity, of pity, of benignity, which being cultivated by sober consideration and good use, under the conduct and aid of heavenly grace, will produce noble fruits of charity.[252]

However, it could be argued that this confusion is more apparent than real, since the latitude-men tend to regard vice, sin, or human degeneracy as very much within human control. Tillotson explicitly says that 'sin is a voluntary

---

[247] *Select Sermons*, Part II, Sermon 4, 382; cf. *Several Discourses*, I, no. 10, 258. The reference is to Hobbes, *Leviathan*, Part I, Chapter 13.

[248] Sermon 28, *Theological Works*, II, 79–80; the reference is to Aristotle, *Nicomachean Ethics*, VIII, i. For similar references to Aristotle see II, 37, 139, 221.

[249] Sermon 33, 'Of Forgiveness of Injuries' (1689), *Works*, II, 403–4.   [250] *Essays*, no. 7, 51.

[251] *Aphorisms*, no. 228; *Select Sermons*, Part I, Sermon 1, 38.

[252] Sermon 26, 'Of the Love of our Neighbour', *Theological Works*, II, 36.

evil which men wilfully bring upon themselves', though in fact he is rather less optimistic than Whichcote in his view of the human capacity to eradicate it.[253] Whichcote habitually regards sin as an abuse of or a deviation from man's natural condition. 'It is not so much the *Disability* of Mens Natures; as their *Neglect* and *Abuse*; that men are not good.' A man becomes bad by putting away 'the Ingenuity of his Nature'. 'We have woful Examples *what Monsters of Rational Agents, on a Moral Account*, some Men become, by unnatural Use of themselves; wrought quite off, from all Ingenuity, Candour, Sweetness.'[254] 'By *Sin*, we part-with the Modesty, and Ingenuity of our Natures; Spoil our Tempers; and Acquire unnatural Principles and Dispositions.' 'Vice is contrary to Nature, and to a Mans Interest; It is against the Reason of Mankind: And till a Man has forced himself, and miserably abused his Natu[r]e he will not consent unto it'.[255]

This way of talking about sin makes it appear an individual choice rather than a universal condition. For Whichcote the good man is the type of humanity, whereas the bad man is a moral monster and therefore atypical. Tillotson, however, regards sin as the normal condition of fallen man, even though he believes that men are responsible for sin and can avoid it, and there is a striking difference in tone between the sermons where he stresses man's rationality and those where he stresses man's sinfulness. In two particularly interesting sermons, 28, 'Objections against the True Religion answered', and 53, 'Of the Education of Children' (the last of three sermons on this subject), Tillotson struggles to reconcile his sense of human degeneracy with his belief in the essential reasonableness of humanity and the power of education to reform men. In Sermon 28 he quotes the first six lines of Fulke Greville's 'Chorus Sacerdotum', which he claims 'are so frequently in the mouths of many who are thought to bear no good-will to religion', and rebuts Greville's Calvinist paradox that there is an impossible gulf between our fallen nature and the demands of religion – 'Created sick, commanded to be sound'. Tillotson uses the doctrine of common notions to insist that 'the law written in GOD's word is not contrary to the law written upon our hearts'; we are not, as Greville's priests claim, 'born under one law, to another bound'. Tillotson argues that men are not equally degenerate: in many there are inclinations to goodness 'which being cultivated by education, may under the ordinary influence of GOD's grace be carried on with great ease to perfection'. Even those with a propensity to vice can be reformed: grace enables men 'if they be not wanting to themselves, to master and subdue all the bad inclinations of nature, even in those who seem to be naturally most corrupt and depraved'.[256]

---

253 Sermon 13, 'The Nature and Benefit of Consideration' (1675), *Works*, I, 309.
254 *Select Sermons*, Part I, Sermon 4, 155, 142, Part II, Sermon 5, 409.
255 *Aphorisms*, no. 488; *Several Discourses*, I, no. 8 (1673), 194–5; cf. *Aphorisms*, no. 212.
256 *Works*, II, 272–7. The reference is probably to Blount, *Anima Mundi* (1679), 71, in *Miscellaneous Works* (1695): Blount objects to 'the Tradition of everlasting Torments, for acting those Vices which their Nature prompted them to: Or, as a Learned Gentleman of our own Nation

Similarly in Sermon 53 he argues that even 'wild and savage natures, monstrous and prodigious tempers' are 'not utterly intractable' to grace and religious education. Tillotson must insist on this point, since the possibility of an intractable temper cannot be reconciled with the latitudinarian idea of God: 'surely there is no temper that is absolutely and irrecoverably prejudiced against that which is good. This would be so terrible an objection against the providence of GOD as would be very hard to be answered.'[257] In terming a propensity to vice an inclination of nature, however unusual, Tillotson is clearly defining nature and vice in a different way from Whichcote and contradicting some of his own statements about human nature.[258] But this does not undercut the crucial point that vice (the use of the term in preference to sin is significant) is always seen to be remediable: degenerate, abused, vicious nature can be restored by the co-operation of human effort with divine grace to its original ingenuity and goodness. This restoration is the only means to happiness, and its achievement is the design of religion.

The latitude-men are agreed that man's end is happiness. However, 'the desire of this is not properly a *Vertue*, or a *Moral Duty*, about which men have a liberty of Acting; but 'tis a *Natural Principle*'.[259] Man's happiness consists in perfecting his faculties, and it is here that choice and moral duty reside. Wilkins continues, 'the Happiness of man must consist in that whereby these faculties are perfected, namely in the favour of God', and the means to this end is religion.[260] There are many overlapping statements by various latitude-men as to the design of religion and the beneficial results it effects for man and society. Whichcote, as might be expected, concentrates on the effect of religion on the temper of the individual: 'Such is the Nature of Religion, that it keeps the Mind in a good Frame and Temper: it establishes a healthful Complexion of Soul, and makes it fit to discharge it self duly in all its Offices towards God, with its self, and with Men.'[261] Glanvill in his account of the divines of Bensalem also stresses this reformation of the individual temper and its consequent effect on society: 'They prest Men to consider, That the *design* of *Religion* was to *perfect humane Nature*; To restore the empire of our *minds* over the *will*, and *affections*; To make them more temperate, and contented in reference to themselves, and more humble, meek, courteous, charitable and just towards others.'[262] Burnet summed up many such statements in his funeral

expresses it, for no[t] being sound, when we are created sick'. Greville's 'Chorus Sacerdotum' from *Mustapha* was first published in 1609.
257 *Works*, IV, 502.
258 Cf. Burnet's account of Article IX, 'Of Original or Birth-Sin', *Thirty-Nine Articles*, and *Rochester*, 85.
259 Wilkins, *Ecclesiastes* (1675), 120; not in 1st edn. Cf. *Natural Religion*, 213; *Sermons*, ed. Tillotson, 12; Whichcote, *Select Sermons*, 216. See p. 44 above.
260 *Ecclesiastes* (1675), 121; cf. *Natural Religion*, Book II, Chapter 1, 'Shewing in general how Religion conduces to our Happiness'.
261 *Select Sermons*, Part I, Sermon 1, 31; cf. Part II, Sermon 6, 431, at the head of this chapter.
262 *Essays*, no. 7, 25; cf. Burnet, *Rochester*, 93–4.

sermon for Tillotson: 'He indeed judged that the great design of Christianity was the reforming Mens Natures, and governing their Actions, the restraining their Appetites, and Passions, the softning their Tempers, and sweetning their Humours, the composing their Affections, and the raising their minds above the Interests and Follies of this Present World, to the hope and pursuit of endless Blessedness.'[263]

The social benefits of religion are sometimes seen to consist in the fostering of the habit of deference to superiors. This kind of observation is aimed especially at the nonconformists, as when Patrick's Conformist claims smugly that he has learnt 'to bridle my tongue, especially when I speak of my superiors; to reverence my governors; to live in obedience to laws, though they happen to hinder my private profit; and for that end to look upon human laws as binding the conscience; to answer my betters with great modesty and humility'.[264] Though this kind of social conservatism is undoubtedly an important element in Anglican thought, especially in the post-Restoration period, it has been overemphasised by modern historians to the neglect of other elements; it is worth stressing that the latitude-men attach much less importance to this restraining aspect of the social benefits of religion than to the positive, reforming effect of religion on the individual and hence on society.

The design of Christianity, as Fowler insists in his book of the same title, is holiness:

the Business that brought the Blessed Jesus by the appointment of God the Father down from Heaven; and the End of His making us the Objects of such Rich and Transcendent Kindness, was the destroying of Sin in us, the Renewing of our depraved Natures, the Ennobling our Souls with Virtuous Qualities and Divine Dispositions and Tempers, and (in one word) *the making us partakers of His Holiness.*

Fowler goes on to define holiness, to Bunyan's disgust, as follows:

It is so sound and healthful a Complexion of Soul, as maintains in life and vigour whatsoever is Essential to it, and suffers not any thing unnatural to mix with that which is so; by the force and power whereof a man is enabled to behave himself as becometh a Creature indued with a principle of Reason; keeps his Supreme Faculty in its Throne, brings into due Subjection all his inferiour ones, his sensual Imagination, his Brutish Passions and Affections.

It is the Purity of the Humane Nature, engaging those in whom it resides, to demean themselves sutably to that state in which God hath placed them, and not to act disbecomingly in any Condition, Circumstance, or Relation.

It is a Divine or God-like Nature, causing an hearty approbation of, and an affectionate Compliance with the Eternal Laws of Righteousness; and a behaviour agreeable to the Essential and Immutable differences of Good and Evil.[265]

263 *Sermon preached at the Funeral of* [Tillotson], 31–2.
264 *Friendly Debate, Works,* V, 376; cf. Glanvill, *Essays,* no. 7, 31.
265 *Design,* Introduction, 3, Chapter 1, 6. For Bunyan's attack see Chapter 3 below, pp. 141–2.

This imitation of or participation in the divine nature is elsewhere called conformity to God,[266] or, in a term peculiar to Whichcote, deiformity: '*Holiness*, in Angels and Men, is their *Dei-formity*; Likeness to God in Goodness, Righteousness, and Truth.'[267] It is achieved partly through Christ working in man to repair his ruined nature, a process Whichcote also calls deification,[268] and partly through man's imitation of the example of Christ.[269] In an extraordinary passage (which conveniently ignores aspects of the New Testament account) Fowler presents Christ for the admiration and emulation of the reader in terms which portray him as the model Anglican gentleman:

His whole Life was one Continued Lecture of the most Excellent *Morals*, the most Sublime and exact Vertue.

For instance; He was a Person of the Greatest *Freedom*, *Affability*, and *Courtesie*, there was nothing in his Conversation that was at all Austere, Crabbed or Unpleasant. Though he was always *serious*, yet was he never *sowr*, sullenly Grave, Morose or Cynical; but of a marvellously conversable, sociable and benign temper.

And Fowler goes on to refer to 'the *Candour* also and *Ingenuity* of his Spirit': Christ exhibits the qualities of the ideal latitude-man.[270] It is not surprising to find Fowler claiming elsewhere that Christ, 'were he now upon the Earth, and conversant here among us, would, I doubt, narrowly escape the reproach of the Long Name', i.e. that of latitudinarian.[271]

Holiness, or conformity to the divine nature, is the essence of happiness: indeed it is a favourite saying of the latitude-men that holiness and happiness are the same thing.[272] Tillotson elaborates this idea of the running together of holiness, happiness and the divine nature as follows:

Happiness must be within us; the foundation of it must be laid in the inward frame and disposition of our spirits: and the very same causes and ingredients which make up the happiness of GOD must be found in us, though in a much inferior degree, or we cannot be happy ... he who is the author and fountain of happiness cannot convey it to us by any other way, than by planting in us such dispositions of mind as are in truth a kind of participation of the divine nature, and by enduing us with such qualities as are the necessary materials of happiness ... There is a certain kind of temper and disposition which is necessary and essential to happiness, and that is holiness and goodness, which is the very nature of GOD.[273]

---

[266] E.g. Smith, *Select Discourses*, no. 5, 147; Burnet, *Rochester*, 64; Barrow, Sermon 1, *Theological Works*, I, 19.

[267] *Aphorisms*, no. 262; cf. Burnet, *History*, I, 187, quoted above, p. 35.

[268] *Select Sermons*, Part II, Sermon 3, 347.

[269] E.g. Tillotson's Sermon 18, 'The Example of Jesus in doing Good', *Works*, I. McGee, *Godly Man*, 107–11, notes Anglican emphasis on the imitation of Christ.

[270] *Design*, 39, 41.   [271] *Principles and Practices*, 341.

[272] E.g. Cudworth, *Sermon Preached before the House of Commons*, in *Cambridge Platonists*, ed. Patrides, 112; Wilkins, *Natural Religion*, 379–80.

[273] Sermon 41 (1692), *Works*, III, 178–9.

Closely associated with this identification of holiness and happiness is the idea that heaven and hell are primarily states of mind (an idea shared by radical sectarians): '*Religion* delivers us from *Hell* by instating us in a possession of True Life and Blisse. *Hell* is *rather a Nature* then *a Place*: and *Heaven* cannot be so truly defined by any thing *without* us, as by something that is *within* us.'[274] The recovery of this state through holiness is the highest pleasure: 'no *Pleasures* are comparable to those that immediately result from vertue & holiness: for that man's Conscience is a very *Heaven* to him that busieth himself in the exercise thereof'.[275]

This emphasis on religion as the means to happiness and on the pleasure to be derived from exercising its duties is the characteristic note of latitudinarian preaching. Burnet argues that the alleged difficulties of following the precepts of religion are experienced only at the outset by those whose natures have been corrupted by vicious habits; the practice of religion becomes easy to those whose natures are restored to their 'Primitive Integrity'.[276] Tillotson, in a charming image, compares the beginning of the religious life to children's fear of going into cold water:

so soon as they have plunged into it the trouble is over, and then they wonder why they were so much afraid. The main difficulty and unpleasantness is in our first entrance into religion; it presently grows tolerable, and soon after easy, and after that by degrees so pleasant and delightful, that the man would not for all the world return to his former evil state and condition of life.[277]

This stress on the easiness of Christianity goes hand in hand with the latitudinarian rejection of the belief that suffering persecution is a necessary aspect of the Christian life, a belief inevitably held by nonconformists like Baxter or Bunyan who experienced such persecution at first hand and who thought (following Luke 14:27) that true Christians must be cross-bearers. Thus Wilkins argues that the biblical texts emphasising the importance of persecution (for example II Timothy 3:12 and Matthew 5:11) refer to the primitive church, and 'are not equally applicable to such other times and places, when and where the true Religion is publickly professed and encouraged ... because in such times and places, the profession of Religion will be so far from hindring, that it will rather promote a Man's secular Advantage'.[278] Wilkins and Tillotson were known friends to the nonconformists and hostile to the penal laws against them, yet they believed that the nonconformists exposed themselves to persecution unnecessarily and that their suffering in no

---

[274] Smith, *Select Discourses*, no. 9, 446–7; cf. Whichcote, *Aphorisms*, no. 464, from *Several Discourses*, I, no. 3, 57.

[275] Fowler, *Design*, 113.   [276] *Rochester*, 117.

[277] Sermon 14, 'The Folly and Danger of Irresolution and Delaying' (1675), *Works*, I, 327.

[278] *Natural Religion*, Book II, Chapter 3, 'How Religion conduces to the Happiness of the Outward-Man, in respect of Liberty, Safety, and Quiet', 328–9; cf. Tillotson, Sermon 6, 'The Precepts of Christianity not Grievous', *Works*, I, 164–5. For the nonconformist attitude to persecution see Chapter 3 below, pp. 156–8.

way constituted a validation of their doctrines. Their voicing of such obtuse or at least tactless remarks on suffering is unfortunately a necessary corollary of their central view that religion, far from turning a man's back on this world in order to prepare him for the next, makes him happier in this world precisely because he has his eye on the next.

This is why so much latitudinarian writing is devoted to urging the prudent man to be religious and demonstrating that the religious life is profitable, advantageous, and in his best interest in this world. This is the argument of Tillotson's early sermons, 1, 'The Wisdom of Being Religious', 3, 'The Advantages of Religion to Societies', and 4, 'The Advantages of Religion to Particular Persons'; of Barrow's two sermons, 2 and 3, on 'The Profitableness of Godliness' (which Tillotson presumably put at the beginning of his first edition of Barrow from the same motives that made him give his own sermons on the same subject prominence); and of Book II of Wilkins's *Natural Religion*, 'Of the Wisdom of practising the Duties of Natural Religion'. From one point of view this constant harping on prudence, profit, advantage, and interest is extremely calculated, and it perhaps sits rather oddly with the latitudinarian conviction of the innately benevolent disposition of man. To some extent it may be seen as an attempt to undermine the persuasiveness of Hobbesian ethics by using Hobbes's vocabulary. This is obviously a different method from the simple stating of man's sociability as a fact in opposition to Hobbes's view of man's selfishness. Burnet's summary of Hobbes's views and the hostile reaction to them of the latitude-men includes the following statement: 'He thought interest and fear were the chief principles of society: And he put all morality in the following that which was our own private will or advantage.'[279] It is perhaps because of this version of interest and advantage that the latitude-men press these terms so much. Tillotson, recognising that 'every man is led by interest', goes on to argue that 'he that would do right to religion, and make a ready way for the entertainment of it among men, cannot take a more effectual course than by reconciling it with the happiness of mankind, and by giving satisfaction to our reason, that it is so far from being an enemy, that it is the greatest friend to our temporal interests'.[280] The deliberate adoption of such vocabulary in the attempt to reconcile religion with interest is illustrated in Barrow's Sermon 5, 'Upright Walking Sure Walking':

The world is much addicted to the politics; the heads of men are very busy in contrivance, and their mouths are full of talk about the ways of consulting our safety, and securing our interests. May we not therefore presume, that an infallible maxim of policy, proposing the most expedite and certain method of security in all our transactions, will be entertained with acceptance?[281]

---

[279] *History*, I, 187, quoted in full above, p. 45.   [280] Sermon 3, *Works*, I, 94–5.
[281] *Theological Works*, I, 113.

The sermon goes on to argue that integrity is the best policy.

However, the calculated rhetorical way in which such an argument is used does not make it cynical. Prudence, properly understood, is a process of rational choice which enables a man to follow the highest good. Wilkins's Sermon 7 on Proverbs 4:7, 'Wisdom is the principal thing, therefore get wisdom', drawing on Aristotle, Cicero and Aquinas as well as Solomon, defines three different ways of attaining three different kinds of happiness: carnal policy, moral prudence, and spiritual wisdom. The end of carnal policy is the gratifying of sensual appetite. The end of moral prudence is 'peace, quiet, safety as to our outward condition, contentment and joy as to our inward frame, and usefulness to those with whom we converse; and such a future state of happiness as the light of nature will inable men to believe and hope for'. Spiritual or Christian wisdom includes the two previous ways of attaining happiness:

Christian Wisdom may be defined to be that habit of mind whereby a man is inabled to propose the true end of eternal blessedness, and to judge aright concerning such means as may be most fit for the attaining of this end, conforming his life and carriage accordingly.

This doth not abolish humane wisdom, so far as we keep within due bounds, in the getting and enjoying these worldly things, much less *moral prudence*; but they may be both comprehended under it, as being subordinate and subservient to it.

Moral prudence is a necessary adjunct of spiritual wisdom. Wilkins concludes that 'grace and holiness is the truest wisdom. He that is truly religious ... is truly wise', and, one might add, truly prudent.[282] It is therefore entirely appropriate for Fowler to emphasise Christ's prudence, the 'wisdom of the serpent' [Matthew 10:16]: '*Prudence* is the first of the primitive vertues, or of those from whence all other take their Original, and are derived: She is the chief Governness of humane actions; and those which are performed without her direction, do want a main circumstance that is necessary to give them the denomination of truly vertuous.'[283]

It is partly because of their use of the language of prudence that the latitudinarians have received a bad press, yet it is difficult to see why the argument that religion brings worldly happiness should be more objectionable than the argument that the test of the truth of a doctrine is the suffering it brings. The latitude-men evidently thought that the appeal to profit, interest, and advantage would make their doctrine more attractive and persuasive, particularly to adherents of libertine or worldly ethics, yet there is no doubt that they believed that religion does make men happy and therefore is in their best interest. Point by point and chapter by chapter in Book II of *Natural*

---

[282] *Sermons*, ed. Tillotson, 205–10, 229. McAdoo, *Spirit of Anglicanism*, 173–4, 207–30, is particularly helpful on the meaning of prudence in Tillotson and Wilkins and their debt to Aquinas.
[283] *Design*, 63.

Religion Wilkins argues that religion conduces to our outward and inward happiness in this world in respect of health, liberty, safety, quiet, riches, pleasure, honour, reputation, regulation of the faculties, and peace and tranquillity of mind. He then urges the reader to verify his doctrine empirically: 'I appeal to the Experience of all considering Men, whether this doth not appear to them, that the generality of those who live most pleasantly in the World, are the most religious and virtuous part of Mankind.'[284]

The central tenets of latitudinarian Christianity are the rational basis of religion and the happiness of the moral life. The contradictions involved in these tenets, and the directions in which they pointed, were largely ignored by their promoters. The latitudinarian emphasis on the reasonableness of Christianity at the expense of its mysteries seemed to its opponents to lead to Socinianism and deism, and though the latitude-men objected strongly to this accusation, which they blamed on high church malice,[285] historians have long concluded that both their methods and some of their principles aided the rise of deism. However, it is misleading to emphasise contradictions in latitudinarian thought by taking certain aspects to their logical conclusion. Eighteenth-century freethinkers like Anthony Collins or Matthew Tindal who claimed Tillotson or Wilkins for their intellectual forebears were deliberately selective in their accounts and gave misleading versions of their thought, as their critic Edmund Gibson showed.[286] Elements which appeared later to be contradictions were held together constructively by the latitude-men: reason and revelation, happiness and holiness, interest and virtue, the demands of this world and of the next. Further, Bunyan's caricature of the latitudinarian point of view in the shape of Mr Worldly Wiseman has been too persuasive. Just as contemporary opponents of both extremes (nonconformist and high church) saw the latitude-men as lukewarm time-servers, so some modern historians have accused them of anxiously cobbling together the remnants of Anglicanism or rationalising the activities of a market society. In contrast, the latitude-men had the highest mutual respect for each other, and were certain of the integrity and consistency of their intellectual and moral position. They regarded themselves as the true heirs of the Christian tradition running from the early church through medieval scholasticism and Renaissance humanism to seventeenth-century Arminianism in its various forms. Their emphasis on their own origins, however, does not disguise the fact that their optimism about human nature and the place of religion in the world illustrates a new and extremely important development in seventeenth-century thought. The

---

[284] *Natural Religion*, 284. See also Rivers, 'Grace, Holiness and the Pursuit of Happiness: Bunyan and Restoration Latitudinarianism', in Keeble, ed., *Bunyan* (1988), Chapter 3.

[285] See e.g. Burnet, *History*, II, 28–9.

[286] The misappropriation of latitudinarian language is treated in *Reason, Grace, and Sentiment*, II.

combination of the tone of careful but confident optimism with the sense of intellectual tradition and community which their writings reveal goes some way towards explaining the extraordinary influence they continued to exercise in English religion in the eighteenth century.

3

The religion of grace: Baxter, Bunyan, and the nonconformist reaction

If you will go with us, you must go against Wind and Tide ... You must also own Religion in his Rags, as well as when in his Silver Slippers, and stand by him too, when bound in Irons, as well as when he walketh the Streets with applause.

Bunyan, *The Pilgrim's Progress* (1678)[1]

The prophane and formal Persecutors on one hand, and the Fanatick dividing Sectary on the other hand, have in all Ages been grinding the spiritual Seed, as the Corn is ground between the Milstones.

Reliquiae Baxterianae (1696)[2]

God's word is large, and man's mind is narrow: and we are apt, when we observe something, to think that it is all. So some are so intent on duty, that they have poor thoughts of grace and mercy; and some think that the magnifying of grace obligeth them to vilify inherent holiness, and performed duty. And nothing is now more common than to set truth against truth, and duty against duty; when they are such as God conjoineth.

Baxter, *The Poor Man's Family Book* (1674)[3]

I saw then in my Dream, so far as this Valley reached, there was on the right hand a very deep Ditch; that Ditch is it into which the blind have led the blind in all Ages, and have both there miserably perished. Again, behold on the left hand, there was a very dangerous Quagg, into which, if even a good Man falls, he can find no bottom for his foot to stand on ... The path-way was here also exceeding narrow, and therefore good *Christian* was the more put to it; for when he sought in the dark to shun the ditch on the one hand, he was ready to tip over into the mire on the other; also when he sought to escape the mire, without great carefulness he would be ready to fall into the ditch.

The Pilgrim's Progress[4]

Faith and holiness are my professed principles, with an endeavour, so far as in me lieth, to be at peace with all men.

Bunyan, *A Confession of my Faith, and a Reason of my Practice* (1672)[5]

[1] Ed. Wharey, rev. Sharrock (1960), 100.   [2] Part I, 103.
[3] *Practical Works*, ed. Orme (1830), XIX, 445.
[4] P. 62   [5] *The Whole Works*, ed. Offor (1862), II, 593.

1 The nonconformist spectrum

The puritan heirs of the sixteenth-century protestant reformers were concerned with two fundamental questions: the nature of the relationship between God and man, and the definition and organisation of the Christian church. During the experimental and unstable period of the 1640s and 1650s a very wide range of answers was given to these questions. In the 1660s the loose grouping of churches, sects, doctrines, and assumptions known as nonconformity came into being as a result of immediate political and legal changes – the restoration of the Church of England and the proscription of those who would not conform to it – but nonconformity also represented a series of developments in traditional protestant theology in reaction to changes in ideas which were thought in different ways to be undermining the religion of grace. In the 1640s and 1650s the principal dangers were thought to be Arminianism at one extreme and antinomianism at the other, both of which were seen as unbalancing the complex and delicate relationship between God and man, in which God's grace must be exalted without man's responsibility for his own actions being denied. Despite these threats, and despite the disagreements both doctrinal and ecclesiastical among the different proponents of the religion of grace, it was the dominant religious and intellectual force in the middle of the century. After the Restoration what had been the basic theology of the English Church for a hundred years became (with some exceptions) the property of proscribed groups, even though theology was not itself the cause of division between conformists and nonconformists, while latitudinarianism gradually took its place as the dominant force. Nonconformity developed in two ways alongside and in response to this reversal: either by incorporating and indeed contributing to some of the rational and moralist features of latitude, or by defining its own values and doctrines sharply in opposition to the coming orthodoxy.[6]

The term nonconformist was in use before the Interregnum to mean much the same as puritan in its technical, disciplinary sense: it referred to those who did not conform to all the ceremonies of the Church of England but wished to purify it from within, not to separate from it. Puritan in its popular sense could be applied to a much wider range of individuals, though after the Restoration it was becoming obsolete: Bunyan's Mr Attentive, in *The Life and Death of Mr. Badman* (1680), feels the need to gloss the term: '*The man was a godly old Puritan,*

---

6 The most useful general works on the ecclesiastical, intellectual, and cultural aspects of nonconformity are: Bolam *et al.*, *The English Presbyterians* (1968); Griffiths, *Religion and Learning* (1935); Keeble, *The Literary Culture of Nonconformity* (1987); Matthews, *Calamy Revised* (1934); Nuttall and Chadwick, eds., *From Uniformity to Unity* (1962); Nuttall *et al.*, *The Beginnings of Nonconformity* (1964); Sommerville, *Popular Religion in Restoration England* (1977); Wallace, *Puritans and Predestination* (1982); Watts, *The Dissenters* (1978); Whiting, *Studies in English Puritanism* (1931).

for so the godly were called in time past.[7] Baxter clearly describes the popular understanding of the term in his account of the people who joined the parliamentary side in 1642, 'who were then called *Puritans, Precisions, Religious Persons*, that used to talk of God, and Heaven, and Scripture, and Holiness, and to follow Sermons, and read Books of Devotion, and pray in their Families, and spend the Lord's Day in Religious Exercises, and plead for Mortification, and serious Devotion, and strict obedience to God', and he goes on to explain how the general took over from the ecclesiastical sense: 'So that the same name in a Bishops mouth signified a Nonconformist, and in an ignorant Drunkards or Swearers mouth, a godly obedient Christian. But the People being the greater number, became among themselves the Masters of the Sense.'[8] The terms puritans preferred to use of themselves were the godly, professors, and the brethren (for ministers).

After the Restoration nonconformist both acquired a very specific legal meaning and also took on the general associations of the earlier puritan.[9] Under the terms of the Act of Uniformity of 1662 the Book of Common Prayer, suspended during the Interregnum, was restored to use, and those clergy, numbering about 2,000, who refused to assent and consent to it in its entirety and among other requirements refused ordination by bishops were ejected from their livings on Bartholomew Day, 24 August 1662, frequently named by Baxter 'the fatal day'. In a detailed analysis of conformists and nonconformists in his posthumously published autobiography, the most remarkable document for the history of nonconformity in this period, Baxter defined the following categories. The conformists were of three sorts: old Presbyterians, latitudinarians (the latter described as 'ingenious Men and Scholars, and of Universal Principles, and free; abhorring at first the *Imposition* of these little things, but thinking them not great enough to stick at when Imposed'), and those who were '*heartily such throughout*' (including the nonconformists' chief scourge, whom Baxter called diocesans and who have become known to historians as high churchmen). The first two parties seemed to Baxter 'the honour of the Conformists, though not heartily theirs'. The nonconformists included the category named by Baxter the reconcilers (among whom he classed himself), i.e. moderate episcopalians who could reluctantly accept the Anglican liturgy but not everything required by the Act, and the two main groupings of the 1640s and 1650s, the Presbyterians and Independents.[10] Baxter's sympathies were very largely with the reconcilers and Presbyterians.

[7] *Mr. Badman*, ed. Forrest and Sharrock (1988), 144. See B. Hall, 'Puritanism: the problem of definition', in Cuming, ed., *Studies in Church History*, II (1965).

[8] *RB*, Part I, 31–2. Cf. Baxter's similar comments in *A Christian Directory* and *The Poor Man's Family Book, Practical Works*, III, 574; XIX, 378.

[9] On the use of the terms nonconformist and dissenter in the period see Keeble, *Literary Culture*, 41–4.

[10] *RB*, Part II, 386–7. See R. Thomas, 'The Rise of the Reconcilers', in Bolam, ed., *English Presbyterians*.

Modern historians have tended to merge the first of these with the second, and to call those to the right of the nonconformist spectrum Presbyterians even if they were not attached to a Presbyterian system of church government, in this respect following contemporary usage: 'Any Man that was for a Spiritual serious way of Worship (though he were for moderate Episcopacy and Liturgy), and that lived according to his Profession, was called commonly a *Presbyterian*, as formerly he was called a *Puritan*, unless he joyned himself to *Independents, Anabaptists*, or some other sect which might afford him a more odious Name.'[11] Baxter did not think that the final category, the sects, should be counted with the nonconformists, and by subsuming the major sects, the Baptists and Quakers, under the name of fanatics he unjustly concealed the great differences between them.[12] It is usual, and more helpful, to speak of four main groups of nonconformists: the Presbyterians (taken in the broad sense), whose leaders were Richard Baxter (1615–91), John Howe (1630–1705), and at a later stage Daniel Williams (1643?–1716); the Independents or Congregationalists, led by John Owen (1616–83), who had been the most powerful divine in England under Cromwell; the Baptists, whose leading writers were John Bunyan (1628–88) and Benjamin Keach (1640–1704); and the Quakers or Religious Society of Friends, founded by George Fox (1624–91), whose later leaders included William Penn (1644–1718), and Robert Barclay (1648–90).

In principle the status of nonconformity in relation to the Act of Uniformity only applied to ministers, not to laymen, and to those such as the Presbyterians who wished to belong to a national church, not to separatists. The majority of ministers ejected from their livings in 1662 were Presbyterians; the sects were largely unaffected, since few sectarian leaders or ministers were incumbents of parish churches. However, the repressive legislation enacted in the 1660s and 1670s in practice defined all those who provided or attended services other than in established churches and according to the Book of Common Prayer as nonconformists and hence as criminals. The most important of these statutes were the Five Mile Act of 1665, which forbade nonconformist ministers who would not take certain oaths from coming within five miles of towns or their former churches and from teaching in schools, and the two Conventicle Acts of 1664 and (more severe) of 1670, which made it a crime for five or more people to assemble together for religious worship other than by the Book of Common Prayer, and which encouraged the use of informers and empowered constables to break into premises in search of such conventicles. The nonconformists responded by systematically breaking these laws, the Presbyterians and Independents cautiously, the sects, especially the Quakers, openly. Some of them suffered appallingly in consequence, through fines, seizure of goods, and imprison-

---

[11] *RB*, Part II, 278.   [12] *RB*, Part II, 387.

ment, and though the last of these penalties for some meant a reasonably comfortable confinement with access to friends, books and writing materials, for many others it meant death from malnutrition, overcrowding, disease, or violence. For the Quakers, ironically, this was a continuation of the persecution they had suffered under the Protectorate; for the Presbyterians, who had preached intolerance in the 1640s and welcomed back the king in 1660, and for the Independents, who had controlled church appointments through the Commission of Triers in the 1650s, this was an unexpected experience, far worse than the Laudian persecution of Puritans in the 1630s. The Quakers had contempt for caution: they met openly and virtually courted arrest, in contrast to Presbyterians and Independents, who often met in secret and disguised the nature of their meetings. Baxter admitted readily that the extraordinary bravery of the 'Fanaticks called *Quakers* did greatly relieve the sober People for a time', as the magistrates had their hands full.[13]

There were periods of respite from this persecution. Charles II's Declaration of Indulgence of 1672 (perhaps issued mainly with the object of obtaining toleration for Roman Catholics, but consistent with the sympathy for 'tender consciences' expressed by the returning king in the Declaration of Breda of 1660) suspended these laws and enabled ministers, if licensed, to preach in meeting places which were also to be licensed. Over 1,400 licences were taken out, and many nonconformists were released from prison. In response to parliamentary pressure, however, the Indulgence was withdrawn the following year. In the last years of Charles's reign (1681–5), following the defeat of the Whig attempt to exclude the Roman Catholic Duke of York from the succession to the throne, persecution of nonconformists intensified. James II's Indulgences of 1687 and 1688, by which he hoped to unite the nonconformists and the Catholics, instead had the effect of totally alienating the Anglicans, reconciling the Anglicans (after a fashion) to the nonconformists, and bringing about his own downfall. For the nonconformists the experience of living alternately and unpredictably under persecution and indulgence is summed up in the contrasted portraits of Vanity Fair in the two parts of Bunyan's *Pilgrim's Progress* (1678 and 1684). In the first part Christian and Faithful after their arrest in Vanity Fair are subjected to violence, imprisonment and a mockery of a trial, reminiscent of contemporary experience (though Faithful's death at the stake is that of an early Christian or Marian martyr). In the second part things are very different at Vanity Fair, as Mr Contrite explains: 'In *those* days we were afraid to walk the Streets, but *now* we

---

[13] *RB*, Part II, 436. For the legislation and subsequent persecution see Watts, *Dissenters*, Chapter 3; Cragg, *Puritanism in the Period of the Great Persecution* (1957), Chapter 4; Keeble, *Literary Culture*, 45–55. Baxter describes the impact of the legislation in *RB*, Part II, 384–5, 435–6; Part III, 2–4, 104–5.

can shew our Heads. *Then* the Name of a Professor was odious, *now* ... Religion is counted Honourable.'[14]

The significance of their suffering was a subject that much exercised the nonconformists.[15] Its effect was not at all that intended by their persecutors. The latter's objectives were clearly summed up in an address published by Bishop Thomas Barlow in 1685, urging that the laws should be enforced 'for the Preservation of the Public Peace and Unity, and for the good of Dissenters themselves: for Afflictio dat Intellectum [Affliction gives Understanding] and their sufferings by the execution of our Just Laws may (by God's blessing) bring them to a sense of Duty and a Desire to do it'.[16] The absurdity of this argument was pointed out in a letter to Barlow by Howe:

> We must, it seems, understand all this Rigour your Lordship shews, to proceed from Love, and that you are for destroying the Dissenters, only to mend their understandings, and because *Afflicto dat Intellectum*. I hope indeed God will sanctify the Affliction which you give and procure them, to blessed purposes ... but for the purposes your Lordship seems to aim at, I wonder what you can expect? Can you, by undoing Men, change the Judgment of their Consciences? Or if they should tell you, we do indeed in our Consciences judge, we shall greatly offend God, by complying with your Injunctions, but yet to save being undone, we will do it: Will this qualify them for your Communion?[17]

The zealots among the conformists had hoped by persecuting nonconformists to drive them back to the Established Church and to stamp nonconformity out. But the terms of allegiance had been so strictly defined that many of those who were anxious to be comprehended within a national church felt obliged to remain outside the Church of England. This was a serious political error on the part of the conformists. The effect was that the Presbyterians and their conservative allies were driven towards the position of the more radical Congregationalists and the sectarians. Although the former in some respects had more in common intellectually with latitudinarian conformists than with more extreme nonconformists, the experience of proscription and persecution gave them a shared view of the nature of the Christian life that was inevitably not available to conformists, and it further caused them to redefine their view of the relationship between church and society, so that ultimately all brands of nonconformists became separatists. Baxter describes this process clearly:

> Presbyterians were forced to forbear all Exercise of their way: they durst not meet together (Synodically) unless in a Goal. They could not (ordinarily) be the Pastors of Parish-Churches, no not for the private part of the Work, being driven five Miles from all their former Charges and Auditors, and from every City and Corporation: Which Law, while they durst not (for the most part of them) obey, they were fain to live privately, as still flying from a Goal, and to preach to none but those that sought to them, and thrust in upon them. So that their Congregations were, through necessity,

---

[14] *Pilgrim's Progress*, 91–7, 275.   [15] See pp. 156–8 below.

[16] Quoted in Brown, *Bunyan*, rev. Harrison (1928), 323–4.

[17] Calamy, *Life of Howe* (1724), 111; Brown, *Bunyan*, 325.

just of Independent and Separating Shape, and outward Practice, though not upon the same Principles.

Baxter, as a self-styled reconciler, saw that persecution made the moderate position virtually untenable and strengthened the position of Independents and sects: 'But whoever be the Sect-Masters, it is notorious, That the Prelates (tho' not they only) are the Sect-makers, by driving the poor People by violence, and the viciousness of too many of their Instruments, into these alienations and extreams'.[18] The successive negotiations conducted by the latitudinarians with the Presbyterians for their comprehension within the Established Church were designed to prevent this state of affairs. Some cautious churchmen favoured comprehension for the Presbyterians with no indulgence for those who would not join a more broadly defined national church; some Congregationalists and sectarians supported indulgence and opposed comprehension for precisely this reason, fearing, as Baxter explained, 'that when the most considerable of the Ministry were embodied with the Conformists; their own Exclusion and Suppression would be unavoidable'.[19] But all attempts at comprehension ultimately failed, and the Toleration Act of 1689 identified all orthodox (i.e. trinitarian) protestants who chose to remain outside the Church of England as protestant dissenters, a term that implied voluntary separation.

In the eyes of the law nonconformists belonged to a single category, and the experience of persecution certainly gave them a common identity. But the traditions and intellectual ancestry of the different denominations, and the divergent experiences of their leaders in the Interregnum period, meant that there was a wide range of approaches to doctrine and discipline that led to suspicion, disagreement, and sometimes outright hostility between the groups. The three denominations (as they later came to be known) of Presbyterians, Congregationalists, and Baptists were agreed in their opposition to the Quakers, whose doctrinal differences set them apart from other nonconformists as a special case. Yet the gap between these three was also great, despite the fact that Congregationalists had links of different kinds with both Presbyterians and Baptists. In *The Poor Man's Family Book* Baxter's spokesman Paul gives his convert Saul a succinct and useful summary of contemporary religious controversies in order to warn him against the temptation of involvement in them:

I.   In doctrinals, you will hear some on one side, and some on the other, hotly contending about predestination and providence, and universal redemption, and free-will, and man's merits, and in what sense Christ's righteousness is imputed to us, and about justification, and the law, and the covenants of works and of grace; and of the nature of faith, and repentance, of assurance of salvation, and whether any fall away from grace, with many such like.

II.   In matters of church government and God's worship, you will meet with some

18 *RB*, Part III, 43.   19 *RB*, Part II, 433; see also Part III, 23–36, 100, 131, 156–7.

that are for prelacy, and some against it; some for government by the pastors in equality, some for the people's power of the keys, and some for an universal government of all the world by the pope of Rome. And you will find some against all praying by the book, or a set form of words; and some against all other praying save that, at least, in public; some for images, and many symbolical ceremonies of men's making, in God's public worship, and some against them; some for keeping all from the sacrament, of whose conversion of holiness the people are not satisfied; and some for admitting the scandalous and ignorant, and some for a middle way; with many other differences about words, and gestures, and manner of serving God.[20]

This analysis, of course, includes the views of Roman Catholics and Anglicans. But it also clearly indicates the grounds on which Presbyterians, Congregationalists, and Baptists differed among themselves.[21] In terms of doctrine, the crucial point of disagreement was the extent of human responsibility in the process of conversion. The Congregationalists and Particular (i.e. Calvinist) Baptists saw any attempts to present the process of justification as one involving co-operation between man and God or conditions to be performed by man as a derogation from the power and grace of God and a heathenish elevation of man's natural faculties, usually covered by the derogatory labels of Arminian or papist. Conversely, the Presbyterians attached far more importance to the role of reason and choice, and feared that the Congregational and Baptist emphasis on the imputation of Christ's righteousness to the elect implied moral passivity and unintentionally opened the door to antinomianism, in which the quality of the moral life of the elect had no bearing on the question of their salvation. These theoretical differences, however, did not prevent the majority of nonconformists from agreeing closely about the importance of practice, about the centrality in the life of the elect of holiness or 'walking with God'. In terms of discipline one of the main points of disagreement was the definition of church membership. Congregationalists and Baptists required from their members evidence of conversion in the form of public testimony to their experience; members of such 'gathered' churches were thus clearly marked as separate from the rest of society. A church was by definition a gathering of saints.[22] Presbyterians were suspicious of this assumption that the elect could be identified through the judgement of their fellows on their experience, and were more flexible in their requirement for membership, asking for a 'credible profession of faith' (and in this approximating more closely to the Anglican position).[23] All nonconformists were agreed on the fundamental opposition between the godly and the ungodly; the problem was the method whereby the godly were to be identified.

---

[20] *Practical Works*, XIX, 424–5.
[21] A very useful summary is provided by Nuttall, 'Relations between Presbyterians and Congregationalists' (1964).
[22] See Nuttall, *Visible Saints* (1957).
[23] On 'credible profession' see *RB*, Part I, 114; Part II, 143.

A further significant disagreement was over the status of the minister. Presbyterian and Congregational ministers tended to be university-educated, and regarded a trained ministry as essential; the Baptists, like the Quakers, attached no importance to human learning as a ministerial qualification. Unlike the Presbyterians, Congregational and Baptist ministers were chosen by their congregations. Yet all nonconformist ministers rejected the necessity of episcopal ordination, which was one of the main requirements of the Act of Uniformity and over which, according to Baxter, negotiations with the latitudinarians over comprehension foundered.[24]

Differences such as these over doctrine and discipline, exacerbated in some cases by recriminations about the past and personal dislike, hindered the nonconformists' attempts to unite both during and immediately after the period of legal proscription. This is especially true of relations between Presbyterians and Congregationalists in London. Correspondence between Baxter and Owen in 1669 on the subject of unity led to nothing, hardly surprisingly in view of Baxter's downright and hostile statement to Owen of 'the great things which hinder the *Presbyterians* and *Moderate Episcopal Men*, from closing with you':

1. Because they think that your way tends to destroy the Kingdom of Christ, by dividing it, while all Excommunicate Persons, or Hereticks, or humorous Persons, may at any time gather a Church of such as Separate from the Church which they belonged to, though it be on the account of Ungodliness, or Impatience of Disciplines, &c. and then may stand on equal Terms with you ...

2. They think, while you seem to be for a *stricter Discipline* than others, that your way (or usual Practice) tendeth to extirpate Godliness out of the Land; by taking a very few that can talk more than the rest, and making them the Church, and shutting out more that are as worthy, and by neglecting the Souls of all the Parish else, except as to some publick Preaching ...[25]

Despite these insuperable difficulties over discipline, following the Declaration of Indulgence of 1672 a joint lecture of Presbyterians and Congregationalists was established weekly at Pinners' Hall in the City, the preachers including Owen and Baxter, and at a later stage Bunyan. Here doctrinal differences were inevitably exposed. Baxter's sermons were criticised for overstressing the importance of human will, 'especially, if I did but say, That Man's Will had a Natural Liberty, though a *M*oral Thraldom to Vice, and that *M*en might have Christ and Life, if they were truly willing, though Grace must make them willing; and that *M*en have power to do better than they do, It was cryed abroad among all the Party, that I Preached up *Arminianism*, and Free-Will, and *Man's Power*, and O! What an odious Crime was this'.[26] Despite suspicion n the part of Congregationalists that the Presbyterians were in danger of becoming Arminians, and on the part of Presbyterians that the Congregationalists were too sympathetic to anti-nomians, after the Toleration Act the two groups set up a Common Fund and formed a 'Happy Union' agreed by their United.

[24] *RB*, Part III, 37 (mispaginated), *ff* 71.   [25] *RB*, Part III, 67.   [26] *RB*, Part III, 103.

Ministers. But in London this unity of the early 1690s was short-lived. The republication in 1690 of the antinomian Tobias Crisp's sermons, *Christ Alone Exalted* (first published posthumously in 1643), led to a serious dispute which resulted after a pamphlet war in the expulsion of Daniel Williams from Pinners' Hall and the setting up by Williams, Howe and others of a rival Presbyterian lecture at Salters' Hall. The Congregationalists eventually agreed to condemn antinomianism, but the ten-year controversy over 'Crispianism' indicates both the seriousness of theological divergence among the dissenters and the difficulties they faced in attempting to unite after the bond of proscription had been removed.[27]

In the critical period 1662–88, however, disputes between nonconformist groups were less significant than nonconformist responses to Anglicanism in establishing a nonconformist sense of identity. Attacks on the nonconformist position made by both high churchmen and latitudinarians, combined with attempts to redefine the religion of grace so as to place much greater stress on morality, enabled nonconformists to identify what was characteristic of and central to their tradition in comparison with the views of those from whom they were separated. The most important works to have this effect were Patrick's *A Friendly Debate* (1669), Samuel Parker's *A Discourse of Ecclesiastical Politie* (1670), Fowler's *The Design of Christianity* (1671), William Sherlock's *A Discourse concerning the Knowledge of Jesus Christ* (1673), and Stillingfleet's *The Mischief of Separation* (1680) and *The Unreasonableness of Separation* (1681).[28] But the nonconformists, although united in their opposition to the principle of conformity, disagreed in their assessment of their relationship to the different groups of conformists. It appeared to some nonconformists that despite the differences among themselves, these were less striking than the differences between the high church and latitudinarian wings of the Church of England. This view is clearly put by Howe in *The Case of the Protestant Dissenters Represented and Argued*, published in 1689 as a contribution to the debate about comprehension and indulgence before the passing of the Toleration Act:

> But some may think, by Concessions to us, *the Church of England* will be ruin'd, and a great Advantage given to the bringing in of *Popery*.
> To which we say, the generality of the Dissenters differ from *the Church of England*, in no substantials of Doctrine and Worship, no nor of Government, provided it be so manag'd as to attain its true acknowledg'd End: The favouring of us therefore will as much ruin the Church, as its Inlargement and additional Strength will signify to its ruin.
> And doth not the World know, that wherein we differ from them, we differ from the *Papists* too? And that for the most part, wherein they differ from us, they seem to agree with them? ...

[27] On the Union and the Crispian controversy see Bogue and Bennett, *History of Dissenters*, I (1808), 399 ff; R. Thomas, 'Parties in Nonconformity', in Bolam, ed., *English Presbyterians;* Colligan, 'Antinomian Controversy' (1913–15); Griffiths, *Religion and Learning*, 99 ff; Rogers, *Life of Howe* (1836), Chapter 10; Thomas, *Daniel Williams* (1964); Toulmin, *Historical View* (1814), 201 ff.

[28] The response to some of these is discussed in Wallace, *Puritans and Predestination*, Chapter 5.

But 'tis wont to be said, we agree not among our selves, and know not what we would have.

And do all that go under the Name of *the Church of England* agree among themselves? We can shew more considerable Disagreements among them, than any can between the most of us, and a considerable part of them. They all agree, 'tis true, in Conformity: and we all agree in Nonconformity. And is not this merely accidental to Christianity and Protestantism? And herein is it not well known that the far greater part of Reformed Christendom do more agree with us?[29]

Howe is arguing that the majority of the nonconformists (he is presumably excluding antinomians and Quakers) and the latitudinarian wing of the conformists are a continuum, whereas the high church wing approximates more closely to the Roman Catholics. In this assessment the real issue is not conformity or nonconformity, but the betrayal or continuation of the Reformation tradition. The difficulty here is that nonconformists further along the spectrum from the Presbyterians would characterise the betrayers differently. In their alternative assessment the Reformation tradition is represented by the centre parties among the nonconformists, i.e. the Congregationalists and Baptists, whereas the Presbyterians are perceived as allied with the latitudinarians on the wrong side of the dividing line. Response to the views of the latitudinarians thus becomes an interesting test of how nonconformists defined their own position.

How far was nonconformity an artificial, legally defined category which temporarily brought together disparate, heterogeneous groups, and how far did it represent a cohesive body of beliefs and attitudes? Are the similarities more important than the differences? An answer to these questions can be attempted through a comparison of Baxter and Bunyan, the two most enduring prose writers of the nonconformist tradition, who illustrate the two main opposed tendencies in nonconformity and yet who share much common ground. Both formed their views essentially before the Restoration, Baxter in the 1640s and Bunyan in the 1650s; both suffered varying degrees of persecution between 1660 and 1688; both achieved enormous contemporary reputation and popularity as preachers and especially as writers. They differed in their education, the sources of their thought, their religious affiliation and friendships, their doctrinal statements, and their assessment of the significance of contemporary latitudinarian thought. In spite of intellectual and social differences they agreed on the nature of their ministerial role; both saw the Christian life as a developing process which required particular kinds of skill and effort on the part of both teacher and learner, and both saw the antithetical temptations to legalism and antinomianism (though they defined them rather differently) as the chief doctrinal obstacles to this life.[30]

[29] Calamy, *Life of Howe*, 157–8; cf. Nuttall, *Holy Spirit* (1946), 9.

[30] The most useful works on Baxter are: Keeble, *Baxter* (1982); Nuttall, *Baxter* (1965); W. Orme, 'The Life and Times of Richard Baxter' and 'The Life and Writings of Richard Baxter', *Practical Works*, I (to be used with caution); Packer, 'Redemption and Restoration' (1954); Powicke, *Baxter* (1924) and *Baxter under the Cross* (1927).

Baxter's early and lifelong sympathy was for the mainstream puritan tradition of the late sixteenth and early seventeenth centuries, for practical writers such as Perkins, Dod, Preston, Sibbes, and Bolton, 'our old, solid divines' as he calls them in the Dedication to *The Saint's Everlasting Rest*.[31] His experience as a chaplain in the army in the mid-1640s of what he regarded as the damaging influence of books by antinomians '(*more fitly called Libertines*)' such as Crisp and Saltmarsh led him to an important reassessment of the doctrine of the covenants and of justification in his first published work, *Aphorismes of Justification* (1649).[32] He was highly unsympathetic to what he saw as the misappropriation of the doctrine of free grace, and to counterbalance this put great stress in all his practical works on obedience and repentance as a necessary part of the process of justification. In the Interregnum he identified his position on matters of church government closely with that of moderate churchmen such as Hall and especially Ussher, and by rejecting the Calvinist doctrine of limited atonement and double predestination he aligned himself doctrinally with the school of French protestants of Saumur.[33] Baxter contributed significantly to the changing theological climate in the middle of the century, and for this he incurred the hostility of those whom he characterised as 'over-orthodox', particularly Owen, whose religious and political views he consistently attacked.[34] Of subsequent nonconformists he was perhaps intellectually closest to Howe, who responded enthusiastically to the *Aphorismes*.[35]

The respect in which Baxter was held by moderate Anglicans is evidenced by the fact that in 1660, when a moderate church policy for a short time seemed possible, Charles II made him one of his chaplains and offered him the see of Hereford, an offer he refused. Baxter was very critical of and was distrusted by Hammond's followers, the 'diocesan' or 'prelatical party', with whom he negotiated unsuccessfully for reform of the liturgy at the Savoy Conference in 1661 and who were responsible for the divisive church settlement in 1662.[36] He thought the two kinds of episcopalians differed from each other much more than the moderate episcopalians from the Presbyterians, and his respect for the latitudinarians, especially Wilkins ('a lover of Mankind, and of honesty, peace and Impartiality and Justice'), Tillotson, Whichcote, and Stillingfleet, emerges at several points in his autobiography.[37]

[31] *Practical Works*, XXII, 4.
[32] See the account in the Preface to 'A Breviate of the Doctrine of Justification', *The Scripture Gospel Defended* (1690); also *RB*, Part I, 111.
[33] For his friendship with Ussher see *RB*, Part II, 206. Packer, 'Redemption and Restoration', Chapters 8 and 9, discusses Baxter's debt to Saumur. For the beliefs of the Saumur theologians Cameron and Amyraut see Armstrong, *Calvinism and the Amyraut Heresy* (1969).
[34] See e.g. *RB*, Part I, 103–4; Part II, 199; Part III, 198. For excised passages critical of Owen see Nuttall, 'The MS of *Reliquiae Baxterianae*' (1955), 77–8.
[35] Rogers, *Howe*, Chapter 3.
[36] See *RB*, Part II, 141, 145, 207 on the diocesans, and 305–64 on the Savoy Conference.
[37] On the kinds of episcopalians see *RB*, Part II, 149; on Wilkins Part III, 131; also Part II, 386, 437; Part III, 19.

Yet he observed with regret a change in the temper of some of the latitudinarians:

At first they were only *Cambridge Arminians*, and some of them not so much; and were much for new and free Philosophy, and especially for *Cartes* [i.e Descartes]; and not at all for any thing Ceremonious; But being not so strict in their Theology or way of piety as some others, they thought that Conformity was too small a matter to keep them out of the Ministry. But afterwards many of them grew into such a distaste of the Weakness of many serious Christians, who would have some harsh phrases in Prayer, Preaching and discourse, that thence they seemed to be out of Love with their very Doctrines, and their manner of worshiping God.[38]

Baxter almost certainly has in mind here Patrick's *Friendly Debate*, the unfair judgements and damaging consequences of which he deplored. Baxter sympathised with Patrick's doctrinal views as expressed in *The Parable of the Pilgrim* (1665), especially Patrick's insistence that '*Obedience must enter the definition of Justifying Faith*', but he objected strongly to Patrick's assumption that the nonconformists represented a uniform group and that the language and methods of preaching and worship of the more extreme Congregationalists were typical of nonconformists as a whole. He further thought that the book played into the hands of religious sceptics as well as persecutors by making both nonconformity and piety appear ridiculous.[39] Baxter's astute comments show him to have been aware that conformists and nonconformists were being pushed apart despite the links between them. He observed a similar process in the horrified response of some nonconformists to Fowler's *The Design of Christianity*, the opinions expressed in which he was accused of 'breeding' through his *Aphorismes* and which he defended with qualifications in *How far Holinesse is the Design of Christianity* (1671).[40] Privately he warned Fowler of the danger of being driven by nonconformist criticism into the arms of the prelates.[41]

In the period of persecution Baxter held a difficult and lonely position, constantly trying to keep ways open between conformists and nonconformists, yet distrusted by both prelatists and Congregationalists. Barred in 1661 from preaching to his former parishioners at Kidderminster, he spent the last thirty years of his life in or near London, often attending Church of England services yet also preaching and ministering when he had the opportunity, both illegally and legally when the Declarations of Indulgence made the latter possible. He had difficulty in getting his books licensed for publication, and on various occasions he was subjected to arrest, fines, the loss of his library, trial, and imprisonment.[42] One of these imprisonments, in 1669, was a relatively agreeable experience shared by his wife;[43] the last, in 1685–6, followed a humiliating trial before Judge Jeffreys.[44]

---

[38] *RB*, Part III, 19–20.   [39] *RB*, Part III, 39–40.
[40] He reports the accusation in *How Far Holinesse* (1671), 3.
[41] *RB*, Part III, 85.   [42] *RB*, Part III, 48–51, 171, 192, 199.
[43] Described in *A Breviate of the Life of Margaret ... Baxter* (1681), in *Richard Baxter and Margaret Charlton*, ed. Wilkinson (1928), 113 and *RB*, Part III, 50–1.
[44] See *The Autobiography of Richard Baxter*, abridged Lloyd Thomas, ed. Keeble, rev. edn (1985), Appendix I.

Baxter felt that the terms of the Act of Uniformity gave him no choice but nonconformity. But he was a nonconformist reluctantly; his own terms for his position were reconciler, Catholic, and Christian.[45] His wish was for the churches to unite 'upon the Terms of primitive Simplicity' and to have '*Unity in things necessary, and Liberty in things unnecessary, and Charity in all*'; he thought the essentials of Christianity were summed up in the baptismal covenant ('*I believe in God the Father, Son and Holy Ghost, and give up my self in Covenant to him, renouncing the Flesh, the World and the Devil*') and that no more detailed definition of Christianity was required than the Creed, the Lord's Prayer, and the Decalogue.[46] The convert Saul in *The Poor Man's Family Book* exclaims, 'I think you will make the baptismal covenant serve for all things, from first to last!'[47] For particular churches to insist on forms of ecclesiastical authority and worship peculiar to themselves or on particular doctrines was irrelevant to the practice of Christianity and indeed was destructive of it. Baxter was involved in much controversial writing, but ironically with the hope of ending controversy and of bringing together the opposing parties and churches, not merely Presbyterians and Congregationalists, conformists and nonconformists, but Roman Catholics, Greek Orthodox, and even Socinians. His huge theological work, *Catholick Theologie* (1675), was written, in the words of the Preface, '*against Clergie Mens Contentions, and Church-distracting Controversies*', and was intended to show that doctrinal divisions were largely about words, not things. In the dialogues of Book II B[axter], the Reconciler, attempts to persuade an Arminian and a Calvinist that there is only one real point of difference, concerning perseverance, between them, and that this 'is not worthy to be insisted on, to the breach of Charity, or the Churches peace, but must consist with toleration and mutal love'.[48] In *A Christian Directory* (1673) Baxter advises the young student, 'experience will tell you at long running, that among ancients and moderns, Greeks and Latins, Papists and Protestants, Lutherans and Calvinists, Remonstrants and Contra-remonstrants, Prelatists, Presbyterians, Independents &c., commonly the moderators are not only the best and most charitable, but the wisest, most judicious men'.[49] Baxter's extreme and at times hysterical hostility to sects, expressed at many points in his autobiography,[50] is certainly inconsistent with charity; yet his response is understandable, given his assumptions about the effects of separation:

the Interest of *Christianity*, *Catholicism* and *Charity*, is contrary to the Interest of *Sects*, *as such*. And it is the nature of a *Sectary*, that he preferreth the Interest of his Opinion, Sect or Party, before the Interest of Christianity, Catholicism and Charity, and will sacrifice the latter to the Service of the former.[51]

[45] See Keeble, *Baxter*, 22–4, and *Autobiography*, 'Introduction', xx–xxi.
[46] *RB*, Part I, 103; Part II, 198.
[47] *Practical Works*, XIX, 451.
[48] *Richard Baxter's Catholick Theologie*, Preface, c5ᵛ; Book II, 3.
[49] Part I, Chapter 7, *Practical Works*, III, 255.   [50] E.g. *RB*, Part I, 39, 53, 102, 130.
[51] *RB*, Part II, 144.

It is important to note that Baxter supported the toleration of sects provided they kept the peace and did not oppose the substantials of Christianity.[52] He objected to the principles of separation, which he thought drove Christians apart, and similarly he objected to all doctrinal extremes because they omitted essential truths and had the effect of driving those who reacted against them into the contrary extreme.[53] Thus he believed 'almost all the Libertine *Antinomian* errors' to have resulted from 'an injudicious opposition to Popery'; in turn, many were driven to popery by these extremes.[54]

Towards the end of his life Baxter returned to the battle against the antinomians in *The Scripture Gospel Defended, and Christ, Grace and Free Justification Vindicated against the Libertines,* his response to the republication of Crisp. This work (some of which was, he says, written long before 1690, its date of publication) contains two critical references to books by Bunyan: his early work on the covenants, i.e. *The Doctrine of the Law and Grace Unfolded* (1659), listed with books by other authors '*which ignorantly subverted the Gospel of Christ*', and his attack on Fowler's *Design of Christianity*, entitled *A Defence of the Doctrine of Justification by Faith* (1672).[55] Yet the Reconciling Monitor (Baxter's spokesman) tells his opponent the Orthodox Zealot that Bunyan's bad opinions co-existed with sincere holiness: '*Bunnian*, an unlearned Antinomian-Anabaptist, wrote against the foresaid Book of Dr. *Fowler*; yet (abating his separation) I never heard that *Bunnian* was not an honest Godly man. If then he attained the design of Christianity, was he not a Christian?'. He further suggests that Bunyan's later sermons contradicted the antinomian tendencies of his earlier works: '*Bunnians* last preachings give me hope that he repented of his Errors; for he Zealously preached but the common acknowledged doctrine of Christ's readiness to receive and pardon converted sinners.'[56] Baxter seems to have misunderstood the implications of Bunyan's views on grace and justification. The important point is that he recognised and shared Bunyan's concern with practical holiness. This made Bunyan a Christian, despite his erroneous opinions – and Baxter thought antinomian views about justification, grace, faith, and works much more erroneous than papist views.[57] It is because of this practical emphasis that in *A Christian Directory* he warns against attaching too much importance to intellectual error, even though he himself spent so much energy combating it:

If a Papist or a Sectary live a holy life, take heed of making a scorn of their persons, notwithstanding thou takest the rise of thy derision from their mistakes: for even a mistaking saint is dearly beloved and honoured of God: and wherever holiness is, it is the greatest, most resplendent, and predominant thing in him that hath it: and

---

52 *RB*, Part I, 87.   53 This idea is explored further on pp. 130–1.
54 *Catholick Theologie*, Book II, 289.
55 *The Scripture Gospel Defended* (1690), 'A Breviate of the Doctrine of Justification', A2; 'A Defence of Christ, and Free Grace', 49.
56 'A Defence of Christ', 49.   57 *Catholick Theologie*, Book II, 289.

therefore puts a greater honour on him, than any mistake or infirmity can dishonour him.[58]

Bunyan acquired his orthodox Calvinist beliefs through the influence of the Bedford Congregational church, which he joined in the early 1650s, and its founder, John Gifford.[59] The principle of church membership was 'faith in Christ and holines of life, without respect to this or that circumstance or opinion in outward and circumstantiall things'.[60] Though he served in the army as an adolescent in the mid 1640s there is no evidence that he responded at that stage to the religious experimentation that shocked Baxter. After a long and painful process of conversion, described in his autobiography *Grace Abounding* (1666), he reached a theological position which on the whole he adhered to, though in the 1670s and 1680s he altered the emphasis that he placed on it. Another early influence was William Dell, former army chaplain, Congregational Master of Caius, Cambridge, and opponent of the university training of ministers, who in 1659 invited Bunyan to preach in his parish church in Bedfordshire, to the disgust of some of his parishioners. (Baxter regarded Dell as typical of the irrational anti-intellectual spirit he was trying to combat – 'one, who took *Reason, Sound Doctrine, Order* and *Concord* to be the intollerable Maladies of Church and State, because they were the greatest Strangers to his Mind'.)[61] Earlier in the same year Bunyan's activities as a lay preacher aroused the wrath of the Professor of Arabic at Cambridge.[62] His writing career began in response to the activities of Quaker preachers in Bedfordshire in the 1650s. In *Some Gospel-Truths Opened* (1656) and *A Vindication* (1657, a further attack in response to a reply by the Quaker Edward Burrough), Bunyan accused the Quakers of being false prophets who taught a metaphorical, unhistorical religion, and by emphasising the light within man undermined the work of grace and the spirit of Christ and obliterated the crucial distinction between the regenerate and the unregenerate.[63] He regarded the Quakers as a more respectable version of the Ranters, whose books and arguments he had been tempted by and resisted earlier: 'the very opinions that are held at this day by the *Quakers*, are the same that long ago were held by the *Ranters*. Only the *Ranters* had made them thred-bare at an Ale-House, and the *Quakers* have set a new glosse upon them again, by an

[58] Part I, Chapter 9, *Practical Works*, III, 575.
[59] The most useful works on Bunyan are: Brown, *Bunyan*, rev. Harrison (1928), the standard biography; Greaves, *Bunyan* (1969), on his theology; Hill, *Turbulent, Seditious, and Factious People* (1988), which concentrates on political and social contexts; Keeble, ed., *Bunyan* (1988); Tindall, *Bunyan* (1934).
[60] *Minutes of the Independent Church at Bedford*, ed. Tibbutt (1976), 17.   [61] *RB*, Part I, 64.
[62] Brown, *Bunyan*, 114, 118.
[63] Bunyan summarised Quaker errors in *A Vindication of Some Gospel-Truths Opened, Miscellaneous Works*, ed. Sharrock *et al.*, I, 123–4, and *Grace Abounding to the Chief of Sinners*, ed. Sharrock (1962), 39.

outward legall holinesse, or righteousnesse.'[64] This is a characteristic identification, often to be repeated in Bunyan's work, of libertinism and legalism as
the joint enemies of the gospel. In his first collection of sermon material, *A Few
Sighs from Hell* (1658), he warned his audience to escape 'these dangerous
rocks on the right hand and on the left' of legal holiness and 'Ranter-like'
'wantonness'.[65] In his account of his own theological position in *The Doctrine of
the Law and Grace* he placed great emphasis on the primacy of grace and the gift
of faith, and on the enormous difference between the erroneous doctrine of
acting legally in order to be justified and the true doctrine of acting
evangelically as a consequence of being justified. He was highly critical of a
Baxterian kind of emphasis on conditions for justification (though he never
names Baxter), yet he was anxious to stress that his doctrine of the covenants
did not have antinomian, libertine implications.

Subsequently the most famous victim of Restoration church policy, Bunyan
was arrested in 1660 under a revived Elizabethan Act and tried in 1661 for
keeping a conventicle, well before the passing of the Act of Uniformity.[66] He
consistently refused to undertake not to preach, just as he had refused to avoid
arrest, and as a result he was imprisoned for twelve years until released in
1672 under the terms of the Declaration of Indulgence. (He described the
circumstances of his arrest, trial, and imprisonment in *A Relation of the
Imprisonment of Mr. John Bunyan*, first published in 1765.) Bunyan was afraid
both for his family – 'O I saw in this condition I was as a man who was pulling
down his house upon the head of his Wife and Children; yet, thought I, I must
do it, I must do it' – and for his life, yet he saw his imprisonment, in the
tradition of the Acts of the Apostles and of Foxe's *Acts and Monuments*, one of his
favourite books, as another way of preaching and giving testimony, 'to
confirm the Truth by way of Suffering'.[67] Ironically, this prolonged period of
imprisonment gave Bunyan the opportunity to preach, both inside and
outside the jail, and, more important, to write among others his two
best-known books, *Grace Abounding* and much of the first part of *The Pilgrim's
Progress*.[68]

There was no common ground between Bunyan and the conformists in
terms of either discipline or doctrine. Bunyan would have nothing to do with
the Book of Common Prayer, and insisted that the gift of preaching should be
used by anyone who had it.[69] He assumed that the conformists were
temporisers and their motives purely selfish. Thus in *The Pilgrim's Progress*
By-ends explains to his companions Mony-love, Save-all and Hold-the-world

---

[64] *Vindication, Miscellaneous Works*, I, 139. On Bunyan's response to the Ranters see *Grace
Abounding*, 16–17.
[65] *Miscellaneous Works*, I, 381–2.   [66] *Grace Abounding*, 'Introduction', xxii–iii.
[67] *Grace Abounding*, 98, 100, 86.
[68] See Charles Doe, *The Struggler*, in *Works*, ed. Offor, III, 766.
[69] *A Relation*, in *Grace Abounding*, 108, 114–18.

the difference between his position and that of the pilgrims Christian and
Hopeful:

Why they after their head-strong manner, conclude that it is duty to rush on their
Journy *all* weathers, and I am for waiting for *Wind* and *Tide*. They are for hazzarding
all for God, at a clap, and I am for taking *all* advantages to secure my life and estate.
They are for holding *their notions*, though all other men are against them, but I am for
Religion in what, and so far as the times, and my safety will bear it. They are for
Religion, when in rags, and contempt, but I am for him when he walks in his golden
slipers in the Sunshine, and with applause.[70]

Bunyan was especially critical of those conformists, like Fowler, who had been
Presbyterians in the 1650s. Writing in 1672 in his attack on Fowler's *Design*, he
blamed the failure of the gospel in his day in large part on such men:

so many ignorant Sir Johns, on the one hand, and so many that have done violence to
their former light, and that have damned themselves in their former anathematizing of
others, have now for a long time, as a judgment of God, been permitted to be, and made
the mouth to the people: persons whose lives are debauched, and who in the face of the
world, after seeming serious detestings of wickedness, have for the love of filthy lucre,
and the pampering their idle carcasses, made shipwreck of their former faith, and that
feigned good conscience they had.

If, as Fowler suggests, in matters of religion men have leave to do what custom
or their superiors command, then Fowler can suit himself 'for every fashion,
mode, and way of religion. Here you may hop from Presbyterianism, to a
prelatical mode; and if time and chance should serve you, backwards, and
forwards again'. Fowler is 'a glorious Latitudinarian, that can, as to religion,
turn and twist like an eel on the angle; or rather like the weather-cock that
stands on the steeple'. More significant was Bunyan's reaction to Fowler's
central arguments about human nature, justification, and holiness: quite
simply, they were heathen, naturalist, opposed to the teaching of the gospel,
and, ironically, contrary to the Articles of the Church of England (notably
nos. X, XI, and XIII) to which Fowler had elected to belong. Bunyan sums
up Fowler's system as 'Papistical Quakerism'.[71] In turn, the anonymous reply
to Bunyan's attack on Fowler, entitled *Dirt Wip't Off: or A Manifest Discovery of
the Gross Ignorance, Erroneousness and most Unchristian and Wicked Spirit of one John
Bunyan*, charged him with being 'as rank and Ranting an Antinomian as ever
foul'd paper' (Baxter's views on justification and holiness are brought forward
as ammunition) and suggested vindictively that he should not be allowed 'to
enjoy any interest in his Majesties *Toleration*'.[72]

Bunyan was, however, released and licensed as a preacher as a result of the

[70] *Pilgrim's Progress*, 101–2.
[71] *A Defence of the Doctrine of Justification by Faith, Works*, ed. Offor, II, 313, 322, 331. See below,
pp. 141–2. Cf. the portrait of the 'temporizing latitudinarian' in *The Strait Gate* (1676),
Miscellaneous Works, V, 126.
[72] *Dirt Wip't Off* (1672), 17, 49, 70, 73.

Declaration of Indulgence before this riposte appeared, and apart from one
brief period of imprisonment in 1677 he became an increasingly public figure,
preaching regularly in London as well as Bedford – he was elected minister of
the Bedford church in 1672 before his release – and after the publication of the
first part of *Pilgrim's Progress* in 1678 reaching an enormous readership, in
Europe and New England as well as at home. His London friends included
Owen (who helped secure his release in 1677) and other Congregational
ministers in whose meeting houses he preached.[73] His numerous audiences
certainly included some who were not entirely sympathetic to his views:
Baxter may have heard him,[74] and in 1704 Samuel Wesley (father of John), a
defector from the dissenters, gave as an instance of the dubious principles of
the pupils at the academy of the Presbyterian Charles Morton that they and
their tutor went to hear Bunyan preach, even though he was not ordained.[75]
The anonymous author of *A Continuation of Mr. Bunyan's Life* suggests that such
hearers were won over:

even some, to whom he had been misrepresented, upon the account of his Education,
were convinced of his Worth and Knowledge in Sacred Things, as perceiving him to be
a man of sound Judgment, delivering himself, plainly and powerfully; insomuch that
many who came meer Spectators, for novelty sake, rather than to edifie and be
improved, went away well satisfied with what they heard, and wondered, as the *Jews*
did at the Apostles, viz., whence this Man should have these things.[76]

   In this period of his growing reputation and authority Bunyan found
himself both fighting a rearguard action against the encroachment of legalism, the overvaluing of merely human attributes that he saw as characteristic
of both Quakers and conformists, and also trying to combat the sectarianism
and complacency in their doctrinal superiority of nonconformists. In *The
Heavenly Footman* (not published till 1698 but perhaps written in the late 1660s)
Bunyan observes, 'Here is one runs a *Quaking*, another a *Ranting*; one again
runs after the *Baptism*, and another after the *Independency*: Here's one for
Free-will, and another for *Presbytery*, and yet possibly most of all these Sects run
quite the wrong way', and he warns the reader, 'fly *Seducers* Company, keep
Company with the soundest Christians, that have most Experience of Christ,
and be sure thou have a care of *Quakers, Ranters, Free-Willers*: Also do not have
too much Company with some *Anabaptists*, though I go under that name my
self'.[77] Bunyan's own attitude to the insistence by some Baptists on adult
baptism as a requirement for church membership is summed up in the title of
Differences in Judgment about Water Baptism, no Bar to Communion (1673). When

[73] On Bunyan's relationship with Owen see Asty, 'Memoirs of the Life of John Owen', *Sermons of
   ... Owen* (1721), xxx; Orme, *Owen*, 2nd edn (1826), 305; Powicke, *Baxter under the Cross*, 58–9;
   Toon, *Owen* (1971), 161–2. On his London connections see Greaves, 'Bunyan's *Holy War*'
   (1975), 158–68.
[74] See 'A Defence of Christ', quoted above, p. 103.   [75] Wesley, *Defence of a Letter* (1704), 48.
[76] *Grace Abounding*, 171.   [77] *Miscellaneous Works*, V, 152–3.

his Baptist opponents challenged him to identify himself as one, he countered in *Peaceable Principles and True* (?1674) by choosing the name Christian or believer, 'or other such name which is approved by the Holy Ghost'. He continues, 'And as for those factious titles of Anabaptists, Independents, Presbyterians, or the like, I conclude, that they came neither from Jerusalem, nor Antioch, but rather from hell and Babylon; for they naturally tend to divisions'.[78] Thus in *A Holy Life, The Beauty of Christianity* (1684) he objects that men are so wedded to their own opinions that they cannot unite as Christians: 'Here's a *Presbyter*, heres an *Independent*, an *Anabaptist*, so joyned each man to his own opinion, that they cannot have that communion one with another, as by the testament of the Lord Jesus, they are commanded and injoyned'; as a result nonconformists pay little attention to the moral quality of their lives, and have betrayed their spiritual forebears: 'Did we but look back to the *Puritans*, but specially to those that but a little before them, suffered for the word of God, in the *Marian* days, we should see another life than is now among men, another manner of conversation [i.e. behaviour], than now is among professors.'[79] The fiercest attack on this complacency appears in *The Strait Gate* (1676), a deliberately 'sharp' work which emphasises the great difficulty professors will have in reaching heaven; those who will fail include the opinionist, the formalist, the legalist, the libertine, the latitudinarian, the ignorant, the freewiller, the Socinian, and the Quaker. Only the elect who have faith and holiness, and who persevere in them, will enter the kingdom.[80]

Despite their very different assessments of the barriers dividing conformists and nonconformists and the meaning of antinomianism and legalism, Baxter and Bunyan were agreed that the crucial division was not between groups of Christians, under whatever doctrinal or denominational label, but between the godly and the world. The sufferings of the nonconformists in the Restoration period were, properly viewed, a local manifestation of a recurrent pattern. Baxter frequently refers to the perpetual enmity between the woman's and the serpent's seed as an inevitable fact of human history. Thus he writes in *Reliquae Baxterianae*: 'There is an universal and radicated Enmity between the *Carnal* and the *Spiritual*, the *Serpent's* and the *Woman's* Seed, the *fleshly Mind*, and the *spiritual Law of God*, through all the World, in all Generations.'[81] In *A Christian Directory* he summarises briefly the 'holy war' of Bunyan's allegory: 'the world is formed into two armies, that lies in continual war: the devil is the prince and general of one, and his angels and wicked men are his armies: Christ is the king and general of the other, and his angels, and saints are his army. Between these two armies are the greatest conflicts in the

[78] *Works*, ed. Offor, II, 649. See Brown, *Bunyan*, 219–24, 238.
[79] *Miscellaneous Works*, IX, 327, 345.
[80] *Miscellaneous Works*, V, 69, 100–1, 125–7.
[81] *RB*, Part I, 31; cf. *Poor Man's Family Book, Practical Works*, XIX, 367.

world.'[82] There can be no compromise; one or the other must conquer, as Bunyan argues in *The Strait Gate*:

They, for their part, have devised all manner of cruel torments to make us submit, as slaying with the sword, stoning, sawing asunder, flames, wild beasts, banishments, hunger, and a thousand miseryes; we again on the other side have laboured by praiers, and tears, by patience, and long-suffering, by gentleness, and love, by sound doctrine, and faithful witness-bearing against their enormities, to bring them over to us, but yet the enmitie remains; so that they must conquer us, or we must conquer them.[83]

The godly must conquer the world by separating themselves from it but not by withdrawing from it: they must, unavoidably, pass through Vanity Fair, but as strangers and pilgrims going to their own country.[84] The role of the minister is to turn the godly away from the world and lead them by means of preaching, writing and monitoring through every stage of this journey. Baxter and Bunyan might disagree strongly as to the nature of conversion and the definition of the doctrine of justification by faith, but like their puritan forebears they are agreed both that the life of faith is an active and often arduous process which is indissolubly linked with and expresses itself in holiness, and that the godly can be taught how to live it.

2 The function of the book

In their attitudes to the relationship between human and divine learning Baxter and Bunyan represent the extremes which in the 1650s had resulted in the dispute over the function of the universities and the status of a trained ministry, with the 'rabbis' ranged against the 'rustics'.[85] Baxter to his regret did not go to university, but his attitudes and learning were those of a university-educated divine: through his long life he was a passionate lover of books and master of an extraordinary range of reading in theology, philosophy, and ecclesiastical history. Yet he maintained a dual attitude to learning. He insisted in *Gildas Salvianus: The Reformed Pastor* (1656) on the need for an educated ministry: 'It is not now and then an idle snatch, or taste of studies that will serve to make a sound divine. I know that laziness hath lately learned to pretend the lowness of all our studies, and how wholly, and only the Spirit must qualify and assist us to the work ... As if God commanded us the use of the means, and then would warrant us to neglect them!'[86] This view is repeated in *Reliquiae Baxterianae*: '*Education* is God's ordinary way for the Conveyance of his Grace, and ought no more to be set in opposition to the

[82] Part I, Chapter 3, *Practical Works*, II, 260.
[83] *Miscellaneous Works*, V, 84, referring to Hebrews 11:37.
[84] *Pilgrim's Progress*, 89–90, based on Hebrews 11:13–14.
[85] See Hill, *World Turned Upside Down* (1973 edn), Chapter 14, 241–4; Keeble, *Baxter*, Chapter 2, and *Literary Culture*, Chapter 5.
[86] *Practical Works*, XIV, 57.

Spirit, than the preaching of the Word'; specifically, 'he that is ignorant of *Politicks* and of the *Law of Nature*, will be ignorant and erroneous in Divinity and the sacred Scriptures'.[87] In *A Treatise of Knowledge and Love Compared* (1689), he listed the fields of his own reading as grammar, physic, metaphysic, history, and scholastic philosophy, and in several of his works there is evidence of his thorough and up-to-date knowledge of disputes in contemporary theology and philosophy (for example his refutation of Lord Herbert in *More Reasons For the Christian Religion*, 1672).[88] Yet at the same time Baxter was certain that the fundamental end of knowledge was practice. Thus in *The Reformed Pastor* he attacks Christian academies for teaching physics, metaphysics and mathematics before theology, and requiring students to give so much time to languages and philosophy that 'instead of reading philosophy like divines, they read divinity like philosophers'. Schoolmasters and tutors should 'begin and end with the things of God'.[89] His own extensive knowledge was grounded on an early love of practical divinity, described in the first few pages of his autobiography. He attributed his first serious interest in religion to his reading at the age of fifteen of Bunny's *Resolution*, 'an old torn Book' lent to his father by a poor labourer, followed by Sibbes's *Bruised Reed*, bought by his father from a poor pedlar, and some works of Perkins, lent by a servant. The image conveyed of this precious collection of popular godly books and the circumstances in which they were acquired is deliberately anti-academic. Early ill health and the fear of death confirmed the importance of such reading: 'it caused me to study *Practical Divinity* first, in the most *Practical Books*, in a *Practical Order*; doing all purposely for the informing and reforming of my own Soul ... By which means my *Affection* was carried on with my Judgment.'[90] Baxter goes on to discuss his youthful delight in logic, metaphysics, and the work of the medieval scholastics, yet in the very careful and judicious summary of the development of his views on religion at the end of Part I of *Reliquiae Baxterianae*, written in 1664, he records how his attitude to knowledge has changed: he prefers the catechism, creed, Lord's prayer, and Ten Commandments to 'any of the School Niceties, which once so much pleased me'; he values study insofar as it makes men better; he recognises that the more he knows the more ignorant he is, so that now he has less admiration for 'Reverend Learned Men' – 'the better I am acquainted with them, the more I perceive that we are all yet in the dark: And the more I am acquainted with holy Men, that are all for Heaven, and pretend not much to Subtilties, the more I value and honour them'.[91] But it is important to note that these are the views of a deeply learned man who traces a circular pattern in his intellectual and religious life, who values practical simplicity again after a

---

[87] *RB*, Part I, 7, 108.   [88] *Practical Works*, XV, 15; XXI, 556–93.
[89] *Practical Works*, XIV, 219–22.
[90] *RB*, Part I, 3–4, 5–6.
[91] *RB*, Part I, 126–7, 129. Cf. *Knowledge and Love Compared, Practical Works*, XV, 16.

journey through speculation, argument, and controversy, but who is to continue on this journey for nearly thirty years. Baxter can only allow those who fully appreciate the meaning of learning to depreciate it in comparison with practice: 'I abhor the Folly of those unlearned Persons, who revile or despise Learning because they know not what it is'.[92] To him, it is his own intellectual attainments that validate his adoption of intellectual humility.

Bunyan not only despised learning and set the Spirit in opposition to education in the way that Baxter deplored, he also concealed the extent of the learning he had.[93] Bunyan tends to associate knowledge of Greek and Latin and of classical philosophy with heathenism and the suppression of the gospel. In *A Few Sighs from Hell* (1658) he attacks 'carnal priests' who 'tickle the ears of their hearers with vain Philosophy and deceit, and thereby harden their hearts against the simplicity of the Gospel', and he warns that those 'who nuzzle up [their] people in ignorance with *Aristotle*, *Plato*, and the rest of the heathenish Philosophers, and preach little, if any thing of Christ rightly' will be blamed by God for bringing many thousands to damnation. Knowledge of Hebrew, Greek and Latin is something gentlemen share with Pontius Pilate.[94] In contrast, Bunyan is introduced to the readers of his first book, *Some Gospel-Truths Opened* (1656), by his minister John Burton (Gifford's successor) as one chosen 'out of the heavenly University, the Church of Christ', as a recipient of a higher form of education: '*He hath through grace, taken these three heavenly degrees, to wit, union with Christ, the anointing of the spirit, and experience of the temptations of Satan, which doe more fit a man for that weighty work of preaching the Gospell, then all University Learning and degrees that can be had.*'[95] This early portrait of a man specially chosen by God despite his ignorance was repeated many years later by Charles Doe in *The Struggler* (1691), an appeal for subscriptions to the printing of Bunyan's works in folio: 'God is not bound to human means of learned education (though learning may be useful in its place), but can, when he will, make a minister of the gospel without man's forecast of education, and in spite of all the men in the world that would oppose it, though it be above sixteen hundred years after the apostles.'[96] Bunyan deliberately cultivated this portrait of himself as an author whose apparent deficiencies proved his strength. Thus in the 'Epistle to the Reader' prefacing *The Doctrine of the Law and Grace Unfolded* he explains:

Reader, if thou do finde this book empty of Fantastical expressions, and without light, vain, whimsical Scholar-like terms, thou must understand, it is because I never went to School to *Aristotle* or *Plato*, but was brought up at my fathers house, in a very mean condition, among a company of poor Countrey-men. But if thou do finde a parcel of

[92] *RB*, Part I, 127.
[93] See Tindall, *Bunyan*, Chapters 4 and 9, and R. L. Greaves, 'Introduction', *Miscellaneous Works*, II, xvi-xxi.
[94] *Miscellaneous Works*, I, 345, 304.
[95] *Miscellaneous Works*, I, 11; cf. 'To the Reader' prefacing *A Few Sighs from Hell*, I, 243-4.
[96] *Works*, ed. Offor, III, 764.

plain, yet sound, true, and home sayings, attribute that to the Lord Jesus, his gifts and abilities, which he hath bestowed upon such a poor Creature, as I am, and have been.[97]

He insisted that in preaching he never made use of other men's lines, and that he had not borrowed his doctrine from libraries.[98] It is unlikely that Bunyan was being consciously duplicit in such claims: the doctrines he learned (almost certainly from reading books as well as hearing sermons) and passed on to his own audiences seemed to him to be the work of the Spirit, not of men, and to represent the obvious meaning of Scripture.

Bunyan's account of the place of books in his religious experience is thus different from Baxter's. The popular godly books his wife inherited and brought him on their marriage, Dent's *The Plaine Mans Path-way to Heaven* and Bayly's *The Practice of Pietie*, succeeded in interesting him in religion but not in converting him.[99] Interestingly, the two books he mentions in his autobiography as having a profound effect on him – Luther's *Commentary on Galatians* and Nathaniel Bacon's *Relation of the Fearful Estate of Francis Spira* – were both disapproved of by Baxter, the first as a source of antinomian error and the second as a cause of melancholy.[100] Bunyan's response to these books shows clearly that he regarded reading as a kind of mirror providentially given him to reflect and reinforce his own experience. He describes Luther's book as cast into his hand by God in response to a longing 'to see some ancient Godly man's Experience'; 'the which, when I had but a little way perused, I found my condition in his experience, so largely and profoundly handled, as if his Book had been written out of my heart'. It is an experience he is eager to share: 'I must let fall before all men, I do prefer this book of Mr. *Luther* upon the *Galathians*, (excepting the Holy Bible) before all the books that ever I have seen, as most fit for a wounded Conscience.' Conversely, his reading of the 'dreadful story of that miserable mortal, *Francis Spira* [who died of despair]; A book that was to my troubled spirit as salt, when rubbed into a fresh wound', served to aggravate his own suffering.[101] Of the handful of other Reformation and puritan books Bunyan mentions in his works, the most important in shaping his experience was Foxe's *Acts and Monuments* (or Book of Martyrs), according to an eyewitness the only book he had in prison besides the Bible.[102]

It is in their attitudes to the Bible that Baxter and Bunyan stand in sharpest contrast. For Bunyan the Bible is the sufficient source of all his knowledge: as he explains in 'The Epistle to Four Sorts of Readers' prefacing *The Holy City*

---

[97] *Miscellaneous Works*, II, 16.
[98] *Grace Abounding*, 87; *Light for Them that Sit in Darkness*, *Miscellaneous Works*, VIII, 51.
[99] *Grace Abounding*, 8. For Bayly see Chapter 1 above, pp. 12–13.
[100] 'A Defence of Christ', *The Scripture Gospel Defended*, 46; *Christian Directory*, *Practical Works*, III, 220. See below, p. 155.
[101] *Grace Abounding*, 41–1, 49.
[102] See *Grace Abounding*, 153, and the references collected there.

(1665), the Spirit operating in him enables him to interpret the Spirit speaking through the Bible without the assistance of human learning. To rely on the works of the learned would be to derogate from the powers of God: 'had I all their aid and assistance at command, I durst not make use of ought thereof, and that for fear lest that Grace, and those Gifts that the LORD hath given me, should be attributed to their Wits, rather then the Light of the Word and Spirit of GOD'. Conversely, to rely on the Bible is to give himself far greater authority: 'having that still with me, I count my self far better furnished than if I had (without it) all the Libraries of the two Universities: Besides, I am for *drinking Water out of my own Cistern*: what GOD makes mine by the evidence of his Word and Spirit, that I dare make bold with'.[103] The power of texts of Scripture to seize hold of Bunyan's mind, to terrify and liberate him, is forcefully described in the central section of *Grace Abounding*; one sentence of Scripture is more powerful than an army of 40,000 men coming against him, an image that recurs in *The Holy War* (1682), where the army of Prince Emanuel marching against Mansoul consists of above 40,000 true men, equipped with forty-four battering rams and twelve slings, all of pure gold.[104] Hence when Bunyan states in *Solomon's Temple Spiritualised* (1688) that his Bible and concordance are his only library in his writings, he is laying claim to irresistible power.[105] His view is summarised succinctly in *A Confession of my Faith* (1672): 'I believe that the holy scriptures, of themselves, without the addition of human inventions, are able to make the man of God perfect in all things'.[106]

Baxter was suspicious of this kind of radical, sectarian approach to Scripture. He records in his autobiography that his father acquired his religion from the Bible 'without either Preaching, or Godly Company, or any other Books', but his own intellectual sympathies convinced him that the Bible could not be interpreted simply in its own light.[107] His second book, the vast and influential work of devotion *The Saint's Everlasting Rest* (1650), illustrates both sides of his views on the subject. He wrote the first draft while very ill and away from his books, as he explains in his autobiography: 'The Marginal Citations I put in after I came home to my Books; but almost all the Book it self was written when I had no Book but a Bible and a Concordance: And I found that the Transcript of the Heart hath the greatest force on the Hearts of others'.[108] Baxter partly, like Bunyan, found this a source of strength; yet this did not prevent him shoring up the book with quotations from the classics and the fathers. Baxter gives Scripture supremacy, but not in isolation. Thus in *The Reformed Pastor* he warns ministers too fond of philosophy and 'the wisdom of the world' not to undervalue Scripture:

[103] *Miscellaneous Works*, III, 71–2.
[104] *Grace Abounding*, 77; *The Holy War*, ed. Sharrock and Forrest (1980), 36, 69.
[105] *Works*, ed. Offor, III, 464.   [106] *Works*, ed. Offor, II, 601.   [107] *RB*, Part I, 2.
[108] *RB*, Part I, 108.

Let all writers have their due esteem, but compare none of them with the word of God. We will not refuse their service, but we must abhor them as competitors. It is a sign of a distempered heart that loseth the relish of Scripture excellency. For there is a connaturality in a spiritual heart to the word of God, because this is the seed that did regenerate him.[109]

Yet other books and sources of knowledge are essential, as he argues in defending the extent of his own writing in the 'Advertisement' to *A Christian Directory*; the dichotomy between human and divine learning is false: 'Are we not men before we are Christians? And is not the light and law of nature, divine? And was the Scripture written to be instead of reason, or of logic, or other subservient sciences?' Those who refuse to accept this position undermine the basis of religion: 'he that will have no books but his creed and Bible, may follow that sectary, who when he had burnt all his other books as human inventions, at last burnt the Bible, when he grew learned enough to understand, that the translation of that was human too'.[110]

Despite this fundamental disagreement over the value of education and the means necessary to the understanding of Scripture, Baxter and Bunyan held very similar views about their pastoral roles, about the relationship between preaching and writing (on the part of the minister) and hearing and reading (on the part of his audience). Judging from their contemporaries' assessments, both were powerful and moving preachers, capable of gathering and holding huge audiences, and they were aware of this power. In 'A brief Account of the Author's Call to the Work of the Ministry' Bunyan describes how in the early years of his preaching he conveyed to his hearers exactly what he felt at each stage of his experience: he first preached the terrors of the law 'as one sent to them from the dead', then proceeded to Christ's offices and finally to union with Christ – 'for still I preached what I saw and felt'. In this process of moulding his hearers to the shape of his own experience it seemed to him 'as if an Angel of God had stood by at my back to encourage me'.[111] Baxter as a young man was impelled by a belief in his own impending death (a recurrent obsession in his work) to convert sinners: he was 'conscious of a thirsty desire of Mens Conversion and Salvation, and of some competent perswading Faculty of Expression, which fervent Affections might help to actuate'. Looking back he rebukes himself for his naive confidence in his abilities, but these were manifest in the success of his Kidderminster ministry in the 1650s: 'I was in the Vigour of my Spirits, and had naturally a familiar moving Voice (which is a great matter with the common Hearers); and doing all in bodily Weakness, as a dying Man, my Soul was the more easily brought to Seriousness, and to preach as a dying Man to dying Men'.[112] This sense of being on the edge of another world evidently gave Baxter a power as a

[109] *Practical Works*, XIV, 128.   [110] *Practical Works*, II, xiii–xiv.
[111] *Grace Abounding*, 85–7.
[112] *RB*, Part I, 12, 86.

preacher that he never lost; Calamy describes hearing him preach in 1691, the last year of his life:

He talked in the pulpit with great freedom about another world, like one that had been there, and was come as a sort of an express from thence to make a report concerning it. He was well advanced in years, but delivered himself in public, as well as in private, with great vivacity and freedom, and his thoughts had a peculiar edge.[113]

This idea of the power of the preacher to transfix and transform his hearers through the combined weight of his own experience, divine assistance, and the spoken word, is encapsulated by Bunyan in the sketch in *Pilgrim's Progress* Part II of the man on Mount-Marvel *'that tumbled the Hills about with Words'*, who is 'set there to teach Pilgrims how to believe down, or to tumble out of their ways, what Difficulties they shall meet with, by faith', and at greater length in *The Holy War*, in the portrait of the four captains sent against Mansoul with commissions from King Shaddai, who after a long siege and with the help of Prince Emanuel succeed in breaking open Eargate and entering the city.[114] But the hearer is not simply a passive recipient of the words of the preacher. Eargate is the means by which the power of the word reaches Mansoul, but Mouthgate also has a crucial function. Emanuel invents an irresistible instrument, managed by Captain Credence, by means of which stones are hurled from Mouthgate; because of the efficacy of Mouthgate as a sally port for petitions addressed to the Prince, Diabolus is keen to block it with dirt.[115] Bunyan is here comparing two kinds of spoken word, the power of preaching with that of prayer: prayer is one of the means whereby the hearer takes an active part. Similarly, Baxter stresses that the relationship between preacher and hearer should be reciprocal. In 'Directions for Profitable Hearing the Word Preached' he gives instruction for 'holy Resolutions and Affections in Hearing'. The hearer must choose to 'live under the most convincing, lively, serious preacher' possible and respond actively to what he hears: 'You have work to do as well as the preacher, and should all the while be as busy as he ... Therefore be all the while at work, and abhor an idle heart in hearing, as well as an idle minister.'[116]

This emphasis on the interdependent roles of preacher and hearer is repeated in the relationship between writer and reader. For both Baxter and Bunyan there was a close connection between preaching and writing, a connection that was reinforced by the legal restrictions imposed on their preaching as nonconformists.[117] Baxter made some very interesting reflections on the subject. In analysing his ministerial work at Kidderminster in his

---

[113] Calamy, *My Own Life*, I, 220–1.
[114] *Pilgrim's Progress*, 285; *Holy War*, 36–7, 39–41, 50–1, 87.
[115] *Holy War*, 117, 195.
[116] *Christian Directory*, Part II, Chapter 19, *Practical Works*, IV, 257–8. Cf. *Poor Man's Family Book*, *Practical Works*, XIX, 447.
[117] See Keeble, *Literary Culture*, Chapter 2; Nuttall, *Baxter*, Chapter 6.

autobiography, he noted 'my Writings were my chiefest daily Labour', and he
attributed his success (among many other reasons) to his habit of distributing
these to his parishioners – 'I had found my self the benefit of reading to be so
great, that I could not but think it would be profitable to others' (he had
admitted earlier to being 'somewhat excessively in love with good Books').
Baxter attached so much importance to his own books that he says he turned
down Charles II's offer of a bishopric in 1660 partly because 'I knew that it
would take me off my Writing.' After the ejection of the nonconformist
ministers writing achieved particular importance as a substitute for rather
than an addition to preaching: 'I now bless God that his poor Servants have
the private help of Books, which are the best Teachers, under God, that many
thousand Persons have.'[118] Baxter wrote *A Christian Directory* in 1664–5
(though it was not published until 1673) 'That when I could not preach the
Gospel as I would, I might do it as I could'.[119] Despite the considerable efforts
made by the government under the Licensing Act of 1662 (which lapsed in
1679 and was renewed in 1685) to prevent nonconformist writing from getting
into print, these were to a large extent unsuccessful; Baxter expressed
gratitude to two of the chaplains who worked as licensers for letting many of
his books through, and thus ensuring that his work and life were not in
vain.[120] In *A Christian Directory* he provided a full and extremely valuable
statement of his view of the relationship between writing and preaching and
the advantages of the former over the latter:

The writings of Divines are nothing else but a preaching the Gospel to the eye, as the
voice preacheth it to the ear. Vocal preaching hath the pre-eminence in moving the
affections, and being diversified according to the state of the congregations which
attend it: this way the milk cometh warmest from the breast. But books have the advantage in many other respects: you may read an able preacher, when you have but a mean
one to hear. Every congregation cannot hear the most judicious or powerful preachers;
but every single person may read the books of the most powerful and judicious.
Preachers may be silenced or banished, when books may be at hand: books may be kept
at a smaller charge than preachers: we may choose books which treat of that very
subject which we desire to hear of; but we cannot choose what subject the preacher shall
treat of. Books we may have at hand every day and hour; when we can have sermons
but seldom, and at set times. If sermons be forgotten, they are gone. But a book we may
read over and over until we remember it; and, if we forget it, may again peruse it at our
pleasure, or at our leisure. So that good books are a very great mercy to the world.[121]

This analysis stresses the personal, domestic, social, economic, and political
advantages of reading over hearing, with particular emphasis on the freedom
of the individual reader to choose books most suitable to his or her condition.
    A marked feature of nonconformist writing, which differentiates it strik-

118 *RB*, Part I, 84, 89, 5; Part II, 281; Part I, 106.
119 'Advertisement', *Practical Works*, II, v, viii.
120 *RB*, Part III, 86. See Keeble, *Literary Culture*, Chapter 3.
121 Part I, Chapter 2, *Practical Works*, II, 151; cf. Part II, Chapter 21, IV, 266.

ingly from Anglican writing of the same period discussed in the previous chapter, is an interest in different classes of reader with gradations both social and spiritual, in the characteristics and needs of different members of the audience, in the different stages of Christian experience which require different kinds of instruction and different methods of awakening, exhortation, and encouragement. Both Baxter and Bunyan express this interest in their own writing, but Baxter in addition (in line with his views on the place of learning in the Christian life) gives a good deal of advice about the importance of reading, with detailed instructions as to the kinds of books to be read by different classes of reader. He insists that children should learn to read, however poor their parents, and he laments that poverty is causing a generation of barbarians, since the poor are too exhausted by work to read to their families and can spare neither time nor money for their children's education.[122] He urges charitable people to set up schools for poor children in London, as his wife did.[123] Masters of families should read to their children and servants, and ministers should ensure that they are supplied with suitable books.[124] Baxter supplies lists of books for different classes of reader, some brief, some of extraordinary length. Particularly interesting are the detailed lists in *A Christian Directory*, in Part I, Chapter 21 for a common family, and in Part III, Questions 173 and 174 for young students and divines.[125] The number of books recommended for the last group (Baxter astonishingly describes the largest as 'the poor man's library') might well provoke Bunyan's warning in *A Holy Life* against a particular form of the iniquity of the closet, the pride of a library. This occurs:

1. When men secretly please themselves to think 'tis known what a stock of Books they have; or when they take more pleasure in the number of, than the matter contained in their books.
2. When they buy books rather to make up a number, than to learn to be good and godly men thereby.
3. When, though they own their books to be good and godly, yet they will not conform thereto.[126]

Anyone following Baxter's most ambitious programme through would spend an inordinate amount of time reading (the lists of books recommended for children and families in *The Poor Man's Family Book* are much shorter).[127] Yet Baxter's emphasis is always ultimately practical; he would not have disagreed with Bunyan's strictures. Reading is never an end in itself. Hence in the

[122] *The Reformed Pastor, Practical Works*, XIV, 99; *Christian Directory, Practical Works*, IV, 271; *Poor Man's Family Book, Practical Works*, XIX, 364.
[123] *Breviate*, 119.
[124] *Poor Man's Family Book, Practical Works*, XIX, 505; *Christian Directory, Practical Works*, IV, 267; *Reformed Pastor, Practical Works*, XIV, 98–9.
[125] *Practical Works*, II, 152; IV, 268–70; V, 577–83, 587 ff. See Keeble, *Baxter*, 36–43.
[126] *Miscellaneous Works*, IX, 324.
[127] *Practical Works*, XIX, 491, 494, 509.

epistle 'To the Reader' prefacing his biography of his wife he recommends the young to read 'true and useful history' in the form of Scripture history, lives of holy persons, and church history.[128] As he explains in his introduction to *The Life & Death of ... Joseph Alleine* (1673), ' it is a notable benefit of this kind of History, that it is fitted to Insinuate the Reverence and Love of Piety into *Young unexperienced Persons*: For before they can read much of *Theological* Treatises with understanding or delight, Nature enclineth them to a pleasure in History'.[129] The object of such reading is to stimulate young Christians to emulation and imitation. Again and again Baxter emphasises the importance of reading affectionate, practical works that awaken the conscience, move the heart, and direct every stage of life. Conversely, he is emphatic as to the books that must not be read because they guide their readers straight to hell: romances, play books, wanton tales, and ballads.[130] Bunyan agrees whole-heartedly with these injunctions against 'profane and wicked Books', 'beastly Romances, and books full of Ribbauldry', 'filthy Ballads & Romances full of baldry'.[131] The damned soul in *A Few Sighs from Hell* laments his neglect of Scripture for 'a Ballad, a Newsbook, *George* on horseback, or *Bevis* of *Southampton*',[132] echoing Dent's warning in *The Plaine Mans Path-way* that such books 'were deuised by the diuel: seene, and allowed by the Pope: Printed in hel ... And all to this ende, that thereby men might be kept from the reading of the scriptures.'[133]

It is noticeable how often Baxter recommends his own books, particularly in *A Christian Directory*. This is because he had a very clear sense of the needs of the particular ranks of Christian readers and deliberately set out to supply them. This sense can be closely related to his pastoral experience at Kidderminster, which involved 'a special care and oversight of each member of the flock':[134] he attempted in his books to provide a literary equivalent to this personal oversight. In the Preface to *A Call to the Unconverted* (1658) he described a scheme suggested to him by Archbishop Ussher for 'a Directory for the several ranks of professed Christians, which might distinctly give each one their portion; beginning with the unconverted, and then proceeding to the babes in Christ, and then to the strong' (referring to I Corinthians 3:1–2 and Hebrews 5:12–14). After initial reluctance he decided on the following plan:

First, to speak to the impenitent, unconverted sinners, who are not yet so much as purposing to turn ... My next work must be for those that have some purposes to turn, and are about the work ... The third part must be directions for the younger and

128 *Breviate*, 63.   129 [T. Alleine *et al.*], *Life & Death of Alleine* (1673), 16.
130 See especially *Christian Directory*, Part I, Chapters 2, 8, *Practical Works*, II, 152–3; III, 457–8.
131 *Mr. Badman*, 39–40; *Holy War*, 31.
132 *Miscellaneous Works*, I, 333. On Bunyan's reading of such works see Golder, 'Bunyan's Valley of the Shadow' (1929).
133 Dent, *The Plaine Mans Path-way* (1601), 395.
134 *The Reformed Pastor*, Chapter 2, *Practical Works*, XIV, 96; see the categories of those the pastor should oversee, pp. 87–94.

weaker sort of Christians ... The fourth part, directions for lapsed and backsliding Christians ... And then the last part is intended more especially for families.[135]

Each of these ranks required different methods of persuasion and exhortation. Bunyan nowhere sets out a systematic programme such as this, but the same assumptions about the range of his readers and the methods appropriate to them underlie his work. In 'The Author's Apology for his Book' prefacing *Pilgrim's Progress* Part I and 'The Author to the Reader' prefacing *Mr. Badman* he uses the images of the fisherman, the fowler, the archer, the king's messenger, and the knight at arms to express his role in relation to his audience. The author must employ various 'Engins', 'Snares, Lines, Angles, Hooks and Nets', to catch his various readers, some of whom 'must be grop'd for, and be tickled too'.[136] With hostile ungodly readers more violent methods are necessary: *'twill be as impossible for this Book to go into several Families, and not to arrest some, as for the Kings Messenger to rush into an house full of Traitors, and find none but honest men there'.* The author who sets about this task is a heroic figure: *'The man ... that writeth Mr.* Badmans *life, had need be fenced with a* Coat of Mail, *and with the Staffe of a Spear'.*[137]

The range of readers aimed at and methods employed can be illustrated by a brief list of examples. Baxter's *The Unreasonableness of Infidelity* (1655) and *The Reasons of the Christian Religion* (1667) are designed for unsettled Christians tempted to infidelity, recoverable apostates, and unbelievers;[138] both are complex doctrinal works investigating the foundations of natural religion and the evidences of Christianity which assume an intellectually sophisticated readership attracted to Hobbesian ideas, not the ignorant sinners for whom *A Call to the Unconverted* is written. Bunyan's *A Few Sighs from Hell* (1658) and *Come, & Welcome, to Jesus Christ* (1678) are popular works aimed at the unconverted, but the first employs terror as a weapon whereas the second entices by offering love. Many of Bunyan's works are designed for different kinds of professor – *The Strait Gate* (1676) and *A Holy Life* (1684) to shake them out of their complacency and teach them the need for holiness, *Light for Them that Sit in Darkness* (1675) to recover those who have fallen away, *Seasonable Counsel: Or, Advice to Sufferers* (1684) to help them bear persecution. Sometimes books are intended to replace works by other authors which are unsuitable for a variety of reasons: Bunyan's *Christian Behaviour* (1663) is a brief family handbook written because comparable earlier books either are not 'gospelized' in their treatment of good works or are too long and expensive;[139] Baxter's *Poor Man's Family Book* is designed as a replacement for Dent's once popular but now dated *Plaine Mans Path-way to Heaven*, as Bunyan's *Mr.*

---

[135] *Practical Works*, VII, cccxxxi–ii. For Baxter's categorisation of his own works see Keeble, 'A Baxter Bibliography', *Baxter*, 157.
[136] *Pilgrim's Progress*, 3.   [137] *Mr. Badman*, 2, 5.   [138] *Practical Works*, XX, xxiii, 451.
[139] *Miscellaneous Works*, III, 9.

Badman may have been.[140] The needs of those reluctant to read long works were also catered for by single sheets, such as Baxter's *One Sheet against the Quakers*, *A Winding Sheet for Popery*, and others published in 1657,[141] and Bunyan's *Of the Trinity, and a Christian*, *Of the Law, and a Christian*, published posthumously in Doe's folio of 1692 but presumably intended for this format.[142] One work might be designed with several classes of reader in mind. On some occasions this is impracticable, either deliberately so, as when Bunyan addresses *The Holy City* 'To Four Sorts of Readers', the godly, the learned, the captious, and 'the Mother of Harlots' – the last two are clearly objects of attack, not intended audiences;[143] or because of authorial incompetence, as when Baxter implausibly addresses Part III, Chapter 5 of the enormous *Saint's Everlasting Rest* (1650) in turn to the 'carnal, worldly-minded man', the ungodly multitude, lazy professors, and the godly.[144]

The most interesting and successful works are those which carefully lead their readers through from the state of unbeliever to that of godly professor, not only addressing different kinds of reader but also endeavouring to lead them from the lowest to the highest rank, to introduce them to the whole range of Christian experience, and to transform them in the process. This is Baxter's method in *A Christian Directory* (1673) and Bunyan's in the two parts of *Pilgrim's Progress* (1678 and 1684). *A Christian Directory* is divided into four parts, covering Christian ethics, economics, ecclesiastics, and politics. The first, and most important, part is designed:

1. To direct ungodly, carnal minds, how to attain to a state of grace. 2. To direct those that have saving grace, how to use it; both in the contemplative and active parts of their lives; in their duties of religion, both private and public; in their duties to men, both in their ecclesiastical, civil, and family relations. And, by the way, to direct those that have grace, how to discern it, and take the comfort of it; and to direct them how to grow in grace, and persevere unto the end.[145]

The book is intended for the use of three groups: young, inexperienced ministers, judicious masters of families, and private Christians. Baxter realised that its size and comprehensiveness made it impracticable for some, and so wrote the second version of *The Life of Faith* (1670) as 'a breviate and substitute'.[146] He provided another kind of substitute in *The Poor Man's Family Book*, designed to teach the poor man how to become a Christian and live and

---

[140] *Practical Works*, XIX, 296; *RB*, Part III, 147. On Bunyan's debt to Dent see Hussey, 'Bunyan and Dent' (1949).

[141] *RB*, Part I, 116. These were not broadsheets, but folded and bound as tracts. (I owe this point to G. F. Nuttall.)

[142] *Works*, ed. Offor, II, 386.   [143] *Miscellaneous Works*, III, 69–72.

[144] *Practical Works*, XXII, 438, 441, 447, 450. Cf. Keeble, *Baxter*, 67.

[145] *Practical Works*, II, 3–4. Calamy thought 'Christian Ethics' 'perhaps the best Body of Practical Divinity; that is extant in our own or any other Tongue', Baxter, *Practical Works* (1707), I, Preface, xvi.

[146] *Practical Works*, II, viii; *RB*, Part I, 122.

die as one.[147] Dent had aimed especially at 'the ignorant, and vulgar sort' and stressed the importance of preachers' methods that were appropriate for such an audience.[148] Baxter attempted to imitate him, but deliberately altered the style in the second half, 'Because I may suppose, that riper Christians need not so loose a style, or method, as the ignorant or vulgar do: and the latter part of the book supposeth the reader to be got above the lowest form, though not to be a learned, accurate man.'[149] But the 'scholars of Christ' must not pass to the next form before they are ready;[150] Baxter warns young Christians in *A Christian Directory*: 'If you will be gnawing bones, when you should be sucking milk, and have no patience to stay till you are past your childhood, no marvel if you find them hard, and if they stick in your throats, or break your teeth.'[151]

Baxter's graduated approach in these directories may be compared with Bunyan's more varied method in the two parts of *Pilgrim's Progress*. Bunyan of course traces Christian's progress from this world to the next, from his setting out through his dangerous journey to his safe arrival (in the words of the title page), i.e. from unbelief and conversion through the varieties of Christian experience to godly death. But true to his account in the 'Apology' of the different engines he must employ, Bunyan interweaves and superimposes different methods for different kinds of reader. Thus *The Pilgrim's Progress* is to be read both by the strong and by babes, by theologically able and experienced Christians and by the intellectually and morally weak. Indeed, there is more emphasis on the latter in Part II, with Great-heart's company consisting of women, children, and hesitant pilgrims such as Mr Ready-to-halt, Mr Feeble-mind, and Mr Dispondencie and his daughter Much-afraid, so that Bunyan appears in effect to have inverted the expected pattern. However, it would be wrong to infer that Part I is for the strong and Part II for babes, for one of Bunyan's characteristic methods in both parts is to present the same doctrinal point in a number of different ways, including pictorial emblem, dramatic narrative, catechetical questioning, and reasoned argument, which make different kinds of demand on different readers but which lead all readers to the same end.

Because such works were essentially practical, or reduced 'theoretical knowledge into serious Christian practice' in Baxter's statement of the 'great work' of *A Christian Directory*,[152] they took precedence over controversial works in their authors' eyes. In his autobiography Baxter regretted his involvement in controversies (which was far more extensive then Bunyan's), his keen and provoking language, and his use of a disputing rather than a learning or teaching way. He observed that such methods drove men to 'defend their

---

[147] *Practical Works*, XIX, 298.   [148] *Plaine Mans Path-way*, A3, 353–4.
[149] *Poor Man's Family Book, Practical Works*, XIX, 296.
[150] On Baxter's school metaphor see Keeble, *Baxter*, 44.
[151] Part I, Chapter 2, *Practical Works*, II, 137, referring to I Corinthians 3:2 and Hebrews 5:12–14.
[152] *Practical Works*, II, vi.

Errors as themselves' and diverted them from a holy life, and he quoted Bacon
with approval to the effect that 'it's one great Benefit of Church-Peace and
Concord, that writing Controversies is turned into Books of practical Devotion for increase of Piety and Virtue'.[153] He illustrated his view of the opposite
effects of controversial and practical writing in an emblematic (and surely
provocative) comparison of Simon Patrick with his brother John in 'The
Epistle to the Reader' prefacing *Poetical Fragments* (1681):

*We have two Brothers in this City, of whom one hath written a Book, called, A Friendly Debate,
to make those seem odious or contemptible who are against his way: It had too much success, and so far
destroyed Love and Concord, as will not easily be recovered in this Age. His Brother (Mr.* Patrike *of
the* Charter-house*) hath with pious Skill and seriousness turned into a new Metre many of*
David's Psalms, *and the advantage for holy affections and harmony, hath so far reconciled the
Non-Conformists, that divers of them use his Psalms in their Congregations.*[154]

Yet there is no such absolute distinction to be made between controversial and
practical works. For nonconformist writers, controversy is an integral part of
practical writing, since in their view theoretical *error* makes serious Christian
practice impossible. This is nowhere better illustrated than in Bunyan's
portrait of Ignorance in *Pilgrim's Progress* Part I: the concluding note is not
Christian's triumphant death, but the putting through a door to hell of the
figure who has argued a theoretical basis for Christian practice resembling
Fowler's and, indeed, Baxter's.

The success of these books, especially the most popular, *A Call to the
Unconverted* and the first part of *Pilgrim's Progress*, was astonishing.[155] The
numbers involved indicate that they were widely read beyond the limited
groups of nonconformists, by conformists in England and by protestants in
Europe and America. They went through repeated editions, were translated
into several languages, and were widely distributed, in Baxter's case often by
being given away free. In the introductory poem to the second part of *Pilgrim's
Progress*, Bunyan surveys the countries and classes which have welcomed his
book: France, Flanders, Holland, and New England, highlanders and wild
Irish, city and country, brave gallants, young gentlewomen, and children,
and so he confidently sends out his second part, '*For Young, for Old, for Stag'ring
and for stable*'.[156] This account is corroborated by Doe in *The Struggler*: 'none
but priest-ridden people know how to cavil at it, it wins so smoothly upon
their affections, and so insensibly distils the gospel into them, and hath been
printed in France, Holland, New England, and in Welsh, and about a
hundred thousand in England'.[157] In his autobiography Baxter provided

---

[153] *RB*, Part I, 137, 126. The reference is to Bacon's essay 'Of Unity in Religion'. Cf. Keeble, 'The
   Autobiographer as Apologist' (1986).
[154] *Poetical Fragments*, 2nd edn (1689), n.p.
[155] On sales and distribution see Sommerville, *Popular Religion*, Chapters 2 and 3, and Keeble,
   Literary Culture, 127–35.
[156] *Pilgrim's Progress*, 169–70.   [157] *Works*, ed. Offor, III, 766.

extremely useful surveys of his activities as a writer and promoter of his own books.[158] Of *A Call to the Unconverted* he claimed: 'In a little more than a Year there were about twenty thousand of them printed by my own Consent, and about ten thousand since, besides many thousands by stollen Impressions, which poor Men stole for Lucre sake'. Baxter received from his booksellers every fifteenth copy of his books, all of which he gave away;[159] he repeatedly urged ministers and the wealthy to follow this example and to distribute books to the poor.[160] *The Poor Man's Family Book* was designed to be distributed in this way: 'I hope rich citizens, and ladies, and rich women, who cannot themselves go talk to poor families, will send them such a messenger as this, or some fitter book to instruct them, seeing no preacher can be got at so cheap a rate.'[161] He was so pleased with its success that he wrote a sequel, *The Catechizing of Families* (1683), and he regarded 'these two Family-books to be of the greatest Common use of any' he had published. His next comment clearly sums up his view of the place of the book in the relationship between pastor and people: 'If Housholders would but do their parts in reading good books to their Households, it might be a great Supply where the Ministry is defective: and no Ministry will serve sufficiently without Men's own Endeavours for themselves and families.'[162] The way that such books travelled across the boundary between nonconformity and conformity is illustrated in Baxter's account of his wife's charities: 'If she could hire the poor to hear God's word, from Conformist or Nonconformist, or to read good serious practical books, whether written by Conformists or Nonconformists, it answered her end and desire: and many an hundred books hath she given to those ends.'[163]

Although popular nonconformist books, including those by Baxter and Bunyan, must have circulated among sympathetic conformist readers, conformist critics of nonconformist writing – both latitude-men such as Patrick and Tillotson and high churchmen such as Robert South and Samuel Parker – were agreed that it was characterised by peculiarities of language, style, and literary method which identified it as the property of an exclusive, self-defined group.[164] Patrick's Conformist objects to Non-conformist: 'Is it a commendable thing to be singular without any need? and to separate from us even in your words and forms of speech? Or is this a part of the language of Canaan (so much talked of in late times), to be learnt of all those that will be accounted

---

[158] *RB*, Part I, 89, 106–24; Part II, 61, 190–1; Appendix VII.
[159] *RB*, Part I, 115; Part III, 142.
[160] E.g. *The Reformed Pastor, Practical Works*, XIV, 99.   [161] *Practical Works*, XIX, 295.
[162] *RB*, Part III, 191.
[163] *Breviate*, 112. Cf. the account of the work of Thomas Gouge's trust in Nuttall, ed., *Beginnings of Nonconformity*, 26–31.
[164] On the clash between conformist and nonconformist styles see the works cited in Chapter 2, n. 100, and Keeble, *Literary Culture*, Chapter 8; Pooley, 'Language and Loyalty' (1980). On other aspects of puritan and nonconformist style see Murdock, *Literature and Theology in Colonial New England* (1949), Chapter 2; Sasek, *Literary Temper of the English Puritans* (1961), Chapter 3; Watkins, *Puritan Experience* (1972), Chapter 12.

the people of God?'[165] The charges levelled by the latitude-men and the reasons underlying them have been examined in Chapter 2 above. However misguided, these charges were brought by men who had seriously considered the relationship between language, religion, and ethics. Parker in *A Discourse of Ecclesiastical Politie*, the main object of which was to insist on the duty of the state to stamp out religious dissent, opportunistically picked up and caricatured latitudinarian ideas about language and moral religion without bothering to think about them seriously. His views, though crude, are significant as a useful summary of conformist objections to nonconformity and because of the response they provoked. Thus he asserts with reference to religious language:

And herein lies the most material difference between the sober Christians of the Church of *England*, and our modern Sectaries, That we express the Precepts and Duties of the Gospel in plain and intelligible Terms, whilst they trifle them away by childish Metaphors and Allegories, and will not talk of Religion but in barbarous and uncouth Similitudes; and (what is more) the different Subdivisions among the Sects themselves are not so much distinguish'd by any real diversity of Opinions, as by variety of Phrases and forms of Speech, that are the peculiar *Shibboleths* of each Tribe.[166]

Nonconformist language, conformists were agreed, employed specialised and unnecessary terms and phrases and was metaphorical and allegorical where it should have been plain and explanatory. As a result it obscured instead of clarifying the meaning of religion and formed an impassable barrier between nonconformists and the rest. How accurate are these generalisations when applied to specific writers? Can Baxter and Bunyan plausibly be linked as speakers of the same language of Canaan?

Baxter loathed the *Friendly Debate* precisely because it lumped all nonconformists together: he would certainly not have identified himself with Bunyan in this way. Because of the range of his writing and intended audiences, from Latin metaphysics and theology for fellow divines to popular handbooks for poor families, and because of his crucial involvement in the mid-century shift away from Calvinist theology together with his separation as a nonconformist from those who were most sympathetic to his views, it is impossible to characterise Baxter's style as a whole.[167] Sometimes he sounds like a latitudinarian, at other times like a critic of latitudinarianism, and occasionally like Bunyan. Like the latitudinarians, Baxter is interested in the place of reason in religion and in the relationship between religion and philosophy, and like them he uses philosophical terminology when it suits him. This differentiates him sharply not only from Bunyan, as is to be expected, but also from an orthodox Calvinist like Owen whose learning is as extensive as Baxter's but who regards 'the mixing of evangelical revelations

---

[165] Patrick, *A Continuation of The Friendly Debate, Works*, V, 441.
[166] *Ecclesiastical Politie* (1670), 75.
[167] On Baxter's style see Keeble, *Baxter*, Chapter 3.

with philosophical notions' as the 'poison of religion'.[168] Like the latitudinarians Baxter believes that *'the greatest enemy to knowledge of all, is mens studying only names and words, in stead of things'*, that no particular words are essentials of religion,[169] and that ambiguous and equivocal words are at the bottom of most doctrinal controversies:

All *words* (being *arbitrary signs*) are *Ambiguous*; and few *Disputers* have the *jealousie* and *skill* which is necessary to discuss *equivocations*, and to agree of the meaning of all their terms before they use them in disputing: And so taking *Verbal* differences for *Material*, doth keep up most of the wretched Academical and Theological Wars of the World.[170]

He does not insist on the indispensability of Scripture expressions, and he avoids using a specialised vocabulary that might be identified with particular sectarian or doctrinal positions.

However, Baxter differs from the latitudinarians in his emphasis on the role of the heart and affections in transforming understanding into practice. This emphasis is especially noticeable in the widely read *Saint's Everlasting Rest*. Though in its personal tone and fervent language it stands out from his subsequent work, the theory of style it embodies underlies all his practical writing. In Part IV, Chapter 6, having explained the physiological and psychological basis of his theory, Baxter urges the reader to undertake the great task of getting the truths of heaven from his head to his heart so that 'all the sermons which thou hast heard of heaven, and all the notions that thou hast conceived of this rest, may be turned into the blood and spirits of affection'.[171] The same point is made more briefly and clearly in *A Christian Directory* (Baxter complained of the latter work that 'necessary brevity hath deprived it of all life and lustre of Stile'):[172] 'The understanding and memory are but the passage to the heart, and the practice is but the expression of the heart: therefore how to work upon the heart is the principal business.'[173] In accounts of his own style and advice to others to adopt a style that will reach the heart Baxter frequently speaks in terms of plainness, warmth, and penetration. In 'A Premonition' to *The Saint's Rest* he is satisfied if he speaks 'pertinently, plainly, piercingly, and somewhat properly',[174] and he urges the preacher in *The Reformed Pastor* to make his teaching plain and evident, to speak to the capacity of his hearers, to be affectionate, serious, and zealous: 'If our words be not sharpened, and pierce as nails, they will hardly be felt by stony hearts. To speak coldly and slightly of heavenly things, is nearly as bad as to say nothing of them.' The worst thing is for the preacher to tend 'to make

---

[168] *The Doctrine of Justification by Faith, through the Imputation of the Righteousness of Christ; Explained, Confirmed, and Vindicated* (1677), *Works*, ed. Goold, V (1851), 10. See also p. 139 below.
[169] *Aphorismes of Justification* (1649), a4ᵛ; *RB*, Part II, 198.   [170] *Catholick Theologie*, b3.
[171] *Practical Works*, XXIII, 314. See also below, p. 145.
[172] *RB*, Part I, 122.   [173] *Christian Directory*, Part II, Chapter 19, *Practical Works*, IV, 257.
[174] *Practical Works*, XXII, 19.

the hearers laugh, or to move their mind with tickling levity, and affect them as stage-players use to do'.[175] Lively, warm, and quickening are favourite terms for describing the most effective books: 'As going to the fire is our way when we are cold, to cure our benumbedness, so reading over some part of a warm and quickening book, will do much to warm and quicken a benumbed soul'.[176] The best teacher has three abilities: he explicates the gospel clearly; he has 'the most convincing and persuading reasons to resolve the will', and he does this 'in the most serious, affectionate, lively manner, together with practical directions, to quicken up the soul to practice, and direct it therein'.[177] Contemporaries clearly felt that these qualities were peculiarly Baxter's; thus Glanvill writes to Baxter in the early 1660s that in practical subjects he admires 'your affectionate piercing, heart-affecting quickness: And that experimental, searching, solid, connective way of speaking, which are your peculiars; for their [sic] is a smartness accompanying your pen that forces what you write into the heart, by a sweet kind of irresistible violence'.[178] Burnet told Calamy in 1702 that he owed to reading Baxter's practical works in his younger days what acquaintance he had with 'serious vital religion'.[179]

Baxter shared the latitudinarian belief in clarity, intelligibility, and the importance of rational persuasion, combined with an emphasis on affection, zeal, warmth, and the heart which is untypical of latitudinarian writing, though latitudinarians might admire it, and which was imitated by his eighteenth-century dissenting heirs, Watts and Doddridge. To use his own terms, he attempted to combine the light and heat of the gospel.[180] The generalisations of conformist critics about nonconformist style are scarcely relevant to him, since he shared some of their stylistic and intellectual values and did not regard himself as employing an exclusive language. These generalisations apply to a much greater extent to Bunyan.[181] Bunyan was very much aware of the godly as marked off from other human beings by the language they speak: the ungodly may be hostile or envious when they hear it, or they may attempt to appropriate it for their own ends. When Christian and Faithful come to Vanity Fair, they cause a hubbub among the inhabitants in part because of the strangeness of their speech: 'for few could understand what they said; they naturally spoke the Language of *Canaan*; But they that kept the *fair*, were the men of this World: So that from one end of the *fair* to the other, they seemed *Barbarians* each to the other'. After Christiana has decided to set

[175] *Practical Works*, XIV, Chapter 3, 123, 127; cf. Chapter 4, 154.
[176] *Christian Directory*, Part I, Chapter 10, *Practical Works*, III, 612–13.
[177] *Poor Man's Family Book*, *Practical Works*, XIX, 510.
[178] Cope, *Glanvill*, 147; cf. Baxter's comment on Glanvill as 'one that had a too excessive estimation of me', *RB*, Part II, 378.
[179] Calamy, *My Own Life*, I, 468.
[180] *Christian Directory*, Part I, Chapter 2, *Practical Works*, II, 90.
[181] On Bunyan's style see Tindall, *Bunyan*, Chapter 8, and R. Pooley, 'Plain and Simple: Bunyan and Style', in Keeble, ed., *Bunyan*, Chapter 5.

out on the same journey as her husband, the new godly language that drops from her lips stuns her old neighbours.[182] In *Grace Abounding* Bunyan vividly describes his sense of exclusion in his unconverted state when he hears 'three or four poor women sitting at a door in the Sun, and talking about the things of God'; he is unable to understand their discourse about 'a new birth, the work of God on their hearts', 'their miserable state by nature', the love of Jesus, the temptations of Satan, and the filthiness of their own righteousness, because he does not understand the doctrines to which these phrases refer. He sums up his sense of their separation:

And me thought they spake as if joy did make them speak: they spake with such pleasantness of Scripture language, and with such appearance of grace in all they said, that they were to me as if they had found a new world, as if they were people that dwelt alone, and were not to be reckoned among their neighbours, Num.23.9.

And he goes on to describe the profound effect these words have on him in making him question his own state.[183] Such discourse is often presented by Bunyan as one of the joys and supports of the godly: Christian has much discourse with Piety, Prudence, and Charity in the Palace Beautiful; Christian and Faithful have 'sweet discourse of all things that . . . happened to them in their Pilgrimage'; Christian and Hopeful '*fall into good discourse*' to prevent drowsiness at the Enchanted Ground.[184] Because it has distinctive characteristics, this language can be imitated; thus Mr Badman woos his wife by godly talk, though 'he knew that he made use of the name of God, of Religion, good Men, and good Books, but as a stalking-Horse, thereby the better to catch his game', and she is easily deceived.[185] The archetypal example of someone hypocritically appropriating the language of Canaan is Talkative, who reproduces the terms employed by the women of Bedford and initially takes in Faithful; but Christian is as severe on him as Patrick could be:

Hearing is but as the sowing of the Seed; talking is not sufficient to prove that fruit is indeed in the heart and life; and let us assure ourselves, that at the day of Doom, men shall be judged according to their fruits. It will not be said then *Did you believe?* but, Were you *Doers*, or *Talkers* only? and accordingly shall they be judged.[186]

The validity of godly language can be judged in two ways. First, it must be preceded by the experience of conversion, as Bunyan argues in *The Doctrine of the Law and Grace*:

Reckon thy self therefore, I say, the biggest sinner in the world, and be perswaded that there is none worse then thy self; then let the guilt of it seize on thy heart, then also go in that case and condition to Jesus Christ, and plunge thy self into his Merits, and the vertue of his Blood; and after that thou shalt speak of the things of the Law, and of

---

[182] *Pilgrim's Progress*, 90, 101.   [183] *Grace Abounding*, 14–15.
[184] *Pilgrim's Progress*, 47–53; 66, 136.
[185] *Mr. Badman*, 68.
[186] *Pilgrim's Progress*, 76, 79–80, referring to Matthew 13: 3–30, 25: 31–46; James 1: 22–7.

the Gospel, experimentally; and the very Language of the Children of God shall feelingly drop from thy lips, and not till then.[187]

Second, as he insists in *Christian Behaviour*, it must issue in deeds: 'Words without deeds is but a half-faced Religion.'[188] Here, as in the case of Talkative, Bunyan cites the ethical definition in James 1:27 of 'pure religion and undefiled'. He is well aware of the dangers of a peculiar religious language. But the true language cannot be divorced from doctrine on the one hand and practice on the other. These implications are summed up in the term conversation, which had in the seventeenth century the meanings of informal talk and social intercourse, but which also retained the archaic meaning of behaviour. In Bunyan it always means the last. Talkative represents a contradiction between talk and conversation: 'Religion hath no place in his heart, or house, or conversation; all he hath lieth in his *tongue*, and his Religion is to make a noise *therewith*.'[189]

The phrase 'the language of Canaan' implies both a particular pattern for the Christian life (discussed in section 3) and a dependence on Scripture for vocabulary, allusion, metaphor, and literary method. Its practitioners disagreed sharply with the latitudinarian view that religious ideas could be clearly explained in non-metaphorical language and that Scripture metaphors should be employed only as illustration and with caution.[190] Thus in *Justification by Faith* Owen objects that 'the lively scriptural expressions of faith, by receiving of Christ, leaning on him, rolling ourselves or our burden on him, tasting how gracious the Lord is, and the like, which of late, have been reproached, yea, blasphemed, by many ... convey a better understanding of the nature, work, and object of justifying faith, unto the minds of men spiritually enlightened, than the most accurate *definitions* that many pretend unto; some whereof are destructive and exclusive of them all', and in *Truth and Innocence Vindicated*, his reply to Parker's *Ecclesiastical Politie*, he asks rhetorically: 'what if the metaphors they are charged with are no other but their expression of gospel mysteries, not in the words which man's wisdom teacheth, but which the Holy Ghost teacheth, comparing spiritual things with spiritual?'[191] In his 'Apology' for *Pilgrim's Progress* Bunyan anticipates possible objections to his method; among them are that such writing lacks

---

[187] *Miscellaneous Works*, II, 14.   [188] *Miscellaneous Works*, III, 44.
[189] *Pilgrim's Progress*, 78; cf. several uses of the term on pp. 80–4.
[190] See the quotation from Tillotson above, Chapter 2, p. 56.
[191] *Works*, ed. Goold, V, 107; XIII, 350. *Truth and Innocence* is dated 1669 but appeared after *Ecclesiastical Politie*, dated 1670. In 'The Scribe Instructed', a sermon preached on 29 July 1660 but not published till the eighteenth century, South attacked 'the whimsical Cant of *Issues, Products, Tendencies, Breathings, Indwellings, Rollings, Recumbencies*, and Scriptures misapplyed'; the added footnote reads: '*Terms often and much used by one* J.O. *a great Leader and Oracle in those Times*', Simon, *Three Restoration Divines*, II, 246–7. Cf. Patrick, *Friendly Debate, Works*, ed. Taylor, V, 291–2; Glanvill, *Essay concerning Preaching* (1678), 26; Bunyan, *Miscellaneous Works*, V, ed. G. Midgley, xxxiii.

'solidness' and that 'Metaphors make us blind'. In reply Bunyan validates speaking through allegory, similitude, and metaphor by biblical precedent. God's laws are held forth '*By Types, Shadows and Metaphors*'; God speaks to the reader '*By Birds and Herbs, and by the blood of Lambs*', and the reader must seek out the meaning; the prophets spoke through metaphors, and Christ and the apostles through parables. Similarly, Bunyan's dark words '*Make truth to spangle*'; '*they do but hold / The Truth, as Cabinets inclose the Gold*'.[192] Within the narrative Bunyan will sometimes make one of his characters intervene to explain the method: thus in Part II Great-heart, using a musical analogy for Mr Fearing's frame of mind, explains, 'I make bold to talk thus Metaphorically, for the ripening of the Wits of young Readers, and because in the Book of the Revelations, the Saved are compared to a company of Musicians that play upon their *Trumpets* and Harps, and sing their Songs before the Throne.'[193] In the verses 'To the Reader' prefacing *The Holy War* Bunyan tells him that lest he should lose his way the key to the riddle lies in the window, i.e. the margin.[194] The marginal glosses contain summaries of the narrative, explications of the allegory, exhortation, and biblical source texts. Bunyan's method is exactly that derided by Patrick:

It was a trick of the Separatists from the beginning, to paint the margin of their books with the chapter and verse of many Scriptures, which were the ornaments also of their preaching and familiar discourse. This very much astonished the simple and credulous, who persuaded themselves that the cause of those men stood upon the ground of God's word, which they had so ready at their finger's end.[195]

One motive for employing allegory is to allure the reader: it is one kind of engine with which the fisherman catches the fish. As Richard Bernard explained at the conclusion of the revised edition of *The Isle of Man* (1627), a work Bunyan probably drew on in *The Holy War*, 'I knew the natures of men in the world: I perswaded my selfe that the allegorie would draw many to reade, which might bee as a baite to catch them, perhaps, at vnawares, and to mooue them to fall into a meditation at the length of the spirituall vse thereof'. The reader is encouraged to enjoy the book: 'I forbid you not to be Christianly merry with him'.[196] But this method has its dangers, as Bunyan warns in the concluding verses to Part I of *Pilgrim's Progress*: the reader must take heed of misinterpreting and of '*playing with the* out-side *of my Dream*'.[197] The delight of the writer in employing biblical figures and of the reader in interpreting them correctly must not be confused with play. In the Preface to *Grace Abounding*

---

[192] *Pilgrim's Progress*, 4. In *The Grounds and Occasions of the Contempt of the Clergy* (1670), 50–1, Eachard objects specifically to the argument that because Christ used metaphors and parables therefore preachers should do so.
[193] *Pilgrim's Progress*, 253.   [194] *The Holy War*, 5.
[195] *A Further Continuation and Defence, or The Third Part of The Friendly Debate, Works*, ed. Taylor, VI, 11.
[196] *The Isle of Man*, 9th edn (1634), n.p.   [197] *Pilgrim's Progress*, 164.

Bunyan insists that his style is deliberately unadorned and unplayful: God did not play in convincing him nor the devil in tempting him, '*wherefore I may not play in my relating of them, but be plain and simple, and lay down the thing as it was*'. This plainness and simplicity is perfectly compatible with allegory, as is shown in the final words of the Preface, a striking example of the language of Canaan: 'The Milk and Honey is beyond this Wilderness: God be merciful to you, and grant that you be not slothful to go in to possess the Land.'[198]

These important differences in approach to language and literary method should not obscure the fundamental agreement of Baxter and Bunyan about the function of the book in the Christian life. A juxtaposition of two accounts of this function, one in *Pilgrim's Progress*, the other in the biography of Margaret Baxter, shows this clearly. When Christian and Hopeful escape from Doubting Castle, they set up a pillar with a warning engraved on it: '*Over this Stile is the way to* Doubting-*Castle, which is kept by Giant Despair, who despiseth the King of the Coelestial Countrey, and seeks to destroy his holy Pilgrims.*' The narrator continues: 'Many therefore that followed after, read what was written, and escaped the danger.' The two pilgrims then come to the Delectable Mountains. Bunyan's writing is an interpretation, based on experience, of the hazards and rewards of the Christian life: it functions as a guide or map to its readers, and if they read it in the right spirit (just as Great-heart does his map, the Bible) it will help them avoid the former and reap the latter.[199] Margaret Baxter had her own period of imprisonment in Doubting Castle, on which Baxter comments: 'this history may teach us, that though God usually begin (as is said) our conversion in fears and penitent sorrows, it is holy and heavenly joy which it tendeth to, as more desirable; and we should chiefly seek, and should labour to moderate fear and sorrow, and not think we can never have enough'. In Chapter 10, some 'Uses proposed to the Reader from this History, as the Reasons why I wrote it' (from which this passage comes), Baxter explains at length how an account of the experience of one Christian can make its writer and its readers 'feel and see' (a phrase repeated several times) doctrine brought to life and hence alter the pattern of their own lives.[200] Both Baxter and Bunyan assume that the writer has the power to transcribe, communicate, and direct his own and others' experience. This can only be achieved with the active partnership of the reader, who (in the words of Bunyan's 'Apology') must lay book, head, and heart together:[201] he must read, interpret, respond, and act.

3 Faith and holiness

In several key chapters in Part I of *A Christian Directory* Baxter warns the beginner of the danger of extremes. In Chapter 2, 'Directions to Young

---

[198] *Grace Abounding*, 3–4, based on Numbers, 13; cf. Pooley, 'Language and Loyalty', 9–10. See also Keeble, *Literary Culture*, Chapter 9.
[199] *Pilgrim's Progress*, 118, 297.   [200] *Breviate*, 153, 151.   [201] *Pilgrim's Progress*, 7.

Christians, or Beginners in Religion, for their Establishment and Safe Proceeding' (which covers similar ground to *The Pilgrim's Progress*), he warns of the need when avoiding one extreme to fear the contrary one: 'See that you look round about you; as well to the error that you may run into on the other side, as into that which you have run into already ... True mediocrity is the only way that is safe'. This warning is elaborated in Chapter 3, 'The General Grand Directions for Walking with God, in a Life of Faith and Holiness': 'you must know in every duty you do, and every sin which you avoid, and every truth you receive, what is the contrary extreme to that particular truth, or sin, or duty; and keep it in your eye. If you do not thus watch, you will reel like a drunken man from side to side, and never walk uprightly with God.' In 'Directions for Young Students', a subsection of Chapter 6, the doctrinal implications of this warning are spelled out. The student must not make the fundamental, but very common, error of assuming 'co-ordinates or subordinates to be opposites', or of separating what God has conjoined. And Baxter goes on to give a list of these essential conjunctions, including the omniscience of God and the liberty of man, nature and grace, fear and love, the word and the Spirit, faith and obedience.[202] Bunyan implies a similar warning in his image of the narrow path Christian must tread between the ditch and the mire (quoted in the heading to this chapter) – though the effect of the image on the reader is very different from Baxter's Aristotelian mediocrity between extremes – and he makes a similar doctrinal point in *A Holy Life*. His text here is II Timothy 2:19, in which, he argues, Paul joins election and exhortation to depart from iniquity: 'Two truths strangely, but necessarily joyned together, because so apt to be severed by the children of men; for many under the pretence of their being elected, neglect to pursue Holiness; and many of them again that pretend to be for Holiness, quite exclude the Doctrine, and motives that election gives thereto.' Bunyan later elaborates this point, a precise illustration of the twin dangers of the ditch and the mire, when he urges the reader to depart from iniquity cleaving to opinions. However good the opinion, some entail iniquity to it:

I need instance in none other for proof hereof, but the doctrine of *faith*, and *holiness*. If faith be preached as that which is absolutely necessary to *Justification*; then faith-fantastical, and loosness and remisness in life (with some) are joyned therewith. If holiness of life be preached, as necessary to *salvation*, then faith is undervalued, and set below its place; and works as to justification with God set up and made co-partners with Christs merits in the remission of sins.[203]

It is assumed by some modern readers, as it was by some seventeenth-century participants in the debate, that in the conflict between nonconformists and conformists or between Calvinists and Arminians such conjunctions became separated: grace from morality, faith from works. Those who were

[202] *Practical Works*, II, 126, 302; III, 248–54.   [203] *Miscellaneous Works*, IX, 262, 326.

thought to undervalue grace were castigated as legalists or heathen moralists, and those who were thought to ignore works were castigated as antinomians. Bunyan was prone to make the first charge and Baxter the second. But it is important to understand that such charges were made at the time because those making them were anxious to reconcile apparently conflicting terms and concepts. Faith and works were not perceived as opposites; rather, grace, faith, holiness, and works properly understood were an inevitable continuum. The disagreements, and they were serious ones, were about the meaning of and the relationship between the different elements in the continuum. Baxter and Bunyan disagreed profoundly about the meaning of faith, the process of justification, the relationship between grace and morality, and the part played by human nature, but they were agreed that faith and holiness were indissolubly linked.

Justification by faith

Although Baxter's *Aphorismes of Justification* (1649), a work which greatly angered Calvinists such as Owen and influenced the thinking of latitude-men such as Fowler and Patrick, was published ten years before Bunyan's *Doctrine of the Law and Grace Unfolded*, it is helpful to consider Bunyan's views on justification first, as expressed in this and other works, since they derive from the orthodox Calvinism of the 1640s that Baxter was reacting against.[204] Bunyan's object is to disabuse the sinner of the view that he has any part in his own salvation. He admits that men find the doctrine of grace as he presents it hard to swallow, since they think that they must be responsible for initiating the process of reconciliation to God:

> why? saith the soul, I am a *sinner*, and God is *righteous*, *holy*, and *just*; his holy Law therefore having been broken by *me*, I must by all means, if ever I look to be saved; In the first place be sorry for my sins. Secondly, turn from the same. Thirdly, follow after good duties, and practise the good things of the Law, and ordinances of the Gospel, and so hope that God for Christs sake may forgive all my sins.

Bunyan sets out to expose what seem to him the fundamental errors in this train of argument. Anyone acting on this assumption is under bondage to the law, and is acting in a legal, not an evangelical spirit, indeed from 'a meer moral principle'.[205] His righteousness is legal, not evangelical, and however obedient he may be, he is unacceptable to God precisely because he thinks his performance of duty makes him acceptable. The legalist, in the definition given in *The Strait Gate*, is a man 'that hath no life but what he makes out of duties', and who thus destroys himself: he 'hath chosen to stand and fall by *Moses* who is the condemner of the world'.[206] Hence in *Pilgrim's Progress* Mount

---

[204] See Greaves, *Bunyan*, for a survey of his theology.
[205] *Law and Grace, Miscellaneous Works*, II, 69, 71.
[206] *Miscellaneous Works*, V, 125.

Sinai threatens Christian with fire, and Moses knocks Faithful down.[207] The
basic error is to assume that there is a condition to be performed by man for
God to accept him. Thus the Mansoulians in *The Holy War* must not send Mr
Good-deed with a petition to Emanuel since it will rebound on them.[208] There
is a condition in the gospel, but it is a very different one: it is to believe that sins
are forgiven without works. If this condition is fulfilled, its efficacy will enable
the sinner to fulfil the other conditions of the gospel: 'then thou wilt not act,
and do, because thou wouldest be accepted of God; but because thou hast
some good hope in thy heart, that thou art accepted of him already'; 'though
there be several conditions in the Gospell to be done, yet Christ Jesus doth not
look that they should be done by man, as man, but by his own Spirit in them'.
To the objection that faith is thus made a condition that the sinner must fulfil,
Bunyan answers that 'the same God that doth command that the condition be
fulfilled, even he, doth help his children by his holy Spirit to fulfill the same
condition'.[209] A man does not choose to have faith: the movement is not from
him. As Bunyan puts it in *Come, & Welcome, to Jesus Christ*, 'a willingness in us'
is not 'a condition of Gods making of us willing'.[210] Faith is not the cause of
salvation, but the instrument; the cause is God's grace, which gives man
faith.[211]

With reference to Romans 6:14, 'ye are not under the law, but under grace',
Bunyan defines grace as 'the free love of God in Christ to sinners, by vertue of
the new Covenant, in delivering them from the power of sin, from the curse
and condemning power of the Old Covenant, from the destroying nature of
sin, by its continual workings ... it is a pardon not conditional but freely
given'.[212] Under the covenant of grace the soul, killed by its own righteousness, is brought to life by the imputed righteousness of Christ. Bunyan
illustrates the process and meaning of the imputation of Christ's righteousness from his own experience:

For upon a time when I was under many condemnings of heart, and feared because of
my sins my soul would misse of eternal glory; methought I felt in my soul such a secret
motion as this, *Thy righteousness is in heaven*, together with the splendour and shining of
the spirit of grace in my soul, which gave me to see clearly, that my righteousnesse by
which I should be justified (from all that could condemn) was the Son of God himself,
in his own person now at the right hand of his Father representing me compleat before
the mercy-seat in his own self: so that I saw clearly, that night and day, where ever I
was, or what ever I was a doing, still there was my righteousnesse just before the eyes of
divine glory; so that the Father could never finde fault with me for any insufficiency
that was in my righteousnesse, being it was compleat; neither could he say, where is it?
because it was continually at his right hand.[213]

---

[207] *Pilgrim's Progress*, 20, 70–1.   [208] *Holy War*, 98.
[209] *Law and Grace, Miscellaneous Works*, II, 78, 165, 81.
[210] *Miscellaneous Works*, VIII, 276.   [211] *Law and Grace, Miscellaneous Works*, II, 81.
[212] *Miscellaneous Works*, II, 84, 85.
[213] *Miscellaneous Works*, II, 142, 146, 147. There is a similar account in *Grace Abounding*, 72;
Sharrock points out Bunyan's debt to Luther here (p. 150).

Bunyan goes on to stress the radical alteration in the nature of those to whom Christ's righteousness is imputed, and the impassable gulf between this righteousness and the righteousness of the law. The sanctified soul 'findes a change in the understanding, in the will, in the minde, in the affections, in the judgement, and also in the conscience; through the inward man a change, and through the outward man a change, from head to foot'. One crucial effect of this change is that 'that fiery Law, that it could not once endure, nor could not once delight in; I say, now it can delight in it after the inward man, now this Law is its delight, it would alwayes be walking in it, and alwayes be delighting in it, being offended with any sin, or any corruption, that would be any wayes an hinderance to it'. Yet this delight in the law has no part in salvation and is utterly different from a legal spirit. 'That is a Legal and Old Covenant-Spirit, that secretly perswades the soul, that if ever it will be saved by Christ, it must first be fitted for Christ, by its getting of a good heart and good intentions to do this and that for Christ'. Bunyan tries to overthrow the whole legalist, moralist position with the question, 'Friend, if thou canst fit thy self, what need hast thou of Christ?'[214] It is this fatal confidence in his own good heart and his obedience that damns Ignorance at the end of the first part of *Pilgrim's Progress*; his definition of justification is a legalistic one: 'I shall be justified before God from the curse, through his gracious acceptance of my obedience to his Law: Or thus, Christ makes my Duties that are Religious, acceptable to his Father by vertue of his Merits'. Hopeful, on the other hand, knows that his own duties are worthless.[215]

Yet Bunyan insists that this doctrine does not have antinomian impli-cations. To the objections that, since no works are required from the believer and no sin is charged to him, he is therefore free to sin as he chooses, Bunyan replies that those in Christ have the spirit of Christ, and 'are so far off from delighting in sin, that sin is the greatest thing that troubleth them ... and in all their prayers to God, the breathings of their souls is as much for sanctifying grace, as pardoning grace, that they might live a holy life'. Those living freely under the covenant of grace embrace the law in a way that is impossible to those who are crushed under the covenant of works: 'the Doctrine of the New Covenant doth call for holiness, engage to holiness, and maketh the Children of the Covenant to take pleasure therein. Let no man therefore conclude on this, that the Doctrine of the Gospel is a licentious Doctrine'.[216]

In *A Confession of my Faith* (1672) the relation between the stages of the sequence – grace, election, calling, faith, imputation of righteousness, holi-ness, the whole comprehended in justification by faith – is briefly and simply set out. Imputation of righteousness is 'an act of grace, a free gift without deserving'; 'the offer of this righteousness ... is to be received by faith'. This

[214] *Law and Grace, Miscellaneous Works*, II, 154, 155–6, 184.
[215] *Pilgrim's Progress*, 145–7, 140–4.
[216] *Law and Grace, Miscellaneous Works*, II, 169–71, 200.

faith is only found in those 'in whom the Spirit of God by mighty power doth work it'. Further, they were elect, freely and permanently, 'before the foundation of the world'. The elect are not chosen because God foresees their good works; on the contrary, election provides 'the graces that accompany their salvation'. Nothing 'can hinder their conversion, and eternal salvation'.[217] As the Judge explains at the trial of the Election-doubter in *The Holy War*, the doctrine of election is an essential element in the doctrine of grace: 'To question Election is to overthrow a great Doctrine of the Gospel, to wit, the *Omnisciency*, and *Power*, and *Will* of God, to take away the liberty of God with his Creature, to stumble the faith of the Town of *Mansoul*, and to make Salvation to depend upon works, and not upon Grace.'[218] 'No man can know his election, but by his calling.' Effectual calling produces faith, hope, repentance, and love. The objects of this love are 'the name ... and word, and truth of God in Christ, together with the sincerity of grace, of faith, and holiness in us ... In a word, [love] designeth a holy conversation in this world'.[219]

Bunyan does not seem to have been troubled by any of the links in this chain of argument, once he had become convinced in the mid-1650s of the doctrine of justification by faith and of his own election. He was certain of the inevitable progression from grace to holiness. He was also certain that he should persuade sinners to have faith, come to Christ, and be holy. In his writing he habitually combines an emphasis on free grace and faith as a gift to the elect from which holiness inevitably springs with urgent exhortation to his readers to pray, repent, will, strive, and do. This does not seem to have struck him as a contradiction, but it was precisely this logical gap in the work of writers such as Tobias Crisp and John Saltmarsh in the 1640s that caused Baxter to redefine the doctrine of justification. Several of Bunyan's views can be paralleled in Crisp's *Christ Alone Exalted* (1643), as the titles of some of the sermons show: 'Mens own Righteousness their grand Idol', 'God remembers not our Sins', 'Reconciliation by Christ alone', 'Christ is ours before we have gracious Qualifications'. In 'Christian Liberty no Licentious Doctrine' Crisp challenges those who interpret his doctrine as licentious by defining a libertine not in the corrupt but true sense of the term as 'one that is *truly free by Christ*'. Crisp's preferred term is freeman of Christ. Christ does all the freeman's work for him. As a result 'the free-men of Christ, having Christ and his Spirit for their Life and Strength, they may go infinitely beyond the exactest Legalist in the World, in more chearful Obedience than they can perform'. There is a simple test for knowing whether one is a freeman or not: 'if thou canst believe and roll thy self upon Christ, cleave to Christ, and say, *I will not let thee go*; this is security enough, Christ was sent to deliver thee'.[220]

[217] *Works*, ed. Offor, II, 597–8.   [218] *Holy War*, 240–1.
[219] *Confession of my Faith*, *Works*, ed. Offor, II, 598–601.
[220] Crisp, *Christ Alone Exalted* (1690 edn), Volume I, Sermon 8, 114, 124, 126, 128.

Baxter's complicated jugglings in the *Aphorismes* with the meaning of justification have one main object: to prevent emphasis on the free grace of God from removing responsibility for works from man.[221] He returned to the subject again and again, notably in his *Confession of his Faith* (1655), *Catholick Theologie* (1675), and *The Scripture Gospel Defended* (1690). His account of faith, righteousness, obedience, and the conditions for man's acceptance by God differs significantly from that of Bunyan and has much in common with that of Hammond and also (though it is much more elaborate than) that of Fowler. It is not necessary to look at the details of Baxter's quarrels with the 'antinomianism' of the 1640s.[222] The important points in his definition of justification are as follows. The imputation of Christ's righteousness to sinners as understood by contemporaries is not a Scripture doctrine, nor does the phrase appear in Scripture, a point made much later by John Wesley.[223] Its misrepresentation has been extremely damaging to the cause of reformed Christianity, 'especially by those men, who affirm that we are justified even before we repent or believe, and that through the imputation of Christs Righteousness, God judgeth the most swinish impenitent wretch, (so he be elect) to be righteous in his sight, and the object of his complacency'.[224] There is no gulf as there is for Bunyan between legal and evangelical righteousness. '*Those only shall have part in Christs satisfaction, and so in him be legally righteous, who do beleive, and obey the Gospel, and so are in themselves Evangelically Righteous.*' Evangelical righteousness is not a consequence of faith: it must be achieved by human effort, by the performance of conditions. '*Though Christ performed the conditions of the Law, and satisfied for our non-performance; yet it is our selves that must perform the conditions of the Gospel.*' These conditions cannot be performed without grace, but Christ enables men to perform them. Baxter tries unsatisfactorily to suggest that men's performance is an insignificant part of the covenant of grace in relation to Christ's satisfaction for sin by means of a parable of a landlord negotiating with his tenant: 'he maketh him a new Lease in this Tenor, That if in acknowledgement of the favor of his Redemption [of the old law], he will but pay a pepper corn, he shall be restored to his former possession, and much more'. Justification is not absolute but conditional and continuous: men conditionally pardoned and justified can be unpardoned and unjustified for non-performance of the conditions.[225] The view that grace cannot be lost is one of Satan's temptations.[226] (Conversely, Bunyan argues that men cannot fall from grace, but only from the false assumption that they

---

[221] On Baxter's doctrine of justification see Packer, 'Redemption and Restoration', Chapter 10; and Allison, *Rise of Moralism*, Chapter 8.

[222] See Orme, *Practical Works*, I, 'The Life and Writings of Richard Baxter', Chapter 9; Packer, 'Redemption and Restoration', Chapters 8 and 14; Kendall, *Calvin and English Calvinism*, Chapter 13; Wallace, *Puritans and Predestination*, Chapter 4.

[223] *Aphorismes*, 47. See Chapter 5 below, p. 223.   [224] *Confession*, a3.

[225] *Aphorismes*, 107–8, 115, 153, 196–7.

[226] *Christian Directory*, *Practical Works*, II, 300; IV, 374.

had grace.)[227] The conditions entail not simply belief, but duties such as repentance, love, obedience, and the works of love. Faith may be called the only condition, since all others are reducible to it.[228] Baxter's inclusive definition of justifying faith is as follows (despite the awkward shift from singular to plural it is worth quoting in full):

> It is, when a sinner by the Word and Spirit of Christ being throughly convinced of the Righteousness of the Law, the truth of its threatening, the evil of his own sin, and the greatness of his misery hereupon, and withall of the Nature and Offices, Sufficiency and Excellency of Jesus Christ, the Satisfaction he hath made, his willingness to save, and his free offer to all that will accept him for their Lord and Savior; doth hereupon believe the truth of this Gospel, and accept of Christ as his only Lord and Saviour, to bring them to God their chiefest good, and to present them pardoned and just before him, and to bestow upon them a more glorious inheritance, and do accordingly rest on him as their Saviour, and sincerely (though imperfectly) obey him as their Lord, forgiving others, loving his people, bearing what sufferings are imposed, diligently using his means and Ordinances, and confessing and bewailing their sins against him, and praying for pardon; and all this sincerely, and to the end.[229]

Obedience to Christ as lord is as much part of justifying faith as affiance in him as saviour. Faith does not justify in opposition to works: works justify as secondary parts of the condition. Baxter anticipates the outcry of 'Heresie, Popery, Socinianism!' that this last statement will raise against him (as indeed it did), but he insists that he only arrived at this doctrine with much reluctance: 'I resisted the light of this Conclusion as long as I was able.' He insists that there is no contradiction between Paul and James on works, and that Paul excludes only the works of the law, not the works of the gospel, from justification. He objects very strongly to 'that dangerous pillar of the Antinomian Doctrine, That we must not work or perform our duties for Life and Salvation; but only from Life and Salvation: That we must not make the attaining of Justification or Salvation an End of our Endeavors, but obey in thankfulness only, because we are saved and justified'.[230] Baxter insists that men will be judged according to their works, and that the 'main drift' of Scripture is that men must act for their salvation: it 'so presseth men to pray for pardon, and to pardon others ... and to strive to enter, and run that they may obtain, and doe Christs Com[man]dments that they may have right to the Tree of life, and enter in by the gate into the City'.[231] Bunyan would agree wholeheartedly with this last statement; it is explicit in his comment on Luke 13:24: 'Therefore, when he saith, strive, it is as much as to say, run for heaven, fight for heaven, labour for heaven, wrestle for heaven, or you are like to go without it.'[232] But Baxter assumes that this emphasis is incompatible with a definition of faith that excludes obedience as an essential part of it; indeed, he asserts that such a doctrine tends to drive obedience out of the world.[233]

[227] Law and Grace, Miscellaneous Works, II, 133.   [228] Aphorismes, 235–6, 238.
[229] Aphorismes, 279–80.
[230] Aphorismes, 286, 290–3, 324–5.   [231] An Appeal to the Light (1674), 3; Aphorismes, 317, 330.
[232] The Strait Gate, Miscellaneous Works, V, 81.   [233] Aphorismes, 325.

Baxter's view of election also differs significantly from Bunyan's. In Chapter 7 of his *Confession* he sets out in tabular form the difference between his position (which later came to be known as the middle way or Baxterianism) and antinomianism on the one hand and Arminianism on the other, the true mediocrity between contrary extremes.[234] The tripartite structure of Book II of *Catholick Theologie*, with Baxter as Reconciler attempting to bring together the positions of Calvinists and Arminians, is a much more elaborate and carefully argued defence of the middle way. Baxter sums up his position in the preface to the *Confession*. God offers pardon and right to eternal life to all, provided they will believe and repent.

> Antecedently to Believing, All have an equal Conditional Gift of pardon, and None have an absolute, nor an Actual Right: The Gospel findeth us equal, and makes no inequality, till we first make it our selves: But the secret unsearchable workings of Divine Grace do begin the difference,and make it *in* us, before it is made *by* us.[235]

Although Christ died for all (a direct contradiction of the doctrine of limited atonement, to which Bunyan adhered),[236] not all receive the same internal grace to enable them to believe and repent. All have sufficient objective grace; not all have sufficient internal grace or effectual grace.

> That this is denied to *any*, is long of themselves, who abuse that Commoner Grace which was sufficient to have made them *Better*: That it is Granted to *Any*, is from the Bounty of God: That it is Granted to *This* man rather then to *That*, is from his Absolute Dominion, and Will, and his Differencing Grace.[237]

Baxter is attempting to safeguard both free grace, God's right to elect arbitrarily one man and not another (contrary to the Arminian view that grace is offered to all and that those who repent and believe are the elect), and man's freedom to repent and believe (contrary to the predestinarian view that the elect believe as a consequence of their election).

Although the theoretical argument in *Catholick Theologie* about predestination, universal and special redemption, natural corruption and free will, sufficient and effectual grace, and perseverance is extremely detailed and complex, covering 218 folio pages, and although Baxter admits that the controversy as to whether God's promise is conditional or absolute is harder than he once thought,[238] in his practical works he insists that in terms of experience the issue of election is not a complicated one. For example, in *A Christian Directory*, Part I, Chapter 6 he argues that those who fear that they are not elect and that nothing they do can save them (very much the position Bunyan describes in *Grace Abounding*) have simply misunderstood the doctrine of election. God elects 'to the end and means together; . . . all that will repent

---

[234] See above, p. 131.   [235] *Confession*, a.
[236] See e.g. *Come, & Welcome, Miscellaneous Works*, VIII, 242–3.
[237] *Confession*, aᵛ. Cf. Armstrong, *Amyraut Heresy*, Chapter 4.
[238] *Catholick Theologie*, Book II, 213.

and choose Christ and a holy life, are elected to salvation, because they are elected to the means and condition of salvation, which if they persevere they shall enjoy'.[239] In *The Poor Man's Family Book*, Baxter puts the point as simply as he can: 'when men believe in Christ, and depart from iniquity, then they have his seal of election on them, and by it they may know themselves that they are his'.[240] As always for Baxter, the crucial question is the relation of theory to practice. In *Catholick Theologie* he points out that puritan preachers of the first half of the seventeenth century who emphasised Christian practice were inevitably concerned with preparations for grace in the form of 'humiliation, desire, endeavour'. 'The truth is, practical Preachers in these practical cases, are carried with full sail into that truth which Disputers would wrangle out of Doors.'[241] In the *Confession* this truth is given special emphasis: Baxter wishes

to leave it even in Capital letters to posterity, THAT PRACTICE IS THE EXCELLENT HELP TO BE TRULY ORTHODOX; THE PRACTICAL EXPERIMENTAL PREACHERS AND PEOPLE, DO HOLD FAST THOSE TRUTHS TO SALVATION WHICH OPINIONATISTS AND MEER DISPUTERS ARE EITHER EASILY DRAWN FROM, OR HOLD BUT SPECULATIVELY TO THEIR OWN PERDITION.[242]

In *The Poor Man's Family Book* he insists that the antinomians are dangerous because they 'destroy the principles of practice.'[243]

Owen, whose *Salus Electorum* (1647) Baxter had attacked in the *Aphorismes* and who had defended himself in *Of the Death of Christ* (1650), made a final attempt to defend and clarify the orthodox position on justification, now rapidly becoming archaic, in *The Doctrine of Justification by Faith, through the Imputation of the Righteousness of Christ; Explained, Confirmed, and Vindicated* (1677). Owen's basic point is that though the doctrine is regarded by some as undermining the necessity for holiness, works, and obedience, a criticism Paul had to contend with, nevertheless it is 'the chief principle of, and motive unto, all that obedience which is accepted with God, through Jesus Christ'. He insists as does Bunyan that the righteousness recognised by law, natural conscience, and philosophical reason has nothing to do with the imputed righteousness of Christ, which is 'alien from those other principles' and revealed to men in an entirely different way. Significantly, he objects (with some justice) to the names 'solifidian' and 'antinomian' being attached to the doctrine of justification by faith. Obedience does not give life and form to faith, but faith gives life and form to evangelical obedience. He also objects to the view that repentance and faith are conditions of justification, and sees the use of the term 'condition' itself as ambiguous and confusing: it leads to an assertion of personal inherent righteousness. Personal righteousness, or

---

[239] *Practical Works*, III, 219; *Grace Abounding*, 20 ff.   [240] *Practical Works*, XIX, 301.
[241] *Catholick Theologie*, Book II, 170.
[242] *Confession*, 115.   [243] *Practical Works*, XIX, 513.

sanctification, is distinct from justification and is a consequence of it.[245] Thus for Owen, far from justification by faith alone being inconsistent with personal holiness, it is the only true source of it.

Owen's wish to detach the label of antinomianism from the doctrine of justification by faith alone has a bearing on the difference between Baxter and Bunyan. Baxter tends to use the terms antinomianism and libertinism interchangeably. He argues that the doctrine he opposes logically inhibits preaching against sin and encourages indifference to works. Theoretical antinomianism is thus held responsible for practical libertinism, and both are condemned. Unfortunately, in *The Scripture Gospel Defended* Baxter falls into an absurd inconsistency on this point: not only does he grant that 'antinomians' such as Bunyan, though holding bad opinions, are themselves men of sincere holiness, he also asserts that 'it is the Piety and Strictness of the lives of many of them, which hath drawn many well-meaning ignorant persons to their Errors'. But these doctrinal errors are attacked because they lead men away from holiness.[246] For Bunyan, however, libertinism has no connection with doctrine, and he is not concerned with the issue that obsesses Baxter, theoretical antinomianism. He regards the belief and behaviour of Ranters as a separate phenomenon.[247] The libertine is 'he that pretendeth to be against forms, and duties, as things that gender to bondage, neglecting the order of God'.[248] The accusation that the doctrine of justification by faith leads to libertinism – 'For what matter how we live if we may be Justified by Christs personal righteousness from all, when we believe it?' – is made by Ignorance, who epitomises latitudinarian and Baxterian error.[249] One of Bunyan's motives for writing his domestic conduct book, *Christian Behaviour*, was '*To take away those Aspersions that the Adversaries cast upon our Doctrine. (Rom, 3.8. as also in the dayes of Paul) that because we preach Justification without the Works of the Law; therefore they pretend we plead for looseness of Life*'.[250] Baxter and Bunyan thus arrived at a view of the essential connection between faith and holiness by radically different routes.

Grace and morality

How far do these doctrinal differences affect their account of holiness and the holy life? This question can be answered in part by looking at their contributions to the debate between nonconformists and conformists in the 1670s about the relationship between grace and morality. The extreme positions on each side were summed up by Parker and Owen; in response to Parker's contention that grace and morality or virtue are the same thing,[250]

[244] *Works*, ed. Goold, V, 4, 24–5, 73, 104, 105–6, Chapter 6.
[245] 'A Defence of Christ, and Free Grace', *The Scripture Gospel Defended*, B2ᵛ, 49.
[246] *Grace Abounding*, 16–17, 49; cf. the portrait of Mr Self-will, *Pilgrim's Progress*, 255–7.
[247] *The Strait Gate, Miscellaneous Works*, V, 125.   [248] *Pilgrim's Progress*, 148.
[249] *Miscellaneous Works*, III, 9.
[250] Parker, *Ecclesiastical Politie*, 71–2. See Chapter 2 above, pp. 74–5.

Owen asserts that the distinction between virtue and grace is 'the known and avowed religion of Christianity'. He regrets the adulteration of Scripture language with 'exotic' philosophical terms such as 'virtue' and 'moral' which have their source in Aristotle and which were introduced into divinity by the schoolmen. He admits that he will not be able to eliminate the phrase 'moral virtue' from theology, it 'having absolutely possessed itself of the fancies and discourses of all, and, it may be, of the understanding of some', but suggests that if Scripture expressions only, such as 'holiness, righteousness, living unto God, walking with God, and before him', had been used 'many vain, wordy perplexities' would have been avoided: 'for let but the Scripture express what it is to be religious, and there will be no contesting about the difference or no difference between grace and moral virtue.'[251]

Bunyan shares this disapproval of the heathen vocabulary of moral virtue. The village to which Mr Worldly-Wiseman directs Christian in order to have his burden removed by Legality is named Morality; Evangelist in redirecting Christian to the strait gate warns him against following 'the Doctrine of this World' which is designed to save its adherents from the cross.[252] Benjamin Keach makes a similar point, probably borrowed from Bunyan, in his allegories *The Travels of True Godliness* (1683) and *The Progress of Sin* (1684): Mr Legalist mistakes True Godliness for Morality, and the deist and Quaker inhabitants of the town Morality wrongly think they dwell in Religion.[253] In *A Defence of the Doctrine of Justification* Bunyan castigates Fowler's language in *The Design of Christianity* as heathen and 'naturalist', objecting particularly to his definition of holiness as 'the sound complexion of soul', 'the purity of the human nature', 'the divine or God-like nature': 'These are but words' since 'there is no such thing'.[254] Human nature is corrupt and sinful, and it has no intrinsic righteousness or holiness. Fowler's conception of holiness is fundamentally unchristian: 'the excellency that you have discoursed of, is none other than the excellency and goodness that is of this world, such as in the first principles of it, is common to Heathens, Pagans, Turks, Infidels'. His view is the same as the Quakers', but whereas they misuse Christian terms, Fowler at least honestly gives his version of holiness 'the names due thereto, viz. A complexion or complication and combination of all the virtue of the soul, the human nature, the dictates of it, the principles of reason, such as are self-evident'.[255] Bunyan accurately puts his finger on latitudinarian terminology and its implications here. He argues that there are three things essential

251 Owen, *Truth and Innocence Vindicated, Works*, ed. Goold, XIII, 426, 412–13.
252 *Pilgrim's Progress*, 19, 22.
253 *The Travels of True Godliness*, 3rd edn (1684), Chapter 8, 83–4; *The Progress of Sin*, 4th edn (1707), Chapter 7, 143–4.
254 *Works*, ed. Offor, II, 288, 282. For Fowler's definition in full see Chapter 2 above, p. 82. See also I. Rivers, 'Grace, Holiness and the Pursuit of Happiness: Bunyan and Restoration Latitudinarianism', in Keeble, ed., *Bunyan*, Chapter 3.
255 *Works*, ed. Offor, II, 286. Cf. Chapter 8 above, p. 77, on the latitudinarian use of the co-prefix.

to inward gospel holiness of which Fowler's account is 'utterly destitute': '1. *The Holy Ghost.* 2. *Faith in Christ.* 3. *A new heart, and a new spirit.*' Citing Paul's distinction between the spirit and of the world and the spirit of God (1 Corinthians 2:12), he identifies the former with Fowler's 'principles of humanity' and with the 'candle of the Lord' (Proverbs 20:27): it represents 'human principles, good motions to moral duties, workings of reason, dictates of nature', 'the virtues of the world'.[256] He sees no possible connexion between the holiness that is supposed to be achieved through the restoration of natural faculties and the imitation of Christ, and the holiness that is the fruit of the new heart and spirit of the justified believer. In the counter-attack on Bunyan, *Dirt Wip't Off*, this distinction, essential to Bunyan's argument, is itself perceived from a characteristically latitudinarian perspective as consisting merely of words: 'And then for *a new heart and a new spirit*, What difference is there between *these* and *Purity of nature*, and *a Sound complexion of Soul*, and *a Divine or Godlike nature?* doth not every body know that these are but several expressions of the very same thing?'[257] The distinction for Bunyan is summed up in two entirely different conceptions of Christ's role. Christ is emphatically not a moral example to be followed, and Fowler's account of his life and conversation is 'heathenish'. Since Christ is saviour, mediator, and sacrifice, not 'the instructor, and schoolmaster only of human nature', 'it is blasphemy for any to presume to imitate him'. The only sense in which Christ is an example, and an example only to the justified, is 'as he carried it meekly and patiently, and self-denyingly towards the world'.[258] Throughout the *Defence* Bunyan separates the pagan and natural and human from the Christian and spiritual and godly. For him Fowler, armed with John Smith and Plato instead of Scripture, is talking about morality, not about grace.

Baxter characteristically attempts to reconcile these contrary extremes. The eleventh day's conference in *Catholick Theologie* between Saul, Paul, and a libertine teacher (a continuation of the format of *The Poor Man's Family Book*), in which the libertine confronts Paul with a list of his errors, reads to some extent like a critical comment on the tone and content of Bunyan's *Defence*.[259] But this does not mean that Baxter entirely concurs with the argument of *The Design of Christianity*. He certainly opposed extreme forms of the tendency to make grace and virtue or morality mean the same thing. Thus one of the 'uses' of his biography of his wife is that it clarifies the distinction:

It may help to convince those that are inclined to Sadducism, or infidelity, and believe not the testimony of the sanctifying spirit as to the truth of the word of God, but take holiness, as it differs from heathen-morality, to be but fancy, hypocrisie, custom or

[256] *Works*, ed. Offor, II, 288–9. For the latitudinarian interpretation of the 'candle of the Lord' see Chapter 2 above, p. 60.
[257] *Dirt Wip't Off*, 33.
[258] *Works*, ed. Offor, II, 300, 329–39, 302. For Fowler's portrait of Christ see Chapter 2 above, p. 83.
[259] *Catholick Theologie*, Book II, 220.

self-conceit. A man that never felt the workings of God's special grace in his own heart is hardly brought to believe that others have that which he never had himself ... But acquaintance, if intimate with gracious persons, might convince them of their moral error.[260]

In the *Aphorismes* Baxter firmly dissociates himself from the Socinian view that Christ is merely a pattern, guide, and law-giver,[261] but he does not regard Fowler as having fallen into this error. In Part I, Chapter 3 of *A Christian Directory* he frequently uses the phrase 'Christ your pattern' and is careful to explain what he means by it:

'Fix your eye upon himself, as your pattern and study, with earnest desire to follow his holy example, and to be made conformable to him.' – Not to imitate him in the works which were proper to him as God, or as Mediator; but in his holiness, which he hath proposed to his disciples for their imitation.[262]

In *How Far Holinesse is the Design of Christianity* he defends Fowler against the accusation of describing 'such a Holiness as is but the meer morality of a Heathen', and sees his erroneous emphasis on human holiness as the only end of Christianity, instead of one of its ends, as a natural reaction to antinomian error at the other extreme. He recommends the *Design* as a book 'of very much worth and use, to call men more seriously to consider of the Design of mans Redemption, and of the nature of true Religion and Felicity'.[263]

Baxter used the occasion of the dispute between Fowler and the non-conformists to clarify his own views about the relationship between grace, holiness, and morality. Unfortunately this pamphlet and its companion piece, *The Judgment of Non-Conformists About the Difference between Grace and Morality* (1676), illustrate only too well Burnet's criticism of Baxter, as recorded by Calamy, that 'the multitude of his distinctions ... created confusion, instead of giving light'.[264] The complexity of his analysis of terms is far removed from latitudinarian simplicity. His essential point is that morality is incorrectly defined when it is divorced from holiness and grace. 'Some ... confine the sense to the Duties of our common Conversation *towards man*, as distinct from *Holiness* or our Duty to God: And so they distinguish a meer *moral honest* man, from a *godly* or *religious* man.' But duty to man cannot be separated from duty to God. The former must depend on the latter; if not, it 'is no *Duty*, no *Morality* at all'. Morality in its most comprehensive sense is 'the Relation of the *Manners* or *Acts* of an Intelligent free Agent to the Governing Will and Law of God'.[265] 'All things commanded by God are directly, and all things *forbidden*, reductively, the parts of Morality: That is all Moral Good and Evil: and so faith in

---

260 *Breviate*, 150; cf. Parker's assertion that grace distinct from morality is 'but a Phantasm, and an Imaginary thing', *Ecclesiastical Politie*, 71.
261 *Aphorismes*, 112, 247, 307.   262 *Practical Works*, II, 223, 227.
263 *How Far Holinesse*, 3, 13–14, 20, 4.
264 Calamy, *My Own Life*, I, 468.   265 *Judgment of Non-Conformists*, 8, 16, 7.

Christ is a great part of our true Morality.'[266] 'All *truly moral Good in lapsed man*' had its origin in God's grace, and is itself grace.[267] 'The sum of Holiness and Morality (which is all one) is, the Love of God as God . . . and the *Love* of man and all things for God appearing in them'. Baxter is thus critical of those such as Owen and Bunyan who restrict the meaning of morality: 'they that will needs take the word in any narrower private sense, prepare for quarrels'. But at the same time his attempt to link the meaning of grace, morality, and holiness is very different from the characteristic latitudinarian attempt to do the same thing, as the following statement shows:

> If either Heathens or wicked nominal Christians do take *Holiness* or *Morality* to be only the Love of our selves, and our neighbours, and a disposition of mind, and course of life, in which we live orderly, justly and charitably to all, and soberly to our own minds and bodies, and all this only for the maintaining of the temporal prosperity of ourselves and others, or for the meriting of a prosperity in the life to come; not at all referring all this to GOD, as the Beginning, the Guide and the ultimate *End* of all; It is but Analogically called either *Holiness* or *Morality*, and not in a proper or univocal sense; because the *End* is left out which must give being to all true Holiness and Morality.[268]

Despite his sympathy for Fowler – and in this dispute he is certainly closer to Fowler than to Bunyan – Baxter is critical of the self-interested, prudential, and human-oriented emphasis of latitudinarian religion.

Mansoul

The differences between Baxter and Bunyan over the definition of justifying faith and the relationship between grace, morality, and holiness can be related to differences in their view of human nature and the operation of the Spirit on human faculties. On the whole they use the same terms to describe the separate faculties which are seen as constituting human nature, or 'mansoul' as Bunyan terms it in *The Holy War*, but they give them a different emphasis. Baxter tends to be precise and careful in his use of terms to denote different faculties, whereas Bunyan is often much looser, and allows his terms to run into each other. In *The Greatness of the Soul* (1682) Bunyan lists the powers of the soul (which is also synonymous with heart) as understanding, conscience, judgement, fancy, mind, memory, affections (the last are 'the Hands and Arms of the Soul', which 'take hold of, receive and imbrace what is liked by the Soul'), and will ('which may be called the *Foot* of the Soul, because by that the Soul, yea, the whole man is carried, hither and thither, or else held back, and kept from moving').[269] Baxter tends to see man as essentially divided into head (which includes understanding, conscience, and judgement) and heart (which includes will and affection), and he often uses the term reason in

---

[266] *How Far Holinesse*, 9.   [267] *Judgment of Non-Conformists*, 9.
[268] *How Far Holinesse*, 9. See below, pp. 161–2.
[269] *Miscellaneous Works*, IX, 146–8.

connection with the first category, a term that is much less important for Bunyan. Bunyan often links will, mind, and affection together as a triad, a usage that is foreign to Baxter. Both are concerned above all with the ways in which will and affection are transformed and moved to practice, and indeed they agree very closely on this process and its importance, but Baxter, as is to be expected, attributes a far greater role to understanding and is particularly interested in the relationship between head and heart.

In Part II of *The Divine Life* (1664), 'Walking with God', Baxter argues for the importance of reason in terms familiar in contemporary latitudinarian preaching:

> though the blindness and disease of reason, is contrary to faith and holiness, yet reason itself is so much for it, as that faith itself is but the act of elevated well informed reason; and supernatural revelation is but the means to inform our reason, about things which have not a natural evidence, discernable by us. And sanctification (actively taken) is but the healing of our reason and rational appetite: and holiness is but the health or soundness of them. The error of reason must be renounced by believers, but not the use of reason.[270]

Reason for Baxter is the means not only to knowledge but to putting knowledge into practice. He insists in the dedication to *The Saint's Everlasting Rest*, in a condensed allegory of the holy war, that the understanding is a crucially important faculty: 'Your understandings are the inlet or entrance to the whole soul; and if you be weak there, your souls are like a garrison that hath open or ill-guarded gates; and if the enemy be once let in there, the whole city will quickly be his own.' However, its function is limited. In Part IV, Chapters 6 and 8, in his account of contemplation (or meditation) and consideration, Baxter explains the relationship between the faculties of the soul and the way in which head and heart, knowledge and practice are linked:

> As God hath made several parts in man to perform their several offices for his nourishing and life, so hath he ordained the faculties of the soul to perform their several offices for his spiritual life . . . the understanding must take in truths, and prepare them for the will, and it must receive them, and commend them to the affections. The best digestion is in the bottom of the stomach; the affections are, as it were, the bottom of the soul; and therefore the best digestion is there.

The highest faculty is useless without the active assistance of the lowest. The instrument for transferring truths from understanding to will and affection, from head to heart, is called by Baxter consideration, which is synonymous with ratiocination, reasoning, discourse of mind, cogitation, and thinking. Consideration makes reason into an active faculty: 'Consideration doth, as it were, open the door between the head and the heart: the understanding having received truths, lays them up in the memory: now, consideration is the

---

[270] *Practical Works*, XIII, 238; cf. *Christian Directory*, Part I, Chapter 1, *Practical Works*, II, 24. For the latitudinarian view of reason see Chapter 2 above, pp. 63 ff. For the view that Baxter is close to Whichcote in his emphasis on reason see Powicke, *Baxter under the Cross*, 239.

conveyer of them from thence to the affections'; 'consideration awakeneth our reason from its sleep, till it rouse up itself, as Sampson'; 'meditation produceth reason into act.'[271]

Bunyan would agree that the faculties represented by the head and the heart in Baxter's categories must be linked, but he is altogether more suspicious of the head. Reason is a term he hardly uses. The expression '*Who could have thought that had been ruled by his reason*', which appears in *The Holy War* and in a slightly different form in *Pilgrim's Progress*, suggests precisely the inadequacy of reason, and indeed Mr Reason plays an almost invisible part in the allegory of *The Holy War*.[272] Bunyan does have a good deal to say about understanding, judgement, and conscience. On their own, these are weak and deceptive faculties. In *A Holy Life* he gives as one of the reasons why professors do not depart from iniquity the fact that 'Their understandings, their Judgments and Consciences have been dealt with, but the power of God has not been upon their wills and minds, and affections rightly to subdue them to the grace of the gospel.' Instead of a work of God having subdued all the powers of the soul, in such cases 'reflex acts' of the understanding, judgement, and conscience temporarily affect the will, mind, and affections. When the effect wears off, the professors return to their former ways:

> willingness, mindfulness of, and affection for this Gospel, lasted no longer than the light shined in their understandings, or than the things were relished by their judgment and conscience. So that when the light of their Candle went out, and when the taste of this sugar-plumb was out of their mouth, their wills and affections, not being possessed with the fear of God, they returned again to their course.

The understanding, judgement, and conscience, even if temporarily enlightened, cannot of themselves influence and motivate the other powers of the soul, but if these other powers are unaffected the professor must inevitably return to iniquity, since 'departing from iniquity must be with the mind and affections, or with the heart: but how can that be, where the heart is not sanctified and made holy?'[273] The so-called powers of the soul are in themselves powerless; without the help of divine agency – the Spirit of Christ, the Holy Ghost, grace, and faith – they can only achieve their own confusion.

This is essentially the subject of *The Holy War*. The powers or faculties are leading citizens of Mansoul: the Lord Mayor Lord Understanding, the Recorder Mr Conscience, and Lord Willbewill, with Mr Affection his deputy and Mr Mind his clerk. When Diabolus enters the town Lord Understanding loses his post and is confined to his darkened house, and so long as Diabolus has control of Mansoul Understanding is simply an impediment in the town. At the same time Diabolus debauches Mr Conscience, potentially a danger-

---

[271] *Practical Works*, XXII, 4, XXIII, 313, 339, 340, 342.

[272] *Holy War*, 112, 114, 198; *Pilgrim's Progress*, 102.

[273] *Miscellaneous Works*, IX, 286–7, 279; cf. Baxter, *Poor Man's Family Book*, *Practical Works*, XIX, 319.

ous opponent, and persuades the town that he is mad and that his irregular fits are not to be regarded.[274] This episode parallels Bunyan's attack on Fowler's exaltation of the 'supreme faculty' of conscience: Fowler's words 'suppose that *this* conscience is perfectly clear and light, when the scriptures say they have the understanding darkened'.[275] Lord Willbewill, the other principal figure, readily serves under Diabolus, turns against Conscience, and dominates Mansoul together with Mind and Affection. After Emanuel has won back the town, the three chief faculties, Understanding, Conscience, and Willbewill, admit their responsibility for co-operating with Diabolus, but instead of condemning them Emanuel pardons them and commits them to the charge of Captain Credence (faith).[276] Willbewill is made commander of the gates, Understanding is restored to the office of Mayor, and Conscience is promoted to a new office, that of subordinate minister to the principal minister and teacher, the Lord Secretary (the Holy Spirit). The distinction between these last two roles is very important. Emanuel explains to Conscience the limits of his role:

thou must (said the Prince) confine thy self to the teaching of Moral Vertues, to Civil and Natural duties, but thou must not attempt to presume to be a revealer of those high and supernatural Mysteries that are kept close in the bosome of *Shaddai* my Father: for those things know no man, nor can any reveal them but my Fathers *Secretary* only.

Emanuel clarifies the difference to Mansoul: the Lord Secretary will teach them 'all high and sublime Mysteries', while Conscience will teach them 'all things humane and domestick'.[277]

In the continuing struggle with Diabolus, when Emanuel withdraws from Mansoul after it has fallen away from him and the Diabolonians break into the town and besiege the citadel of the heart (the palace built for Shaddai, turned into a fortified castle by Diabolus), Understanding, Conscience, and Willbewill all play their part in the defence and in attempting to bring Emanuel back. But the successful negotiations are conducted not by Mansoulians, not by human faculties or powers of the soul, but by the crucial agents placed in Mansoul by Emanuel: the Lord Secretary and Captain Credence. Emanuel rejects all petitions from Mansoul until one is drawn up by the Lord Secretary. Nevertheless the latter insists to the townsmen that it is not his petition alone: '*True, the hand and pen shall be mine, but the ink and paper must be yours, else how can you say it is your Petition?*' The petition is carried by Credence, who brings back from Emanuel notes to Understanding, Willbewill, Conscience, and Godlyfear (who has taken an active part in the petitioning), thanking them for supporting his cause.[278] The Lord Secretary then puts

[274] *Holy War*, 18–20.
[275] *Defence of the Doctrine of Justification, Works*, ed. Offor, II, 283, referring to Ephesians 4:18.
[276] *Holy War*, 22–3, 27, 104–7.   [277] *Holy War*, 140, 142.
[278] *Holy War*, 207–8, 211–13. On the importance of the fear of God see below, pp. 152–3.

Credence in charge of all the forces of Mansoul. Interestingly, the Mansoulians, before they know of the Secretary's decision, themselves request that this should be done. When Credence and his forces are joined by Emanuel with his, the Diabolonians are routed and the prince enters the town.[279] Though Bunyan stresses through his allegory that the powers of the soul can achieve nothing without the help of the Spirit working through faith, at the same time he portrays these powers as constantly active in the narrative. Yet Emanuel, in his final speech, reveals that he has been the source of all action for good in Mansoul:

Nor did thy goodness fetch me again unto thee, after that I for thy transgressions have hid my face, and withdrawn my presence from thee. The way of back-sliding was thine, but the way and means of thy recovery was mine. I invented the means of thy return . . . 'Twas I that set Mr. Godlyfear *to work in* Mansoul. *'Twas I that stirred up thy* Conscience *and* Understanding, *thy* Will *and thy* Affections, *after thy great and woful decay. 'Twas I that put life into thee, O* Mansoul, *to seek me, that thou mightest find me, and in thy finding find thine own health, happiness and salvation.*[280]

This combined emphasis on the determining operation of the spirit of Christ on the soul and the active participation of the faculties or powers, particularly the will, is characteristic of Bunyan's teaching. The holy war is a struggle between God and Satan for the human will, as he explains in *The Heavenly Footman*: 'I tell you *the Will is all*, that's one of the chief things which turns the Wheel either backwards or forwards; and God knoweth that full well, and so likewise doth the Devil, and therefore they both endeavour very much to strengthen the Will of their servants'.[281] Satan's temptations must be actively resisted and God's call actively followed, but only God strengthening the will makes this active process possible. This participatory relationship is explained in *Come, & Welcome, to Jesus Christ*, the text for which is John 6:37, 'All that the Father giveth me [which Bunyan interprets to mean the saved], shall come to me; and him that cometh to me, I will in no wise cast out'. Coming to Christ involves the mind, the will, and the affections: it is 'a moving of the mind towards him', it is 'through the inclining of the will', and it is expressed in Scripture by the bowels: 'My bowels; the passions of my mind and affections; which passions of the affections, are expressed by the yerning, and sounding of the bowels'.[282] Why does the sinner come?

because God has INCLINED *thine heart to come; God hath called thee, illuminated thee, and inclined thy heart to come, and therefore thou comest to Jesus Christ . . . It is God that giveth thee* POWER; *power to pursue thy Will in the matters of thy Salvation, is the gift of*

---

279 *Holy War*, 213–14, 219–23.
280 *Holy War*, 246; cf. the account of the sanctified soul, *Law and Grace, Miscellaneous Works*, II, 154, quoted above, p. 134.
281 *Miscellaneous Works*, V, 165.
282 *Miscellaneous Works*, VIII, 255; cf. Hopeful's account of his coming to Christ, *Pilgrim's Progress*, 143.

God ... *Will* to come, and *power* to pursue thy will, is a double Mercy, coming Sinner.[283]

It could be argued that this double emphasis leaves Bunyan, in respect of the role of the human will in promoting action, in a similar position to Baxter. Baxter attaches enormous importance to the will, which is the seat of morality;[284] it is a more important faculty than the intellect, as he explains in his expository work *The Reasons of the Christian Religion* (1667):

It is man's will, which is his ultimate, perfective, imperant faculty; it is the proper subject of moral habits, and principal agent of moral acts; and therefore in all laws and converse, the will is taken for the man, and nothing is further morally good or evil, virtuous or culpably vicious, than it is voluntary. The intellect is but the director of the will; its actions are not the perfect actions of the man; if it apprehend bare truth, without respect to goodness, its object is not the highest, or felicitating, or attractive object, and therefore the act can be no higher: if it apprehend any being or truth as good, it apprehendeth it but as a servant or guide to the will, to bring it thither to be received by love. The perfect excellency on the object of human acts is goodness, and not mere entity or verity. Therefore, the most excellent faculty is the will.[285]

For the will to be a moral agent with goodness as its object it must be free, but this freedom must co-exist with grace. In *Catholick Theologie* Baxter undertakes

To prove, that in the points of Predestination and Redemption, there is no difference between moderate men of each Party, but what is resolved into the points of Grace and Free-Will; and in the points of Grace and Free-Will there is no real difference, but what is resolved into the question of the degree of Gods co-operating influx, compared with mans agency ... which will prove either no difference at all, or else about a thing past mans Understanding.

He refuses to be reconciled to the position of the predeterminants, those who believe in the will's necessitation (indeed he argues that God has purposely allowed Hobbes to bring discredit on the theory).[286] There is no doubt that for Baxter Bunyan's theology is necessitarian, yet Bunyan, though he never employs such terminology, is centrally concerned with the relationship between 'Gods co-operating influx' and 'mans agency'. From Baxter's point of view Bunyan's attempt to attribute all power of the human will to God and yet to insist on human responsibility in exercising that power is illogical. Yet at the same time Baxter certainly agrees that it is grace that activates the will, the Spirit that transforms the faculties and makes them capable of pursuing holiness.

Surprisingly, given their significant intellectual differences and the different kinds of nonconformity that they represent, Baxter and Bunyan are much

---

[283] *Miscellaneous Works*, VIII, 391–2.   [284] *Judgment of Non-Conformists*, 9.
[285] *Practical Works*, XXI, 17–18. Cf. Ames's emphasis on faith as an act of will as well as understanding, *Marrow of Sacred Divinity* (1642), 5.
[286] *Catholick Theologie*, Book II, 3–4.

closer on the meaning of the work of the Spirit than might be expected.[287]
Baxter confesses in his autobigraphy to have long overlooked the importance
of the witness of the Spirit because of fanatics treating it as enthusiastic
inspiration, whereas he now believes the 'the Spirit by Renovation, Sanctification, Illumination and Consolation, assimilating the Soul to Christ and
Heaven is the continued Witness to all true Believers'.[288] In *The Poor Man's
Family Book* he is careful to distinguish what he regards as false interpretations
of the witness of the Spirit from the true. Paul tells Saul that 'Fanatics mean,
an inward impulse, or actual word, or suggestion of the Spirit within them,
saying, or persuading their minds, that this is the word of God' (an account
which might be thought to fit the Bunyan of *Grace Abounding*). He goes on to
explain that every believer has the spirit of power, of wisdom, and of love, and
that the witness of the Spirit means not an inward suggestion but evidence:

> Even as the being of a rational soul in all men, having the faculties of vital action,
> understanding, and free-will, do prove by evidence, that a God who hath life,
> understanding, and will, is their Creator; so the regenerating of (not one or few, but) all
> true believers, by the quickening, illuminating, and converting work of the word and
> Spirit conjunct, powerfully giving us a new vital activity, wisdom, and love to God and
> holiness, doth in the same sort prove, by way of evidence, that God is the author of the
> new creature, and consequently the owner of the Gospel that is used thereunto.

The works of the Spirit 'are such that a stander-by, that is rational and true to
his own conscience, cannot deny'.[289] In his preface to Howe's *The Blessedness of
the Righteous* (1668) Baxter argues that the life of faith involves more than faith:
'Between faith and glory, there is the spirit of holiness, the love of God, the
heavenly desires, which are kindled by faith, and are those branches on which
the happy flower and fruit must grow: they are the name and mark of God
upon us'. This is the true witness of the Spirit, 'the objective and the sealing
testimony, the divine nature, the renewed image of God, whose children are
known by being like to their heavenly Father, even by being holy as he is
holy'.[290] Though in part these arguments and their expression are alien to
Bunyan, in particular the emphasis on rationality and free will and the
dismissal of inward suggestion, nevertheless in terms of practical consequences the similarities are more important. The view that the work of the
Spirit means a renovation of all the faculties of the soul issuing in a life of
holiness and love which can be objectively verified by observers is essentially
the one that Faithful puts to Talkative. A work of grace in the soul discovers
itself to standers by in two ways: '1. *By an experimental confession of his Faith in
Christ. 2. By a life answerable to that confession,* to wit, *a life of holiness; heart-holiness;
family-holiness (if he hath a Family) and by Conversation-holiness in the world*'.[291]

---

287 On this subject generally see Nuttall, *Holy Spirit* (1946).   288 *RB*, I, 127–8.
289 *Practical Works*, XIX, 452–6; cf. *Christian Directory*, Part I, Chapter 3, Grand Direction 3,
    Practical Works, II, 188–98.
290 Howe, *Works*, ed. Hunt (1822), III, 9–10.   291 *Pilgrim's Progress*, 83.

Baxter would insist that the first point is not verifiable in itself. But as to the second point there is no dispute between them: the life of faith *is* the life of holiness, and only the soul whose powers have been renewed by faith can live it.

The life of holiness

In *The Poor Man's Family Book* Paul tells the newly converted Saul:

you are but entered into the holy war. You have many a temptation yet to resist and conquer; temptations from Satan and from men, and from your flesh; temptations of prosperity and adversity. You have constant and various duties to perform, which require strength, and skill, and willingness. You have remaining corruptions yet to mortify, which will be striving to break out against, and to undo, you. You know not how many burdens you have to bear, where flesh, and heart, and friends may fail you. I tell you all the rest of your life must be the practice of what you have promised in your covenant; a labour, a race, a warfare: and you must defend yourself with one hand, as it were, while you build with the other; and all the way to heaven must, step by step, be carried on by labour and victory conjunct.[292]

Baxter here summarises the recurrent emphasis of seventeenth-century puritan teaching on the arduousness of the Christian life, employing the characteristic puritan metaphors of journey and combat, of the Christian as pilgrim and soldier, which Bunyan elaborated in his allegories.[293] In this view the Christian life entails suffering at the hands of and alienation from the world in return for a heavenly reward, the cessation of all labour, blessedness, joy, the victor's crown. The second cannot be achieved without the first: 'no motion, no rest', in Baxter's words; *No Cross, No Crown*, in Penn's.[294] Or as the visitor Secret tells Christiana, '*The bitter is before the sweet*: Thou must through Troubles, as did he that went before thee, enter this Celestial City.'[295] These are traditional Christian ideas deriving from particular passages in the New Testament, notably the eleventh chapter of Hebrews (which is the basis of *Pilgrim's Progress* and which Baxter urged young Christians to read because it would teach them that 'All that are in heaven have gone this way, and overcome such oppositions and difficulties as these').[296] Yet in the 1660s and 1670s they strike a particular note in the context both of the isolation and persecution of nonconformists and of the emphasis in contemporary latitudinarian writing on the happiness and easiness of the Christian life and its suitability to human nature and to the world. From the conformist point of view, nonconformist religion subjects its followers to unnecessary difficulties, fears, doubts, and sufferings, both internal and external. Whereas both conformists and nonconformists emphasise the central importance of practice,

---

[292] *Practical Works*, XIX, 420.
[293] See Haller, *The Rise of Puritanism* (1938), Chapter 4, and Keeble, *Literary Culture*, Chapter 9.
[294] *The Saint's Everlasting Rest*, *Practical Works*, XXII, 40; Penn, *No Cross, No Crown* (1669).
[295] *Pilgrim's Progress*, 180; cf. the repetition of this phrase, pp. 183, 184; *Holy War*, 112.
[296] *Christian Directory*, Part I, Chapter 2, *Practical Works*, II, 110.

works, and holiness, the prudential latitudinarian calculation that holiness will bring about worldly happiness and is to be pursued for that reason is absent from nonconformist writing. Yet the nonconformists do not offer a life of unmitigated misery in this world in exchange for happiness in the next; on the contrary, though the godly must expect labour, hardship, affliction, and tribulation, though they must be cross-bearers, they will also experience love, joy, and delight now as a foretaste of the blessedness to come.

There is a certain tension here in the nonconformist account of the various stages through which the Christian must pass before experiencing this joy which can be clearly seen in the disagreement between Bunyan and Baxter over the meaning of fear, doubt, and despair. For Bunyan fear is an essential part of the process of conversion. Hopeful and Christian, discussing the parlous stage of Ignorance, agree that 'fear tends much to Mens good, and to make them right, at their beginning to go on Pilgrimage'. The ignorant think these fears come from the devil, not God, and therefore wrongly resist them.[297] Every Christian should experience fear in the course of his progress, as is shown by the response of the pilgrims in Part II to Great-heart's account of Mr Fearing, who had 'a *Slow of Dispond* in his Mind, a *Slow* that he carried every where with him'. His fears are not of the world or persecution, but about his final acceptance. Yet they are groundless: when he passes in terror through the Valley of the Shadow of Death the enemies are quiet, and when he crosses the river, expecting to drown, it is almost dry. In a musical analogy Great-heart suggests that fear is the bass string of the soul on which God first plays to set the soul in tune; Fearing's imperfection was to play no other music till the end. The pilgrims are encouraged by Great-heart's narrative because they all recognise their own lesser fears in this extreme example. The episode underlines the indispensability of the fear of God: 'No fears, no Grace ... Though there is not always Grace where there is the fear of Hell; yet to be sure there is no grace where there is no fear of God.'[298]

Bunyan is anxious to distinguish between on the one hand the true fear of God (to which he devoted *A Treatise of the Fear of God*, 1679) and the doubts about their acceptance and salvation to which the elect are subject and which he had himself experienced (described at length in *Grace Abounding*),[299] and on the other hand the state of despair of the reprobate. Psychologically from the human point of view there seems to be a very narrow line dividing fear and doubt from despair, precisely because it is difficult for the elect to be sure of their election; theologically from the divine point of view they are poles apart. Bunyan's pastoral task is to help the elect to distinguish between true fear and slavish fear, to profit from the first and to free themselves from the second. The Man in the Iron Cage whom Christian questions in the House of the Interpreter is a man of despair whose heart is hardened, who cannot repent,

---

[297] *Pilgrim's Progress*, 150–1.   [298] *Pilgrim's Progress*, 249–54.
[299] Cf. the soul's monologue in *Law and Grace*, *Miscellaneous Works*, II, 150–1.

and who therefore cannot escape his own prison: 'God hath denied me repentance; his Word gives me no encouragement to believe; yea, himself hath shut me up in this Iron Cage: nor can all the men in the World let me out.' The Interpreter warns Christian, 'Let this mans misery be remembred by thee, and be an everlasting caution to thee.'[300] As has often been noted, this episode encapsulates the plight of Francis Spira, who also claims that God has hardened his heart and taken away from him '*all power of repentance*' so that he cannot escape from his prison of despair:

although I can say, I would believe, yet can I not say, I will believe, God hath denied mee the power of will; and it befalls mee in this my miserable estate, as with one that is fast in irons, and his friends comming to see him, do pitie his estate, and do perswade him to shake off his fetters, and to come out of his bonds, which God knows he would fain do, but cannot.

The account of Spira is presented to the reader, as the Man in the Iron Cage is to Christian, as an example from which to profit: he should avoid backsliding and dallying with conscience, and should take heed of Spira's principal errors – disputing overbusily with Satan and concluding from present experience to past reprobation and future damnation. Above all he should hope: 'hope well, while the space of Grace lasteth; *Dum spiras, spera* [while you breathe, hope]; so mayest thou take good and no hurt, by the reading of this terrible Example'.[301] Thus Christian is pulled out of the Slough of Dispond by Help, and could have avoided it altogether had he looked for the steps (the promises); Christian and Hopeful escape from Giant Despair when Christian remembers that he has in his bosom the key called Promise which '*opens any Lock in* Doubting *Castle*'; Great-heart kills Giant Despair, demolishes Doubting Castle, and releases the only survivors, the starving Mr Dispondencie and his daughter Much-afraid, implying that a good pastor can protect his congregation from the affliction of unnecessary doubt and despair, though many may have succumbed to it. Mr Dispondencie's last words of advice to his fellow pilgrims before he crosses the river are to shut the doors on '*Disponds*, and slavish Fears': 'they are *Ghosts*, the which we entertained when we first began to be Pilgrims, and could never shake them off after'.[302]

There are intellectual and moral difficulties in Bunyan's analysis. First, those in a state of despair are implicitly blamed for not availing themselves of the scriptural promises, whereas Bunyan certainly held that God only grants the will to do so to the saved; second, there is a danger that accounts of doubt and despair intended to guide men out of them may have the contrary effect of increasing their fears, a danger Bunyan was aware of, to judge from the more generous tone of Part II of *The Pilgrim's Progress*. Bunyan is here confronting one of the chief problems of the puritan and nonconformist minister in warning and encouraging his flock: he must both frighten the complacent professor (as he does in *The Strait Gate*) and comfort the weak and hesitant (as

[300] *Pilgrim's Progress*, 34–5.   [301] N. Bacon, *Francis Spira* (1649 edn), 36–7, 43–4, 80.
[302] *Pilgrims Progress*, 15, 118, 282, 308.

he does in *Pilgrim's Progress* II). The dilemma is clearly stated by the congregational minister Matthew Meade in *The Almost Christian Discovered*: '*My design herein is that the formal sleepy professor may be awakened, and the close Hypocrite discovered; but my fear is, that weak believers may be hereby discouraged*'.[303] Some relevant advice on this subject was given thirty years earlier by the puritan Richard Sibbes, in *The Bruised Reed and Smoking Flax* (1630), one of the first godly books Baxter read (by bruising Sibbes means the awakening of the conscience):

> It is dangerous, I confess, in some cases with some spirits, to press too much and too long this bruising, because they may die under the wound and burden before they be raised up again. Therefore it is good in mixed assemblies to mingle comfort, that every soul may have its due portion. But if we lay this for a ground, that there is more mercy in Christ than sin in us, there can be no danger in thorough dealing. It is better to go bruised to heaven than sound to hell.[304]

Baxter certainly shared the view that the sinner must be 'bruised' in order to be converted (see, for example, *The Saint's Everlasting Rest*, Part III, Chapters 1–4 and *A Call to the Unconverted*), and he accepted that fear was the beginning of the process: 'experience telleth us, that conversion commonly beginneth in fear'.[305] However, he was convinced that altogether too much stress was laid by many practising Christians on doubts about salvation and scrutiny of the marks of election, and that what was usually interpreted as a spiritual state, despair, was in many cases more likely to be a bodily one, melancholy. These errors were the result of larger errors about the nature of the Christian life. Baxter had much experience of cases of melancholy. Paul claims in *The Poor Man's Family Book*, 'I have had to do with as many melancholy, conscientious [i.e. troubled in conscience] persons as any one that I know of in England.'[306] This claim is autobiographical; in the *Reliquiae* Baxter relates that many melancholy persons were sent to consult him, and he draws certain conclusions from this experience for the benefit of the reader: 'Melancholy Phantasms and Passions' should not be ascribed to God's spirit; religion should not be placed too much 'in Fears, and Tears, and Scruples; or in any other kind of Sorrow', and tears and grief should not in themselves be taken as signs of a converted person.[307] In two interesting chapters in *A Christian Directory* Baxter provides detailed guidance on this subject: 'Directions to the Melancholy about their Thoughts' (in Part I, Chapter 6) and 'Directions for Fearful, Troubled Christians that are perplexed with Doubts of their Sincerity and Justification' (Part II, Chapter 25). (There is similar, more compressed advice in the First and Fifth Days of *The Poor Man's Family*

---

303 *The Almost Christian Discovered* (1662), 'To the Reader'. For Bunyan's connection with Meade in the 1670s see Greaves, 'Bunyan's *Holy War*', 164–5.
304 Sibbes, *Complete Works*, ed. Grosart (1872), I, 46–7. Sibbes's text is Isaiah 42:3.
305 *Christian Directory, Practical Works*, II, 478.
306 *Practical Works*, XIX, 308.   307 *RB*, Part III, 86.

Book.) The first of these chapters provides an astute gloss on *Grace Abounding* (there is no evidence that Baxter had read it, but he was certainly familiar with the case it described). Examples of the signs of such melancholy are when men think that God has forsaken them – 'they are just like a man in a wilderness, forsaken of all his friends and comforts, forlorn and desolate; their continual thought is "I am undone, undone, undone!" ' – or that it is too late to repent, or that they are not elect 'so that they are past help or hope', or that all cases of hardness of heart such as Cain or Pharoah are directed at them. Stories of God's judgements have a damaging effect on such persons: 'The reading of Spira's case, causeth or increaseth melancholy in many; the ignorant author having described a plain melancholy, contracted by the trouble of sinning against conscience, as if it were a damnable despair of a sound understanding.' Further signs are that they consider no one to be as they are (Baxter observes that he has seen many in the course of a few weeks saying the very same thing), or they are so taken up with their own thoughts 'that they feel it just as if something were speaking within them, and all their own violent thoughts were the pleading and impulse of some other: and therefore they are wont to impute all their fantasies, either to some extraordinary actings of the devil, or to some extraordinary motions of the Spirit of God', or they are tempted to blaspheme against God, Christ, and Scripture, or to think that they have committed the sin against the Holy Ghost.[308]

Bunyan exhibits many of these signs in *Grace Abounding*, though he attributes them to the devil, not to his own mental state: he is tempted not to strive about his election, to blaspheme against God, Christ, and Scripture, to desire to sin against the Holy Ghost, to sell Christ; he compares himself to Cain, Esau, Judas, Spira, and many others, and concludes that his own sin of letting Christ go 'was bigger than the sins of a Countrey, of a Kingdom, or of the whole World'.[309] This prolonged mental suffering, lasting several years, is summarised in *Pilgrim's Progress* in Christian's experience in the Valley of the Shadow of Death, though his torments and temptations are somewhat alleviated by the weapon All-prayer and the voice he hears (presumably Faithful's) repeating verse four of the twenty-third psalm.[310] In Part II Christiana and her family are guided through the Valley by Great-heart. Bunyan implies, as he does elsewhere in Part II, that proper pastoral care can alleviate such horrors, but at the same time he suggests the value for Christians in sharing these experiences. Christiana observes: 'Now I see what my poor Husband went through. I have heard much of this place, but I never was here afore now ... Many have spoke of it, but none can tell what the Valley of the shadow of death should mean, until they come in it themselves.' And her son Samuel adds, to Great-heart's approval, '*one reason why*

[308] *Practical Works*, III, 219–24.   [309] *Grace Abounding*, 21–52.
[310] *Pilgrim's Progress*, 62–4.

we must go this way to the House prepared for us, is, that our home might be made the sweeter to us'.[311]

For Baxter, however, these experiences are contrary to the spirit of Christianity. The combination of melancholy with a misunderstanding of the nature of faith produces states in which true believers are consumed with despair because of their own supposed inability to believe or to feel as they think they should.[312] Baxter's prime example of such a state was his friend the minister James Nalton, who was convinced of his gracelessness and died in despondency and self-condemnation, although manifestly a holy man.[313] But Baxter thought such states could be cured, with the help of either a physician or a minister who could teach the true nature of faith. In *A Christian Directory* he advises the melancholy, 'Overvalue not the passionate part of duty, but know that judgment, will, and practice, a high esteem of God and holiness, a resolved choice, and a sincere endeavour, are the life of grace and duty, when feeling passions are but lower, uncertain things.'[314] After their marriage his wife overcame 'all the doubts of her sincerity and salvation and all the fears and sadness thereupon, which cast her into melancholy', and learnt from him that 'religion consists in doing God's commanding will, and quietly and joyfully trusting in His promising and disposing will: and that fear and sorrow are but to remove impediments and further all this'.[315]

Though they differ in their interpretation of the place of inner fears, there is no disagreement between Baxter and Bunyan over the inevitability of outward persecution in the Christian life. In *A Christian Directory* Baxter warns the young convert not to be surprised at persecution: 'It is great weakness in you, to think such usage strange: do you not know that enmity is put, from the beginning, between the woman's and the serpent's seed?'[316] In *A Holy Life* Bunyan states as a fact that 'persecution always attends the word, that of the *Tongue*, or that of the *Sword*'.[317] The divisions in the church after the Restoration convinced Baxter of the truth of this view: 'I am more apprehensive that Sufferings must be the Churches most ordinary lot, and Christians indeed must be *self-denying Cross-bearers* [Luke 9:23, 14:27], even where there are none but formal nominal Christians to be the *Cross-makers*'. One of the reasons he gives is that 'The Tenour of the *Gospel* Predictions, Precepts, Promises and Threatnings, are fitted to a People in a suffering State.'[318] This was seen by conformists as a perverse and partisan interpretation of

[311] *Pilgrim's Progress*, 242–3.
[312] See *Christian Directory, Practical Works*, III, 220–1; *Poor Man's Family Book, Practical Works*, XIX, 416–17.
[313] *RB*, II, 431.
[314] *Practical Works*, III, 232. Cf. Doddridge's advice to Miss Scott, quoted in Chapter 4 below, p. 194.
[315] *Breviate*, 128–9.   [316] Part I, Chapter 2, *Practical Works*, II, 124.
[317] *Miscellaneous Works*, IX, 290.
[318] *RB*, Part I, 132–3.

Scripture. Baxter records a dispute he had with the Bishop of London's chaplain, who refused to license one of his works on the grounds that it referred to the prosperity of the wicked and the adversity of the godly, and to hypocrites forsaking truth for fear of suffering. 'And he askt me, whether I did not think my self that Nonconformists would interpret it as against the Times. I answered him, Yes, I thought they would; and so they do all those Passages of Scripture which speak of Persecution and the Suffering of the Godly; but I hoped Bibles should be licensed for all that.'[319] Baxter is anxious to make clear that the nonconformist interpretation is the correct one. Thus in *The Poor Man's Family Book* Saul (who has obviously been talking to conformists) says he thought 'that this command of forsaking all, and taking up our cross, had been spoken only to such as lived in times of persecution, when they must deny Christ or die, and not to us that live where Christianity is professed'. Paul tells him that 'every one that will be Christ's disciple must forsake the world in heart and resolution, and be a martyr in true preparation and disposition, though no one must cast away his estate or life, nor be a martyr, by suffering, till God call him to it'.[320] Bunyan repeatedly quotes the biblical texts concerning persecution in his attempt to both warn and comfort his readers by insisting on the necessity of suffering and its value. In *The Heavenly Footman* he stresses that 'there is no Man that goeth to Heaven, but he must go by the Cross ... *We must through much tribulation enter into the Kingdom of Heaven. Yea, and all that will live Godly in Christ Jesus, shall suffer Persecution*' (Acts 14:22; II Timothy 3:12).[321] Mr Worldly-Wiseman, in advising Christian against the way pointed out by Evangelist, paradoxically asserts the relevance of such texts: '*thou art like to meet with in the way which thou goest, Wearisomness, Painfulness, Hunger, Perils, Nakedness, Sword, Lions, Dragons, Darkness; and in a word, death, and what not? These things are certainly true, having been confirmed by many testimonies.*' Before Christian and Faithful enter Vanity Fair, Evangelist tells them that they will continue the scriptural tradition: 'you have heard in the words of the truth of the Gospel, that you must through many tribulations enter into the Kingdom of Heaven [Acts 14:22]. And again, that in every City, bonds and afflictions abide in you [Acts 20:23] ... You have found something of the truth of these testimonies upon you already, and more will immediately follow'. The line of descent from the apostles, the early Christian martyrs, the protestant martyrs of Mary's reign, to contemporary nonconformists is made explicit in Gaius's account of Christian's progenitors in Part II.[322]

Two main reasons are given why Christians must suffer in this way: because of the force of example, and because bodily affliction promotes

---

319 *RB*, Part I, 123.
320 *Practical Works*, XIX, 317–18. Cf. Wilkins's strictures on misinterpretation of such scriptural passages, quoted in Chapter 2 above, p. 84.
321 *Miscellaneous Works*, V, 159.
322 *Pilgrim's Progress*, 18, 87, 260; cf. *Grace Abounding*, 99, ∬ 332.

spiritual growth. The meekness and patience of Christian and Faithful win several of the men of Vanity Fair to their side, and the death of Faithful generates the new life of Hopeful: 'Thus one died to make Testimony to the Truth, and another rises out of his Ashes'.[323] The willingness of ministers or preachers to suffer was crucial, hence the importance of Bunyan's resolution to face death if necessary.[324] Margaret Baxter had contempt for ministers who did not show this courage: 'She was exceeding impatient with any Nonconforming minister that shrunk for fear of suffering, or that were overquerulous and sensible of their wants or dangers; and would have no man be minister that had not so much self-denial as to lay down all at the feet of Christ, and count no cost or suffering too dear to serve Him.'[325] Baxter himself thought that sufferers were in the highest form of Christ's disciples, and that his own misfortunes had strengthened his faith: 'It is not long since I found myself in a low (if not a doubting) case, because I had so few enemies, and so little sufferings for the cause of Christ ... and now that doubt is removed by the multitude of furies which God hath let loose against me.'[326] Characteristically, he warned against the experience of suffering being misinterpreted and misused, particularly if it made the persecuted hate their persecutors, who as their superiors must not be wronged. It was one of Satan's designs 'to make us take such a poor Suffering as this [i.e. Baxter's imprisonment in 1669], for a sign of true Grace, instead of Faith, Hope, Love, Mortification, and a Heavenly Mind'.[327] Baxter was clearly afraid that persecution might generate political anger, which he saw as a sin, instead of spiritual submission. A thorough account of what suffering meant in spiritual terms was provided by Bunyan in *Seasonable Counsel: or, Advice to Sufferers* (1684). Suffering is a token and mark that the godly belong to Christ, a means of trying them to see what they are, and, most important, a process whereby they are made more righteous, holy, and fruitful. Only those tested and purified in such a way will be worthy of heaven:

Righteousness thriveth best in affliction, the more afflicted, the more holy man; the more persecuted, the more shining man, (Acts 6.15) ... These things are sent, to better Gods people, and to make them white, to refine them as Silver, and to purge them as gold: and to cause that they that bear *some* fruit, may bring forth *more*: we are afflicted, that we may *grow*. (John 15.1,2). 'Tis also the will of God that they that go to heaven should go thither hardly or with difficulty. *The righteous shall scarcely be saved.* That is, they shall, but yet with great difficulty, that it may be the sweeter.[328]

The path to holiness is thus a much more arduous one for the nonconformist than for the conformist. How far does the meaning of the life of holiness differ? In social and domestic terms 'Walking with God' (the favourite puritan

[323] *Pilgrim's Progress*, 92, 98.   [324] *Grace Abounding*, 97–101.   [325] *Breviate*, 121–2.
[326] *The Divine Life* (1664), *Practical Works*, XIII, 307, 309.
[327] *RB*, Part III, 58–59.
[328] *Miscellaneous Works*, X, 61, 72–3; cf. the letter on this subject written in 1669 to brother Harrington by Bunyan and other members of the Bedford Church, *Minutes*, ed. Tibbutt, 56–8.

phrase used by Baxter in the titles of Part II of *The Divine Life* and Part I, Chapter 3 of *A Christian Directory*), or the godly, righteous life of works, fruit, and practice, means much the same to conformist and nonconformist: love to God and man, charity, the performance of reciprocal duties between husbands and wives, parents and children, masters and servants, and neighbours. In ecclesiastical and political terms there is necessarily a difference in the view of the proper relationship between magistrate and people: for the conformist, the magistrate can require obedience in matters of church discipline; for the nonconformist, if the magistrate attempts to coerce the godly in matters which they regard as sinful it is right and holy for them to disobey. In ethical terms the differences in the approach to holiness are more subtle and interesting. Essentially for the nonconformist, unlike the latitudinarian conformist, the life of holiness cannot be self-interested. Two rather different accounts of this disinterestedness are provided by Bunyan and Baxter. Bunyan's most important works on the meaning and practice of holiness are *Christian Behaviour; Being the Fruits of True Christianity. Teaching Husbands, Wives, Parents, Children, Masters, Servants, &c, how to walk so as to please God* (1663), and *A Holy Life, The Beauty of Christianity: Or, An Exhortation to Christians to be Holy* (1684). What is of interest in these tracts is not the conventional instructions for appropriate behaviour but the reasons for the importance of a holy life that Bunyan gives. Grace, faith, and works are the links of an unbreakable chain, and works both derive from and lead back to grace. Works are a testimony to men of the grace of God. '*For though we are justified,* (Rom. 3.24, &c.) *freely by Grace through Christ before God; yet we are justified before men* (Jam. 2.18) *by our works: Nay, a life of Holiness flowing from Faith in us that are saved by Grace, it doth justifie that Grace before the World that justifies us before God*'.[329] Grace and faith are invisible, but the holy life is a gospel that shows them to men. '*He then that would have Forgiveness of Sins, and so be delivered from the Curse of God, must believe in the Righteousness and Blood of Christ: but he that would shew to his Neighbours that he hath truly received this Mercy of God, must do it by* good Works'.[330] Faith is the only source of works, and works inevitably proceed from faith: 'a life of Holiness and Godliness in this world, doth so inseparably follow a principle of Faith, that it is both monstrous and ridiculous to suppose the contrary'.[331] Works are good not in themselves, but for what they signify: '*Not that Works make a man good; for the Fruit maketh not a good Tree, it is the Principle, to wit, Faith, that makes a Man good, and his works that shew him to be so.*'[332] The way to promote good works is to promote the doctrine of grace: 'as *Faith* animates to *Good Works,* so the *Doctrine of Grace* animates *Faith*: Wherefore, the way to be rich in *Good Works,* it is to be rich in *Faith,* and the way to be rich in *Faith,* is

---

329 *Christian Behaviour, Miscellaneous Works,* III, 9.
330 *Holy Life, Miscellaneous Works,* IX, 251.
331 *Christian Behaviour, Miscellaneous Works,* III, 15.
332 *Holy Life, Miscellaneous Works,* IX, 251.

to be conscientiously affirming the *Doctrine of Grace* to others, and believing it our selves'.[333]

The unresolved problem of human moral effort is at the centre of this account. At times Bunyan suggests that the link between faith and holiness, between the tree and the fruit, is spontaneous. The man who loves God cannot help but be holy. 'A man cannot love God, that loves not holiness; he loves not holiness that loves not Gods word; he loves not Gods word, that doth not do it.'[334] A holy life is the beauty of Christianity. It reveals to men in visible beautiful form the unseen world of faith. But at the same time Bunyan's main emphasis in *A Holy Life* is on the difficulties professors face in attempting to depart from iniquity. One reason he gives for this difficulty is that grace is weak, even in the strongest saints:

we are, while in this world, no where by the word, said to have attained to the mark and point of absolute perfection; but are bid to grow, to follow on, to press forward, and to perfect holiness in the fear of God. Yea, the best of us all, even the Apostles and Prophets, have not only made it manifest by their *imperfections*, that as yet they have not departed from iniquity, as they should; but they have confessed, and denied not, that they were yet in the pursuit of righteousness, and had not already attained.

Perfection belongs not to this but to another world:

1. This is a place to act faith in.
2. This is a place to labour and travel in.
3. This is a place to fight and wrestle in.
4. This is a place to be tryed in.

And therefore this is no place of perfection, and consequently no place, where Gods people can depart from iniquity as they should.

The struggle of the saints to pursue a holiness that they cannot attain on earth is thus another kind of testimony to the truth of the unseen world. But Bunyan laments that there are few who give this testimony. 'Where is the man that walketh with his Cross upon his shoulder? Where is the man that is zealous of moral holiness?' Indifference to practical holiness among professors (especially 'carnal Gospellers' who cast dirt at those they misname 'legal preachers') is thus a negative kind of evidence, which shows how few men have saving faith.[335]

The life of holiness for Bunyan is a fruit and a sign: the consequence of saving faith and the means of making it known to the world. It is a life of struggle: '*The ease that Pilgrims have is but little in this life*',[336] and they commonly experience despondency, fear, difficulty, affliction, and suffering. Notwithstanding, it is also a life of joy, not on earth but in prospect, as Bunyan insists in one of his darkest works, *A Few Sighs from Hell*:

---

[333] *Christian Behaviour, Miscellaneous Works*, III, 53–4.
[334] *Holy Life, Miscellaneous Works*, IX, 283.
[335] *Holy Life, Miscellaneous Works*, IX, 292, 296, 346, 351.   [336] *Pilgrim's Progress*, 106.

though the Saints have all their evil things in their life time, yet even in their life time they have also joy unspeakable and full of glory, while they look not at the things that are seen, but at the things which are not seen. The joy that the Saints have sometimes in their hearts by a believing consideration of the good things to come when this life is ended, doth fill them fuller of joy then all the crosses, troubles, temptations, and evils that accompany them in this life can fill them with grief, 2. *Corinth.* 4.[337]

This joy is the product not of holiness but of faith. Bunyan simply does not concern himself with the issue that figures so largely in latitudinarian writing, the connection between holiness and happiness.

Given the theological differences between Baxter and Bunyan about the meaning of faith, it might be expected that Baxter's view of holiness would approach more closely to that of the latitude-men. And indeed occasionally he treats the subject in the manner of Fowler or Barrow or Whichcote. For example, in *The Divine Life* he writes: 'holiness is called natural to us, in a higher respect [than sin], because it was the primitive, natural constitution of man, and was before sin, and is the perfection or health of nature, and the right employment and improvement of it, and tends to its happiness'.[338] In his exhortation to parents in Part II, Chapter 10 of *A Christian Directory* to bring up their children to live holy lives he stresses the profitableness of holiness: 'Let it be the principal part of your care and labour in all their education, to make holiness appear to them the most necessary, honourable, gainful, pleasant, delightful, amiable state of life; and to keep them from apprehending it either as needless, dishonourable, hurtful, or uncomfortable.'[339] But Baxter does not normally give prudential or self-interested motives for the pursuit of holiness, or offer happiness as a reward to the holy. The terms he usually annexes to the life of holiness are delight, love, and joy: 'a genuine Christian life, is a Life of the greatest joy on earth';[340] 'Diligently labour that God and Holiness may be thy chief Delight: and this holy Delight may be the ordinary temperament of thy religion';[341] Christians should 'live in the constant delights of divine love';[342] 'holiness lies especially in delighting in God, His Word and Works, and in His joyful praise, and hopes of glory, and longing for, and seeking the Heavenly Jerusalem'.[343] This joy or delight has its origin in the disinterested love of God, and is to be distinguished from felicity arising from prudential self-love. In a long appendix to Part I, Chapter 3 of *A Christian Directory*, entitled 'The true Doctrine of Love to God, to Holiness, to Ourselves, and to Others, opened in certain Propositions', Baxter provides an extraordinarily interesting critique of what he sees as the secular implications of latitudinarian ethics (though he does not put it like that). Man's self-love

---

[337] *Miscellaneous Works*, I, 296. Cf. Bunyan's climactic experience of joy prompted by Hebrews 12:22–4, *Grace Abounding*, 82.

[338] *Practical Works*, XIII, 236. Cf. p. 145 above, and n. 270.

[339] *Practical Works*, IV, 180, cf. *Poor Man's Family Book*, *Practical Works*, XIX, 491.

[340] *Life & Death of Alleine*, 'Introduction', 16.   [341] *Christian Directory*, *Practical Works*, II, 408.

[342] *Poor Man's Family Book*, *Practical Works*, XIX, 446.   [343] *Breviate*, 128.

and concern for his own felicity is a 'natural "pondus", or necessitating principle' which both God and the devil use for their own ends. 'God saith, thou lovest felicity, and fearest misery: I and my love are the true felicity'. The carnal man is capable of loving God for the sake of his own felicity. Indeed this is the usual first step to the true love of God: 'self-love, and desire of endless felicity, and fear of endless misery, are the first notable effects or changes on a repenting soul'; 'almost all God's preparing grace consisteth in exciting and improving the natural principle of self-love in man; and manifesting to him, that if he will do as one that loveth himself, he must be a Christian'. At this stage self-love is a much more powerful motivating factor in turning men to a new life than love of God for his own sake. But it is essential to distinguish the two. Love of God is an end in itself; God must not be loved as a means to another end, human felicity:

It is possible to love God, and holiness, and heaven, as a conceited state and means of our sensual felicity, and escape of pain and misery; but to love God as the true felicity of the intellectual nature, and as our spiritual rest, and yet to love him only or chiefly for ourselves, and not rather for himself as our highest end, implieth a contradiction. The same I say of holiness, as loved only for ourselves . . . it is essential to holiness to be the soul's devotion of itself to God as God, and not only to God as our felicity: therefore to love God only or chiefly for ourselves, is to make him only a means to our felicity, and not our chief end; and it is to make ourselves better, and so more amiable than God, that is, to be gods ourselves.

Many make this mistake: 'yet is it very common to have a false, imperfect notion of God and holiness, as being the felicity of man'; many more 'take in no more of God and holiness, but that they are better for us than temporary pleasures'; some 'make the perfection of man's highest faculties (practically) to be their ultimate end; and desire or love God and holiness (defectively and falsely apprehended) for themselves, or their own felicity, and not themselves, and their felicity and holiness, ultimately for God'. Baxter is prepared to grant that 'he that hath only a necessary self-love, even a love to his spiritual, eternal felicity, operating by strong desire and fear, conjunct with a weaker degree of love to God as good in himself . . . hath grace, and may so be saved'. However sanctification, the pure love of God and holiness, is when the soul loves 'God and holiness as such, for their own goodness, above its own felicity as such'.[344] The underlying assumption of this very interesting appendix is that the kind of argument being put forward by contemporary latitudinarian writers, which appeals to human nature and human interest as the principal, not merely the initial, ground for religious behaviour, is in fact misrepresenting the nature of religion and inadvertently promoting a selfish secular ethic which deifies man in God's place. The good man posited by latitudinarian thinking calculates the benefits to himself of virtuous action and is moved to act accordingly. Baxter's sanctified man is not moved by threats or promises, but loves God,

[344] Practical Works, II, 468–71, 474, 478, 481.

holiness, the good, in and for themselves. Hence it is that the holy life is one of joy, delight, and love.

It would not have occurred to contemporary nonconformists or their eighteenth-century dissenting heirs to link Baxter and Bunyan as representatives of a common tradition. In ecclesiastical terms Baxter was descended from the puritans and Bunyan from the separatists, and the general legal categories of nonconformity and dissent did not completely eliminate this distinction. In doctrinal terms Bunyan fought to defend a once-orthodox position which was now outmoded, whereas Baxter contributed to the formation of the new orthodoxy; the Baptist Keach lamented in 1684 that the 'true ancient Orthodox Doctrine about Justification' was 'sadly corrupted by *Baxterian* Notions'.[345] From the point of view of latitudinarian churchmen both these positions might have been expected to become extinct. Burnet, according to Calamy, was convinced that adherents of the Baxterian middle way 'must at last, when pressed, fall into the Arminian scheme'.[346] But this did not happen. The Baxterian tradition continued among eighteenth-century Presbyterians and Congregationalists, and Bunyan's views had a considerable impact on Methodists and evangelicals. However, these differences of ancestry, discipline, doctrine, and influence should not obscure the significance of the similarities between Bunyan and Baxter as nonconformists in contrast to the latitudinarians. What links them particularly is the connection between principles and practice. Their position as nonconformists led them to emphasise the separation of the church and the godly from the world and the difficulty of living the holy life, in contrast to the latitudinarian emphasis on the suitability of religion to the world and the essential congruity of holiness and happiness. Where the latitudinarians deliberately played down doctrine, the emphasis on which had proved so divisive, in order to strengthen ethics, Baxter and Bunyan were agreed that ethics depends on doctrine and is meaningless without it. For nonconformists the separation of doctrine and ethics, for whatever reason, is unchristian: the life of holiness cannot be separated from the life of faith.

[345] Keach, *The Progress of Sin* (1707 edn), 211.   [346] Calamy, *My Own Life*, I, 471.

4

Affectionate religion: Watts, Doddridge, and the tradition of old dissent

We have some pretences above our predecessors, to freedom and justness of thought, to strength of reasoning, to clear ideas, to the generous principles of christian charity; and I wish we had the practice of it too. But as to the savour of piety, and inward religion, as to spiritual-mindedness, and zeal for God, and the good of souls; as to the spirit and power of evangelical ministrations, we may all complain, the glory is much departed from our Israel.

Watts, Dedication to *Sermons*, I (1721)[1]

If the judgment be never so much convinced, yet while the affections remain unmoved, the work of religion will be begun with difficulty, and will drive on but very heavily. This the prophets and apostles well knew; and the great God, who employed them, knew it too, and therefore he sent them armed with the powers of natural and divine oratory, to reach the inmost affections, to penetrate the heart, and to raise holy commotions in the very centre of the soul.

Watts, *Discourses of the Love of God, and the Use and Abuse of the Passions in Religion* (1729)[2]

He who would be generally agreeable to dissenters, must be an evangelical, an experimental, a plain and an affectionate preacher.

Doddridge, *Free Thoughts on the Most Probable Means of Reviving the Dissenting Interest* (1730)[3]

While I have any reverence for scripture, or any knowledge of human nature, I shall never affect to speak of the glories of Christ, and the eternal interest of men, as coldly as if I were reading a lecture of mathematics, or relating an experiment of natural philosophy. I hope I shall always remember, how unworthy the character of a man and a christian it is, to endeavour to transport men's passions, while the understanding is left uninformed, or the judgment unconvinced: But so far as is consistent with a proper regard to these leading powers of our nature, I heartily pray, that I, and all other gospel ministers, may so feel the energy of divine truths on our own souls, as to preach and write concerning them with an holy fervency and ardour.

Doddridge, Preface to *Ten Sermons on the Power and Grace of Christ* (2nd edn, 1741)[4]

[1] *Works*, ed. Parsons (1800), I, xxvii. [2] *Works*, ed. Parsons, II, 311–12.
[3] *Works*, ed. Williams and Parsons (1802–5), IV, 213.
[4] *Works*, ed. Williams and Parsons, II, 212.

The dissenting interest is not like itself: I hardly know it. It used to be famous for faith, holiness, and love. I knew the time when I had no doubt, into whatever place of worship I went among dissenters, but that my heart would be warmed and comforted, and my edification promoted. Now I hear prayers and sermons, which I neither relish nor understand. Evangelical truth and duty are quite oldfashioned things. Many pulpits are not so much as chaste. One's ears are so dinned with reason, the great law of reason, and the eternal law of reason, that it is enough to put one out of conceit with the chief excellency of our nature, because it is idolized, and even deified.

John Barker (Presbyterian minister) to Doddridge (1744)[5]

1 The situation of old dissent

Two basic tendencies can be observed in the attitudes and language of dissent in the first half of the eighteenth century, the first rational, the second evangelical.[6] Historians have sometimes identified them with Presbyterianism and Congregationalism respectively, but this is not an adequate account of a complex state of affairs; in the period up to the beginnings of the Evangelical Revival in the 1730s and 1740s these tendencies were concurrent and interconnected, though later in the century they were to diverge and come into conflict. In both cases there are continuities with and departures from the puritan and nonconformist traditions of the previous century. The development of the rational tendency owes a good deal to the nonconformists' experience of ejection from the Church of England and persecution in the period 1662–88, and the subsequent change in the political circumstances of dissent after the Toleration Act of 1689, which allowed 'protestant dissenters' freedom of worship and immunity from prosecution (while not removing civil disabilities). This side of the rational tendency emphasises toleration, liberty of thought and conscience, free enquiry, hostility to impositions of doctrine or forms of worship, the separation of church and state, and strict limits on the power of the civil magistrate in the sphere of religion. Some of these attitudes had been held by Congregationalists and sectarians before the Restoration, but most had been resisted by the Presbyterians, who learned their value the

5 *Letters to and from Doddridge*, ed. Stedman (1790), 95; cf. *Correspondence and Diary of Doddridge*, ed. Humphreys (1829–31), IV, 358; *Calendar of the Correspondence of Doddridge*, ed. Nuttall (1979), Letter 1009.

6 The most useful general works on the intellectual and cultural history of old dissent are: Ashley Smith, *The Birth of Modern Education* (1954); Barlow, *Citizenship and Conscience* (1962); Bogue and Bennett, *History of Dissenters*, 4 vols. (1808–10); Bolam *et al.*, *The English Presbyterians* (1968); Coomer, *English Dissent under the Early Hanoverians* (1946); Davie, *A Gathered Church* (1978); Griffiths, *Religion and Learning* (1935); McLachlan, *English Education under the Test Acts* (1931); G. F. Nuttall, 'Continental Pietism and the Evangelical Movement in Britain', in van den Berg and van Dooren, eds., *Pietismus und Réveil* (1978); Nuttall, 'Methodism and the Older Dissent: Some Perspectives' (1981); Nuttall, *New College, London and its Library* (1977); Parker, *Dissenting Academies in England* (1914); Spivey, 'Middle Way Men' (1986); Toulmin, *An Historical View* (1814); Watts, *The Dissenters* (1978), Chapter 4.

hard way: as the Congregational Watts commented with regard to Presbyterian intolerance of sects in *Orthodoxy and Charity United* (1745, but written
twenty to thirty years earlier), 'The fathers have been dearly instructed in the
value of toleration and liberty by most abundant retaliations. The children
have learned to preach this part of the gospel well, and I am persuaded they
will never forget it again.'[7] The rationalist view of the proper relationship
between religion and society was summed up for dissenters in the Introduction to Part II of *A Defence of Moderate Non-Conformity* (1704) by the
Presbyterian Edmund Calamy. Calamy (1671–1732), grandson of the
puritan of the same name, became the principal spokesman for and defender
of dissent against the attacks of high churchmen. In his autobiography (not
published until the early nineteenth century) he describes this Introduction as
the most maturely weighed of all his publications; Locke, on whose first *Letter
concerning Toleration* (1689) he drew, 'thought it such a defence of Nonconformity
as could not be answered',[8] and it became the standard account to which
dissenters referred: the Congregational Doddridge, according to his one-time
student and biographer Job Orton, taught his students the principles of
separation from it.[9] Calamy's crucial assertion is that civil government is
concerned only with the civil interests of mankind. 'Every one by being a
Member of a Civil Society has as clear a Right to be Protected in that Mode of
Religious Worship, which he apprehends to be most agreeable to the Will of
God (as long as the Civil Peace is not endanger'd) as in any Matter
whatsoever.'[10] This Lockean principle is repeated in Watts's *New Essay on
Civil Power in Things Sacred* (1739): 'the power of civil government reaches no
further than the preservation of the natural and civil welfare, rights and
properties of mankind with regard to this world, and has nothing to do with
religion further than this requires'.[11] Dissenters were agreed on the rational
and political arguments for their religious separation.

The rational tendency in dissent is also a continuation of the tradition in
seventeenth-century puritanism and nonconformity which emphasised the
essential, but limited, role of reason in religion in opposition to the attacks on
'carnal reason' of the sects, and which converged in this respect with the views
of the latitude-men. Baxter's *The Unreasonableness of Infidelity* (1655) and *The
Reasons of the Christian Religion* (1667) are important works initiating this
tradition, though for eighteenth-century dissenters Book IV of Locke's *Essay*

---

[7] Essay no. 7, 'Against Uncharitableness', *Works*, ed. Parsons, II, 526; for the dating see Preface,
    II, 403.
[8] Calamy, *My Own Life*, II, 29, 31.
[9] Orton, *Memoirs of the Life, Character and Writings of ... Doddridge* (first published 1766), in *Works*,
    ed. Williams and Parsons, I, 65–6.
[10] Calamy, *A Defence of Moderate Non-Conformity*, Part II (1704), Introduction, 29.
[11] *Works*, ed. Parsons, III, 361. Watts is enthusiastic about Locke's *Letter concerning Toleration* in
    the Preface to *Philosophical Essays on Various Subjects* (1733): 'I found myself surprised and
    charmed with truth. There was no room to doubt in the midst of sunbeams.' *Works*, VI, 482.

concerning Human Understanding (1690), which draws together latitudinarian arguments, was more influential. For the Baxterian nonconformists this emphasis on reason had by no means precluded an equally strong emphasis on evangelical doctrine and the importance of the affections in religion. In the eighteenth century, however, especially among some of the Presbyterians, the rational tendency further came to imply hostility to appeals to feeling and the influence of the Spirit in religion, and a growing sympathy not only with the moralist latitudinarian strain in the Established Church (to which Baxter had himself partly contributed) and its Arminian theology, but with the covert Arianism of some of its members. The rational tendency began to be increasingly opposed to the evangelical, until it issued in the later part of the century in the unitarianism of the self-styled rational dissenters.[12] By the end of the century the range of disparate positions and churches covered by the term 'protestant dissent' was much wider than had been allowed for by the Toleration Act a hundred years earlier. Thus paradoxically rationalism is both an essential element in the complex of attitudes and beliefs that constitute early eighteenth-century dissent, and a potential threat to its survival.

The evangelical tendency emphasises the traditional Reformation doctrines of grace, atonement, justification by faith (often covered by the label 'orthodoxy'), the importance of experimental knowledge, meaning both the believer's own experience of religion, and acquaintance with the variety of the experience of others, and the central function of the heart and affections in religion in relation to the will and understanding. In emphasising these things eighteenth-century dissenters were following in the footsteps of their puritan and nonconformist forebears, but with certain important modifications. The Baxterian compromise with the Calvinist doctrine of election, rejecting reprobation, distinguishing special from general grace, and assuming active co-operation with grace on the part of the believer,[13] became widely accepted by 'moderate' or 'reconciling' or 'middle-way' dissenters among both Presbyterians and Congregationalists, although high Calvinists who looked to the theology of John Owen and the Westminster Catechism were hostile to this development. The puritan emphasis on the operation of the Spirit in experimental religion tended to be played down by dissenters; there is evident tension here between the rational and evangelical tendencies of dissent. However, in one area, the emphasis on knowledge of the heart and the religious use of the passions, the dissenters continued an important puritan tradition and developed it further into a practical religious psychology. This 'affectionate religion' both derives from the rational tendency in dissent, in that it is in part a philosophical investigation into human nature, and

---

[12] See J. Goring, 'The Break-up of the Old Dissent', and H. L. Short, 'Presbyterians under a New Name', in Bolam, *English Presbyterians*, Chapters 5–6.
[13] See Chapter 3 above, pp 138–9.

represents a reaction against it; it is thus not merely a continuation into the eighteenth century of certain important features of puritanism and a development of the 'affective-practical science' Baxter defined divinity as being,[14] but a response to an increasingly rational intellectual climate which seemed to be subverting the characteristically evangelical features of the dissenting tradition.

The two men who were largely responsible for defining and disseminating affectionate religion, who tried to balance the rational and evangelical tendencies of dissent and to transmit the attitudes and values of their puritan and nonconformist fathers, modified to suit the changes in the social and intellectual climate, to the new generations of dissenters, were Isaac Watts (1674–1748)[15] and Philip Doddridge (1702–51).[16] Watts was brought up as an orthodox Calvinist; in 1702 he became minister to what had been Owen's congregation in Mark Lane, London, and assured his congregation at his ordination that 'in the chief doctrines of Christianity [he] was of the same mind with' Owen.[17] In a very interesting letter to his brother Enoch (unfortunately undated, but probably early), outlining the differences in doctrine and discipline among the various denominations in England, he clearly differentiates himself from the Baxterians while allowing them to be true Christians.[18] However there is no doubt that Watts later moved away from high Calvinism and became a proponent of moderation, to the dismay of his more orthodox followers.[19] Doddridge was educated by the moderate Calvinist John Jennings, from whom, he says in his letters, he learnt the principles of free enquiry, moderation, and catholicism.[20] As a young man Doddridge was unsympathetic to the Calvinist tradition as represented by Owen and Thomas Goodwin, greatly preferring Tillotson to them and responding enthusiastically to Baxter.[21] After Jennings's early death Doddridge re-established his academy at Northampton (with the encouragement of Watts), and from 1729 to 1751 developed and propagated Jennings's intellectual tradition. He defined his own and his associates' position as that of

[14] Baxter, *The Divine Life* (1664), *Practical Works*, ed. Orme, XIII, 183.
[15] The most useful accounts of Watts are: Davis, *Watts* (1948); Gibbons, *Memoirs of Watts* (1780); Milner, *The Life, Times and Correspondence of Watts* (1845).
[16] The most useful accounts of Doddridge are: Deacon, *Doddridge* (1980); Gordon, 'Philip Doddridge and the Catholicity of the Old Dissent', in *Addresses Biographical and Historical* (1922); Greenall, ed., *Doddridge, Nonconformity and Northampton* (1981); Harris, 'Doddridge' (1950); Nuttall, *Baxter and Doddridge* (1951); Nuttall, ed., *Doddridge: His Contribution to English Religion* (1951); Nuttall, Introduction to *Calendar*; Orton, *Memoirs*.
[17] Milner, *Watts*, 182.   [18] Milner, *Watts*, 194.
[19] E.g. the wealthy lay supporter of orthodoxy William Coward; see *Calendar*, ed. Nuttall, Letter 465; Milner, *Watts*, 620.
[20] *Correspondence*, ed. Humphreys, I, 155–6, 198–9; *Calendar*, ed. Nuttall, Letters 35, 53.
[21] *Correspondence*, ed. Humphreys, I, 44, 368, 460, II, 58; *Calendar*, ed. Nuttall, Letters 8, 120, 155, 185; Nuttall, *Baxter and Doddridge*, 17. For Doddridge's recommendation of Goodwin's *Child of Light*, see Chapter 1 above, p. 16.

moderate or Baxterian Calvinism,[22] in opposition to high Calvinist orthodoxy on the one hand and moralist 'new scheme' rational dissent on the other. Watts and Doddridge were at the same time defensive and confident about their middle position; defensive, because they were under pressure from both extremes; confident, because they were consciously creating a new meaning for dissent in the period of legal toleration. In order to understand their attitudes it is necessary to appreciate the peculiar situation of dissent in the early eighteenth century.

One potential danger of toleration was loss of identity. Calamy in his biography of Howe records Burnet's belief that nonconformity was supported by persons rather than principles, and that it would not outlive the generation of men like Baxter and Howe.[23] Burnet was of course proved wrong, but the experience of ejection and persecution and heroic leadership must have given a sense of identity and commitment to the nonconformists not shared by the succeeding generations of dissenters. Calamy did more than anyone to keep the memory of the heroic period alive; he helped Matthew Sylvester edit Baxter's autobiography, and published an *Abridgment* of it in 1702 with a long and important new chapter giving an account of the ministers ejected in 1662, which he considerably expanded in the second edition of 1713 into a separate volume. In the peroration to this chapter he exhorted the new generation to keep to their fathers' principles:

> if we, who rise up in the Room of those who in so noble a Manner adhaer'd to that Old *Puritannical* Principle (which was indeed that of the first Reformers) *of the Necessity of a farther Reformation in the Church, in order to the more General and Effectual reaching of the great Ends of Christianity*; if we (I say) who rise up in the room of those who ventur'd All that was dear to them in bearing their Testimony to this Principle, rather than they would do violence to their Consciences; do but imitate their Faith and Patience, Piety and Purity; do but partake of the same Divine Spirit whereby they were Acted; and have but the same Presence of God with us, to Guide and Assist us, to Prosper and Succeed us, to Comfort and Support us; we are fearless of the Issue ...[24]

Yet many did not follow in the steps of the nonconformists. The numbers of dissenters in the early eighteenth century were declining, particularly among the gentry;[25] there was disquiet at the fact that several younger dissenters educated for the ministry in dissenting academies transferred to the universities and conformed to the Established Church. (The most notable examples are Joseph Butler and Thomas Secker; Doddridge was offered support at university in return for conforming but refused it.) Calamy's comments in his autobiography on the climate in which these defections took place are very illuminating. He points out that those who conformed at an earlier period (like Samuel Wesley, father of John and Charles, who became a high

---

[22] E.g. *Calendar*, ed. Nuttall, Letters 663, 1402.   [23] Calamy, *Life of Howe*, 127–9.
[24] Calamy, *Abridgment of Baxter's History* (1702), Chapter 9, 496–7.
[25] On numbers and social composition see Watts, *Dissenters*, Chapter 4.

churchman) turned bitterly against the dissenters, whereas those conforming under the Hanoverians kept their tempers.[26] The likely explanation is that by then latitudinarian control of the church was complete, and the threat posed to dissenters by high churchmen in Queen Anne's reign was eliminated: the Occasional Conformity Act (1711), designed to prevent dissenters from qualifying for public office by taking communion in parish churches, and the Schism Act (1714), designed to prevent them from maintaining their own educational establishments, were ineffective and were repealed early in the new reign.[27] Many dissenters of a rational persuasion were now more sympathetic to latitudinarians than to the Calvinists among themselves. Calamy comments of those who conformed that many complained of 'a spirit of imposition working among the Dissenters'.[28] He is referring here to the Salters' Hall debates of 1719 among the three bodies of the dissenters (Presbyterian, Congregationalist, and Baptist) concerning the principle of demanding subscription to orthodox Trinitarian doctrine. This demand for subscription was a reaction by some orthodox Calvinists to the spread of rationalism; the 'anti-subscribers' resisting the demand included not only the rationalists but the moderates. Toleration had in effect produced a split between the wings of dissent which the moderates attempted to bridge.[29] The problem for moderates like Watts and Doddridge who wished to combine rational free thought with evangelical orthodoxy was that the rationalists were abandoning the evangelical doctrine central to the dissenting tradition, while the orthodox, in attempting to defend doctrine by imposing tests, were betraying the rationalist principles which made the continued toleration of dissent possible.

One beneficial result of these disputes between the wings of dissent (however damaging they were seen to be at the time) was that they caused a general rethinking among dissenters about their specific identity, the nature of their tradition, and the directions in which they might move. One rational dissenter who later conformed, Strickland Gough, published anonymously in 1730 *An Enquiry into the Causes of the Decay of the Dissenting Interest*, in which he deplored the effects of the disputes, repudiated the frequently asserted view that toleration or the decline of the puritan spirit had weakened dissent, and argued that on the contrary dissenters should discontinue those puritan traditions that had become unfashionable and impolite – 'what was fashion-

---

[26] *My Own Life*, II, 503–6. Samuel Wesley attacked dissenting education and principles in *A Letter from a Country Divine* (1703), *A Defence of a Letter* (1704), and *A Reply to Mr. Palmer* (1707); they were defended by Samuel Palmer in *A Defence of the Dissenters Education* (1703) and *A Vindication* (1705). See Chapter 1 above, p. 14.

[27] On the legislation see Calamy, *My Own Life*, II, Chapter 8; Holmes, *British Politics in the Age of Anne* (1967), Chapter 3; Spivey, 'Middle Way Men', Chapter 8.

[28] *My Own Life*, II, 506.

[29] See R. Thomas, 'The Salters' Hall Watershed, 1719', in Bolam, *English Presbyterians*, Chapter 4; Spivey, 'Middle Way Men', Chapters 11–13.

able to our forefathers is now as disagreeable to us as their dress'. For Gough the future strength of dissent lay in the combination of rational principles (liberty of conscience and rejection of impositions) with polite conduct.[30] Among the replies to Gough were Doddridge's first publication, the anonymous *Free Thoughts on the Most Probable Means of Reviving the Dissenting Interest* (1730), and Watts's *An Humble Attempt towards the Revival of Practical Religion among Christians* (1731). Although they accepted Gough's rational principles and (with some qualifications) his emphasis on politeness, they agreed that the crucial point was the revival of vital practical religion as the puritans had known it, and that the essence of this religion lay in the relationship between minister and congregation, a relationship based on close knowledge of the heart and close application by the minister of evangelical doctrine to the special circumstances of the individual member of the congregation. Doddridge claimed that he had observed the success of these methods with congregations in his part of the country, where the number of dissenters had greatly increased in the last twenty years.[31] Watts frequently emphasises the strength of this affectionate, experimental, evangelical ministry of 'our fathers': 'Our fathers talked much of pious experience, and have left their writings of the same strain behind them: They were surrounded with converts, and helped to fill heaven apace'; '*we have too much left off the Way of our Fathers in distinguishing the Characters of our Hearers, and dividing the Word aright to Saints and Sinners*'; 'Surely this was the fashion and practice of our fathers amongst the puritans and protestant dissenters in their ministry ... and I wish with all my soul this sort of ministration, this manner of *dividing the word of God, and giving to each their due*, may never grow out of fashion in our places of worship'.[32] Doddridge was convinced that to abandon this evangelical tradition in pursuit of rational principles exclusively was to destroy the dissenting interest, as he urges in the second of his *Sermons to Young Persons* (1735):

It is *the good old way*, in which our fathers in the ministry went, and in which they prospered. Let us follow their steps, and exert our most vigorous efforts here ... I hope, God is my witness that I am heartily concerned for the interest of virtue, if by that be meant the advancement of practical religion; but I never expected to see it promoted by the most philosophical speculations concerning its nature, or the finest harangues of its innate beauties, when the name and peculiar doctrines of Christ are thrown off, as unfashionable incumbrances of a discourse. Experienced Christians, who have tasted the *Bread of Life*, will not contentedly be put off with such chaff: And if we imagine that the younger part of our auditors may be trained up to a relish for it, we may, perhaps, succeed in the attempt; but I much fear, that success will be the calamity of the church, and the destruction of souls.

---

[30] Gough, *Enquiry*, 3–6, 34–43.
[31] Doddridge, *Free Thoughts*, *Works*, ed. Williams and Parsons, IV, 220.
[32] Watts, Dedication to *Sermons*, I, *Works*, ed. Parsons, I, xxvii; Preface to Jennings, *Two Discourses* (1723), vii–viii; *Humble Attempt*, *Works*, ed. Parsons, IV, 68. Watts is referring to the *Directory* of 1644; see Chapter 1 above, p. 16.

And Doddridge adds the revealing footnote: 'The author has taken a greater freedom on this head, as the discourse was delivered before several candidates for the ministry, for whom he had some peculiar concern.'[33]

Since the identity of dissent thus depended to a large extent on the preacher and his relationship with his congregation, the nature of ministerial education became a central issue. Paradoxically, in the area of education, the *limited* nature of the toleration granted to dissenters proved the main strength of their interest. For a dissenting minister to officiate, the Toleration Act required subscription only to the thirty-five of the Thirty-Nine Articles that were concerned with doctrine, whereas the universities required all their students to subscribe in full. The dissenters therefore had to make provision for both the training of their ministers and the liberal education of their members intended for the professions. The dissenting academies were essential to the continuation of the tradition (which is why the high churchmen were anxious to have them made illegal): they were the principal means by which the culture, values, and attitudes of puritanism and nonconformity were transmitted to the following generations. At the same time, the rationalism inherent in the educational methods of most academies meant that this culture was profoundly transformed. The importance of Watts and Doddridge in this process cannot be overestimated. Watts was not a teacher, and his poor health restricted his activities as a minister, but he exercised enormous influence through the great range of his writings, educational and philosophical as well as religious, many of them serving as academy textbooks. Doddridge trained several of the most influential ministers of the next generation,[34] and through his educational methods, his ministerial work, and his practical writings furthered the rational as well as the evangelical tendencies of dissent. In addition, the influence of Watts and Doddridge as educationalists and evangelical publicists reached far beyond the confines of the dissenting interest.

Although both men were mainly concerned with the distinctive features of their own tradition, they looked outward as well as inward. There is little reference in their writing to the differences (partly doctrinal, partly disciplinary) that divided the three dissenting bodies: although they were Congregationalists and moderate Calvinists, they preferred to describe themselves simply as protestant dissenters. Similarly, although they regarded dissent as a distinct and superior religious tradition, they did not think that as a body it should exist in isolation, divorced from other churches or religious movements. They took great interest in other manifestations of affectionate religion, among Methodists in England and Wales, Presbyterians in Scotland, Congregationalists in New England, Lutheran pietists and Moravians in

---

[33] *Works*, ed. Williams and Parsons, II, 116–17.

[34] Orton estimated that in the twenty-two years Doddridge acted as tutor, he educated about 200 students of whom about 120 became ministers. *Works*, ed. Williams and Parsons, I, 78; *Correspondence*, ed. Humphreys, V, 546–52. See n. 162 below.

Germany, and in missions in India and North America; they corresponded or had dealings with the leaders of these movements, for example George Whitefield, John Wesley, the Countess of Huntingdon, Jonathan Edwards, and Count Zinzendorf.[35] However, they were cautious in their welcoming of these manifestations (Watts more so than Doddridge) wherever they appeared to be without a rational basis and hence enthusiastic rather than truly affectionate and evangelical. (Watts, for example, was more critical than Doddridge of Whitefield.)[36] In addition, Watts and Doddridge maintained close links with the Established Church, and evidently valued highly their associations with men who were sometimes notably unsympathetic to affectionate religion. Watts's friendship with Edmund Gibson, Bishop of London, and Doddridge's with William Warburton, future Bishop of Gloucester, are cases in point. The terms used by Doddridge in particular to designate this open-mindedness towards other denominations, movements and churches are candour and catholicism. In a letter of 14 March 1748 to another Anglican friend, George Lyttelton, Doddridge claimed that none of the dissenting ministers he had trained was a bigot against the Establishment, and that in the last twenty five years 'a generous and catholick temper' had spread in his part of the country.[37] In Free Thoughts (1730) he had expressed the hope that the new generation of dissenters would learn the 'united principles of piety and catholicism':[38] in other words, the distinctive values of the dissenting tradition should be maintained together with friendship for other churches and movements not necessarily sympathetic to all those values. The possible inconsistency of these aims, like the tension between the rational and evangelical sides of dissent, may explain some of the difficulties faced by Watts and Doddridge in defining and propagating their idea of affectionate religion, and some of the differences in language and rhetoric employed in works addressed to audiences belonging to different traditions.

2 The audiences of Watts and Doddridge

In his dedication to Watts of The Rise and Progress of Religion in the Soul (1745) Doddridge, praising Watts for the range and influence of his writings and his capacity to reach different kinds of audience, imagines him addressing these

---

35 See Calendar, ed. Nuttall, Introduction; Davis, Watts, Chapter 3. For relationships with pietists see Nuttall, 'Continental Pietists and the Evangelical Movement'; for Watts's relation to the New England revival see Edwards, The Great Awakening, ed. Goen (1972) and Pratt, Watts and His Gifts of Books to Yale College (1938); for Doddridge's relationship with Wesley see I. Rivers, 'Dissenting and Methodist Books of Practical Divinity', in Rivers, ed., Books and their Readers (1982), 145–52.

36 See e.g. Milner, Watts, 638; Correspondence, ed. Humphreys, IV, 56, 292; Calendar, ed. Nuttall, Letters 705, 934, 1611.

37 Calendar, ed. Nuttall, Letter 1322.   38 Works, ed. Williams and Parsons, IV, 219.

audiences simultaneously, children, students in academies and universities, ministers, congregations, families, individuals:

> I congratulate you, dear Sir, that while you are in a multitude of families and schools of the lower class, condescending to the humble, yet important work of forming infant minds to the first rudiments of religious knowledge, and devout impressions, by your various catechisms and divine songs; you are also daily reading lectures of logic, and other useful branches of philosophy, to studious youths; and this not only in private academies, but in the most public and celebrated seats of learning; nor merely in Scotland, and in our American colonies ... but through the amiable candor of some excellent men and accomplished tutors, in our English universities too. I congratulate you, that you are teaching, no doubt, hundreds of ministers, and thousands of private Christians, by your sermons, and other theological writings ... But above all, I congratulate you, that by your sacred poetry, especially by your psalms, and your hymns, you are leading the worship, and I trust also animating the devotion of myriads, in our public assemblies every sabbath, and in their families or closets every day.[39]

This image of the different books representing so many voices, of the infant teacher, lecturer, or minister, adapted to particular hearers, effectively draws attention to Watts's oratorical instinct. Watts's sense of the needs of any particular audience is always very strong: in Part I, Chapter 8 of *The Improvement of the Mind* (1741), 'Of enquiring into the Sense and Meaning of any Writer or Speaker', he advises, 'Consider not only the person who is introduced speaking, *but the persons to whom the speech is directed*, the circumstances of time and place, the temper and spirit of the speaker, as well as the temper and spirit of the hearers', and in Part II (1751) he writes of Ergates, his model of the good preacher (which his friend and biographer Thomas Gibbons said could be applied to Watts himself), 'He makes the nature of his subject, and the necessity of his hearers, the great rule to direct him what method he shall choose in every sermon, that he may the better enlighten, convince and persuade.'[40] This sense of the importance of the relationship between writer and reader and the obligations it imposes informs all Watts's work.

Watts's writings can be classified according to subject and intention as practical and evangelical, controversial, educational, and speculative; the audiences he addresses on different occasions range in religious affiliation from his own particular congregation at Bury Street, London,[41] congregations of dissenters in general, disputing dissenters, all protestants regardless of

[39] *Works*, ed. Williams and Parsons, I, 212.
[40] *Works*, ed. Parsons, VI, 221, 336; see Gibbons, *Memoirs*, 200.
[41] The Mark Lane congregation moved to a new chapel in Bury Street in 1708; see Milner, *Watts*, 209–10. It became a centre of moderate Calvinism. See the 'Bury Street Sermons', i.e. *Faith and Practice Represented in fifty-four Sermons on the Principal Heads of the Christian Religion*, 2 vols. (1735), by Watts *et al.*, strongly recommended by Doddridge in the Preface to *Ten Sermons*, *Works*, ed. Williams and Parsons, II, 212, and in his letter to John Wesley, 18 June 1746, *Correspondence*, ed. Humphreys, IV, 489.

denomination, doubting Christians, to those who in varying degrees have placed themselves beyond the bounds of Christianity – Arians, Socinians, and deists. They also range in age and intellectual attainment from small children and students to philosophers, and in social class from the 'mean' and 'vulgar' to the 'polite'. The greatest contrast is between works of an evangelical and of a speculative or non-religious kind, and Watts on several occasions draws attention to the difference between the cold rational language of philosophical argument, which is intended to work demonstratively on the reader's intellect, and the warm affectionate language of evangelical preaching, which is aimed at arousing the passions. Watts warns the dissenting minister in *An Humble Attempt*:

remember you are a minister of Christ and the gospel, sent to publish to men what God has revealed by his prophets and apostles, and by his Son Jesus; and not a heathen philosopher to teach the people merely what the light of reason can search out: you are not to stand up here as a professor of ancient or modern philosophy, nor an usher in the school of Plato or Seneca, or Mr. Locke; but as a teacher in the school of Christ, as a preacher of the New Testament.[42]

Doddridge similarly contrasts the roles of the heathen philosopher and the Christian minister, and the polite philosophical essay and the lively evangelical discourse.[43] The model Watts recommends for 'sacred oratory' – 'bright, warm and pathetic language, to strike the imagination or to affect the heart, to kindle the divine passions or to melt the soul' – is Scripture, especially the prophets, psalms, and epistles of Paul.[44] The contrast of cold and heat runs through Watts's dedication of his first volume of sermons to his own congregation:

A statue hung round with moral sentences, or a marble pillar with divine truths inscribed upon it, may preach coldly to the understanding, while devotion freezes at the heart: But the prophets and apostles were *burning and shining lights* [John 5:35]; they were all taught by inspiration to make the words of truth glitter like sun-beams, and to operate like a *hammer*, and *a fire* [Jeremiah 23:29] and *a two-edged sword* [Hebrews 4:12]. The movements of sacred passion may be the ridicule of an age which pretends to nothing but calm reasoning. Life and zeal in the ministry of the word, may be despised by men of luke-warm and dying religion: *Fervency of spirit in the service of the Lord* [Acts 18:25], may become the scoff and jest of the critic and the profane: But this very life and zeal, this sacred fervency, shall still remain one bright character of a christian preacher . . .[45]

Conversely, Watts ridicules Shaftesbury in *The Improvement of the Mind*, I for his display of 'what some folks now-a-days call politeness' and the inefficacy of

---

42 *Works*, ed. Parsons, IV, 14.
43 *Lectures on Preaching, Works*, ed. Williams and Parsons, V, 459–60; *Ordination Sermons, Works*, II, 243.
44 *Humble Attempt, Works*, ed. Parsons, IV, 31; cf. II, 311–12 (quoted at the head of this chapter), and *The Improvement of the Mind* I, *Works*, VI, 258.
45 *Works*, ed. Parsons, I, xxvi.

his style: 'How many have you ever actually reclaimed by this smooth soft method, and these fine words? . . . the wild passions and appetites of men are too violent to be restrained by such mild and silken language'.[46] And Gibbons records Watts's saying that 'Polished and harmonious language is oftentimes like oil flowing smoothly over marble which leaves no traces behind it.'[47]

Watts's recurrent emphasis upon the passions and their function will be examined in the next section. Here it should be stressed that Watts uses this 'warm' style sparingly: it is the style of ministerial exhortation, found in the volumes of *Sermons on Various Subjects* (1721, 1723, 1729), *The World to Come* (1739, 1745) and *Evangelical Discourses* (1747), though Watts is always firmly in control of his 'sacred fervency' – as Gibbons notes, 'in proper places the sermons are both cool and argumentative, and again flaming and pathetic'.[48] It is also, though again with some qualification, the style of the poems, hymns, and psalms, *Horae Lyricae* (1706, enlarged 1709), *Hymns and Spiritual Songs* (1707, enlarged 1709), and *The Psalms of David* (1719). In the Preface to *Hymns and Spiritual Songs* Watts says that he intended in the first of these volumes to 'please and profit the politer part of mankind, without offending the plainer sort of christians', and in the second 'to promote the pious entertainment of souls truly serious, even of the meanest capacity' without giving 'disgust to persons of richer sense, and nicer education'. With the 'plain' or 'mean' audience in mind, Watts finds himself obliged to restrain his language: 'The metaphors are generally sunk to the level of vulgar capacities . . . some of the beauties of poesy are neglected, and some wilfully defaced: I have thrown out the lines that were too sonorous, and have given an allay to the verse, lest a more exalted turn of thought or language should darken or disturb the devotion of the weakest souls.'[49]

In spite of his disclaimer in the dedication of the first volume of sermons – 'nor have I affected that easy indolence of style which is the dry delight of some modish writers, the cold and insipid pleasure of men who pretend to politeness'[50] – Watts does in the majority of his writings, of a controversial or educational or theoretical kind, use polite language and accommodate his tone and attitudes to the expectations of polite society. Samuel Johnson exaggerated the point from the perspective of a churchman: 'Dr. *Watts* was one of the first who taught the Dissenters to write and speak like other men, by shewing them that elegance might consist with piety'.[51] In the controversial writings this 'politeness' is an essential attribute of Watts's moderate, rationalist position and his appeal to audiences with values other than those assumed by the evangelical writings. This difference of tone between categories undoubtedly creates problems of interpretation.

---

[46] *Works*, ed. Parsons, VI, 207, 236–7.   [47] *Memoirs*, 156.   [48] *Memoirs*, 199.

[49] *Works*, ed. Parsons, VII, 122. On Watts's poetics see Davie, *A Gathered Church*, Lecture 2.

[50] *Works*, ed. Parsons, I, xxvi.

[51] *Boswell's Life of Johnson*, ed. Hill, rev. Powell (1934–50), I, 312.

In works addressed chiefly to dissenters but sometimes assuming also a wider readership, such as the three sermons entitled 'A Rational Defence of the Gospel' (1723), *The Ruin and Recovery of Mankind* (1740), *Orthodoxy and Charity United* (1745), and *The Rational Foundation of a Christian Church and The Terms of Christian Communion* (1747), Watts makes plain his own position and his hostility to certain beliefs and attitudes. He insists on his own orthodoxy, aligning himself broadly in the Preface to *Orthodoxy and Charity* with the doctrinal position of the puritans and protestant reformers: 'By the word orthodoxy, the author means all those christian doctrines, which were generally approved in the last age ... by almost all the protestant dissenters in the nation; even those great doctrines, on which the reformation from the church of Rome was built.' They are summarised as the doctrines of the fall, the pardon of sin and sanctifying grace, the sacrifice and atonement of Christ, the repentance of sinners, justification by faith, obedience to the law, and the resurrection.[52] He explicitly condemns those who are undermining this traditional orthodoxy: Socinians who deny the divinity and sacrifice of Christ are little better than deists who have substituted natural religion for the gospel. Watts repeats these charges again and again, but they are summarised most urgently in *Orthodoxy and Charity*:

In this present age, the popish and pelagian doctrines of justification by works, and salvation by the power of our own free-will, are publicly maintained and preached abundantly through the land: The socinian and the arminian errors are revived and spread exceedingly, whereby Jesus Christ is robbed of his godhead, or his satisfaction, or both, and the blessed Spirit denied in the glory of his offices: For deism and natural religion, in opposition to Christianity, daily prevail.

Though some may be willing to accommodate themselves to this drift towards rationalism, and may hope 'by preaching the gospel a little more conformably to natural religion, in a mere rational or legal form, to bring it down as near as may be to their scheme', Watts is adamant 'that we should in such a day stand up for the defence of the gospel in the full glory of its most important doctrines, and in the full freedom of its grace; that we should preach it in its divinest and most evangelical form'.[53] And in *The Terms of Christian Communion* he ridicules the idea of a congregation containing members of widely differing or contradictory beliefs, or a preacher attempting to address such a congregation:

He can scarce express any thing about the redemption and atonement of Christ, but he awakens either the calvinist or the socinian, to jealousy, and affronts their sacred doctrines: He must not ascribe glory to the Father, Son and Spirit, lest he displease the unitarians in his assembly; nor must he neglect it, lest the trinitarian take umbrage. He dares not name the word perseverance, lest the arminian be angry; and if he should talk of falling from grace, the calvinist trembles, and half despairs ... He must not pray for forgiveness of sins, for the antinomian believer does not want it; nor for almighty

[52] *Works*, ed. Parsons, II, 403.   [53] *Works*, ed. Parsons, II, 442.

sanctifying grace, for the remonstrant christian knows no need of it: He must not confess original sin, for the pelagian disowns himself guilty; nor dares he mention a word of *the imputed righteousness of Christ, or justification by faith alone*, lest half the assembly rise in arms against him ...[54]

Watts is very precise as to the limits of charity: it must not be extended to 'a socinian, a professed pelagian, or an antinomian of the grossest kind'.[55]

This tone of embattled orthodoxy is not, however, typical of Watts's controversial writing. The position he usually adopts, doctrinally and rhetorically, is that of a moderate or reconciler or advocate of the middle way, and there is some tension evident between his desire to uphold evangelical principles and his wish to bring together disputing factions and wherever possible to demonstrate that differences of opinion are insignificant. In *Orthodoxy and Charity*, the hand of moderation is withheld from the extremists: 'as for the high-flyers, or extreme and rigid party-men of either side', says Watts, 'I leave them out in my present account, while I mention the little differences among the men of moderation, among whom I reckon far the greatest part of the protestant dissenters in England, to be at this time'.[56] He defines what he means by moderate in *The Terms of Christian Communion*, in the process of arguing that although those who differ over doctrine or practice cannot join in the same communion, they can have occasional communion together (he instances here moderate episcopalians, Baptists, Lutherans, and Calvinists): 'Those I call moderate, who are not so strict and rigid in their opinions, nor run into such extremes, nor place so great a necessity in their particular modes of worship or discipline, but being persons of serious piety and of extensive charity, they think it proper to omit or alter, on particular occasions, what may be offensive to either side'.[57] In Essay 2 of *Orthodoxy and Charity*, 'The Form of the Gospel', and Questions 13 and 14 of *Ruin and Recovery*, 'How far has the glorious Undertaking of our Lord Jesus Christ provided any Hope of Salvation for those who were not eternally chosen, and given into the Hands of Christ, to be redeemed and saved?', and 'Can the different Opinions of Christians, concerning the Operations of divine Grace on the Souls of Men, be reconciled?', Watts attempts to reconcile the 'little differences' between those who lean towards Calvinist or Arminian accounts of grace and free will by arguing that both are true and compatible with each other: apparently contradictory texts of Scripture can be reconciled by combining the Calvinist doctrine of absolute salvation for the elect and the Arminian doctrine of conditional salvation for all, so that there is absolute salvation for the elect and conditional salvation for the non-elect. 'The calm doctrinal truth, stripped of all rhetoric and figures, lies nearer to the middle, or at least ... some of these appearing extremes, are more reconcileable than

---

[54] *Works*, ed. Parsons, III, 288.   [55] *Works*, ed. Parsons, III, 266; cf. II, 404; VI, 388.
[56] *Works*, ed. Parsons, II, 433.
[57] *Works*, ed. Parsons, III, 293.

angry men will generally allow.'[58] Watts's Baxterian compromise here is of course not original, and his tone and method of arguing are of more interest than his doctrinal solutions. In Question 14 of *Ruin and Recovery*, following Baxter's model in Book II of *Catholick Theologie* (1675), he characterises the representatives of the opposing and reconciling views as A (Arminian), C (Calvinist), and R (Reconciler), and in the conclusion he explains that he has endeavoured to see what relief can be given to harsh-sounding doctrines.[59] This habit not so much of personifying doctrines as of seeing them in terms of their human and social consequences is typical of Watts, and throws some light on what he means by charity: in *The Terms of Christian Communion* he writes, 'I hope I have kept the middle way between a libertinism of principles, and a narrow uncharitable spirit.'[60] The emphasis on charity and reconciliation does not lead Watts into 'libertinism of principles' (by which presumably he means the view that one person's principles are as good as another's), but it does lead him deliberately to play down doctrinal difference and to stress human sympathy.

This tendency is apparent even in works addressed to those he thinks should be excluded from charity. Watts appeals directly to Arians in *The Arian Invited to the Orthodox Faith* (1724), to Socinians in *The Redeemer and the Sanctifier, or The Sacrifice of Christ* (1736), to 'doubting Christians' in *A Caveat against Infidelity* (1729), and to deists in *Self-Love and Virtue Reconciled only by Religion* (1739), *The Strength and Weakness of Human Reason* (1731), and part of *The Ruin and Recovery*. The assumption underlying these works is that differences of doctrine are exacerbated by unnecessary enmity between their adherents. Although Watts does not think that protestants of different opinions should be members of the same congregation, he does approve of occasional communion between them; similarly, although he holds the views of Socinians and deists to be erroneous, he believes that closer contact between orthodox and heterodox will soften their differences. Thus in *The Sacrifice of Christ* and *The Strength and Weakness of Human Reason* he uses the familiar device of a dialogue between representatives of opposing views, showing how those moving towards the extremes can be brought back to the middle ground. In *The Sacrifice of Christ* Agrippa represents the Socinian and Paulinus the orthodox position; Cavenor, who is sympathetic to Agrippa, is won over to Paulinus' view not by Paulinus' supporter Ferventio but by the moderate, rational summing up of Charistes. In *The Strength and Weakness of Human Reason* Logisto, who is, Watts stresses, 'an enquiring deist, not a resolved and obstinate unbeliever',[61] debates the question whether reason is an adequate guide to

---

58 *Orthodoxy and Charity, Works*, ed. Parsons, II, 441; *Ruin and Recovery, Works*, III, 468–72. Watts points out that 'Calvin himself has frequently intimated in his comments on scripture, that Christ did in some sense die for all men', *Works*, III, 472.

59 *Works*, ed. Parsons, III, 503. See Chapter 3 above, pp. 102, 138.

60 *Works*, ed. Parsons, III, 262.   61 *Works*, ed. Parsons, III, vi.

religion, morality and happiness; here also it is the summing up of the moderator Sophronius, who agrees with Logisto that reason is speculatively sufficient, but with Pithander that it is practically insufficient, which convinces Logisto.

The outcome of these debates is of course already decided: Watts has no doubt about the difference between truth and error. What is important is the tone of these works, the intellectual climate they are intended to foster, the emphasis on converse between men of different opinions, the assumption that open-minded enquiry will support truth. Such assumptions pervade Watts's principal educational writings, *Logick: or The Right Use of Reason in the Enquiry after Truth* (1725) and *The Improvement of the Mind* (Part I 1741, Part II 1751),[62] the works which (apart from the hymns) probably gained him his widest audience at the time. He advocates wide reading, converse, and travel to combat dogmatism, open-mindedness combined with settled principles, and the rational testing of ideas.[63] The account of Agathus' education of his son Eugenio, in *A Discourse on the Education of Children and Youth* (1753), section x, clearly illustrates Watts's view that evangelical principles are compatible with and indeed supported by rational free thought. The whole chapter, entitled 'Of the proper Degrees of Liberty and Restraint in the Education of a Son', is a parable of the problems facing dissenters in their attempt to reconcile traditional and rational values. Modern youth turn against *'the practices of our fathers'* because they were *'precise and foolish'*, and their faith because it was *'absurd and mysterious'*, but there is a middle way between severity and indulgence. Eugenio is taught scriptural doctrine, but he is encouraged to reason about everything and given 'liberty of thought'. Watts characteristically and optimistically assumes that free thought will lead to evangelical conclusions: Eugenio 'dares to believe the doctrines *of original sin, the satisfaction of Christ, the influences of the blessed spirit,* and other despised truths of the gospel; and this not because his ancestors believed them, but because he cannot avoid the evidence of them in scripture'. He is ready to give reasons for his beliefs, but he will not argue with those who ridicule religion. 'Thus he supports the character of a Christian with honour; he confines his faith to his bible, and his practice to all the rules of piety; and yet thinks as freely as that vain herd of atheists and deists who arrogate the name of free-thinkers to themselves.'[64]

Doddridge was entirely in sympathy with the diversity of Watts's aims and with the rational and evangelical tendencies of his thought. However, partly from deliberate choice, and partly because of the demands of his career, the

---

[62] Part II appeared posthumously, edited by Doddridge and David Jennings, Watts's literary executors.

[63] *Logick*, Part I, Chapter 5; *The Improvement of the Mind*, Part I, Chapters 4, 18, *Works*, ed. Parsons, VI.

[64] *Works*, ed. Parsons, VI, 383–8.

range of Doddridge's writings and the kinds of audience he addressed were more limited, though this did not prevent several of his books from having a very wide readership. Watts's work as a minister, which he was unable to carry out for long periods of time, took second place to his writing; Doddridge's primary obligations were to his academy and church, and his writings are an extension of his roles as tutor and pastor. Apart from his involvement in the debate about the future of dissent in *Free Thoughts* and in the anti-deist controversy in three letters he published in answer to Henry Dodwell's *Christianity Not Founded on Argument* (1742–3), he avoided controversial writing. He did not think that the rehearsal of disagreements was profitable – 'The event of many a voluminous controversy has been this; that men of contrary parties have sat down more attached to their own opinions than they were at the beginning, and much more estranged in their affections' – and he warned against different sects insisting 'too rigorously on the history of former wrongs and injuries' ('Christian Candour and Unanimity', 1750).[65] Though he described himself in a letter of 1724 as 'in all the most important points a Calvinist',[66] and his treatment of Calvinist doctrines in Part VIII of his *Lectures on Divinity* bears this out,[67] he warned his ministerial students against preaching on 'the highest points of Calvinism' (such as the imputation of Adam's sin to Christ, reprobation, and irresistible grace), because 'these doctrines may be abused, and prejudice some against the more necessary doctrines of Calvinism' (the mediation and atonement of Christ, and the influence of the Spirit).[68] He did not insist on his own orthodoxy to others, and indeed regarded the term itself with some distrust; in 1727 he rejected an invitation from a congregation in Norfolk because they insisted on it too much: 'there is a certain equivocal word beginning with an O— which prevents my entertaining any thought of the matter, for we are here [i.e. Harborough] the most catholic people in the world'.[69] Doddridge hoped that distinctions between parties and denominations might be broken down by mutual candour (i.e. trust and generosity) and by an emphasis on catholic rather than sectarian principles. One reason for his support for the County Infirmary at Northampton was that churchmen and dissenters were jointly involved in the venture: 'as it is necessarily concerted upon a plan, in which all parties and denominations are equally concerned, it will probably be a means of promoting more candid and catholic sentiments, in consequence of repeated opportunities of mutual converse' ('The Duty of Compassion to the Sick', 1743).[70] He hoped that his edition of the *Expository Works* of the Scottish episcopalian Robert Leighton (1748) might 'promote that spirit of catholi-

---

[65] *Ordination Sermons, Works*, ed. Williams and Parsons, III, 266, 278.
[66] *Correspondence*, ed. Humphreys, I, 439; *Calendar*, ed. Nuttall, Letter 150.
[67] *Works*, ed. Williams and Parsons, IV, especially Lectures 184–7.
[68] *Lectures on Preaching, Works*, ed. Williams and Parsons, V, 441.
[69] *Correspondence*, ed. Humphreys, II, 322.
[70] *Sermons on Public Occasions, Works*, ed. Williams and Parsons, III, 109.

cism, for which our Author was so remarkable',[71] and that his own writings might have a similar effect: 'as I endeavour to write on the common general principles of christianity, and not in the narrow spirit of any particular party, I bless God I have the pleasure to see my writings, imperfect as they are, favoured by many excellent persons of different denominations; and I hope therefore, they may be a means of spreading a serious and candid spirit'.[72]

Doddridge's writings fall into two main categories, educational and practical. His educational works consist of lectures delivered to his students over many years and published posthumously: *A Course of Lectures on the Principal Subjects in Pneumatology, Ethics, and Divinity* (1763), forming the centre of the course taken by all the students, and *Lectures on Preaching* (1804), addressed to the ministerial students. Both the substance and structure of his teaching, and the educational and intellectual principle of free enquiry underlying it, owed much to his own tutor, John Jennings. Doddridge's course of pneumatology,[73] ethics, and divinity begins with the faculties of the human mind, continues with natural religion (the being of God, the nature of moral virtue, the immortality of the soul), goes on to the evidences for revelation, and concludes with evangelical doctrine. The lecturing method (described by Orton in his *Memoirs of Doddridge*, Chapter 6) shows the way in which Doddridge encouraged free enquiry: he assembled from several authors arguments pro and con a particular subject, discussed their merits, and indicated his own position; the students then followed up the references for themselves and at the next lecture were questioned on their reading and conclusions. By this means they acquired a wide knowledge of contemporary moral and religious thought (Doddridge's interest in contemporary moral philosophy is striking) and were introduced to a heterogeneous group of authors ranging from dissenters and churchmen to deists and sceptics. For example in Lecture 23, 'On the Existence of God', the students were directed to Hume's *Philosophical Essays*. Doddridge believed, with Watts, that such freedom of enquiry would necessarily lend support to evangelical doctrine: he told John Wesley, in a letter of 18 June 1746 based on material from *Lectures on Preaching* recommending books for Wesley's *Christian Library*, 'you will not by any means imagine that I intend to recommend the particular notions of all the writers I here mention, which may, indeed, sufficiently appear from their absolute contrariety to each other in a multitude of instances; but I think that, in order to defend the truth, it is very proper that a young minister should know the chief strength of error'.[74] Doddridge's Miltonic

---

71 Leighton, *The Whole Works*, ed. Pearson (1825), 'Dr Doddridge's Preface', I, cciii.
72 Preface to *Ten Sermons* (2nd edn, 1741), *Works*, ed. Williams and Parsons, II, 211.
73 For the changes in the meaning of pneumatology in the seventeenth century from the study of grace to that of separated souls, hence psychology, see Fiering, *Moral Philosophy* (1981), 211 ff. Pneumatology is also broadly used in the eighteenth century, especially at Scottish universities, to mean natural religion.
74 *Correspondence*, ed. Humphreys, IV, 492–3; *Calendar*, ed. Nuttall, Letter 1166. This is not a view Wesley shared. For the principles underlying the *Christian Library* see Chapter 5 below, pp. 218–19.

confidence seems ill-founded in retrospect: he does not recognise any conflict between his rationalist intellectual and his practical evangelical aims. His *Course of Lectures* was widely used in other academies by tutors who had been his pupils, and though some continued to uphold his evangelical views, there is no doubt that the kind of speculative freedom he had encouraged lent support in the period after his death to the spread of unitarianism.

However, despite his wide reading and his educational principles, Doddridge's interest in theoretical speculation was strictly subordinated to his practical aims. Unlike Watts, whose *Doctrine of the Passions* and *Philosophical Essays* deal with problems of psychology and epistemology, Doddridge wrote no theoretical works. In the *Lectures on Preaching*, the culmination of the course for ministerial students and an extremely useful guide to the temper of his religion, Doddridge emphasises throughout the importance of practice. He recommends a wide range of practical writers to be used as models, drawing his examples from puritans, including Bolton and Sibbes, nonconformists, including Owen and Goodwin ('Both highly evangelical, but both very obscure'), dissenters, including Baxter and Howe, and members of the Established Church, including Tillotson, Barrow, and Wilkins. His analyses concentrate on the authors' style and rhetoric; he is not concerned here with their doctrinal positions. Both doctrinal difficulties and irrelevant speculation are out of place in sermons. Thus in Lecture 5, 'Rules for composing Sermons', he warns his students against dealing with subjects such as 'the doctrines of natural religion', 'the evidences of Christianity', 'the inexplicable mysteries of the gospel', and 'the highest points of Calvinism'. They are urged instead to preach on subjects such as 'those which relate immediately to Christ', 'the Spirit and his operations', 'the privileges of the children of God', 'the love of Christ and a devotional temper', and 'the temptations and exercises of a pious soul'. In Lecture 6, 'On different Strains of Preaching' (i.e. 'the general manner in which the whole discourse is composed'), of the evangelical strain he stresses: 'Let it be a maxim with you, never to preach without introducing Christ, and the Holy Spirit.' In Lecture 8, 'On the Choice of Thoughts', he insists that these must be useful ('An ingenious man, by attentive thought, may find out a set of just and rational, yet trifling and useless speculation. – BUTLER'S sermons furnish us with some examples of this kind') and popular – 'that is, suited to the people in general'.[75]

Doddridge may have felt occasional regret that he deliberately avoided speculative writing for a learned audience in order to devote himself to practical writing for a popular one; in the Introduction to *The Rise and Progress of Religion in the Soul* (1745), a devotional handbook written at Watts's suggestion, he states with awkward condescension that for the sake of 'real religion' 'he is willing to lay aside many of those curious amusements in

---

[75] *Works*, ed. Williams and Parsons, V, 439–44, 446–7, 453–4.

science which might suit his own private taste, and perhaps open a way for some reputation in the learned world. For this he is willing to wave [*sic*] the laboured ornaments of speech, that he may, if possible, descend to the capacity of the lowest part of mankind.'[76] In the Preface to *Ten Sermons*, however, there is none of this defensiveness: 'If any ask, why I publish so many things on these practical subjects, so often handled by a variety of writers; I answer in a few words, with all simplicity ... "Because I know the gospel to be true, and through divine grace I feel in my heart, an ardent concern for the salvation of men's souls." '[77] These practical works fall broadly into two main categories: the sermons, addressed to the immediate audience of his own or neighbouring dissenting congregations, and three works addressed to a much wider public including members of the Established Church. Within these broad groups, Doddridge is always careful to define his specific audience. Thus in the sermons particular sections of the congregation are singled out – for example parents in *Sermons on the Religious Education of Children* (1732), ministerial students in various *Ordination Sermons*, the young in *Sermons to Young Persons* (1735) and *Ten Sermons on the Power and Grace of Christ* (1736). The works which were intended for and reached a wide public are similarly differentiated. *The Family Expositor* (6 volumes, 1738–56), a detailed commentary on the New Testament, was written 'chiefly to promote *family religion*' and especially for the use of those without a learned education.[78] *The Rise and Progress of Religion* caters for all the ranks of Christian readers (distinguished as in Baxter's scheme by spiritual status rather than age or social class or denomination), from the careless sinner to the experienced Christian, and under Watts's close supervision Doddridge tried to make the book suitable to as large an audience as possible: 'I have studied the greatest plainness of speech, that the lowest of my readers may, if possible, be able to understand every word'.[79] He clearly found this very difficult to do. Watts had hoped, as he says in a letter of 10 April 1744, 'for a small Book for the Poor, like Baxters *Call to the Unconverted*', and he tested Doddridge's writing for intelligibility by reading it to his servants.[80] Doddridge to some extent followed Watts's advice to shorten his sentences and use easier words, but was reluctant to abandon his typically more expansive polite style.[81] He had his eye on the polite audience as well as the popular one, and did not wish to lose the former by addressing the latter. *Some Remarkable Passages in the Life of the Honourable Col. James Gardiner* (1747), an exemplary biography and conversion

---

[76] *Works*, ed. Williams and Parsons, I, 218–19.
[77] *Works*, ed. Williams and Parsons, II, 211.
[78] *Works*, ed. Williams and Parsons, VI, 9.   [79] *Works*, ed. Williams and Parsons, I, 215.
[80] *Calendar*, ed. Nuttall, Letter 963. For Baxter's scheme see Chapter 3 above, pp. 118–19. See Nuttall, *Baxter and Doddridge*, and Rivers, 'Dissenting and Methodist Books', 139–45.
[81] This can be seen by comparing the two versions he printed of the form of self-dedication to God, the second an abridgement of the first, in Chapter 17 of *The Rise and Progress*.

narrative of the close friend whom Doddridge regarded as a 'Christian hero',[82] is in contrast intended for an educated audience, some of whom are assumed to be, if not sympathetic to deism, then certainly antipathetic to enthusiasm. It is characteristic of Doddridge's practical works that he attempts to sustain the fiction of the author's speaking voice, so that his audience almost literally become hearers rather than readers. Hence in his dedication to his congregation of *Sermons on the Religious Education of Children* he explains that he wanted the sermons when first delivered to be 'a warm and serious address to you. I have likewise, for the same reason, retained that form in transcribing them for the press; though I am sensible it might have appeared more fashionable and polite, to have cast them into a different mould, and to have proposed my remarks in a more cool and general way.'[83] In *The Rise and Progress* the voice is more intimate, no longer that of a preacher to a congregation: 'I shall here speak in a looser and freer manner, as a friend to a friend, just as I would do, if I were to be in person admitted to a private audience, by one whom I tenderly loved, and whose circumstances and character I knew to be like that, which the title of one chapter or another of this treatise describes.'[84] In these and similar statements of intent learning, politeness, the written word, coolness, generality, are set against practical use, plainness, the speaking voice, warmth, liveliness, immediacy, intimacy. This opposition, and the preference of the second mode, is carefully calculated: it represents an attempt both to revive in an eighteenth-century context certain characteristics of the puritan tradition, and to strengthen those characteristics by basing them on a new religious psychology. It is this attempt that gives the work of Watts and Doddridge its importance.

3 The rhetoric of the affections

In the Preface to *Philosophical Essays on Various Subjects* (1733) Watts writes: 'Many advantages in moral sciences attend a right notion of the union of soul and body, the sensations, the appetites, the passions, and various operations which are derived thence. This hath been, I confess, a favourite employment of my thoughts'.[85] The unassuming tone of Watts's 'confession' here, appropriate as it is to the speculative, tentative arguments of the essays, belies his seriousness. His principal motive for wishing to investigate the relationship between the various faculties of soul and body, in particular the reason, will and affections, is in order to establish the part played by these faculties in religion, and hence the ways in which the minister or religious writer can work on these faculties for practical religious ends. Watts explores this relationship

---

[82] *Works*, ed. Williams and Parsons, IV, 104.   [83] *Works*, ed. Williams and Parsons, II, vii.
[84] *Works*, ed. Williams and Parsons, I, 223.
[85] *Works*, ed. Parsons, VI, 481. On Watts's philosophical interests see Laird, 'Concerning Dr Isaac Watts', in *Philosophical Incursions into English Literature* (1946).

in two connected works, *The Doctrine of the Passions Explained and Improved* and *Discourses of the Love of God, and the Use and Abuse of the Passions in Religion* (1729, revised and enlarged 1732), and illustrates how this doctrine should be put to practical use in *An Humble Attempt towards the Revival of Practical Religion*. Doddridge's interest in the theory is evident in the first part of *A Course of Lectures* and *Lectures on Preaching*; in turn the implications of the theory can be seen to have had a considerable influence on the method and style of *The Rise and Progress of Religion* and *The Life of Gardiner*.

Watts and Doddridge are agreed as to both the essential role of reason in religion, and its limitations. This dual treatment approximates to Locke's, which is optimistic in Book IV of the *Essay concerning Human Understanding* and more cautious in *The Reasonableness of Christianity*. Watts's views on reason are summed up in his notes of 1705 on Martin Clifford's *A Treatise of Human Reason* (1674),[86] and restated many times, notably in 'A Rational Defence of the Gospel', *The Strength and Weakness of Human Reason*, and *The Rational Foundation of a Christian Church*. It is through reason that man receives, tests, and accepts revelation: 'It must be granted, that men of sense and learning and inquiry, are led by reason to the acknowledgement of the divinity of scripture; deducing this conclusion from a hundred moral arguments and probabilities, which united amount to a certainty and demonstration. Thus by reason we find out the rule of religion which is infallible; but then our reason must subject itself to be guided by that rule which is divine and infallible' (notes on Clifford).[87] 'Man is obliged to religion because he is a reasonable creature. Reason directs and obliges us not only to search out and practise the will of God, as far as natural conscience will lead us, but also to examine, receive, and obey, all the revelations which come from God, where we are placed within the reach of their proper evidences' (*The Rational Foundation of a Christian Church*).[88] The two springs of light in man are reason and revelation, which cannot contradict but rather mutually support each other: 'Now as the revelation of God in an illustrious manner supplies the deficiencies of our reason, and enlightens our natural darkness in the knowledge of divine things, so the exercise of our reasoning powers is very necessary to assist us not only in the understanding of the several parts of revelation, but in reconciling them to each other as well as to the dictates of right reason' (Preface to *Ruin and Recovery*).[89] The believer must be rationally satisfied of the basis of his beliefs before acting on them: 'Even the most mysterious and sublime doctrines of revelation, are not to be believed without a just reason for it; nor should our pious affections be engaged in the defence of them, till we have plain and

---

[86] In Milner, *Watts*, 122 ff; Palmer, *Life of Watts by Johnson* (2nd edn, 1791), Appendix I. On the controversy caused by Clifford's book see Harth, *Contexts of Dryden's Thought* (1968), 236–42.
[87] Milner, *Watts*, 125.   [88] *Works*, ed. Parsons, III, 195.
[89] *Works*, ed. Parsons, III, 369; cf. *Logick, Works*, VI, 120.

convincing proof that they are certainly revealed' (*The Improvement of the Mind,* Part I).[90]

This assumption that religion must be 'a reasonable service' (Romans 12:1)[91] is fully shared by Doddridge and underlies his answer to Dodwell, as he explains in a letter to his wife of 2 January 1743: 'It is far from being my design to satisfy weak Christians in the grounds of their faith, but to show (what has never yet been fully shown by any author I have met with) that they may have a rational satisfaction; and that the arguments with which we have been again and again insulted by the Deists, to prove Christianity incapable of any rational proof, are inconclusive.'[92] Hence it is essential that the young should be made familiar with both the objections to and the evidence for Christianity. Doddridge explains to Dodwell that this is done in dissenting academies: 'in several of [the protestant dissenters'] little seminaries, to my certain knowledge, the rational evidences of natural and revealed religion, with such a view of the objections against both, are as regularly, and as methodically taught, as logic or geometry, or any of the other sciences'.[93] Doddridge is describing his own practice here: Part V of *A Course of Lectures,* 'Of the Reason to expect and desire a Revelation: and the internal and external Evidence with which we may suppose it should be attended', concludes with three lectures (108–10) in which the arguments of the deists against revelation are considered. In his sermons on 'The Evidences of Christianity', where some of this material is also presented, Doddridge is confident that the deist controversy has strengthened Christianity by allowing its rational basis to be demonstrated: 'The cause of christianity has greatly gained by debate, and the gospel comes like fine gold out of the furnace, which the more it is tried, the more it is approved.'[94]

However, Watts is emphatic in stressing what reason cannot do. It is limited on two grounds, as a means of knowledge, and as an impetus to action. First, very little can be known of religion by the light of nature alone. In 'A Rational Defence of the Gospel', Part II Watts insists that 'The light of nature and reason is a poor dark bewildered thing, if it hath no commerce, nor communication with persons who have been favoured with divine revelation. It is only the scripture that has established and ascertained the doctrines of natural religion'.[95] The basic argument of *The Strength and Weakness of Human Reason* is that reason cannot teach the individual everything he needs to know about religious doctrines and duties, for which the promises and aids of

---

[90] *Works,* ed. Parsons, VI, 283.
[91] Cited by Doddridge in 'The Absurdity and Iniquity of Persecution', *Sermons on Public Occasions, Works,* ed. Williams and Parsons, III, 127, and *Life of Gardiner, Works,* IV, 90, quoted below, p. 201.
[92] *Correspondence,* ed. Humphreys, IV, 178; *Calendar,* ed. Nuttall, Letter 841.
[93] *An Answer to a Late Pamphlet,* Letter I, *Works,* ed. Williams and Parsons, I, 499.
[94] *Ten Sermons on the Power and Grace of Christ,* 10, *Works,* ed. Williams and Parsons, II, 361.
[95] *Works,* ed. Parsons, I, 192; cf. 'The Knowledge of God by the Light of Nature', *Works,* I, 539 ff.

revelation are essential. Pithander, after quoting *The Reasonableness of Christianity*, points out that 'Mr. Locke himself, whom all the world admires as a master of reason, and who allowed as much power to human reason as one could well desire', thought reason insufficient to establish morality.[96]

Second, reason has a restricted function in the human constitution and cannot provide any motive to action. The relation between reason and the passions or affections (the terms are used synonymously by Watts) must be understood. In *The Doctrine of the Passions* they are described as 'those sensible commotions of our whole nature, both soul and body, which are occasioned by the perception of an object according to some special properties that belong to it'; they are 'of a mixed nature, belonging partly to the soul, or mind, and partly to the animal body, that is, the flesh and blood'.[97] These two features of the passions, that they are mixed in origin and that they have the effect of moving, are repeatedly emphasised. Watts points out that the term heart is used to designate the seat of the passions,[98] and in 'An Essay on the Powers and Contests of Flesh and Spirit' (appended to *Evangelical Discourses*, 1747) he implies that this is partly because of the biblical usage in which these features are combined: the Jews 'used the word heart, for all those inward powers of the man whence outward actions proceeded; and this because the springs and motions of the blood and life, as well as the ferments of several passions, were found there'.[99] In *The Doctrine of the Passions* he stresses that the passions are not merely passive indicators of feeling; rather, they instigate action, and this is their essential function. They are 'active and sprightly powers, because some of them include the act of the will in them, and very few of them are so entirely passive, but they have a tendency to excite the person to lively and vigorous actions of some kind or other; And indeed this is the chief design of them in the nature of man.'[100] They exist in a mutually supporting relation with reason. The function of reason is to judge and test, but it is too slow and weak to bring about action; the passions play no part in speculation or judgement, but they are essential to action:

though they were not given us to tell us what is good, and what is evil, yet when our reason, upon a calm survey, has passed a just judgment concerning things, whether they are good or evil, the passions ... are those lively, warm, and vigorous principles and powers in our nature, which animate us to pursue the good, and avoid the evil; and that with vastly greater speed and diligence than the mere calm and indolent dictates of reason would ever do.[101]

The passions or affections thus have an essential role in the religious life, and it is Watts's object in *Discourses of the Love of God* to explain this. It is a dangerous error to assume that religion is essentially a matter of understand-

[96] *Works*, ed. Parsons, III, 17–18.   [97] *Works*, ed. Parsons, II, 218–19.
[98] *Works*, ed. Parsons, II, 220.
[99] *Works*, ed. Parsons, II, 116.   [100] *Works*, ed. Parsons, II, 220.
[101] *Works*, ed. Parsons, II, 224.

ing and that appeals to affection are only necessary for the intellectually weak, because such a religion can have no practical effect:

We are often told, that this warm and affectionate religion belongs only to the weaker parts of mankind, and is not strong and manly enough for persons of sense and good reasoning. But where the religious use of the passions is renounced and abandoned, we do not find this cold and dry reasoning sufficient to raise virtue and piety to any great and honourable degree, even in their men of sense, without the assistance of pious affections.[102]

Cold reason alone is ineffectual, but warm passion will strengthen it: 'It is one great end and design of the passions, to fix the attention strongly upon the objects of them, to settle the thoughts with such intenseness and continuance on that which raises them, that they are not easily taken off ... Now if the passions are strongly engaged for God, the world will have but little power to call off the heart from religion.' The 'Affectionate Christian' is thus 'Vindicated' as the truly strong and active Christian.[103]

It follows from Watts's doctrine that the preacher or practical religious writer must both understand the relative and mutually supporting functions of the faculties of soul and body and know how to address himself to them in order to achieve practical religious ends. He must learn to apply the three parts of rhetoric, as explained in *The Improvement of the Mind*, Part I: '*Conveying the sense of the speaker* to the understanding ... *Persuading the will* effectually to chuse or refuse the thing suggested ... *Raising the passions* in the most vivid and forcible manner, so as to set all the soul and every power of nature at work, to pursue or avoid the thing in debate.' The divine must model himself on Cicero and Demosthenes.[104] But Watts is not simply appealing to an ancient division of the faculties, since his view of their interaction is more complex than is allowed in classical ethics and rhetoric. In 'An Exhortation to Ministers', the first part of *An Humble Attempt*, the work in which he is principally concerned to explain the practical use of this psychological knowledge, Watts argues in effect for both a revival of the puritan tradition of experimental preaching and a reinterpretation of it in the light of contemporary theorising about the inter-relation of the faculties. Watts recommends to preachers the *Two Discourses* of John Jennings (Doddridge's tutor), 'Of Preaching Christ' and 'Of Particular and Experimental Preaching' (1723, with a preface by Watts), in which the puritans are held up as models for their skill in moving the passions by addressing themselves 'to all the Variety of the Hearts of Men, and Sorts and Frames of Christians, according to the true Precepts of Oratory and

---

[102] Preface to *Discourses, Works*, ed. Parsons, II, 272.
[103] *Works*, ed. Parsons, II, 298; Discourse 6. Watts's argument anticipates that developed more fully by Jonathan Edwards in *A Treatise Concerning Religious Affections* (1746); see especially Edwards's discussion of the terminology of the affections, *Religious Affections*, ed. Smith, (1959), Part I, 96–9.
[104] *Works*, ed. Parsons, VI, 305–6.

Christianity'.[105] One of Jennings's epigraphs is from Baxter's *Gildas Salvianus: The Reformed Pastor* (1656), and in his Preface to *Two Discourses* Watts points out that Baxter always practised this method of addressing himself to the different spiritual ranks of Christians.[106] Watts is seeking to redirect contemporary dissenters to this tradition, but at the same time to reinvigorate it by giving it a firmer philosophical basis. Thus in *An Humble Attempt* he urges dissenting ministers, in the paragraph immediately preceding his recommendation of Jennings: 'In addressing your discourse to your hearers, remember to distinguish the different characters of saints and sinners, the converted and the unconverted, the sincere christian and the formal professor, the stupid and the awakened, the diligent and backsliding, the fearful or humble soul, and the obstinate and presumptuous'.[107] He then goes on to explain that in order to reach these different categories of hearer the minister must understand the relationship between the faculties and their function in the religious life:

> Remember that you have to do with the understanding, reason, and memory of man, with the heart and conscience, with the will and affections; and therefore you must use every method of speech, which may be most proper to engage and employ, each of these faculties or powers of human nature, on the side of religion and in the interests of God and the gospel.

Watts goes through these faculties in turn, showing how the minister must engage each of them, and concludes with a summary of the argument of *The Doctrine of the Passions*, that God has deliberately endowed man with passions in order to excite the will to put into practice what the understanding knows to be right. Hence the minister must address the passions of the different categories of hearer in an appropriate manner: 'Try all methods to rouze and awaken the cold, the stupid, the sleepy race of sinners; learn all the language of holy jealousy and terror, to affright the presumptuous; all the compassionate and encouraging manners of speaking, to comfort, encourage and direct the awakened, the penitent, the willing and the humble.'[108]

Watts's linking in Part I of *An Humble Attempt* of the preacher's knowledge of the human faculties and of the methods of oratory encapsulates the progression of Doddridge's educational system from the first part of *A Course of Lectures*, 'Of the Powers and Faculties of the Human Mind', through to the *Lectures on Preaching*. As a young man starting his course at Jennings's academy at Kibworth, Doddridge was urged by his mentor Samuel Clark in a letter of 28 March 1720 'to study the passions and the secret springs by which men are moved' in order to learn the method of applying to their consciences.[109] The division of Doddridge's *Course of Lectures*, in which the study of ethics and natural religion precedes that of revealed religion, was derived from Jenn-

105 *Works*, ed. Parsons, IV, 21; Jennings, *Two Discourses* (1723), 44.
106 *Two Discourses*, viii; see p. 171 above.
107 *Works*, ed. Parsons, IV, 21.   108 *Works*, ed. Parsons, IV, 26, 29.
109 *Correspondence*, ed. Humphreys, I, 33; *Calendar*, ed. Nuttall, Letter 1.

ings's example (see Doddridge's account of Jennings's educational scheme in a letter to Thomas Saunders of 16 November 1725).[110] The reason for this division, and for the progression from knowledge of the faculties through the various aspects of natural and revealed religion to the practical rhetorical lessons and analyses of style in *Lectures on Preaching*, is apparent in the light of Watts's argument in *An Humble Attempt*. In the first part of *A Course of Lectures*, after surveying problems of epistemology, Doddridge devotes Lectures 14 to 'Dr. Watts's Survey of the Passions' and 15 to 'The Original of our Passions'; other authors cited include Locke, Baxter, Hartley, Hutcheson, Descartes, Butler, and Pope. One of the Corollaries to Lecture 15 states:

> It must be of the greatest importance, in order to influence men to a due course of action, to know how to awaken or moderate their passions by proper application to them; and those who act as if they desired entirely to eradicate the passions, are ignorant of the constitution of human nature, and can expect but little success in their attempts to work upon the mind.[111]

The reference here is to the Preface to Doddridge's own *Ten Sermons*:[112] there is thus an explicit link made from the outset of the course between philosophical investigation of the faculties and the preacher's appeal to the passions.

In the *Lectures on Preaching* the term that recurs most often as a commendatory definition of the method of preaching that stimulates and directs the passions is 'pathetic': it is, for example, the style of the puritan Sibbes, the nonconformist Howe, Watts, and occasionally Tillotson; that of Clarke (the Arian) is by contrast 'void of pathos'.[113] Doddridge had early praised Baxter for his pathos, and in turn it is this pathetic quality in his own preaching that his biographer Orton singles out.[114] Doddridge distinguishes several 'strains' of preaching, the argumentative, pathetic, insinuating, evangelical, spiritual and experimental, and scriptural. These strains, he argues, are not only compatible with each other but ought to be found in every sermon; his headings bring together doctrine, exposition, and, under 'pathetic' and 'insinuating', persuasion and personal application, without which the discourse would be useless. Under the heading 'pathetic' he urges that the passions are 'the sails of the soul' which the preacher must fill:

> Have some pathetic strokes even while explaining, as well as in your reflections or improvement; – or else your reasoning will not be attended to, nor of course understood; – and then however strong in itself, it will prove of no avail, – and an address to the passions will appear as irrational as if no such reasoning had been

110 *Works*, ed. Williams and Parsons, V, 559–67; *Correspondence*, ed. Humphreys, II, 462–75; *Calendar*, ed. Nuttall, Letter 190.
111 *Works*, ed. Williams and Parsons, IV, 330.
112 *Works*, ed. Williams and Parsons, II, 211–12; quoted at the head of this chapter.
113 *Works*, ed. Williams and Parsons, V, 429, 431, 433, 435, 437.
114 Letter to John Nettleton, 8 December 1724, *Correspondence*, ed. Humphreys, I, 460; *Calendar*, ed. Nuttall, Letter 155; *Memoirs*, in *Works*, ed. Williams and Parsons, I, 54, 83.

formed. Therefore make your sermons addresses to your hearers, rather than general essays or speculative harangues.

Under 'insinuating' he continues: 'That the passions may be moved by soft touches, and sudden turns, lead them into their own hearts; – shew them the workings of their own minds and passions.'[115] Doddridge is in effect urging the preacher (as Watts does in *An Humble Attempt*)[116] to emulate the pathetic style of Scripture; the influence of this style on the reader is described in extreme terms in the Preface to the third volume of *The Family Expositor*:

[The reader should] leave the heart to be (if I may so express myself) *carried away with the torrent* whither it will . . .
For surely the breast of every well-disposed reader, under the influences of that *blessed Spirit* which guided the *sacred penmen* in these lively and well-chosen narrations, must by every page of them be inflamed with some devout passion; and his progress must often be interrupted with tears of holy delight, or with warm and perhaps rapturous aspirations of soul.[117]

Many other instances could be given of Doddridge's stress on the importance of the passions and affections in religion. Perhaps the best summary is in the sermon 'Of the Nature of Regeneration, with Respect to the Change it produces in Men's Affections', in a passage which links several key terms: 'the heart is melted down into tenderness; it is warmed with generous sentiments; it longs for opportunities of diffusing good of all kinds . . . it beats with an ardour, which sometimes painfully recoils upon a man's self, for want of ability to help others in proportion to his desire to do it . . . These are the ruling affections in the heart of a good man'.[118] However, the recurrent images of weeping and melting, or warming, inflaming, ardour and rapture, suggest certain difficulties involved in putting the doctrine of the passions to practical use. Both Watts and to a greater extent Doddridge were aware of possible inconsistencies and dangers in the use of the rhetoric of the affections, of which they duly warned their readers, and hence they were often themselves remarkably cautious in employing the rhetorical methods they advocated for others. The problem essentially is whether the affections are concerned primarily with action or with feeling. This ought not to be a problem, since the basic assumption of Watts's *Doctrine of the Passions* is that the passions are instigators of action. However, the favourite images of Watts and Doddridge suggest release, dissolution, annihilation of a sense of self, passive enjoyment of a 'frame': the emphasis as a result often appears to rest on feeling rather than on action.

In the Preface to his *Memoirs* Orton makes clear that such cultivation of feeling was an important part of Doddridge's character, and that it was

115 *Works*, ed. Williams and Parsons, V, 446–7.
116 *Works*, ed. Parsons, IV, 31, quoted above, p. 175.
117 *Works*, ed. Williams and Parsons, VII, 215.
118 *Practical Discourses on Regeneration* (1741), Sermon 3, *Works*, ed. Williams and Parsons, II, 414.

disapproved of in some quarters: 'His temper was remarkably affectionate and impressible'; as a result some readers may think him 'an enthusiast, because there was so much of a devotional spirit in him, and he lays some stress on his particular feelings and impressions'.[119] This stress is evident in many of Doddridge's letters, and in his diary entries and 'reflections' after taking the sacrament, for example 'Hints of a Remarkable Experience, April 5, 1747', in which he prayed that 'God would shed abroad something sensible and peculiar upon me' and afterwards 'arose with tears of joy'.[120] It is also evident in his advice 'On the Delivery of Sermons' in *Lectures on Preaching*: 'Let it be *Affectionate. –* Feel all you say. If a tear will fall, do not restrain it, – but it should never be forced.'[121] In 'Advice to Parents', the third of *Sermons on the Religious Education of Children*, he urges, 'if tears should rise while you are speaking, do not suppress them. There is a language in them, which may perhaps affect beyond words. A weeping parent is both an awful, and a melting sight.'[122] However, though at times Doddridge may link affection primarily with feeling, sensation, and the release of emotion through tears, there are other passages in which affection is firmly associated with rational thought and action. Thus in Lecture 92 of *A Course of Lectures* conscience is defined as 'a certain affection of mind, or principle of action', and in *Practical Discourses on Regeneration*, no. 8 he argues that it is often difficult to distinguish the operations of the Spirit from one's own thoughts 'because the Spirit operates by suggesting rational views of things, and awakening rational affections'.[123]

There are three possible explanations of such variations by Watts and Doddridge in their treatment of the passions. The first is that they are genuinely uncertain of the relative importance of feeling and action and that they state their views differently on different occasions, so that to juxtapose separate statements is inevitably to reveal inconsistencies. The second is that they are aware of the difficulties inherent in the subject, so that wherever possible they are at pains to spell out the dangers and to urge caution on their readers. The third is that they are afraid that some sections of their audience will react in a hostile manner, so that they deliberately moderate their terms for some readers and express themselves more freely for others. The variations can thus be attributed to confusion, or principle, or expediency, or a combination of the three; it is not always possible to determine which is the most likely explanation, but the two latter are certainly the most important.

In several passages Doddridge carefully explains that feeling divorced from action is not religion. In some cases this leads him to repudiate the

---

119 *Works*, ed. Williams and Parsons, I, xii.
120 *Correspondence*, ed. Humphreys, V, 474–5. (Volume V includes Doddridge's diary entries and memoranda.)
121 *Works*, ed. Williams and Parsons, V, 461.   122 *Works*, ed. Williams and Parsons, II, 44.
123 *Works*, ed. Williams and Parsons, IV, 519; II, 515.

terminology he employs elsewhere, and hence apparently to deny the theory of the passions. Thus in *Sermons to Young Persons*, no. 2 he warns:

Trust not to the warmth of your passions in matters of religion, as the foundation of your most important hopes ... You might weep at a mournful scene in a well-wrought tragedy, as you have done at the story of a Redeemer's sufferings ... I have often told you, and one can hardly repeat it too often, or insist too earnestly upon it, that there is a very wide difference between a good state, and a good frame; and that religion is not seated either in the understanding, or in the passions, but principally in the will; which in this disjointed state of human nature, is far from being always in due harmony with either.[124]

This public advice is corroborated in a letter of 25 June 1745 to a young friend, Elizabeth Scott, who was suffering from religious depression. She is urged 'To lay it down as a certain principle, that religion consists more in an intelligent, rational, and determinate choice of the will than in any ardent transport of the affections', and to 'be more intent upon the sincerity of the heart, and the calm fixedness of the thoughts, than about the flow of the affections, which are not and cannot be immediately in our own power'.[125] The repudiation of the characteristic terminology in these passages – the separation of the will or the heart from the affections – can be explained in terms of the audiences to whom the warnings are addressed, the impressionable young who overvalue 'frames' of feeling and, as in the case of Miss Scott, who suffer unnecessarily when they are unable to sustain these frames. Doddridge's terminology and attitude are very close to Baxter's here, and suggest a similar concern with the danger of emphasising feeling to the detriment of practice.[126]

In *The Rise and Progress of Religion* Doddridge employs the rhetoric of the affections systematically and at length, yet here especially he warns his readers against the misuse of feeling. Though the voice of *The Rise and Progress* is deliberately more intimate than that of the *Sermons*, Doddridge follows his own precepts in linking the various 'strains' of preaching defined in *Lectures on Preaching*. The pathetic and insinuating strains are particularly evident in his manner of taking individual members of his audience at different stages of spiritual development and addressing them in appropriate terms. For each Doddridge modifies his tone and approach, for example awakening the careless sinner (Chapter 2), threatening the awakened sinner with judgement (4–7), entreating him to accept salvation (10), challenging the infidel (11), cautioning the young convert (21), supporting the Christian 'struggling under great and heavy Afflictions' (25), urging the established Christian to be

---

[124] *Works*, ed. Williams and Parsons, II, 107–9.

[125] *Correspondence*, ed. Humphreys, IV, 414–15 (Humphreys's italics removed); *Calendar*, ed. Nuttall, Letter 1075. Miss Scott married Elisha Williams, later Rector of Yale.

[126] Cf. Baxter's advice to the melancholy in *Christian Directory*, Part I, Chapter 6, quoted above, p. 156.

socially useful (28). *The Rise and Progress* is a practical embodiment of the programme Watts sketches in *An Humble Attempt* for the ideal dissenting minister who unites an understanding of the theory of the passions and the methods of rhetoric with a wide knowledge of the human heart. It is because of the last of these that Doddridge on occasion uses the rhetoric of the affections against the affections themselves. In three particularly interesting chapters, 'The Case of spiritual Decay and Languor in Religion' (22), 'The Case of the Christian under the Hidings of God's Face' (24) and 'The Christian assisted in examining into his Growth in Grace', (26), Doddridge warns against common misapprehensions of the role of feeling in religion. 'Too great a stress is commonly laid on the flow of affections'. The Christian suffering from what he takes to be spiritual distress – the 'Hidings of God's Face' – may have interpreted his symptoms wrongly and be in need of the help of a physician rather than a divine.[127] True religion must not be measured by intensity of feeling or the loss of it; feeling must not be separated from knowledge and the disposition to act:

you are not to measure your growth in grace, only or chiefly by your advances in knowledge, or in zeal, or any other passionate impression of the mind; no, nor by the fervour of devotion alone; but by the habitual determination of the will for God ... It must be allowed, that knowledge and affection in religion, are indeed desirable. Without some degree of the former, religion cannot be rational; and it is very reasonable to believe, that without some degree of the latter that it cannot be sincere, in creatures whose natures are constituted like ours. Yet there may be a great deal of speculative knowledge, and a great deal of rapturous affection, where there is no true religion at all.[128]

The terms impression, fervour, and rapturous, which elsewhere carry favourable connotations, are here treated with some caution. It is arguable that in passages such as these from *The Rise and Progress* or the *Sermons to Young Persons* Doddridge remains true to the theory of the passions and that as a matter of principle he is anxious to enforce the point that their function is to stimulate the will to make men act. Watts issues comparable warnings in *The Love of God*, especially in Discourse 5, 'The Abuse of the Passions in Religion': the passions must not be divorced from holiness; true Christianity of the heart manifests itself in purity of life. Those who 'seem to make all their religion consist in a few warm and pious affections' miss its true end:

Such christians as these live very much by sudden fits and starts of devotion, without that uniform and steady spring of faith and holiness, which would render their religion more even and uniform, more honourable to God, and comfortable to themselves. They are always high on the wing, or else lying moveless on the ground: They are ever in the heights or the depths, travelling on bright mountains with the songs of heaven on

---

[127] *Works*, ed. Williams and Parsons, I, 387, 408.
[128] *Works*, ed. Williams and Parsons, I, 422.

their lips, or groaning and labouring through the dark vallies, and never walking onward, as on an even plain, toward heaven.[129]

And at the end of *The Love of God* Watts puts into the mouth of the reader a summary of what he has learned from the discourse that explicitly repudiates the pursuit of extremes of feeling: 'I have learned so much of religion, as to know that it does not consist in vehement commotions of animal nature, in sublime raptures, and ecstasies: We may be sincere christians in the exercise of repentance and faith, and in the practice of holy obedience, without any overwhelming sorrows, or transporting joys.'[130]

In cautionary statements such as these in which Watts and Doddridge insist that affection must not be separated from knowledge, will, and action and that the stimulation of feeling must not be an end in itself, they are addressing readers whose tendency is to attach the wrong emphasis to affection. However, on several occasions their caution has its origin in a fear of alienating the reader who is unsympathetic to the language of the affections: they are attempting to convince such readers of the importance of the religious use of the passions while at the same time deliberately muting their characteristic terminology so as to avoid incurring the charge of enthusiasm. The critical response of some readers to works employing affectionate language uninhibitedly illustrates why Watts and Doddridge at times felt caution to be necessary. Both men associated themselves with affectionate and even rhapsodic authors. Watts edited and published Elizabeth Rowe's *Devout Exercises of the Heart* at her request (1737); in his Preface he defensively anticipates readers' objections to her use of the 'Language of holy Passion', and suggests that it should be read with the heart rather than the head. After defending her rapturous tone, however, he admits that it is inessential: 'Ten thousand Saints are arrived safe at Paradise, who have not been favoured, like St *Paul*, with a Rapture into the third Heaven, nor could ever arise to the affectionate Transports and devout Joys of Mrs *Rowe*'.[131] The same year, Watts together with John Guyse edited and published a much more important work, Jonathan Edwards's initial account of the Great Awakening in New England, *A Faithful Narrative of the Surprising Work of God*. Watts was sent the account by his Boston correspondent Benjamin Colman, and published it with some misgivings as to the effect of Edwards's style on the rationalist English reader. In a letter to Colman the following year he defended his editorial changes: 'It was necessary to make some alterations of the language, lest we together with the book should have been exposed to

[129] *Works*, ed. Parsons, II, 325, 328–9. There seems to be an implicit criticism of Part I of *Pilgrim's Progress* here.
[130] *Works*, ed. Parsons, II, 349.
[131] Rowe, *Devout Exercises of the Heart*, ed. Watts (8th edn, 1770), Preface, 9–10, 18, 20.

much more contempt and ridicule on this account, tho I may tell my friend that 'tis not a little of that kind we have both met with.'[132]

Just as Watts suffered embarrassment for his association with Mrs Rowe and Edwards, so did Doddridge for his friendship with the evangelical clergyman James Hervey, author of *Meditations among the Tombs* (1746). Doddridge dedicated his early sermon 'Christ's Invitation to Thirsty Souls' (preached in 1729 but not published till 1748) to Hervey, and in the dedication celebrated their common sentiments.[133] This drew a warning from Warburton in a letter of 10 June 1749 that Doddridge was allowing his reputation to suffer: 'I think you do not set a just value on yourself, when you lend your name or countenance to such weak, but well meaning rhapsodies as Hervey's Meditations ... Your charity and love of goodness suffer you to let yourself down in the opinion of those you most value, and whose high opinion you have fairly gained by works of learning and reasoning inferior to none.'[134] Of the same sermon George Whitefield remarked approvingly in a letter to Doddridge of 21 December 1748, 'It contains the very life of preaching, I mean sweet invitations to close with CHRIST. I do not wonder you are dubbed a Methodist on account of it.'[135]

Clearly if the effect of Watts and Doddridge using affectionate language openly, or associating themselves, however cautiously, with affectionate or rhapsodic authors, was to invite at worst contempt and ridicule and at best condescension from readers hostile to or unfamiliar with the tradition of affectionate religion, then if they were to appeal to such readers they would have to restrain their language and present their point of view tentatively, in such a way as to disarm criticism. Assumptions of this sort appear to underlie Doddridge's method in *The Life of Gardiner*, a book which paradoxically attempts to portray Gardiner's rapturous, ardent impressions and experiences in a coolly objective manner in order to win the doubting reader over to affectionate religion, and at the same time to convince the affectionate reader that rapture must not be divorced from reason and action. The curiously inconsistent tone, together with the mixed reception the book had, suggest the difficulty Doddridge faced in addressing these divergent audiences.

A work which throws some light on Doddridge's methods and assumptions in *The Life of Gardiner* is Watts's 'The extraordinary Witness of the Spirit', no. 12 of *Evangelical Discourses* (published in 1747, the same year as the *Life*). Watts appears to have two main aims in this essay: first, to convince rationalists who are wary of anything that smacks of enthusiasm that the extraordinary witness, though very unusual, is perfectly consistent with the ordinary,

---

[132] Edwards, *The Great Awakening*, ed. Goen (1972), editor's Introduction, 44–5; cf. the Preface by Watts and Guyse to *A Faithful Narrative*, in *The Great Awakening*, 136–7.

[133] *Works*, ed. Williams and Parsons, II, 588.

[134] *Correspondence*, ed. Humphreys, V, 125; *Calendar*, ed. Nuttall, Letter 1601.

[135] *Calendar*, ed. Nuttall, Letter 291; Introduction, xxxv.

rational witness which manifests itself in a holy life; and second, to persuade
those (the vast majority) who have never experienced the extraordinary
witness not to be discouraged and not to attach too much importance to rapturous feelings. The extraordinary witness is characterised in two ways,
though Watts does not maintain the distinction: first, as 'some very uncommon and powerful confirmation of the ordinary and rational witness, by
most sensible impressions of divine love on the heart, by which it is raised to
holy raptures, to heavenly joy and assurance', and second, 'when in an
immediate and powerful manner the Holy Spirit impresses the soul with an
assurance of divine love, and gives the heart of a saint such a full discovery of
his adoption or interest in the favour of God, without the more slow and
argumentative method of comparing the dispositions of their souls with
some special characters of the children of God in scripture'.[136] Watts then
proceeds to give examples, introducing them in a cool and careful manner.
Thus he quotes from Howe's account, written in the blank leaf of his
Bible, of his two intense spiritual experiences of 1689 and 1704 (presumably
taken from Calamy's *Life of Howe*), explaining that he cites Howe as 'the
example of a person whose solid sense, whose deep sagacity, whose sedate
judgment, and the superior excellence of [whose] reasoning powers, leave no
room to charge him with vain and delusive raptures of a heated imagination'. There is a deliberate contrast between the rational tone of Watts's
comment on Howe and Howe's own rapturous account of his 'most rav-
ishing and delightful dream, that a wonderful and copious stream of celestial
rays, from the lofty throne of the divine Majesty, did seem to dart into my
open and expanded breast'.[137] However, after attempting to persuade the
sceptical reader that such extraordinary experiences are rational in themselves and have been felt by eminently rational men, Watts proceeds to
retreat from his own seeming boldness by arguing that the extraordinary
witness is not only 'exceeding rare and uncommon, at least in our days' but
also cannot really be communicated to others: 'the extraordinary witness of
the Spirit is like the *white stone* of absolution, and the *new name written in it*;
Rev. ii. 17. *which none knows but he that receives it*'.[138] Exactly this point, based
on the same text, is made by Doddridge in 'The Evidences of Christianity
briefly stated'.[139] The extraordinary witness is thus of no use as a means of
propagating Christianity. Furthermore, as Watts goes on to argue in the
second half of 'The extraordinary Witness', too much emphasis on such
experiences leads to a denigration of the ordinary witness and a separation of
feeling from holiness:

---

[136] *Works*, ed. Parsons, II, 100.
[137] *Works*, ed. Parsons, II, 103; cf. Calamy, *Howe*, 230–1. Howe's account is in Latin; the
translation is Calamy's.
[138] *Works*, ed. Parsons, II, 109.
[139] *Ten Sermons*, VIII, *Works*, ed. Williams and Parsons, II, 314.

There is great danger of depending upon such raptures, if they leave no evident and lasting effects of sanctification behind them ... Perhaps this is one reason why some christians fall under so many doubts and fears, because they live more upon their inward sensations of joy, their transports of pleasure in religion, which they call the extraordinary witness of the Spirit, than they do upon the characters of the children of God, which should be written in their hearts.[140]

Watts is trying at the same time to assert the reality of the extraordinary witness in the face of rationalist ridicule, to convince rationalists by employing their own terminology, to point out the limitations of the extraordinary witness as a means of testimony for others, and to warn affectionate readers against the pursuit of extraordinary experiences, which are of their nature extremely rare, and which may divert them from real religion.

In the case of Colonel Gardiner, Doddridge faced a similar problem: to narrate the man's extraordinary experience in a way that would persuade the rationalist reader to take it seriously, to avoid the censure of enthusiasm without detracting from the importance of the experience, and to remind the reader that the experience was extraordinary and therefore not in itself exemplary, but that its real importance lay in its effect on Gardiner's life and hence on the life of the reader. Doddridge is thus at different stages in the narrative both closely involved with the distant from his subject, both stimulating and restraining the passions of his reader. He appears reluctant to let Gardiner's experiences speak for themselves, and is careful to act as mediator between Gardiner and the reader, cooling Gardiner's warm and affectionate language with passages of deliberation and explanation. Doddridge's anxiety at the need to express extraordinary experiences in rational language is explained in 'Of the Nature of Regeneration, with Respect to the Change it produces in Men's Affections':

Should we place [the experience of regeneration] in any mechanical transports of animal nature, in any blind impulse, in any strong feelings, not to be described, or accounted for, or argued upon, but known by some inward inexplicable sensation to be divine; we could not wonder, if calm and prudent men were slow to admit the pretension to it, and were fearful it might end in the most dangerous enthusiasm, made impious by excessive appearances of piety.[141]

Though his aim in writing the *Life of Gardiner* is to spread 'a warm and lively sense of religion',[142] he is anxious not to frighten off such 'calm and prudent men': he therefore introduces his account of Gardiner's conversion with details of his own doubts about publishing it, emphasising the circumstances in which Gardiner told him the story and his own veracity in recording it, and acknowledging that he is exposing himself to censure. Doddridge then proceeds with the account of what happened to Gardiner one night while he

---

[140] *Works*, ed. Parsons, II, 110.
[141] *Practical Discourses on Regeneration*, no. 3, *Works*, ed. Williams and Parsons, II, 426–7.
[142] *Works*, ed. Williams and Parsons, IV, 10.

was waiting to meet a married woman. Though Gardiner told Doddridge that
he actually saw, and did not simply imagine, what is described, and that he
had not dreamt it, Doddridge in his narration carefully anticipates rationalist
doubts:

> He *thought* he saw an unusual blaze of light fall upon the book, while he was reading,
> which, he at first *imagined, might* happen by some accident in the candle. But lifting up
> his eyes, he apprehended, to his extreme amazement, that there was before him, *as it
> were*, suspended in the air, a visible representation of the Lord Jesus Christ upon the
> cross, surrounded on all sides with a glory; and was impressed, *as if* a voice, or *something
> equivalent to* a voice, had come to him, to this effect (*for he was not confident as to the very
> words*): "Oh sinner! did I suffer this for thee, and are these thy returns?" But *whether this
> were* an audible voice, *or only* a strong impression on his mind equally striking, *he did
> not seem very confident*; though, to the best of my remembrance, he *rather judged it* to be the
> former. Struck with so amazing a phenomenon as this, there remained hardly any life
> in him; so that he sunk down in the arm-chair in which he sat, and continued, *he knew
> not very exactly* how long, insensible: (which was one circumstance that made me several
> times take the liberty to suggest, that he *might possibly* be all this while asleep). But
> *however that were*, he quickly after opened his eyes, and saw nothing more than usual.[143]

The extent of Doddridge's caution (and the way he thereby dissipates the
impact of the account) is more apparent when this passage is set beside
another describing a comparable experience, which aims to involve the reader
directly and makes no attempt to appeal to his rational judgement. The
passage comes from John Wesley's edition of the life of Sampson Staniforth,
one of the Methodist preachers, published in 1783 in the *Arminian Magazine*:

> As soon as I was alone, I kneeled down, and determined not to rise, but to continue
> crying and wrestling with God, till he had mercy on me. How long I was in that agony I
> cannot tell: but as I looked up to heaven, I saw the clouds open exceeding bright, and I
> saw Jesus hanging on the cross. At the same moment these words were applied to my
> heart, "Thy sins are forgiven thee." My chains fell off; my heart was free [cf. Acts
> 12:7]. All guilt was gone, and my soul was filled with unutterable peace. I loved God
> and all mankind, and the fear of death and hell was vanished away. I was filled with
> wonder and astonishment. I then closed my eyes: but the impression was still the same.
> And for about ten weeks, while I was awake, let me be where I would, the same
> Appearance was still before my eyes, and the same impression upon my heart, "Thy
> sins are forgiven thee."[144]

Doddridge first alluded to Gardiner's conversion in *Practical Discourses on
Regeneration*, no. 8, but he stressed that such experiences are untypical and that
the operations of the Spirit are usually indistinguishable from one's own

---

[143] *Works*, ed. Williams and Parsons, IV, 25; my italics.
[144] 'A Short Account of Mr. Sampson Staniforth', *Arminian Magazine*, VI (1783), 72. Wesley's
usual aim as editor was by simplifying and shortening to emphasise the essential argument of
a work. See I. Rivers, '" Strangers and Pilgrims": Sources and Patterns of Methodist
Narrative', in *Augustan Worlds*, ed. Hilson *et al.* (1978), and Chapter 5 below, p. 222.

thoughts.[145] Throughout the *Life* Doddridge balances his attempts to give the
reader a vivid sense of Gardiner's experiences and modes of expression with
hesitations, warnings, and a self-conscious defensiveness about his own
position as narrator. Thus he quotes extracts from Gardiner's letters and
private papers, introducing them with his doubts about publishing them
because they may provoke ridicule in some, and discourage others; he
anticipates the various responses of 'proud scorners', 'strangers to religion',
and 'pious readers', pitying the first category, but hoping to convince the
second and 'quicken' the third.[146] After citing examples of Gardiner's
'ardours and elevations' Doddridge goes on to consider the charge of
enthusiasm that he expects will be laid against his subject and himself. He
insists that Gardiner claimed no 'immediate revelations from God' and was
governed by no irrational 'secret impulses upon his mind', but that his 'ardent
expressions' and 'strong impressions' were evidence of a spiritual experience
that might be much better understood by those familiar with scriptural
phraseology than by 'persons who are themselves strangers to elevated
devotion, and perhaps converse but little with their bible'.[147] After this careful
wooing of the unsympathetic, anti-enthusiastic reader, Doddridge comes out
openly with a positive identification of his own religious position with that of
Gardiner:

On the whole, if habitual love to God, firm faith in the Lord Jesus Christ, a steady
dependence on the divine promises, a full persuasion of the wisdom and goodness of all
the dispensations of providence, a high esteem for the blessings of the heavenly world,
and a sincere contempt for the vanities of this, can properly be called enthusiasm; then
was Colonel Gardiner, indeed, one of the greatest enthusiasts, our age has produced;
and in proportion to the degree, in which he was so, I must esteem him one of the wisest
and happiest of mankind; nor do I fear to tell the world, that it is the design of my
writing these memoirs, and of every thing else, that I undertake in life, to spread this
glorious and blessed enthusiasm; which I know to be the anticipation of heaven, as well
as the most certain way to it.[148]

Doddridge of course knows that this is not what the hostile reader means by
enthusiasm, and later in the book he carefully distinguishes what he describes
as Gardiner's 'steady and judicious' and rational religion from real, irrational
enthusiasm (these comments are probably directed at the Methodists):

he always wished, so far as I could observe, to have these topics [religious duties and
spiritual exercises] treated in a rational as well as a spiritual manner, with solidity, and
order of thought, with perspicuity and weight of expression; as well knowing that
religion is a most reasonable service [Romans 12:1]; that God has not chosen idiots or
lunatics as the instruments, or nonsense as the means, of building up his church; and

145 *Works*, ed. Williams and Parsons, II, 510, 515 (quoted above, p. 193). The passage on
     Gardiner is quoted in the *Life*, *Works*, IV, 28.
146 *Works*, ed. Williams and Parsons, IV, 42–3.
147 *Works*, ed. Williams and Parsons, IV, 47–9.
148 *Works*, ed. Williams and Parsons, IV, 49.

that, though the charge of enthusiasm is often fixed on christianity and its ministers, in a wild, undeserved and indeed (on the whole) enthusiastical manner, by some of the loudest or most solemn pretenders to reason, yet there is really such a thing as enthusiasm, against which it becomes the true friends of the Revelation, to be diligently on their guard.[149]

But Doddridge is consistent in urging that it is the *tendency* of all religious impressions that must be taken into account (the same argument is put forward in Lecture 182, 'Of Assurance of Salvation – extraordinary Impressions – particular Revelations'):[150] it is because Gardiner's experiences resulted in a totally changed way of life that Doddridge thought he must communicate them, in spite of his misgivings as to the effect they might have in different ways on sceptical or affectionate readers.

However, it is difficult to claim consistency for Doddridge's method of procedure in *The Life of Gardiner*. If extraordinary impressions are remote from the ordinary man's experience and cannot really be communicated to him, if they are likely to disgust the rational and discourage the pious, then why does Doddridge make them the dramatic centre of his book? If, on the other hand, Doddridge's essential aim is to animate and quicken the pious reader by means of Gardiner's example, is it not possible that he may dissipate this effect by attempting at the same time to convince the rationalist reader? Contemporary reactions were very varied, and suggest that different kinds of reader responded to different aspects of the book, not necessarily in the ways Doddridge hoped. Richard Pearsall of Taunton read it to his congregation, and 'had a great number hanging their ears upon my lips', but he warned Doddridge that it might provoke hostility: 'you will not wonder if in this *rational*, self-opinionated, erroneous and unbelieving age, some may call it a scene of enthusiasm, and load it and you with reproaches'.[151] David Fordyce of Aberdeen 'felt his heart melted in many places', but pointed out that Doddridge's criticism of Gardiner's Calvinist views had brought his own orthodoxy into question.[152] Warburton, interestingly, praised Doddridge for occupying a middle ground: 'The distinction you settle between piety and enthusiasm ... is highly just and important, and very necessary for these times, when men are apt to fall into the opposite extremes.'[153] However, as one would expect, Doddridge failed to convince some more cautious Anglican readers: Gilbert West wished that Doddridge had omitted Gardiner's 'rapturous strains of piety' because 'men of cool hearts' and 'men of the world'

---

[149] *Works*, ed. Williams and Parsons, IV, 90.
[150] *Course of Lectures*, *Works*, ed. Williams and Parsons, V, 253. The recommended reading here includes the *Life of Howe*, 229–31 (see n. 137 above), and Watts's *Evangelical Discourses*, no. 12.
[151] *Correspondence*, ed. Humphreys, IV, 573; *Calendar*, ed. Nuttall, Letter 1296.
[152] *Correspondence*, ed. Humphreys, V, 55; *Calendar*, ed. Nuttall, Letter 1325. For Doddridge's cautious criticism of Gardiner's Calvinism see *Works*, ed. Williams and Parsons, IV, 73.
[153] *Correspondence*, ed. Humphreys, IV, 565; *Calendar*, ed. Nuttall, Letter 1282. The passage to which Warburton refers is in *Works*, ed. Williams and Parsons, IV, 48.

would find them unnatural and affected and Gardiner's whole character enthusiastic;[154] George Lyttelton approved of the book but wished that Gardiner's 'conversion had rather been the effect of sober reason, than the impression of a dream', and he thought Gardiner's language 'the common cant of enthusiasts';[155] William Oliver (Dr Oliver of Bath) commented sceptically that 'The spirit of man, assisted by a lively imagination and warm passions, is capable, we know, of working strong delusions in the mind, even the hearing of voices never uttered, and seeing visions without real objects.'[156]

In *The Life of Gardiner* Doddridge was attempting to write a catholic work, rational and affectionate, designed for the sceptical and pious reader, both cool and warm. In writing in this manner, Doddridge may have been modifying the theory of the passions and neglecting his own rhetorical advice; on the other hand, in bearing in mind the specific needs and interests of the different audiences he set himself to reach, he may arguably have been true to the rhetoric of the affections. The *Life* is an interesting case because it illustrates particularly well both the problems involved in the attempt to reconcile the rational and evangelical tendencies in dissent, and the limits beyond which Doddridge was not prepared to go. The problems were partly literary and rhetorical, and partly intellectual and religious. Both Watts and Doddridge were aware of the difficulty of finding a literary style appropriate to their position: each criticised the other for writing in a way that was too diffuse,[157] and though Doddridge confessed that 'the great labour of my life is to bring down my discourses to common apprehensions',[158] it is doubtful whether he achieved this. Lyttelton found Doddridge's paraphrases and commentaries in *The Family Expositor* too florid, and begged him 'to avoid these phrases which (though many Dissenting writers are fond of the use of them) most readers of our Church will call *cant*',[159] a criticism that is stylistic rather than theological, since Lyttelton sympathised with Doddridge's *'evangelical strain'* and was a devoted reader of the *Expositor*.[160] The problem of appropriate style was closely related to the problem of maintaining the balance between the evangelical and the rational, the middle way of moderate Calvinism. Both Watts and Doddridge believed firmly that free thought, rational enquiry, the liberty to test contradictory opinions were essential to the religious life, and that they would support evangelical orthodoxy. The

[154] *Correspondence*, ed. Humphreys, V, 51–2; *Calendar*, ed. Nuttall, Letter 1323.

[155] Phillimore, *Memoirs and Correspondence of Lyttelton* (1845), I, 377–8; *Calendar*, ed. Nuttall, Letter 1286.

[156] *Correspondence*, ed. Humphreys, V, 66; *Calendar*, ed. Nuttall, Letter 1342.

[157] *Calendar*, ed. Nuttall, Letter 963; *Lectures on Preaching*, no. 3, *Works*, ed. Williams and Parsons, V, 433. Surprisingly, Doddridge's editors blame the defects of his style on his partiality for Tillotson, *Works*, ed. Williams and Parsons, V, 451.

[158] Preface to *Sermons on the Religious Education of Children*, *Works*, ed. Williams and Parsons, II, viii.

[159] Phillimore, *Memoirs and Correspondence of Lyttelton*, I, 423; *Calendar*, ed. Nuttall, Letter 1601.

[160] Preface to *The Family Expositor*, *Works*, ed. Williams and Parsons, VI, 12; *Calendar*, ed. Nuttall, Letter 1673.

careers of some of Doddridge's pupils show that this was not necessarily the case. In a letter of 12 December 1743 defending his relationship with Whitefield but distancing himself from Methodists and Moravians, Doddridge wrote, 'I am sure I see no danger that any of my pupils will prove methodists: I wish many of them may not run into the contrary extreme.'[161] Some, like Risdon Darracott at Wellington and Benjamin Fawcett (who edited Baxter) at Taunton and Kidderminster continued the tradition; others, like John Aikin at Warrington, joined the ranks of rational dissent.[162] By the end of the century there was a gulf between rational dissent on the one hand and evangelicalism in its various manifestations on the other. Doddridge's advice to dissenting ministers in *Free Thoughts* was to become 'all things to all men' (1 Corinthians 9:22),[163] but his attempt to fulfil Paul's maxim aroused suspicion and distrust among those more rational or more orthodox than he was. Orton, who himself tried to follow Doddridge's pattern, commented: 'He was represented by the bigots on both sides as a trimmer and a double dealer. So have many of the greatest eminence for wisdom, holiness and zeal been represented; and he used to take comfort in this, that he was no worse treated, than those four excellent divines, whose writings, above all others, he admired, the Archbishops Leighton and Tillotson, Mr. Baxter and Dr. Watts.'[164]

---

161   *Correspondence*, ed. Humphreys, IV, 293; *Calendar*, ed. Nuttall, Letter 934.
162   See A. V. Murray, 'Doddridge and Education', in Nuttall, ed., *Doddridge*, 120; Harris, 'Doddridge', 187 ff.
163   *Works*, ed. Williams and Parsons, IV, 218.
164   *Memoirs*, in *Works*, ed. Williams and Parsons, I, 152.

5

John Wesley and the language of Scripture, reason, and experience

Nothing can be more intricate, complex, and hard to be understood, than religion as it has often been described ... Yet how easy to be understood, how plain and simple a thing, is the genuine religion of Jesus Christ! Provided only that we take it in its native form, just as it is described in the oracles of God.

Sermon 43, *The Scripture Way of Salvation* (1765)[1]

I have endeavoured to describe the true, the scriptural, experimental religion ... And herein it is more especially my desire, first, to guard those who are just setting their faces towards heaven ... from formality, from mere outside religion, which has almost driven heart-religion out of the world; and, secondly, to warn those who know the religion of the heart, the faith which worketh by love [Galatians 5:6], lest at any time they make void the law through faith [Romans 3:31] and so fall back into the snare of the devil.

Preface to *Sermons on Several Occasions*, Volume I (1746)[2]

It is ... a great blessing given to this people [the Methodists] that, as they do not think or speak of justification so as to supersede sanctification, so neither do they think or speak of sanctification so as to supersede justification. They take care to keep each in its own place, laying equal stress on one and the other. They know God has joined these together, and it is not for man to put them asunder. Therefore they maintain with equal zeal and diligence the doctrine of free, full, present justification on the one hand, and of entire sanctification both of heart and life on the other – being as tenacious of inward holiness as any mystic, and of outward as any Pharisee.

Sermon 107, 'On God's Vineyard' (1788)[3]

1 Wesley and his contemporaries

The most significant challenge to the dominant Anglican tradition of moral and rational religion in the middle of the eighteenth century came not from dissent but from within the Established Church itself. This was the large and

---

[1] *Works*, ed. Baker *et al.*, I–IV: *Sermons*, ed. Outler (1984–87), II, 155–6.

[2] *Sermons*, ed. Outler, I, 106.

[3] *Sermons*, ed. Outler, III, 507.

diverse movement known as the Evangelical Revival, which began in the
1730s and increased in size and influence throughout the century. The label
covers a number of groups of different origins, who sometimes co-operated
and sometimes clashed with each other over issues of organisation and
doctrine. Two main features characterised these groups: in terms of organisation they employed irregular practices and structures (such as open-air,
itinerant, and lay preaching, private chapels and meeting houses, religious
societies, conferences, and 'connexions') that functioned alongside and
ostensibly not in opposition to the existing parochial system, though
inevitably these caused much friction with the Established Church; in terms
of theology they dissociated themselves from the largely ethical preaching
typical of the Anglican clergy and returned to the Reformation doctrines of
justification and regeneration as expounded in the Thirty-Nine Articles. The
reinterpretation of these doctrines was by no means a straightforward matter,
and there were long-lasting and sometimes bitter disputes between those
evangelical groups which taught Calvinist and those which taught Arminian
versions of the relationship between grace, faith, and works. The leaders of the
former groups were the Welsh itinerant lay preacher and founder of Welsh
Calvinist Methodism, Howell Harris (1714–73); the itinerant clergyman
George Whitefield (1714–70), a member of the Oxford Methodists in the
1730s, associate of the Wesleys, and evangelist in England, Scotland, Wales,
and especially North America; and the Countess of Huntingdon (1707–91),
founder of a theological college at Trevecca in Wales and ultimately of her
own Connexion, together with the group of clergy she gathered round her as
her chaplains. The leaders of the latter group, the Societies of People called
Methodists, were the Wesley brothers, John (1703–91) and Charles
(1707–88), both itinerant clergy, together with their subordinate itinerant lay
preachers. In addition there were several evangelical or 'gospel' clergy with
parish livings, such as the Calvinist John Berridge of Everton (1716–93) and
the Arminian John William Fletcher of Madeley (1729–85), who contributed
in various ways to the spread of the revival. Some of these clergy, however,
though sympathising with the doctrinal and pastoral aims of the revival, were
hostile to the forming of extra-parochial connexions, which they regarded,
with justice, as a movement away from the Established Church towards dissent.
Despite such differences, the leaders of the revival maintained close contact and
friendship with each other. They were also deeply interested in and influenced
by the contemporary revival movements in New England and Germany,
the most significant figures being Jonathan Edwards, leader of the Great
Awakening in Massachusetts in the 1730s, and Count Zinzendorf, pietist and
Bishop of the Unitas Fratrum or Moravians, whose members were active in
Europe, America, and Asia. The revival was an international movement of
reaction and reform, hostile to the secularist tendency of much con-

temporary religion and philosophy, and confident of its own ultimate success.[4]

The most interesting and important of the leaders of the revival is John Wesley, partly because of his extraordinary effectiveness in establishing the organisation that was eventually to become, after his death and against his wishes, the dissenting Methodist Church, but especially because of his theology, which constitutes a complex and subtle attempt to resolve the problem that dominated English thought from the time of the Reformation, the relationship between religion and ethics.[5] Throughout his adult life Wesley regarded true religion as under attack from two distinct quarters. On the one hand it was threatened by the development of the religion of reason, both within and outside Christianity. Wesley thought the deists less dangerous than those he variously called moralists or heathens or formal, nominal, almost or outside Christians: both groups overvalued reason, but whereas the deists made their position clear by denying revelation and the authority of Scripture, the moralists insidiously undermined Scripture from within by misinterpreting and misapplying it, in particular by ignoring the meaning of faith, the essential place of feeling and experience in religion. On the other hand religion was threatened by the various groups Wesley designated unjustly as antinomians, including the Moravians, the Calvinists, and from some points of view the mystics. These groups in different ways laid too much stress on faith, feeling, experience, and inward religion: they slighted the law, morality, social holiness, the outward ordinances of religion, reason, and human learning. The Moravians and Calvinists travestied Scripture, the mystics virtually ignored it. Wesley's characteristic ideas, language, and rhetorical methods were developed in response to the separate challenges represented by the moralists and antinomians. The reader of Wesley must always bear in mind the particular emphases of his various opponents, which evoked particular responses from him; thus to the men of reason he stressed faith and experience, the inward witness of the Spirit; to the antinomians he stressed the fulfilment of the law, the need for works and holiness. To some of Wesley's contemporaries, in particular his Calvinist opponents, these changes of emphasis looked like self-contradiction. Wesley himself was certain that his

---

[4] On the revival in general see Bebbington, *Evangelicalism* (1989), Chapter 2; Overton, *Evangelical Revival* (1886); J. D. Walsh, 'Origins of the Evangelical Revival', in *Essays in Modern English Church History*, ed. Bennett and Walsh (1966), and 'Methodism at the End of the Eighteenth Century', in *History of the Methodist Church*, ed. Davies and Rupp, I (1965); Watts, *The Dissenters*, Chapter 5.

[5] The most useful studies of Wesley's life and thought are: Baker, *Wesley and the Church of England* (1970); Flew, *The Idea of Perfection in Christian Theology* (1934), Chapter 19; Green, *The Young Mr. Wesley* (1961); Lindström, *Wesley and Sanctification* (1966); J. Orcibal, 'The Theological Originality of John Wesley and Continental Spirituality', in *History of the Methodist Church*, ed. Davies and Rupp, I; Outler, ed., *John Wesley* (New York, 1964), and *Sermons* (see n. 1); Rack, *Reasonable Enthusiast* (1989); Sangster, *The Path to Perfection* (1957); Schmidt, *Wesley*, 2 vols. in 3 (1962–73); Semmel, *The Methodist Revolution* (1974); Simon, *Wesley*, 5 vols. (1921–34); Tyerman, *Wesley*, 3 vols. (1870).

teaching was of a piece. His appeal to the threefold authority of Scripture, reason, and experience as sources of religious truth was intended as a kind of self-regulating check against the errors into which moralists and antinomians fell. Wesley had contempt for much current theorising about natural religion and the role of unaided reason. Man cannot know God through reason, but only through revelation – Scripture – and experience – the inward witness. But the role of reason is essential. Only through reason can man interpret Scripture: only through the rational comparison of Scripture and experience can the truth of both be assessed. If a particular interpretation of Scripture is not borne out by the evidence of experience, then the interpretation must be wrong (this was an important argument in Wesley's doctrine of perfection). Conversely, if a particular experience does not follow a scriptural pattern (for example, if an individual's claim to be justified does not issue in the fruits of a holy life), then the experience is invalid. By means of this threefold appeal Wesley could refute the charges of enthusiasm levelled against him by the moralists and of legalism by the antinomians.

However, although Wesley claimed that his religious position was whole and self-consistent, he consciously drew its elements from widely disparate sources, and over the course of his long career he modified those aspects that came to seem dangerous and ceased to attach the same importance he once had to certain concepts. The chief influences on his thought and the opponents against whom he defined his position can conveniently be divided into three phases (though there is some chronological overlapping between them). In the first phase, that of Oxford Methodism from 1725 to 1735 (he was educated at Christ Church, Oxford from 1720 to 1724 and elected a Fellow of Lincoln in 1726), Wesley worked out his central ideas of inward or heart religion, purity of intention, and holiness of heart and life. He owed these ideas to certain key works he never ceased to venerate: Jeremy Taylor's *Holy Living* (1650) and *Holy Dying* (1651), Thomas à Kempis's *Imitatio Christi*, always called by Wesley *The Christian's Pattern*, and William Law's *Christian Perfection* (1726) and *Serious Call to a Devout and Holy Life* (1729). He stressed the influence of these works on his thought in the review in his *Journal* of his life up to 24 May 1738,[6] in the letter to the evangelical clergyman John Newton of 14 May 1765,[7] and in the opening pages of *A Plain Account of Christian Perfection* (1766).[8] However, he later came to believe that he had concentrated too much in this period on righteousness without knowing how to attain it.

In the second phase, including his voyage to Georgia (1735–7), his visit to the Moravians in Germany (1738), the beginning of his itinerancy and field preaching (1739), the establishment of the Methodist societies in England, and the defence of Methodism from the charge of enthusiasm made by leading

---

[6] *Journal*, ed. Curnock (1909–16), I, 466–7.
[7] *Journal*, ed. Curnock, V, 115–18, and *Letters*, ed. Telford (1931), IV, 297–300.
[8] *Works*, ed. Jackson (3rd edn, 1831), XI, 366–7.

members of the Established Church (the 1740s and beyond), Wesley altered the emphasis of his thought considerably by adopting the Reformation doctrine of justification by faith alone. He learnt this doctrine from the Moravians, particularly Peter Böhler, as he testifies in the second part of his *Journal* (see especially the entries for 18 February, 4 March and 24 May 1738).[9] The doctrine involved Wesley in a new interpretation of faith not merely as a rational assent to the truth of Scripture but as a spiritual sensation, an inward witness, an assurance of his own salvation; in the words of his experience of 24 May 1738 at Aldersgate Street, 'I felt I did trust in Christ, Christ alone for salvation; and an assurance was given me that He had taken away *my* sins, even *mine*, and saved *me* from the law of sin and death.'[10] On the one hand this doctrine implied an emphasis on internal evidence, the invisible operations of the Spirit, and in general on the importance of the part played by feeling in religion; on the other hand it implied a repudiation of works as a condition, but not as a necessary fruit, of justification. Wesley made a careful study of the Edwardian Homilies, the Book of Common Prayer, and the Thirty-Nine Articles in comparison with the Bible, especially the Pauline epistles, and established to his own satisfaction that the doctrine of justification by faith was scriptural, that it was the official doctrine of the Church of England, but that it was neither taught nor understood by its clergy – rather, they expressly repudiated it.[11] To the clergy who reacted with anger and often with violence to the growth of the new Methodist organisation, Wesley's teaching on the Spirit made him an enthusiast and on works an antinomian. Wesley insisted that the doctrine he taught was 'the plain old religion of the Church of England, which is now almost everywhere spoken against [Acts 28:22], under the new name of Methodism'.[12] In the *Journal* entry for 13 September 1739 he set out the doctrinal differences between the Methodists and those clergy who had given up the Reformation doctrine, differences which he summed up in their respective interpretations of the terms justification, sanctification, and the new birth. The erring clergy regarded good works as a condition of justification; the new birth meant simply a virtuous life.[13] These differences were the grounds for the repeated attacks, some unintelligent and ill-informed, some serious and questioning, made on Wesley by senior representatives of the clergy, among the former Bishops Lavington, Gibson, and Warburton, among the latter Dr Church and the anonymous 'John Smith'. The controversial works in which Wesley rebutted these attacks provided him with an excellent opportunity to clarify his own position. The most important of these are the letter to Dr Stebbing of

---

[9] *Journal*, ed. Curnock, I, 440, 442, 465 ff.   [10] *Journal*, ed. Curnock, I, 476.
[11] He published an abridgement of the Homilies as *The Doctrine of Salvation, Faith and Good Works* (1738); see *Journal*, ed. Curnock, II, 101, also Sermon 107, 'On God's Vineyard', *Sermons*, ed. Outler, III, 505.
[12] *Journal*, ed. Curnock, II, 293.   [13] *Journal*, ed. Curnock, II, 275.

July 1739;[14] *An Earnest Appeal to Men of Reason and Religion* (1743) and *A Farther Appeal to Men of Reason and Religion* (1745);[15] *An Answer to the Rev. Mr. Church's Remarks* (1745) and *The Principles of a Methodist Farther Explained* (1746);[16] and the letters to 'John Smith' (especially those of 28 September and 30 December 1745, 25 June 1746, and 25 March 1747).[17] With this group should be included *A Letter to the Reverend Dr. Conyers Middleton* (1749),[18] though this is an answer not to a personal attack but to Middleton's *Free Inquiry into the Miraculous Powers* of the same year, and Wesley regarded him not as an Anglican but as a covert deist. The concluding section of Wesley's letter (published separately in 1753 as *A Plain Account of Genuine Christianity*) contains an important statement on the internal evidence of religion.

The third major phase, from the 1740s to Wesley's death in 1791, includes the breach with the Moravians and Calvinists, the repudiation of various antinomians who seceded from his own societies, his failure to persuade the evangelical or 'gospel' clergy of the Church of England to join with him, and, in spite of these repeated difficulties, the gradual establishment of the Methodist societies throughout the British Isles and in North America. In this phase Wesley developed his most interesting and controversial doctrine, that of Christian perfection, which was for him another term for holiness or sanctification. This doctrine was in part (as he repeatedly asserted) a logical continuation of what he had believed in his moralistic, 'self-righteous' phase in the 1720s; it was also the culmination of the doctrine of justification by faith that he had learnt in 1738.[19] Wesley claimed that no group of Christians properly understood the relationship between justification and sanctification except the Methodists. Thus Luther and modern Calvinists understood justification but not sanctification; Roman Catholics and modern mystics understood sanctification but not justification.[20]

Wesley's complicated but revealing attitude to his early mentor Law can best be understood in terms of the phases of his thought.[21] In the first phase Wesley's admiration was wholehearted. In the second phase, under the initial impact of the Moravians, Wesley reacted sharply against Law; in his letters of

---

[14] *Journal*, ed. Curnock, II, 249–51, and *Works*, ed. Baker, XXV–XXVI: *Letters*, ed. Baker (1980–2), I, 669–72. Stebbing's attack was directed at Whitefield.

[15] *Works*, ed. Baker, XI: *The Appeals*, ed. Cragg (1975).   [16] *Works*, ed. Jackson, VIII.

[17] The complete correspondence between 'Smith' and Wesley, which was not published in Wesley's lifetime, is in *Letters*, ed. Baker, II.

[18] *Works*, ed. Jackson, X.

[19] He habitually dated the origins of his own teaching and of Methodism not from 1738–9 but from 1725–9. See notes 6–8, and *Sermons*, ed. Outler, no. 81, 'In what Sense we are to leave the World' (1784), III, 152; no. 94, 'On Family Religion' (1783), III, 335; no. 107, 'On God's Vineyard' (1788), III, 503; no. 112, 'On Laying the Foundations of the New Chapel' (1777), III, 580–5; no. 127, 'On the Wedding Garment' (1791), IV, 147.

[20] 'On God's Vineyard', *Sermons*, ed. Outler, III, 505–6. See above, p. 205.

[21] On their relationship see Baker, *A Herald of the Evangelical Revival* (1948). See also the references in *Sermons*, ed. Outler, III, 268, 330.

14 and 20 May 1738, he uncharitably blamed Law for not teaching him justification by faith and for not having living faith in Christ.[22] He subsequently criticised Law in detail in a published letter of 6 January 1756 for not understanding the doctrine of justification and for adulterating and subverting scriptural Christianity in his later works with mystical and philosophical jargon.[23] However, he remained under the influence of and continued to propagate Law's teaching on perfection. Wesley's editions of Law's devotional works were required reading for his preachers,[24] and in a late sermon of 1790, 'On a Single Eye', he reiterated the link between Kempis, Taylor, and Law as teachers of perfection, and claimed that Law's *Serious Call* was one of the most important books in English.[25] Wesley's consideration of Law's case raised doubts about his own single-minded insistence in his second phase on the necessity of believing the doctrine of justification by faith alone. In an important *Journal* entry for 1 December 1767, Wesley came to the conclusion that it was not necessary for salvation for a man to have clear conceptions of justification by faith: 'a Mystic, who denies Justification by Faith (Mr. Law, for instance) may be saved. But, if so, what becomes of *articulus stantis vel cadentis ecclesiae* ['the article by which the church stands or falls' – Luther's claim for the doctrine]?[26] He repeated this view in a posthumously published sermon, 'On Living without God' (1792): it is not necessary for true Christians to have 'clear views of those capital doctrines, the fall of man, justification by faith, and of the atonement made by the death of Christ, and of his righteousness transferred to them', in order to benefit from his death. 'I believe the merciful God regards the lives and tempers of men more than their ideas. I believe he respects the goodness of the heart rather than the clearness of the head.'[27] It was this kind of argument that made Wesley's Calvinist opponents accuse him of being an enemy to grace and a champion of justification by works. They were wrong to do so, but there is no doubt that in this, the third and dominant phase of Wesley's thought, he valued those who taught sanctification while remaining ignorant of justification by faith above those who taught justification by faith but either denied the possibility of sanctification in this life or defined sanctification irresponsibly.

Wesley broke with the Moravians in 1740, not long after coming under their influence. He had first met a group of Moravians on the journey to

---

22 *Letters*, ed. Baker, II, 540–50.

23 *Letters*, ed. Telford, III, 332–70. See also Wesley's letter of 17 September 1760 to the *London Chronicle* on the dispute, in *Journal*, ed. Curnock, IV, 409–11, and *Letters*, ed. Telford, IV, 105–7.

24 See I. Rivers, 'Dissenting and Methodist Books of Practical Divinity', in Rivers, ed., *Books and their Readers*, 152–9.

25 *Sermons*, ed. Outler, no. 125, IV, 121. Sermon 79, 'On Dissipation' (1784), is imbued with Law's influence.

26 *Journal*, ed. Curnock, V, 244.   27 *Sermons*, ed. Outler, IV, 175.

Georgia in 1735, and had been in constant contact with them there; in 1738 he had formed a religious society jointly with Moravians in London, and had visited Count Zinzendorf's religious settlement at Herrnhut in Saxony. The grounds for the breach included Wesley's disapproval of the Moravian doctrine of 'stillness' (i.e. their slighting of the means of grace – prayer, communicating, reading the Bible – and the practice of good works), which he regarded as antinomian, combined with Moravian disapproval of Wesley's doctrine of perfection, which Zinzendorf regarded as legalist. The fourth part of Wesley's *Journal*, published in 1744, was intended to explain this breach.[28] Wesley also incorporated part of his crucial conversation with Zinzendorf on 3 September 1741, recorded in the *Journal*, in *A Dialogue between an Antinomian and his Friend* (1745).[29] Afterwards Methodists and Moravians went their separate ways.

Wesley's conflicts with the Calvinists were more bitter and long-lasting, and had a more profound effect on his thought. In the period 1739–41 Wesley's differences with Whitefield came into the open with the publication of Wesley's sermon *Free Grace* (1739) and Whitefield's letter of reply (1740),[30] and after carefully investigating the history of predestinarianism Wesley came to the conclusion that its central tenets – unconditional election, irresistible grace and final perseverance – have a natural tendency to obstruct holiness (*Predestination Calmly Considered*, 1752).[31] This was to remain the essence of his primarily practical objection to Calvinism. However, Wesley's relations with Whitefield remained on the whole cordial. In his funeral sermon for Whitefield (preached on 18 November 1770) Wesley stressed the essential, fundamental, scriptural doctrines taught by Whitefield, the new birth and justification by faith, and ignored the 'less essential' doctrines (Whitefield's Calvinist tenets).[32] This approach naturally aroused the anger of Whitefield's Calvinist supporters. The disagreement between Wesley and the Calvinists (who included Calvinist Methodists, followers of the Countess of Huntingdon, and evangelical clergy of the Church of England) came to a head in 1770 after Whitefield's death with the publication of the minutes of the twenty-seventh annual Methodist Conference. For years Wesley had expressed doubts about the antinomian tendencies of Calvinism. In the 1770 minutes he clarified the grounds of his opposition once and for all (the statement was incorporated in Questions 74 to 77 of the so-called *Large Minutes*): Calvinism is 'the direct antidote to Methodism, the doctrine of heart-holiness'; though a man is not saved by the merit of his works, works are a necessary condition of salvation.[33] The result was a flood of controversial writing from associates of

---

[28] *Journal*, ed. Curnock, II, especially 328–31, 488–98. See Towlson, *Moravian and Methodist* (1957).

[29] *Works*, ed. Jackson, X, 266–76.   [30] *Sermons*, ed. Outler, no. 110, II, 542–3.

[31] *Works*, ed. Jackson, X, 258.

[32] *Sermons*, ed. Outler, no. 53, II, 341–3.

[33] *Works*, ed. Jackson, VIII, 336–7. See also pp. 278, 284–5, for comments on Calvinism in the minutes of 1744 and 1745.

the Countess of Huntingdon and others who accused Wesley of abandoning the essential doctrines of evangelical or true protestantism. Wesley tried to avoid becoming caught up in this controversy himself, relying to some extent on the support of his associates, notably John Fletcher, who published a series of *Checks to Antinomianism* (1771–5) defending Wesley's dual stress on faith and holiness.[34] Wesley did not write a major doctrinal work nor did he redefine his ideas in response to these attacks: his thinking on perfection had been worked out over many years, as he told Lady Huntingdon in a letter of 19 June 1771,[35] and its stages are carefully traced in *A Plain Account of Christian Perfection* (1766).

However, the prolonged dispute with Calvinism culminating in the 1770s had important consequences. Wesley found himself towards the end of his life far more in sympathy with the moralist strain in the Church of England than would have been conceivable in the late 1730s and 1740s. An interesting letter of 18 October 1778 criticising Calvinist dissent makes this change of emphasis clear: 'Calvinism is not the gospel; nay, it is farther from it than most of the sermons I hear at church. These are very frequently un-evangelical; but those are anti-evangelical ... Nay, I find more profit in sermons on either good temper or good works than in what are vulgarly called gospel sermons.'[36] In response to the Calvinist denial of the freedom of the will and the possibility of the individual contributing anything to his own salvation, Wesley identified himself as an Arminian and, more daringly, on occasion as a Pelagian. *The Arminian Magazine*, which he began publishing in monthly parts in 1778, was specifically designed to propagate the doctrine of universal redemption in contradiction to the Calvinist doctrine taught by the *Spiritual* and *Gospel Magazines*.[37] He insisted on the label 'Arminian' rather than the equivocal terms 'Scriptural' or 'Christian',[38] though these would undoubtedly have satisfied him forty years before. The adoption of the label must have seemed to his opponents deliberate provocation: Wesley himself pointed out that 'to say, "This man is an Arminian," has the same effect on many hearers, as to say, "This is a mad dog"'.[39] Wesley's reasons for wishing to rehabilitate the term are clear enough. But his association of himself with Pelagius is more difficult to understand. The moralist, unevangelical, latitudinarian wing of the Church of England had been repeatedly denounced as Pelagian by non-conformists, dissenters, and evangelicals, and this was the tradition Wesley labelled 'almost Christian'. But Wesley did not see Pelagius as the ancestor of the moralists: interestingly, he characterises Pelagius as a scriptural Christian like himself whose doctrines were travestied by his opponent, the arch-

---

[34] Fletcher, *Works* (1825), I–II. See Tyerman, *Wesley*, III, 1770 and years ff, under 'Calvinian Controversy'; Tyerman, *Wesley's Designated Successor* (1882), Chapters 8 ff.

[35] *Letters*, ed. Telford, V, 259.   [36] *Letters*, ed. Telford, VI, 326.

[37] *Arminian*, I (1778), iii, 'To the Reader'.

[38] *Letters*, ed. Telford, VI, 284.

[39] *The Question, 'What is an Arminian?' Answered* (1770), *Works*, ed. Jackson, X, 358.

predestinarian Augustine: 'I verily believe the real heresy of Pelagius was neither more nor less than this, the holding that Christians may by the grace of God (not without it; that I take to be a mere slander) "go on to perfection" [Hebrews 6:1]; or, in other words, "fulfill the law of Christ" [Galatians 6:2].'[40] The identification is explicit in a letter to Fletcher of 18 August 1775 on predestinarianism: 'It was hatched by Augustine in spite to Pelagius (who very probably held no other heresy than you and I do now)'.[41] (The parenthesis suggests that Wesley did not know very much about Pelagius.) Thus though Wesley was well aware that his opponents would attach to him the moralist connotations of the label, his linking of himself with Pelagius, supposedly a scriptural Christian who joined grace and holiness, was paradoxically intended to stress that there was no discontinuity between the second and third phases of his thought, that his doctrine of perfection was scriptural and consistent with justification by faith.

2 Wesley as publicist

In 1761 Wesley replied to an opponent, the Dean of Lincoln, who had found his writings perplexing: 'Very few lay obscurity or intricacy to my charge. Those who do not allow them to be true do not deny them to be plain. And if they believe me to have done any good at all by writing, they suppose it is by this very thing – by speaking on practical and experimental religion more plainly than others have done.'[42] This statement, linking a plain style with practical and experimental religion, points to the most important aspects of Wesley's aims and methods as a religious writer.[43] The audience to whom he principally addressed his writing was popular, and his style was correspondingly intended to be clear and intelligible. His material and method were practical and experimental in that he accumulated through a variety of means large numbers of examples of Christian experience, in order both to demonstrate the validity of his doctrines and to persuade his readers to use these examples as models for their own conduct.

Wesley's disputes with moralists and antinomians inevitably involved him, though reluctantly, in much controversial writing: 'How much rather would I write practically than controversially! But even this talent I dare not bury in the earth.'[44] In such cases, his argument, tone, style, and language were carefully tailored to his particular audience. One of the best examples of this kind of directed writing is *An Earnest Appeal to Men of Reason and Religion*, in

[40] *Sermons*, ed. Outler, no. 68, 'The Wisdom of God's Counsels' (1784), II, 556.

[41] *Letters*, ed. Telford, VI, 175.

[42] *Letters*, ed. Telford, IV, 145.

[43] On Wesley's style and literary methods see *Letters*, ed. Baker, I, 129–40; Herbert, *Wesley as Editor and Author* (1940); Lawton, *Wesley's English* (1962); Shepherd, *Methodism and the Literature of the Eighteenth Century* (1940).

[44] *Journal*, ed. Curnock, IV, 247.

which Wesley addresses and adopts the language and mode of argument of a 'reasonable man'.[45] In *A Farther Appeal*, Part II he extends this method to include in turn Anglicans, dissenters, Catholics, Jews, and deists. However in his far more numerous practical works, which were designed for the use of his preachers and the members of his societies, Wesley does not define his audience in this way by doctrinal or denominational affiliation. Instead, he assumes an audience of plain, common people, who are unfamiliar with the terminology of philosophy and divinity. The Preface to the first volume of *Sermons* (first published 1746), which is an important manifesto for the whole of Wesley's thought, begins with an account of his style in relation to his chosen audience:

I now write (as I generally speak) *ad populum*, – to the bulk of mankind – to those who neither relish nor understand the art of speaking, but who notwithstanding are competent judges of those truths which are necessary to present and future happiness . . .

I design plain truth for plain people. Therefore of set purpose I abstain from all nice and philosophical speculations, from all perplexed and intricate reasonings, and as far as possible from even the show of learning, unless in sometimes citing the original Scriptures. I labour to avoid all words which are not easy to be understood, all which are not used in common life; and in particular those kinds of technical terms that so frequently occur in bodies of divinity, those modes of speaking which men of reading are intimately acquainted with, but which to common people are an unknown tongue.[46]

Wesley later came to believe that the gap between the learned and unlearned need not be so great as is implied here; in *The Arminian Magazine*, as he explained in a letter of 9 November 1783, 'I apply to both; chiefly, indeed, to the unlearned, because these are the far greater number.'[47] In the preface 'To the Reader' in Volume VII of the *Arminian* (1784) he defends publishing his abridgement of Locke's *Essay*, though it is 'not intelligible to common Readers', on the grounds that he aims at both categories. But he was concerned that other writers whose sentiments and doctrines he approved dissipated the effect of their argument by failing to take into account the intellectual and educational limitations of their intended audience. He twice criticised Joseph Butler's *Analogy of Religion* (1736) in his *Journal* on these grounds: 'I doubt it is too hard for most of those for whom it is chiefly intended. *Freethinkers*, so called, are seldom *close thinkers*. They will not be at the pains of reading such a book as this. One that would profit them must dilute his sense, or they will neither swallow nor digest it.'[48] Wesley rarely addressed himself to precisely this audience, but his comments here have a bearing both

---

[45] *Appeals*, ed. Cragg, 49 ff. [46] *Sermons*, ed. Outler, I, 103–4. See also p. 205.
[47] *Letters*, ed. Telford, VII, 195.
[48] *Journal*, ed. Curnock, V, 265; see also III, 232. Butler is treated in *Reason, Grace, and Sentiment*, II.

on his attempts to make Christian doctrine intelligible through his own work, and on his editorial treatment of the work of others.

Wesley's views on style and his reasons for insisting that a preacher must speak and write in the plain language of the common people are most clearly set out in three letters to Samuel Furly of 6 March, 15 July and 11 October 1764. Wesley felt that Furly had been to some extent hindered by his Cambridge education, as he himself was at Oxford, from expressing himself intelligibly to the unlearned, and he explains how he has altered his own style since his Oxford days. The criteria of a good style are 'perspicuity and purity, propriety, strength, and easiness, joined together'. '*Stiffness, apparent* exactness, *artificialness* of style' are particularly to be avoided. Strength comes from conciseness. 'Clearness in particular is necessary for you and me, because we are to instruct people of the lowest understanding. Therefore we, above all, if we think with the wise, yet must speak with the vulgar. We should constantly use the most common, little, easy words (so they are pure and proper) which our language affords.'[49]

Wesley's advocacy of a plain style for an unlearned audience did not mean that he thought the ideas it expressed should be simplified or debased. Simplicity and ease of language were for him in no way incompatible with depth of thought. On separate occasions he recommended South, Swift, and the nonconformists Bates and (surprisingly) Howe as models of the style he admired. In the Preface to the four volumes of sermons published in 1788, which had originally appeared in the *Arminian*, he defended his chosen plainness against the charge that with age he had lost the capacity for fine writing: 'give me the plain, nervous style of Dr. South, Dr. Bates, or Mr. John Howe'. A comparison of the prefaces of 1746 and 1788 shows the consistency of his approach. However, Wesley more often sets up Scripture as the stylistic model for himself and his preachers, in particular the first Epistle of John. In the 1788 Preface he recommends St John's as 'the style, the most excellent style, for every gospel preacher'.[50] This choice is explained in the *Journal* entry for 18 July 1764:

I began expounding the deepest part of the Holy Scripture, namely, the first Epistle of St. John, by which, above all other, even inspired writings, I advise every young preacher to form his style. Here are sublimity and simplicity together, the strongest sense and the plainest language! How can any one that would 'speak as the oracles of God' [I Peter 4:11] use harder words than are found here?[51]

The implications of Wesley's use of scriptural language for the expression of his own religious ideas will be explored further in the next section. In connexion with his intended audience it is worth stressing here that he believed that the most important religious ideas could and indeed should be

[49] *Letters*, ed. Telford, IV, 232, 256–8.   [50] *Sermons*, ed. Outler, II, 357.
[51] *Journal*, ed. Curnock, V, 137.

expressed in a plain language, and that they were readily intelligible to common men because they were expressible in a language and appealed to experience common to all.

Wesley wrote and edited a wide range of works for this audience. True to his principles, he made no attempt to write a large work of systematic theology. His central doctrinal tenets, together with their practical application for the life of the believer (the two were rarely separated in his work), were expounded in the sermons he preached all over the British Isles and published, some as single pamphlets, but the majority in four volumes as *Sermons on Several Occasions* (1746, 1748, 1750, 1760).[52] In addition Wesley wrote a large number of important sermons for the *Arminian*, the majority of which were reprinted in 1788 as Volumes V to VIII of *Sermons on Several Occasions*. A further collection of sermons from the *Arminian* was published in 1800.[53] Among the most important sermons for the reader who wishes to grasp Wesley's essential ideas are no. 5, 'Justification by Faith'; 10–11, 'The Witness of the Spirit'; 12, 'The Witness of our own Spirit'; 17, 'The Circumcision of the Heart'; 20, 'The Lord our Righteousness'; 35–6, 'The Law Established through Faith'; 37, 'The Nature of Enthusiasm'; 40, 'Christian Perfection'; 43, 'The Scripture Way of Salvation' (all from *Sermons*, Volumes I–IV); 62, 'The End of Christ's Coming'; 70, 'The Case of Reason Impartially Considered'; 76, 'On Perfection'; 85, 'On Working out our own Salvation'; 99, 'The Reward of Righteousness'; 105, 'On Conscience'; 107, 'On God's Vineyard' (all from *Sermons*, Volumes V–VIII). In addition to sermons, Wesley published a number of short practical treatises for the guidance of Methodists and the clarification of his own doctrines. The most important of these are *The Character of a Methodist* (1742),[54] *A Plain Account of Genuine Christianity* (the conclusion of *A Letter to the Reverend Dr. Conyers Middleton*, 1749; published separately in 1753),[55] and in particular *A Plain Account of Christian Perfection* (1766, but incorporating a good deal of material published earlier).[56]

However, to a large extent Wesley expounded his ideas through the writings of others. Throughout his career he edited, abridged, printed, and distributed on a wide scale different kinds of religious writing by authors belonging to a number of different religious traditions, from Greek Orthodox, Roman Catholic, and high church to puritan and nonconformist. He issued

---

52 With a few additions they were reprinted in 1771 as the first four volumes of *The Works*, 32 vols. (Bristol, 1771–4), and with some deletions in 1788 as the first four volumes of *Sermons on Several Occasions*.

53 For full details see Outler's edition of *Sermons*, especially I, 38–54; II, 349–53; IV, 1–2.

54 *Works*, ed. Jackson, VIII, 339–47.

55 *Works*, ed. Jackson, X, 67–79.

56 *Works*, ed. Jackson, XI, 366–446. It includes extracts from sermons, prefaces, minutes, letters, and tracts, notably *Thoughts on Christian Perfection* (1760) and *Farther Thoughts on Christian Perfection* (1763).

many of these in individual editions, but he also published them in collected form. The principal collection is *A Christian Library* (50 volumes, Bristol, 1749–55), intended primarily for the use of his preachers, for them to expound to the societies; much edited material is included in the 1771–4 edition of the *Works*; the *Arminian* is a remarkable anthology of such material, interspersed with Wesley's own writing. The English authors of practical and doctrinal works he abridged include, from the high church wing of the Church of England, Taylor, the author of *The Whole Duty of Man*, South, John Norris, and Law; from the latitude-men Cudworth, Smith, Patrick, Barrow, and Tillotson; and from the puritan and nonconformist tradition Bolton, Sibbes, Thomas Goodwin, Dell, Owen, Bunyan, Baxter, Howe, and Annesley (his maternal grandfather).[57] Recent authors outside the English churches include the German Lutheran pietist A. H. Francke and the New England Calvinist Edwards. No adequate study of Wesley's position as a religious writer and publicist can fail to take account of these works.[58]

He applied to the works he edited the same criteria by which he judged his own writing. His editorial principles are explained in the Preface to the first volume of *A Christian Library*: he greatly admired the English practical divinity of the seventeenth and eighteenth centuries, but he found it in many ways marred by doctrinal error, controversial tone, unintelligible style, superficiality, mysticism, or self-contradiction. By judicious excisions and additions, he intended to improve the works he edited by in effect reducing them to a clear, coherent, self-consistent whole. Thus he says that he has 'endeavoured to extract such a collection of English Divinity, as (I believe) is all true, all agreeable to the oracles of God; as is all practical, unmixed with controversy of any kind, and all intelligible to plain men; such as is not superficial, but going down to the depth, and describing the height, of Christianity; and yet not mystical, not obscure to any of those who are experienced in the ways of God'.[59] Of the many practical treatises he subjected to this editorial method, undoubtedly the most important are his editions of à Kempis's *The Christian's Pattern* and Law's *A Practical Treatise upon Christian Perfection* and *A Serious Call to a Devout and Holy Life* (all reprinted many times in separate editions, and included in Volumes IV to VIII of the *Works* (1771–2)).[60]

Wesley's editorial practice created certain problems. His decision to delete what he regarded as error and to make all his chosen authors consistent with one another meant that he drastically misrepresented some of them. A

[57] On Wesley's editions of and sympathies with puritans and nonconformists see Monk, *John Wesley: His Puritan Heritage* (1966); also Newton, *Susanna Wesley and the Puritan Tradition in Methodism* (1968).

[58] See Green, *Bibliography* (1896); Baker, *Union Catalogue* (1966); *Works*, ed. Baker, XXXIII–IV (forthcoming). The second edition of *A Christian Library* published by Jackson (30 vols., 1819–27) incorporates Wesley's revisions.

[59] *Works*, ed. Jackson, XIV, 220–2; *Christian Library*, ed. Jackson, I (1819), v–ix.

[60] I have examined these further in 'Dissenting and Methodist Books', 153–7.

striking example of this is Bunyan. In his abridged edition of Part I of *Pilgrim's Progress* (1743),[61] among other changes Wesley criticised Bunyan's portrayal of the Valley of the Shadow of Death, altered Faithful's account of the work of grace in the soul, emphasised joy in Hopeful's account of his conversion, and rewrote part of the dialogue with Ignorance.[62] In his abridged edition of *The Holy War* in *A Christian Library* he cut the trial of the Doubters, thereby suppressing Bunyan's predestinarianism.[63] He even went so far as to argue in a late sermon of 1785, 'On Perfection', that Bunyan unwittingly admitted the doctrine of perfection in *The Holy War*, though it was incompatible with his own system.[64] This reshaping of Bunyan's beliefs justly brought down on Wesley's head the wrath of his Calvinist opponent Richard Hill, who in *A Review of all the Doctrines taught by the Rev. Mr. John Wesley* (1772) characterised Wesley's abridged Bunyan as a counterfeit. Declaring 'I cannot find the smallest traces of your system in any of his works, except where he is describing the faith of one *Mr. Ignorance*', Hill asserted that Ignorance's definition of justification contained 'the very quintessence ... of all Mr. Wesley's writings'.[65] He showed that Wesley's attempt to make the works he edited consistent with themselves and with his own writings had failed, and he compiled a list of contradictions entitled 'A Farrago'. In reply Wesley somewhat pusillanimously disclaimed responsibility for much of the text of *A Christian Library*, on the grounds that many of his editorial revisions were ignored by his printers, and he might himself have overlooked some unsuitable passages. He refused to answer any of Hill's criticisms that included quotations from the authors he had edited. He dealt with one such set of criticisms by saying: 'I am no way engaged to defend every expression of ... Richard Baxter's Aphorisms. The sense ... I generally approve, the language many times I do not.' Further on he insisted peremptorily: 'Baxter's Aphorisms go for nothing. Richard Baxter is not John Wesley.'[66] Even if we allow for Wesley's printing difficulties and his hasty and careless editorial work, it is still hard to reconcile such statements with the claims of the Preface to *A Christian Library*.

Wesley's widespread propagation of the writings of others is an important aspect of his conception of experimental religion. The individual knows God

---

[61] Reissued many times, also in *Works*, IX (1772).   [62] *Works*, IX (1772), 79, 90, 116–18.

[63] *Christian Library*, ed. Jackson, XIX (1825), 220–3. See Chapter 3 above, p. 135.

[64] *Sermons*, ed. Outler, no. 76, III, 86.

[65] Hill, *Review*, 2nd edn (1772), 20–1, 41, 123. For Ignorance's definition see Chapter 3 above, p. 134.

[66] *Some Remarks on Mr. Hill's 'Review of all the Doctrines taught by Mr. John Wesley'* (1772), *Works*, ed. Jackson, X, 382–4, 387. In fact Wesley attached considerable importance to Baxter's *Aphorisms*. He published a thirty-six-page extract in 1745 (reprinted several times, also in *Works*, 1773, XXII), with the hope that God might '*once again make it a powerful Antidote against the spreading Poison of* Antinomianism' (1745, 'To the Reader'). See the Conference minutes of 1 August 1745, *Works*, ed. Jackson, VIII, 282. On his abridgement of *The Saint's Everlasting Rest* see Rivers, 'Dissenting and Methodist Books', 141–2.

through Scripture and through experience. He can readily compare the two, but he also needs the testimony of others, partly in order to test whether his own experience coheres with common experience, and is not peculiar to himself and hence invalid, and partly to encourage him to persevere. Hence Wesley's experimental method, by which he systematically collected accounts of the experiences of others and published them in a variety of forms – biographies, autobiographies, conversion narratives, deathbed accounts, letters – had a twofold purpose: to test the validity of his own doctrines, and to give support to his readers. His letters illustrate one way in which he collected this material. In the 1760s and 1770s, for example, he was anxious to compile evidence of Christian perfection, and his letters are full of lists of questions to his correspondents about the details of their experiences. He explained one reason for doing so in a letter of 14 April 1771: 'It is certain no part of Christian history is so profitable as that which relates to great changes wrought in our souls: these, therefore, should be carefully noticed and treasured up for the encouragement of our brethren.'[67] The other reason, to test the validity of a doctrine, is explicit in a letter of 11 June 1777: 'I have lately made diligent inquiry into the experience of many that are perfected in love. And I find a very few of them who have had a clear revelation of the several Persons in the ever-blessed Trinity. It therefore appears that this is by no means essential to Christian perfection.'[68]

The chief means whereby he publicised this material, whether collected by himself or sent to him by others, were the *Journal* and *The Arminian Magazine*. The *Journal* appeared in twenty-one parts at intervals of a few years from 1739 to 1791. Wesley clearly believed that the huge range of times, persons, places, and experiences covered gave him a unique authority to interpret and explain experimental religion. The *Journal* includes, for example, experiences of justification by faith collected among the Moravians at Herrnhut in 1738; of the physical symptoms of the new birth collected in Newcastle in 1743, in Ireland in 1756, and at Everton under the ministry of the evangelical Berridge in 1759; and experiences of perfection collected in 1760 and 1769.[69] The publication of such accounts was one of the principal objects of the *Arminian* (the other was, as noted above, to combat Calvinism). Wesley was convinced of the originality and importance of this project: 'the Letters and the Lives, which will make a considerable part of every number, contain the marrow of experimental and practical religion; so that nothing of the kind has appeared before'.[70] The originality of the magazine lay partly in the fact that it

---

[67] *Letters*, ed. Telford, V, 237.
[68] *Letters*, ed. Telford, VI, 266. See below, nn. 73–4.
[69] *Journal*, ed. Curnock, II, 36–49; III, 69; IV, 169–70; IV, 317–22, and especially 359–60; V, 367–70; V, 297–9.
[70] *Letters*, ed. Telford, VI, 295.

published 'Accounts and Letters, containing the experience of pious persons, the greatest part of whom are still alive'.[71]

However, from the beginning of his career Wesley had published editions of the biographies and autobiographies of those carefully-chosen men of the past whom he regarded as exemplary models of Christian experience. The most important of these were the lives of the Marquis de Renty, a Roman Catholic French nobleman (1741, and in *Works*, Volume XI, 1772); David Brainerd, a New England Calvinist missionary to the Indians (1768, and in *Works*, 1772); Gregory Lopez, a Roman Catholic hermit in Mexico (in *A Christian Library*, Volume L, 1755, and *Arminian*, Volume III, 1780); and Thomas Haliburton, a Scottish Presbyterian minister (1739, and in *Works*, Volumes X–XI, 1772). Wesley repeatedly referred to these men in his published writings and his correspondence; he urged his preachers and members of his societies to read their lives, and explicitly recommended Brainerd as a model for his preachers;[72] he compared details of the experience of his friends with these experimental models, while stressing that they represented the summit of Christian experience. Thus in Sermon 55, 'On the Trinity', he quotes one of his favourite sayings from the life of de Renty: 'I do not say that every real Christian can say with the Marquis de Renty, "I bear about with me continually an experimental verity, and a plenitude of the presence of the ever-blessed Trinity." I apprehend this is not the experience of *babes*, but rather *fathers in Christ* [1 Corinthians 3:1; 1 John 2:13; Hebrews 5: 13–14].'[73] In his letters to some of those he believed had attained perfection he questioned them on their apprehension of de Renty's 'experimental verity'.[74]

Wesley made one contribution himself to the genre he valued so highly: this was *A Short Account of the Life and Death of the Reverend John Fletcher* (1786). He relied heavily on statements collected from others, notably Joseph Benson and Mary Bosanquet, Fletcher's wife. In the concluding chapter Wesley explains the relation of this biography to the earlier ones, and the function of the experimental model in relation to the doctrine of perfection. Fletcher's life was an ideal, but an ideal that every Christian can hope to attain:

For many years I despaired of finding any inhabitant of Great Britain, that could stand in any degree of comparison with Gregory Lopez, or Monsieur de Renty. But let any impartial person judge if Mr. Fletcher was at all inferior to them ...

Within fourscore years, I have known many excellent men, holy in heart and life: But one equal to him, I have not known; one so uniformly and deeply devoted to God. So unblamable a man, in every respect, I have not found either in Europe or America. Nor do I expect to find another such on this side eternity.

Yet it is possible we may be such a one as he was. Let us, then, endeavour to follow him as he followed Christ.[75]

---

[71] *Arminian*, I (1778), vi.   [72] *Large Minutes, Works*, ed. Jackson, VIII, 328.
[73] *Sermons*, ed. Outler, II, 385. For other references to De Renty see I, 344 n.
[74] E.g. 2 June 1776, 2 August 1777; *Letters*, ed. Telford, VI, 223, 270.
[75] *Works*, ed. Jackson, XI, 364–5.

The most important single group of writings that Wesley published as experimental evidence consisted of the autobiographies of his itinerant lay preachers, which he specifically commissioned for publication in the *Arminian*. Some of his preachers had published accounts of their lives independently (John Nelson is the best example), but the majority wrote under Wesley's editorial direction. (Wesley's letters to John Valton from 1780 to 1783 show how successfully insistent he was in demanding an account from a preacher reluctant to supply one: Valton's journal extracts appeared in the volumes for 1783 and 1784.)[76] The autobiographies were published in the *Arminian* and its successor, *The Methodist Magazine*, from 1778 to 1811 (well after Wesley's death); they appeared in monthly instalments of about five to ten pages, usually totalling twenty to forty pages.[77] Though Wesley was ultimately responsible for these writings, their value is intrinsic, rather than merely throwing light on his own work. Among the best accounts are those by John Haime, Alexander Mather, Sampson Staniforth, and Silas Told; Wesley himself seems to have particularly admired those of Mather and Haime.[78]

Since these lives were written by itinerants who had largely given up the ties of work, home, and affection, from some points of view their experience was necessarily untypical. Yet they illustrated, as did all the letters and lives that Wesley published, the essential connexion between doctrine and practice. This was their principal function as experimental models: they demonstrated, clearly and plainly, that the life of the 'altogether Christian', in spite of the apparently intolerable demands made of it, could be lived. William Green's account must stand for them all: 'Though I have left my wife, and children, and dearest friends, and house, and business, and wander about, chiefly on foot, through cold and rain, I find my mind uninterruptedly happy.'[79]

3 Faith working by love

In his first letter to 'John Smith', dated 28 September 1745, Wesley answers 'Smith's' criticism in his letter of May 1745 that Methodist phraseology is singular and anachronistic:

I thoroughly agree that it is best to 'use the most common words, and that in the most obvious sense', and have been diligently labouring after this very thing for little less than twenty years. I am not conscious of using any uncommon word, or any word in an uncommon sense. But I cannot call those uncommon words which are the constant

---

[76] *Letters*, ed. Telford, VII, 17, 35, 44, 100, 180.

[77] Jackson published four editions of the autobiographies (with stylistic revisions) as *The Lives of Early Methodist Preachers* (1837–71); the most recent edition is by Telford, *Wesley's Veterans* (1909–14). A new annotated edition is needed. The lives are analysed further in Rivers, '"Strangers and Pilgrims": Sources and Patterns of Methodist Narrative', in *Augustan Worlds*, ed. Hilson *et al.* (1978).

[78] *Letters*, ed. Telford, VII, 35.   [79] *Arminian*, IV (1781), 308.

language of Holy Writ. These I purposely use, desiring always to express Scripture sense in Scripture phrase.[80]

'Smith' was not satisfied with this answer; in his reply of 27 November 1745 he argued that in many cases this practice would result in cant, burlesque, or unintelligibility: 'It is not therefore the merely being scriptural that makes terms proper; but we must look back to the occasion of their use, and if the circumstances then and now are alike, then and not otherwise we may pronounce their use alike proper'.[81] However, this desire 'to express Scripture sense in Scripture phrase', or, as he has it elsewhere, 'spiritual things in spiritual words' or 'scripture truths in scripture words', remained constant with Wesley.[82] In a letter to John Newton of 1 April 1766, in which he discusses the fact that their ideas are similar though their language is different, Wesley comments that years earlier the Moravians had criticised him for being too sparing in his use of the terms 'Christ' and 'faith': 'My answer was: "The Bible is my standard of *language* as well as sentiment. I endeavour not only to think but to speak *as the oracles of God*. Show me any one of the inspired writers who mentions Christ or faith more frequently than I do, and I will mention them more frequently." '[83]

Wesley was prepared to allow, as this letter suggests, that someone using unscriptural language might not be wrong in his ideas. He carried this argument furthest in Sermon 20, 'The Lord our Righteousness' (1765; intended partly as an answer to the Calvinist James Hervey), which criticised Calvinist insistence on the phrase 'the imputation of Christ's righteousness'. Wesley did not like using this phrase himself, because it was unscriptural and had antinomian implications, though he accepted it as meaning that man is accepted through Christ's merits.[84] In the sermon he argues that this need not be cause for dispute: 'believers may not all speak alike; they may not all use the same language ... But a difference of expression does not necessarily imply a difference of sentiment. Different persons may use different expressions, and yet mean the same thing.' However, he goes on to argue that those who reject not only the term but also the doctrine expressed by the term (for example mystics, Quakers, many members of the Church of England, and unitarian dissenters) may still not be wrong: 'However confused their ideas may be, however improper their language, may there not be many of them whose heart is right toward God ...?'[85] This argument is applied in a different context in the *Journal* for 19 September 1764, where Wesley cites the case of a woman near madness: 'her sentiments are confused, and her expressions odd and indigested: and yet, notwithstanding this, more of the real power of God

[80] *Letters*, ed. Baker, II, 143–4, 155.   [81] *Letters*, ed. Baker, II, 166.
[82] *Letters*, ed. Baker, I, 534; *The Character of a Methodist, Works*, ed. Jackson, VIII, 341.
[83] *Letters*, ed. Telford, V, 7–8.
[84] *Letters*, ed. Telford, III, 230. On Wesley's use of the phrase see *Sermons*, ed. Outler, I, 481n.
[85] *Sermons*, ed. Outler, I, 454, 460–1.

attends these uncouth expressions than the sensible discourses of even good men who have twenty times her understanding'.[86]

Normally Wesley was not willing to make this distinction between true feeling on the one hand and confused ideas and unscriptural expression on the other. He regarded unscriptural language as at best perplexing, at worst dangerous, and on these grounds repeatedly attacked Moravians, antinomians, 'gospel preachers', Roman Catholics, Quakers, and mystics.[87] The reasons for his objections are best set out in a letter of 10 June 1781 criticising the Flemish mystic Antoinette Bourignon:

> What makes many passages, both in her life and writings, so striking is that they are so peculiar; they are so entirely her own, so different from everything which we have seen or read elsewhere. But this is in reality not an excellence, but a capital defect. I avoid, I am afraid of, whatever is peculiar, either in the experience or the language of any one. I desire nothing, I will accept of nothing, but the common faith and common salvation.[88]

This condemnation should be compared with his approval of Elizabeth Rowe's *Devout Exercises of the Heart*: 'Her experience is plain, sound, and scriptural, no way whimsical or mystical; and her language is clear, strong, and simple'.[89]

Wesley similarly regarded moralist language as perplexing and dangerous, but for different reasons. He objected to the substitution of fashionable new terms for familiar scriptural ones, such as 'moral sense' for 'conscience' (Sermon 12, 'The Witness of our own Spirit', 1746);[90] he himself considered that 'what is vulgarly called "natural conscience"' is 'more properly termed "preventing grace"', and should not be considered natural but a 'supernatural gift of God' (Sermon 85, 'On Working Out Our Own Salvation', 1785; Sermon 105, 'On Conscience', 1788).[91] He suspected the motives of those who cultivated this terminology, suggesting that the underlying influence was Satanic:

> It were to be wished that they were better acquainted with this faith who employ much of their time and pains in laying another foundation, in grounding religion on 'the eternal *fitness* of things', on 'the intrinsic *excellence* of virtue', and the *beauty* of actions flowing from it – on the *reasons*, as they term them, of good and evil, and the *relations* of beings to each other. Either these accounts of the grounds of Christian duty coincide with the scriptural or not. If they do, why are well-meaning men perplexed, and drawn

[86] *Journal*, ed. Curnock, V, 97.
[87] For example *Sermons*, ed. Outler, no. 125, IV, 101; *A Second Dialogue between an Antinomian and his Friend, Works*, ed. Jackson, X, 283–4; *Letters*, ed. Baker, II, 486–7; *Letters*, ed. Telford, V, 209, VII, 26.
[88] *Letters*, ed. Telford, VII, 67.
[89] *Journal*, ed. Curnock, V, 326. For Watts's much more cautious account of *Devout Exercises*, which he edited, see Chapter 4 above, p. 196.
[90] *Sermons*, ed. Outler, I, 302.
[91] *Sermons*, ed. Outler, III, 207, 482. See Outler's comments, I, 64n, II, 156–7n.

from the weightier matters of the law by a cloud of terms whereby the easiest truths are explained into obscurity? If they are not, then it behoves them to consider who is the author of this new doctrine, whether he is likely to be 'an angel from heaven' who 'preacheth another gospel' than that of Christ Jesus [Galatians 1:8].

(Sermon 17, 'The Circumcision of the Heart', preached at Oxford in 1733.)[92]

If moralist language converges with scriptural, then it is unnecessary; if it does not, then it is destructive of religion. Wesley is almost never to be found using such language; a rare and surprising exception is when he attempts to define the law of God 'after the manner of men' as 'supreme, unchangeable reason', 'unalterable rectitude', 'the everlasting fitness of all things', 'a copy of the eternal mind, a transcript of the divine nature' (Sermon 34, 'The Original, Nature, Properties, and Use of the Law', 1750).[93] Whenever possible, however, he uses scriptural language for the expression of doctrine, even where, as in his use of the term perfection, it causes offence: 'We may not ... lay these expressions aside, seeing they are the words of God, and not of man' (Sermon 40, 'Christian Perfection').[94]

Wesley often insisted that so-called Methodism was nothing but 'the one old religion; as old as the Reformation, as old as Christianity, as old as Moses, as old as Adam' (letter to *The Westminster Journal*, 7 January 1761).[95] Methodists are not distinguished by their adherence to a particular set of opinions: 'as to all opinions which do not strike at the root of Christianity, we think and let think ... I, and all who follow my judgment, do vehemently refuse to be distinguished from other men, by any but the common principles of Christianity, – the plain, old Christianity that I teach, renouncing and detesting all other marks of distinction' (*The Character of a Methodist*, 1742).[96] However, Wesley's distinction between opinions on the one hand and principles, doctrines, or essentials on the other is not always clear-cut. Opinion sometimes seems to be a kind of optional addition to doctrine, and sometimes doctrine itself. Wesley is certain that there are right and wrong opinions, but whether right or wrong, they do not constitute religion: 'Persons may be quite right in their opinions, and yet have no religion at all. And on the other hand persons may be truly religious who hold many wrong opinions.' (Wesley here gives as examples of the latter his three favourite Catholics – à Kempis, Lopez, and de Renty – and the Calvinists, asserting that 'all the absurd opinions of all the Romanists in the world' are nothing compared to the Calvinist opinion of God's irresistible decrees.) This statement, which occurs in similar form elsewhere, is here soon modified: many mistakes are consistent with religion, but some truths are more important than others, and

[92] *Sermons*, ed. Outler, I, 410–11.
[93] *Sermons*, ed. Outler, II, 10. Contrast Sermon 69, 'The Imperfection of Human Knowledge'.
[94] *Sermons*, ed. Outler, II, 100.
[95] *Journal*, ed. Curnock, IV, 340; also in *Letters*, ed. Telford, IV, 131.
[96] *Works*, ed. Jackson, VIII, 340, 346.

must be known. One of these truths is the Trinity, the subject of this sermon (Sermon 55, 1775).[97] Belief in the Trinity for Wesley is clearly not an opinion, but one of the 'common principles of Christianity' (he does not – he logically cannot – insist on the unscriptural term, but he dismisses the view that the doctrine is unscriptural); an anti-trinitarian could therefore not be truly religious. However, he later abandoned this view; he published the life of the late seventeenth-century unitarian Thomas Firmin in the *Arminian* for 1786, with a note admitting that real piety was consistent with erroneous notions of the Trinity.[98]

An interesting letter to John Newton of 14 May 1765, published in the *Journal* as 'Letter to a Friend', obfuscates the question of which truths are more important than others. Newton, an evangelical Calvinist, disapproved strongly of Wesley's teaching on perfection, regarding it not as an opinion but as a dangerous mistake, subversive of Christian experience. Wesley states, taking up Newton's words, that 'Whatever is "compatible with love to Christ and a work of grace", I term an *opinion*.' He used to regard predestination not as an opinion, but as a dangerous mistake; but since it is compatible with 'real Christian experience' (as in Newton's case) he now regards it as an opinion. The conclusion Newton is required to draw is that, similarly, he should regard perfection as an opinion.[99]

Wesley's conciliatory spirit is admirable, but his argument is disingenuous. Two obvious difficulties arise. The first is that Wesley himself (as he makes clear elsewhere) did not regard perfection or holiness as an opinion, but as an essential doctrine. The second is that he did regard Calvinist opinions as dangerous and capable of striking at the root of Christianity, though he believed many Calvinists, Whitefield in particular, to be holy men. These contradictions may be illuminated (though they cannot be solved) by the sermon 'Catholic Spirit' (1750), in which Wesley tries to explain the relationship between his tolerance and his own fixed beliefs. First, 'a catholic spirit is not *speculative latitudinarianism*. It is not an indifference to all opinions ... A man of a truly catholic spirit has not now his religion to seek. He is as fixed as the sun in his judgment concerning the main branches of Christian doctrine.' Second, 'a catholic spirit is not any kind of *practical latitudinarianism*. It is not indifference as to public worship'. Third, 'a catholic spirit is not indifference to all congregations. This is another sort of latitudinarianism, no less absurd and unscriptural than the former.' The man of catholic spirit has universal love for all mankind, while remaining fixed in his principles, manner of worship, and congregation (i.e. denomination).[100] On the one hand

---

[97] *Sermons*, ed. Outler, II, 374.

[98] *Arminian*, IX, 253. Calamy, by contrast, records that Firmin's charitable acts enabled him to spread Socinian notions, so that it was open to question whether he did more good than harm; *My Own Life*, I, 404.

[99] *Journal*, ed. Curnock, V, 115–17; also in *Letters*, ed. Telford, IV, 297–8.

[100] *Sermons*, ed, Outler, II, 92–4.

Wesley's dislike of controversy and his paramount concern with the pursuit of holiness led him to define as opinion matters which to his opponents and sometimes himself were much more than that; on the other hand he tended to exaggerate the extent to which his own principles remained fixed. His claim in the *Journal* for 1 September 1778, 'Forty years ago I knew and preached every Christian doctrine which I preach now', needs some qualifying (as suggested in section 1).[101] However, it is possible to define what Wesley meant by the most important truths, the common principles, or the essentials of Christianity. In an open letter to the evangelical clergy of 19 April 1764 Wesley unsuccessfully invited them to unite together on three agreed essentials, setting aside differences in opinions (such as predestination and perfection – Wesley's characteristic difficulties emerge here), expressions (such as imputed righteousness and the merits of Christ), and outward order.[102] These three, original sin, justification by faith, and holiness of heart and life, are fundamental categories in Wesley's thought, which only make sense in relation to each other, each category resting on the one before. Original sin is the natural state of mankind; justification by faith is the means of release from this state; holiness of heart and life is the end of Christian experience. Wesley's key terms and concepts can best be explored by means of this tripartite division, yet it must always be remembered that he saw these categories as interdependent.

Original sin

The principal sources for Wesley's view of original sin are *The Doctrine of Original Sin, according to Scripture, Reason, and Experience* (1757), which is an uncharacteristically bulky answer to the attack on the doctrine made by John Taylor, dissenting minister at Norwich, in *The Scripture-Doctrine of Original Sin proposed to free and candid examination* (third edition, 1750),[103] and Sermon 44, 'Original Sin' (1759), though there are many relevant observations scattered throughout Wesley's works. Original sin, in Wesley's view, is the essential underpinning of Christianity, and it is closely linked with his views on the natural man and natural religion, heathenism, atheism, deism, morality, and the role of reason. The central issue involved is dramatically stated in a letter to Taylor of 3 July 1759:

It is Christianity or Heathenism! For take away the scriptural doctrine of redemption, or justification, and that of the new birth, the beginning of sanctification; or, which amounts to the same, explain them as you do, suitably to your doctrine of Original Sin;

---

[101] *Journal*, ed. Curnock, VI, 209. See n. 19 for other retrospective views.

[102] *Journal*, ed. Curnock, V, 60–2; also in *Letters*, ed. Telford, IV, 235–9. See Baker, *Wesley and the Church of England*, Chapter 11.

[103] Watts's *The Ruin and Recovery of Mankind*, which appeared in 1740, the same year as the first edition of *The Scripture-Doctrine of Original Sin*, was attacked by Taylor in a supplement to the second edition (1741); Watts took note of Taylor's criticisms in the second edition of *The Ruin*

and what is Christianity better than heathenism? Wherein (save in rectifying some of our notions) has the religion of St. Paul any pre-eminence over that of Socrates or Epictetus?[104]

Natural man is evil, and man in his natural unaided state is incapable of knowing God. Wesley's view is succinctly summed up in his *Journal* account of a sermon he preached at Bath on 24 January 1743: 'Some of the rich and great were present, to whom, as to the rest, I declared with all plainness of speech: (1) that, by nature, they were all children of wrath; (2) that all their natural tempers were corrupt and abominable; and, (3) all their words and works, which could never be any better but by faith; and that (4) a natural man has no more faith than a devil, if so much.'[105] No man has a natural idea of God; there is no image of God stamped on man's soul; by nature every man is an atheist (Sermon 44, 'Original Sin'; 69, 'The Imperfection of Human Knowledge' (1784); 95, 'On the Education of Children', (1783)).[106] Wesley does not dismiss natural religion entirely. Knowledge that God exists can be deduced from God's works, but this is a knowledge of a very limited kind. At the end of Part II of *A Farther Appeal to Men of Reason and Religion* (1745) he urges those who accept natural but reject revealed religion to acknowledge this fundamental limitation:

I cannot love one whom I know not. How then can I love God till I know him? And how is it possible I should know God, unless he makes himself known unto me? By *analogy* or proportion? Very good. But where is that proportion to be found? What proportion does a creature bear to its creator? What is the proportion between finite and infinite?

I grant, the *existence* of the creatures demonstratively shows the *existence* of their Creator. The whole creation speaks that there is a God. But that is not the point in question. I know there is a God. Thus far is clear. But who will show me what that God is? . . .

O my friend, how will you get one step farther unless God reveal himself to your soul?[107]

In general, Wesley is very critical of the arguments derived from natural religion. After reproducing a Frenchman's account of the cruel and idle way of life of the Chicasaw Indians in the *Journal* for 9 July 1737, he comments, with a sneer at Wollaston, 'See *the religion of Nature truly delineated!*' In *The Doctrine of Grace* (1763) Warburton seizes on this passage to show that Wesley is an enemy to reason and natural religion, quoting another of Wesley's comments on the

---

and Recovery. Wesley joined in this debate, quoting at length and approvingly from Watts in Part IV of *Original Sin*. See Davis, *Watts*, 104–5.

[104] *Journal*, ed. Curnock, IV, 327; also in *Letters*, ed. Telford, IV, 67. In a letter of 9 December 1758 to the Calvinist A. M. Toplady Wesley claimed that Taylor's books had poisoned the clergy and universities of England, Scotland, Holland, and Germany; *Letters*, ed. Telford, IV, 48.

[105] *Journal*, ed. Curnock, III, 65.   [106] *Sermons*, ed. Outler, II, 176–8, 571; III, 350.

[107] *Appeals*, ed. Cragg, 268–9.

Indians: 'hence we could not but remark, What is the religion of nature, properly so called? or, that religion which flows from natural reason, unassisted by revelation'.[108] Wesley's reply in *A Letter to the Right Reverend the Lord Bishop of Gloucester* (1763) shows that he uses the term to mean not a theoretical set of deductions but the way of life of the natural man which is devoid of religion, so that 'natural religion' is a contradiction in terms:

What does your Lordship mean by 'natural religion'? A *system of principles*? But I mean by it, in this place, *men's natural manners*. These certainly 'flow from their *natural passions and appetites*', with that degree of *reason* which they have. And this, in other instances, is not contemptible; though it is not sufficient to teach them true religion.[109]

Wesley is totally disbelieving of the 'fair pictures' of human nature drawn by classical and especially contemporary English moralists, whose views have spread to such an extent that 'it is now quite unfashionable to talk otherwise, to say any thing to the disparagement of human nature' (Sermon 44, 'Original Sin').[110] Such 'fair pictures' are seductive and dangerous, particularly when they are apparently derived from empirical evidence. He is especially critical of the account given by Captain Wilson of the thoroughly good, amiable and benevolent inhabitants of the Pelew Islands, recorded in George Keate's *An Account of the Pelew Islands* (1788), in which their religion is described as follows:

Independant of external ceremony, there may be such a thing as the religion of the heart, by which the mind may, in awful silence, be turned to contemplate the GOD of NATURE; and though unblessed by those lights which have pointed to the Christian world an unerring path to happiness and peace, yet they might, from the light of reason only, have discovered the efficacy of virtue, and the temporal advantages arising from moral rectitude. – The reader will, by this time, have met with sufficient occurrences to convince him, that the inhabitants of these new-discovered regions had a fixed and rooted sense of the great moral duties; this appeared to govern their conduct, glow in all their actions, and grace their lives. – Actuated by such principles, we see them laborious, industrious, and benevolent. In moments of danger firm, and prodigal of life; in misfortunes patient; in death resigned.[111]

In the *Journal* for 16 January 1789 Wesley dismissed Wilson's description of the King of Pelew as 'the finest picture of atheistical religion that ever I saw'.[112] His objections are elaborated in 'Thoughts on a Late Publication'.

---

[108] *Journal*, ed. Curnock, I, 367–8; Warburton, *The Doctrine of Grace* (2nd edn, 1763), 224. Wesley's reference is to Wollaston, *The Religion of Nature Delineated* (1722). See *Sermons*, ed. Outler, III, 280–1n for other references to Wollaston. Cf. Wesley's derogatory definition of the 'natural religion' of American Indians as torture and murder in Sermon 38, 'A Caution against Bigotry' (1750), *Sermons*, ed. Outler, II, 67.

[109] *Appeals*, ed. Cragg, 502.

[110] *Sermons*, ed. Outler, II, 172–3. Cf. Sermon 128, 'The Deceitfulness of the Human Heart' (1792), *Sermons*, IV, 151.

[111] Keate, *Account of the Pelew Islands* (2nd edn, 1788), 324–5.

[112] *Journal*, ed. Curnock, VII, 464.

On the basis of his own experience of American Indians he refuses to believe in naturally good men. But the account contradicts Scripture as well as experience: 'if this account be true, the Bible is not true ... if mankind are faultless by nature, naturally endued with light to see all necessary truth, and with strength to follow it ... revelation is a mere fable; we can do perfectly well without it'.[113]

Though he believes the tendency of such pictures to be atheistical, Wesley does not concentrate his attack on atheists as such, nor on deists, but on moralists, because they are the majority and do not understand the dangerous implications of their own position. There are, in Wesley's opinion, very few speculative atheists – in fifty years' enquiry he claims to have found only two in the British Isles[114] – but those who preach up morality are no better than atheists. Some, like Francis Hutcheson (Wesley's *bête noire* among moralists – 'your smooth-tongued orator of Glasgow, one of the most pleasing writers of the age!'),[115] masquerade as Christians but undermine Christianity by making morality independent of God:

He does not make the least scruple to aver that if any temper or action be produced by any regard to God, or any view to a reward from him, it is not virtuous at all; and that if an action spring partly from benevolence and partly from a view to God, the more there is in it of a view to God, the less there is of virtue. I cannot see this beautiful essay of Mr. Hutcheson's [*An Inquiry into the Original of our Ideas of Beauty and Virtue* (1725)] in any other light than as a decent, and therefore more dangerous, attack upon the whole of the Christian revelation; seeing this asserts the love of God to be the true foundation both of the love of our neighbour and all other virtues.[116]

He sums up his objections in his *Journal* account of 17 December 1772 of Hutcheson's *Essay on the Nature and Conduct of the Passions and Affections* (1728):

He is a beautiful writer, but his scheme cannot stand unless the Bible falls. I know both from Scripture, reason, and experience that his picture of man is not drawn from the life. It is not true that no man is capable of malice, or delight in giving pain; much less that every man is virtuous, and remains so as long as he lives; nor does the Scripture allow that any action is good which is done without any design to please God.[117]

The majority recognise that religion consists of two parts, duty to both God and our neighbour, but in practice they forget the first and put the second for the whole duty of man:

[113] *Works*, ed. Jackson, XIII, 411–13; from *Arminian*, XIII (1790).
[114] Sermon 130, 'On Living without God' (written 1790), *Sermons*, ed. Outler, IV, 171.
[115] Sermon 106, 'On Faith' (1788), *Sermons*, ed. Outler, III, 499.
[116] Sermon 90, 'An Israelite Indeed' (1785), *Sermons*, ed. Outler, III, 279–80. Cf. the attack on Hutcheson in Sermon 105, 'On Conscience' (1788), where Hutcheson comes off worse than John Taylor, *Sermons*, ed. Outler, III, 483–4.
[117] *Journal*, ed. Curnock, V, 492–5. For other references to Hutcheson see *Sermons*, ed. Outler, I, 302n.

Thus almost all men of letters, both in England, France, Germany, yea, and all the civilized countries of Europe, extol 'humanity' to the skies, as the very essence of religion. To this the great triumvirate, Rousseau, Voltaire, and David Hume, have contributed all their labours, sparing no pains to establish a religion which should stand on its own foundation, independent on any revelation whatever, yea, not supposing even the being of a God. So leaving him, if he has any being, to himself, they have found out both a religion and a happiness which have no relation at all to God, nor any dependence upon him.

It is no wonder that this religion should grow fashionable, and spread far and wide in the world. But call it 'humanity', 'virtue', 'morality', or what you please, it is neither better nor worse than atheism.[118]

Wesley draws his arguments against this fashionable religion, as he states in his critique of Hutcheson and in the title of *The Doctrine of Original Sin*, from Scripture, reason, and experience. These corroborate each other, but the last provides the bulk of the evidence. That human nature is degenerate and diseased, that mankind is universally miserable, are facts that our knowledge of history, society, our acquaintance and indeed ourselves confirms. The method of Part I of *The Doctrine of Original Sin* is to survey 'the real state of mankind' in each of these areas. On the degeneracy of society, especially as shown in war, Wesley quotes from *Gulliver's Travels*, Parts II and IV, and comments: 'Surely all our declamations on the strength of human reason, and the eminence of our virtues, are no more than the cant and jargon of pride and ignorance, so long as there is such a thing as war in the world.' He concludes his survey with a summary statement of the obviousness of the fact: 'This is the plain, glaring, apparent condition of human kind'.[119] This fact is emphasised several times in Wesley's correspondence. For example: 'It is no play of imagination, but plain, clear fact. We see it with our eyes and hear it with our ears daily ... No man in his senses can deny it; and none can account for it but upon the supposition of original sin.'[120] Wesley's object in Part II of *The Doctrine of Original Sin* is to show that while experience *confirms* the fact, only the scriptural account of the fall can *explain* it: 'The only true and rational way of accounting for the general wickedness of mankind, in all ages and nations, is pointed out in those words: "In Adam all die" [I Corinthians 15:22].'[121] Only Scripture can both diagnose the disease and provide the cure. The doctrine of original sin (Wesley does not insist on the phrase, which is unscriptural, but on the explanation) is the fundamental difference between Christianity and heathenism, because any system of thought (Wesley lumps all such systems together as heathenism) that supposes man to be a naturally rational and virtuous creature obviates the need for Christ the physician: 'But what need of this, if we are in perfect health? If we are not diseased, we do not

---

[118] Sermon 120, 'The Unity of the Divine Being' (1790), *Sermons*, ed. Outler, IV, 68–9.

[119] *Works*, ed. Jackson, IX, 220–3, 234.

[120] 2 July 1772, *Letters*, ed. Telford, V, 327.   [121] *Works*, ed. Jackson, IX, 258.

want a cure ... If, therefore, we take away this foundation, that man is by nature foolish and sinful ... the Christian system falls at once'.[122]

The great mistake of heathens past and present, in Wesley's view, is to overestimate the role of reason, to attribute to it powers which it cannot have. He quotes in shortened form Taylor's comment on Romans 2:14, the basic scriptural source for natural religion: 'This text clearly proves that natural reason and understanding is a rule of action to all mankind, and that all men ought to follow it. This, therefore, overthrows the whole doctrine of original sin.'[123] Wesley argues that the fact that man has some reason remaining does not prove he is not fallen. On the contrary, Taylor is unable to deal on his terms with the problem of why there is so much vice in the world: 'suppose man a reasonable creature, and supposing virtue to be agreeable to the highest reason, according to all the rules of probability, the majority of mankind must in every age have been on the side of virtue'.[124] Experience demonstrates the absurdity of such a claim for reason. Wesley argues in Sermon 62, 'The End of Christ's Coming', that moralists who extol man's rational capacity to understand and hence to practise virtue fail to recognise that reason cannot restrain passion. The classical heathen moralists were aware that they could see the right but not attain it, yet they could not find a remedy for this problem: 'For they sought it where it never was and never will be found, namely, in themselves – in reason, in philosophy. Broken reeds! Bubbles! Smoke! They did not seek it in God, in whom alone it is possible to find it.'[125]

It is not Wesley's intention to deny the role of reason, rather to clarify its limitations. He strongly criticises Luther's attack on reason in his *Commentary on Galatians* in the *Journal* entry for 15 June 1741: 'How does he ... decry reason, right or wrong, as an irreconcilable enemy to the gospel of Christ! Whereas, what is reason (the faculty so called) but the power of apprehending, judging, and discoursing? Which power is no more to be condemned in the gross than seeing, hearing, or feeling.'[126] In Sermon 70, 'The Case of Reason Impartially Considered' (1781), he attempts to steer a Baxterian middle course between the extremes of those who despise reason as 'carnal', such as the antinomians, and those who overvalue it, such as the deists and Socinians. He complains that neither 'that great master of reason' Locke nor 'the good and great' Watts has succeeded in defining the mean between undervaluing and overvaluing reason, so he sets out to supply this 'grand defect' himself by showing what reason can and cannot do. He defines reason

---

[122] *Works*, ed. Jackson, IX, Preface, 194.

[123] *Works*, ed. Jackson, IX, Part II, 293; cf. Taylor, *Scripture-Doctrine* (3rd edn, 1750), 183.

[124] *Works*, ed. Jackson, IX, Part III, 350.   [125] *Sermons*, ed. Outler, II, 472–3.

[126] *Journal*, ed. Curnock, II, 467. Wesley attributes this definition to Aristotle: 'The operations of the mind are more accurately divided by Aristotle than by Mr. Locke. They are three, and no more: Simple apprehension, judgment and discourse' ('Remarks upon Mr. Locke's *Essay on Human Understanding*', *Works*, ed. Jackson, XIII, 456). Cf. Wilkins's definition of reason in *Ecclesiastes*, quoted above, p. 64.

(as in the criticism of Luther) as the faculty that exerts itself by apprehension, judgement, and discourse, and, having listed its uses in common life, goes on to examine its role in religion. Reason, with the assistance of the Spirit, enables us to understand the essential doctrines of Christianity expressed in Scripture, repentance, saving faith, justification, the new birth, and holiness, and guides us in all our duties. Thus 'there is a large field indeed wherein reason may expatiate and exercise all its powers.' But there are crucial things that it cannot do. It cannot produce faith, because it cannot provide evidence of the invisible world; it cannot produce hope of immortality, nor love of God and our neighbour, nor virtue, nor happiness. And Wesley appeals to his own experience of having unsuccessfully made the attempt in order to support his statement that reason can do none of these things.[127]

In general when Wesley uses the term reason, especially in his favourite phrase 'according to Scripture, reason and experience', he means it in this carefully limited sense as the faculty of reasoning. His caution to some extent derives from the first two books of Locke's *Essay Concerning Human Understanding*. He thus has a much less exalted view of the meaning of reason than a seventeenth-century latitude-man such as Whichcote or an eighteenth-century deist such as Matthew Tindal.[128] On the one occasion where he does use it in the sense a deist would have applauded, in *An Earnest Appeal to Men of Reason and Religion*, it is in order to deflate it. He appears at first to corroborate the 'reasonable man's' definition:

We join with you then in desiring a religion founded on reason, and every way agreeable thereto. But one question still remains to be asked: 'What do you mean by reason?' I suppose you mean the eternal reason, or the nature of things: the nature of God and the nature of man, with the relations necessarily subsisting between them. Why, this is the very religion *we* preach; a religion evidently founded on, and every way agreeable to, eternal reason, to the essential nature of things. Its foundation stands on the nature of God and the nature of man, together with their mutual relations.

But this is parody, as soon appears from Wesley's definition of the nature of man: 'It is every way suited to the nature of man, for it begins in a man's knowing himself: knowing himself to be what he really is – foolish, vicious, miserable.' This, of course, is something that the supporter of 'eternal reason' or 'the essential nature of things' who does not 'believe the Christian system to be of God' would never grant.[129] It is Wesley's object to subvert this definition, and then, moving on to the definition of reason as the faculty of

[127] *Sermons*, ed. Outler, II, 587–600.
[128] For the view of reason of the latitude-men see above, pp. 63–6. Locke and Tindal are treated in *Reason, Grace, and Sentiment*, II.
[129] *Appeals*, ed. Cragg, 55, 49. Contrast Tindal's attack in *Christianity as Old as the Creation* (1730), Chapter 14 on Samuel Clarke's inconsistency in *A Discourse concerning the Unchangeable Obligations of Natural Religion, and the Truth and Certainty of the Christian Revelation* (1706) in stressing the eternal rule of reason in the first part and the corruption of mankind in the second.

reasoning, to show how utterly dependent in matters of religion this faculty is on faith, the only means by which knowledge of the spiritual world is received:

What then will your reason do here? How will it pass from things natural to spiritual? From the things that are seen to those that are not seen? From the visible to the invisible world? What a gulf is here! By what art will reason get over the immense chasm? This cannot be till the Almighty come in to your succour, and give you that faith you have hitherto despised.[130]

Faith

Although Wesley is anxious to refute fashionable optimistic accounts of human nature, and although his own account, particularly in *The Doctrine of Original Sin*, is deliberately unattractive by contrast, in fact very little of his writing deals with this particular question. He is principally concerned not with man in a state of nature, but man in a state of grace, not with what man is in himself, but with what man may become through the gift of faith. Wesley's account is ultimately much more optimistic than those of the moralists, both secular and Christian, whom he attacks: his concept of perfection is much more demanding and ambitious, for example, than the concept of benevolence explored in different ways by Shaftesbury, Hutcheson, or Hume.[131] The crucial difference is that for Wesley the pursuit of perfection can only begin after a radical transformation of the individual's essential nature, the new birth. Though the individual has an important part to play at the beginning of this process, by repenting his natural condition, it is the gift of faith only that makes the completion of the process possible. Wesley normally identifies the stages as repentance, faith, justification (i.e. the individual's pardon and acceptance by God), assurance (his recognition that he is justified), the new birth (the beginning of sanctification), and sanctification, otherwise holiness or perfection. They are clearly set out in the opening pages of *A Farther Appeal to Men of Reason and Religion* (1745), Part I, and in Sermon 43, 'The Scripture Way of Salvation' (1765).[132] Though faith is the essential and the only condition of justification and sanctification, it is a means and not an end. In *The Principles of a Methodist Farther Explained* Wesley provides a telling image for the component parts of the process: 'Our main doctrines, which include all the rest, are three, – that of repentance, of faith, and of holiness. The first of these we account, as it were, the porch of religion; the next the door; the third, religion itself.'[133] Faith is the door of religion because it is only through faith that God is known, only through faith that man is justified and sanctified. But faith is not religion itself. In Sermon 36, 'The Law Established through Faith', II (1750), Wesley makes its subordinate position

---

[130] *Appeals*, ed. Cragg, 57.   [131] See *Reason, Grace, and Sentiment*, II.
[132] *Appeals*, ed. Cragg, 105–8; *Sermons*, ed. Outler, II, 156 ff.
[133] *Works*, ed. Jackson, VIII, 472.

clear: 'faith itself, even Christian faith, the faith of God's elect, the faith of the operation of God, still is only the handmaid of love. As glorious and honourable as it is, it is not the end of the commandment. God hath given this honour to love alone. Love is the end of all the commandments of God.'[134] Describing the function of this essential yet subordinate element in the process of salvation gave Wesley enormous difficulties. Of particular interest are his repeated attempts to define in adequate terms the experience of faith, and at the same time to defend his position against the often levelled charge of enthusiasm.

In *Advice to the People called Methodists* (1745) Wesley warns the members of his societies that they will give offence 'to men of form, by insisting so frequently and strongly on the inward power of religion; to moral men, (so called,) by declaring the absolute necessity of faith, in order to acceptance with God. To men of reason [they] will give offence, by talking of inspiration and receiving the Holy Ghost'.[135] The first and last of these 'offensive' doctrines pose particular problems of definition. Wesley sets himself to describe, though he admits he cannot explain, both the effect of faith on the individual, and the way that effect is brought about by the Spirit.

Early in *An Earnest Appeal* Wesley gives the following definition of faith, elaborating Hebrews 11:1: 'Faith is that divine evidence whereby the spiritual man discerneth God and the things of God. It is with regard to the spiritual world what sense is with regard to the natural. It is the spiritual sensation of every soul that is born of God.'[136] This attempt to define the experience of faith by analogy with the experience of physical sensation is repeated many times, and caused Wesley great difficulty with his critics. Sometimes he appears to be making a figurative comparison, drawing directly on biblical terminology, and sometimes to be attempting a scientific description. He wishes to demolish the accepted view that faith is a matter of opinion, of intellectual assent; such a notional or speculative faith is a dead faith. In its place he wishes to substitute the view that faith is a disposition of the heart (Sermon 18, 'The Marks of the New Birth', 1748).[137] The problem he must avoid is of making this appear simply a matter of subjective interpretation. In *An Earnest Appeal*, in his attempt to persuade the 'reasonable man' (who is unlikely to be moved by the kind of appeal to experience made elsewhere), Wesley incorporates biblical terminology with the language of Lockean empiricism, perhaps derived from his reading of Peter Browne's *The Procedure, Extent, and Limits of Human Understanding* (1728).[138] Wesley's view of religious knowledge, however, despite the convergence of terms, is fundamentally very

---

[134] *Sermons*, ed. Outler, II, 38.   [135] *Works*, ed. Jackson, VIII, 355.
[136] *Appeals*, ed. Cragg, 46.
[137] *Sermons*, ed. Outler, I, 418.
[138] On Wesley's debt to Locke and especially Browne in the field of religious epistemology see Hindley's suggestive article, 'The Philosophy of Enthusiasm' (1957).

different from Locke's. Our ideas are not innate but derive from our senses; our senses are of two kinds, natural and spiritual; faith is the means by which we record the impressions made on our spiritual senses, and the means by which reason can form ideas of the spiritual world. Biblical metaphors are put to the service of quasi-philosophical analysis:

It is necessary that you have *the hearing ear*, and the *seeing eye* [Proverbs 20:12], emphatically so called; that you have a new class of senses opened in your soul, not depending on organs of flesh and blood, to be 'the *evidence* of things not seen' [Hebrews 11:1] as your bodily senses are of visible things, to be the avenues to the invisible world, to discern spiritual objects, and to furnish you with ideas of what the outward 'eye hath not seen, neither the ear heard' [adapted from I Corinthians 2:9].[139]

Wesley carries this analysis further in the concluding section of his *Letter to Middleton*. We cannot know anything of the invisible world because we do not have physical senses 'suitable to invisible or eternal objects'. What every thinking man wants is a window in the breast to 'let in light from eternity'. It is faith that does this:

It gives a more extensive knowledge of things invisible, showing what eye had not seen, nor ear heard, neither before could it enter into our heart to conceive. And all these it shows in the clearest light, with the fullest certainty and evidence. For it does not leave us to receive our notices of them by mere reflection from the dull glass of sense; but resolves a thousand enigmas of the highest concern by giving faculties suited to things invisible.

(These 'faculties' are the equivalent of the 'spiritual senses' of *An Earnest Appeal*.) As a result every real Christian can say, 'I now am assured that these things are so: I experience them in my own breast.'

Wesley is again deliberately conflating the language of Scripture with that of philosophical argument. He goes on to claim that such internal evidence is the strongest of the arguments for the truth of Christianity. The traditional evidence may be weakened by time and is complicated, whereas the internal evidence is always present and is plain and simple: 'If, then, it were possible (which I conceive it is not) to shake the traditional evidence of Christianity, still he that has the internal evidence (and every true believer hath the witness or evidence in himself) would stand firm and unshaken.'[140] That Wesley should put forward this argument is consistent with what he says about experience elsewhere. Yet the manner of his argument should be related to its context, his attack on Middleton's historical scepticism, which Wesley believes undercuts not only the supposed miracles in the early church (the ostensible subject of *A Free Inquiry*) but also the authority of the New

---

[139] *Appeals*, ed. Cragg, 56–7.
[140] *Works*, ed. Jackson, X, 74–6. The concluding section of the *Letter to Middleton* was also used by Wesley as the conclusion to *A Letter to the Bishop of Gloucester*, *Appeals*, ed. Cragg, 527–38.

Testament. Wesley twice quotes a passage from Middleton's preface which thoroughly alarms him:

The credibility of facts lies open to the trial of our reason and senses. But the credibility of witnesses depends on a variety of principles wholly concealed from us. And though, in many cases, it may reasonably be presumed, yet in none can it certainly be known.

Wesley comments: 'If this be as you assert ... then farewell the credit of all history ... it is plain, all history, sacred or profane, is utterly precarious and uncertain.'[141] Hence he attempts to counter the implications of such scepticism with what he presents as scientific certainty, the unshakeable internal evidence.

In *An Earnest Appeal* and the *Letter to Middleton* Wesley subordinates biblical to philosophical terminology appropriate to his audience for his account of faith. He avoids considering the role of the Spirit, and he does not embellish his account of spiritual or internal sensation. It is when he concentrates not so much on the role of faith in the believer as on the operations of the Spirit on him that he uses a freer, more figurative language, and attempts to illustrate what he means by 'feeling'.[142] In his letter to Dr Stebbing of July 1739 (published in the *Journal* in 1742), in which he defends his doctrine of the new birth, Wesley argues that Stebbing is in no position to contradict him until he himself has experienced these 'inward feelings' for which he has such contempt:

When the Holy Ghost hath fervently kindled *your* love towards God, you will know these to be very *sensible* operations. As you 'hear the wind, and feel it, too', while it 'strikes upon your bodily organs', you will know you are under the guidance of God's Spirit the same way, namely, by *feeling it in your soul*; by the present peace and joy and love which you feel within, as well as by its outward and more distant effects.[143]

This doctrine, that the effects of the Spirit on the soul can be felt in a way analogous to physical sensation, is labelled 'perceptible inspiration' by 'John Smith' in his letter of 27 November 1745.[144] Wesley reacts to the label as follows in his reply of 30 December:

For this I earnestly contend; and so do all who are called Methodist preachers. But be pleased to observe what we mean thereby. We mean that inspiration of God's Holy Spirit whereby he fills us with righteousness, peace, and joy [Romans 14:17], with love to him and to all mankind. And we believe it cannot be, in the nature of things, that a man should be filled with this peace and joy and love by the inspiration of the Holy Ghost without perceiving it, as clearly as he does the light of the sun.[145]

[141] *Works*, ed. Jackson, X, 3, 65; Middleton, *Free Inquiry* (1749), ix.
[142] Cf. Nuttall, *The Holy Spirit in Puritan Faith and Experience* (1946), Chapters 2, 'The Discerning of Spirits', and 3, 'The Witness of the Spirit', for comparable language employed in the 1650s.
[143] *Letters*, ed. Baker, I, 672. The terms and phrases in italics (except the first) and inverted commas are Stebbing's. See also *Journal*, ed. Curnock, II, 251.
[144] *Letters*, ed. Baker, II, 170.   [145] *Letters*, ed. Baker, II, 181–2.

It is a subject Wesley returns to again and again in his dispute with 'Smith' and elsewhere, because of both the hostility it arouses and the difficulty he has in making himself understood.[146] In Part I of *A Farther Appeal to Men of Reason and Religion* Wesley devotes some space to showing that his views on 'the ordinary operations of the Holy Spirit', in spite of attacks made on his *Journals*, are orthodox: he quotes a long passage from a standard work, Pearson's *Exposition of the Creed* (1659), and several short passages from the Book of Common Prayer and the Homilies in support of his position and in defence of his terminology.[147] He concludes by restating his views in the terms that have given offence: the Spirit 'reveals' what we did not know before, it 'inspires' us with the faith, peace, joy, and love we could not have of ourselves:

And as we are figuratively said to *see* the light of faith, so by a like figure of speech we are said to *feel* this peace and joy and love; that is, we have an inward experience of them, which we cannot find any fitter word to express.

The reasons why in speaking of these things I use those terms (*inspiration* particularly) are, (1), because they are scriptural; (2), because they are used by our Church; (3), because I know none better.[148]

The importance he attaches to this account can be seen from the fact that he refers 'John Smith' to it (25 June 1746) and quotes from it in his answer to Warburton.[149]

In the important Sermon 10, 'The Witness of the Spirit', I (1746), Wesley deals with what 'John Smith' calls perceptible inspiration in very similar terms, while stressing the difficulty of adequate definition, especially philosophical definition. Yet because of the problem his opponents have set him, precise definition is essential. The problem is that because some enthusiasts 'have mistaken the voice of their own imagination for this "witness of the Spirit" of God', 'many reasonable men . . . are almost ready to set all down for "enthusiasts" who use the expressions which have been so terribly abused'. Expanding his text, Romans 8:16, and acknowledging that no words 'will adequately express what the children of God experience', Wesley states: 'the testimony of the Spirit is an inward impression on the soul, whereby the Spirit of God directly "witnesses to my spirit that I am a child of God"'.[150] The process cannot be explained, but the experience is as immediate as physical sensation:

the fact we know; namely, that the Spirit of God does give a believer such a testimony of his adoption that while it is present to the soul he can no more doubt the reality of his

---

[146] See 'Smith's' letters of 26 February 1746 and 27 April 1747, and Wesley's of 25 June 1746, 25 March 1747, and 10 July 1747, *Letters*, ed. Baker, II, 188, 202–3, 230–3, 240–1, 246–8.

[147] *Appeals*, ed. Cragg, 163–70.   [148] *Appeals*, ed. Cragg, 171.

[149] *Letters*, ed. Baker, II, 203; *Appeals*, ed. Cragg, 519–25.

[150] *Sermons*, ed. Outler, I, 269–70, 274.

sonship than he can doubt of the shining of the sun while he stands in the full blaze of his beams.[151]

Wesley is certain that this real witness can be distinguished from false witness, whether presumption or delusion, as easily as light from dark, 'provided your senses are rightly disposed'. Again he provides an analogy with physical sensation, stressing that this is the only method available:

In like manner, there is an inherent, essential difference between spiritual light and spiritual darkness . . . And this difference also is immediately and directly perceived, if our spiritual senses are rightly disposed.

To require a more minute and philosophical account of the *manner* whereby we distinguish these, and of the *criteria* or intrinsic marks whereby we know the voice of God, is to make a demand which can never be answered.[152]

It is worth pointing out that in Sermon 11, his second discourse on 'The Witness of the Spirit', written twenty years later (1767), Wesley quotes and reaffirms his definition of testimony, adding that he cannot see any way of making his expressions more intelligible.[153]

There are certain unresolved and perhaps unresolvable difficulties in Wesley's use of the language of feeling. Sometimes he uses it figuratively, as the only way of expressing the inexpressible, sometimes it appears to be intended literally. One of 'John Smith's' complaints in his letter of 27 November 1745 is that the reader cannot tell which is meant: 'the insisting too strongly even on Scripture metaphors has something in it misguiding to the reader . . . Thus the hanging so much on faith being the eye, the ear, the finger, the palate etc. of the soul, inclines a reader to think that you mean something more than mere metaphor'.[154] An example combining literal and figurative usage is in a letter of June 1744 to the lay preacher John Bennet insisting that no one is a Christian who does not have the biblical marks of one: 'One of these is, the love of God, which must be felt, if it is in the soul, as much as fire upon the body'.[155] Physical burning is an analogy for a literal feeling in the soul. Wesley sometimes makes it clear that he is using feeling or sensation as reliable empirical evidence: feeling is our basic source of knowledge. In the very interesting *Journal* entry for 8 January 1738 (on the voyage home from Georgia) he lists his own shortcomings, including unbelief, pride, and levity, and prays for faith, humility, and seriousness. He knows that he lacks these things 'by the most infallible of proofs, inward feeling'.[156] Similarly, in the entry for 4 January 1739, in which he presents his own difficulties as the

---

[151] *Sermons*, ed. Outler, I, 276; cf. the letter to Smith of 30 December 1745 quoted above. Outler, I, 276–7n, sees Wesley's theory of religious knowledge as deriving from Christian Platonism and distinct from his Thomist and Lockeian theory of empirical knowledge, and collects many of Wesley's references to the subject.

[152] *Sermons*, ed. Outler, I, 282.   [153] *Sermons*, ed. Outler, I, 287.

[154] *Letters*, ed. Baker, II, 167, referring to *An Earnest Appeal, Appeals*, ed. Cragg, 46–7.

[155] *Letters*, ed. Baker, II, 108.   [156] *Journal*, ed. Curnock, I, 415.

reflections of 'one who had the form of godliness many years', he accuses himself of not being a Christian because he does not love God. He answers a hypothetical question as to how he knows this: 'I *feel* this moment I do not love God; which therefore I *know* because I *feel* it. There is no word more proper, more clear, or more strong'.[157]

These statements, in which feeling is presented as certain knowledge, exemplify further difficulties in Wesley's use of the language of feeling. He is indignant when Bishop Lavington misapplies the first of these two passages from the *Journal*. In *A Second Letter to the Author of 'The Enthusiasm of Methodists and Papists Compared'* (1751) Wesley quotes Lavington: 'With what pertinacious confidence have impulses, impressions, feelings, etc., been advanced into *certain rules* of conduct? [The Methodists] have been taught to depend upon them, as sure guides and *infallible proofs*.'[158] Wesley is right to insist that he does not make feeling a certain rule of conduct. But the difficulty implied in making feeling a certain source of knowledge seems insuperable. On the one hand it seems that the validity of such feeling can only be asserted by the individual who has experienced it, while to the outsider it must appear simple enthusiasm. Wesley makes this point several times, in the letter to Stebbing, for example (see above), and in his *Journal* comment of 12 November 1739 on the traveller he met who criticised Whitefield's *Journals* as 'd—d cant, enthusiasm from end to end': 'Whatever is spoke of the religion of the heart, and of the inward workings of the Spirit of God, must appear enthusiasm to those who have not felt them.'[159] In Sermon 18, 'The Marks of the New Birth', he argues that the individual will know the truth of what he has experienced, will know that he is a child of God: 'Is the Spirit of adoption now in your heart? To your own heart let the appeal be made.'[160] This argument seems circular in precisely the way identified by Locke in Book IV, Chapter 19 of the *Essay concerning Human Understanding*, 'Of Enthusiasm'. Locke is attacking those in the puritan and nonconformist tradition who have contempt for the carefully worked out Anglican view of the mutually confirming relationship of reason and revelation, a view Wesley fully endorsed. Yet much of what Locke says fits Wesley's language, images, and arguments:

Reason is lost upon them, they are above it: they see the Light infused into their Understandings, and cannot be mistaken; 'tis clear and visible there; like the Light of bright Sunshine, shews it self, and needs no other Proof, but its own Evidence: they feel the Hand of GOD moving them within, and the impulses of the Spirit, and cannot be mistaken in what they feel ...

This is the way of talking of these Men: they are sure, because they are sure: and their Perswasions are right, only because they are strong in them. For, when what they say is strip'd of the Metaphor of seeing and feeling, this is all it amounts to: and yet

---

[157] *Journal*, ed. Curnock, II, 125–6.   [158] *Appeals*, ed. Cragg, 399.
[159] *Journal*, ed. Curnock, II, 319.
[160] *Sermons*, ed. Outler, I, 428.

these Similes so impose on them, that they serve them for certainty in themselves, and demonstration to others.

Locke insists that they must examine the grounds on which they claim the impression is from God,

or else all their Confidence is mere Presumption: and this Light, they are so dazled with, is nothing, but an *ignis fatuus* that leads them continually round in this Circle. *It is a Revelation, because they firmly believe it*, and *they believe it, because it is a Revelation*.[161]

Wesley is aware of this danger, yet his solution would not meet Locke's objection. It is only by appeal to the Spirit that the individual will know if his experience is from the Spirit, as he explains in a letter of 2 May 1771: 'There is a danger of every believer's mistaking the voice of the enemy or of their own imagination for the voice of God. And you can distinguish one from the other, not by any written rule, but only by *the unction of the Holy One*' [I John 2:20].[162] Such an argument would suggest that Wesley's appeal to feeling is solipsistic and that contemporaries were justified in their criticism.

On the other hand, Wesley's experimental method, his frequent appeals to experimental models, suggest that the individual can have experimental knowledge at second hand, that the feelings of others, although he may not share them, can be a valid testimony for him. There is evidence in the *Journal* and elsewhere to suggest that Wesley did not think himself capable of such feeling, or, as he sometimes calls it, 'the assurance of faith', and that his experience of assurance on 24 May 1738 was temporary (see, for example, his *Journal* entry of 14 October 1738, in which after self-examination he finds that he does not have lasting joy in the Holy Ghost or the full assurance of faith, and of 4 January 1739).[163] In an extraordinary and candid letter to his brother Charles of 27 June 1766, he clearly states that his faith is and always has been of a rational or intellectual and not an experimental kind (the phrases in square brackets were originally in shorthand):

[I am only an] honest heathen ... [I never had any] other 'ἔλεγχος of the eternal or invisible world that [I have] now; and that is [none at all], unless such as fairly shines from reason's glimmering ray. [I have no] direct witness, I do not say that [I am a child of God], but of anything invisible or eternal.[164]

Though this letter was not meant for public consumption, Wesley did not make a secret of the argument implied here. In the conclusion of the *Letter to Middleton*, after insisting on the certainty of internal evidence, Wesley goes on to argue that even if one has not experienced such internal evidence oneself, one can accept it on the testimony of others. Hence the primary importance of the writings of the early fathers (whom Middleton had attacked

---

[161] Locke, *Essay*, ed. Nidditch, IV, xix, *ff* 8–10, 700–2.   [162] *Letters*, ed. Telford, V, 241.
[163] *Journal*, ed. Curnock, II, 91; 125–6, quoted on the previous page.
[164] *Letters*, Telford, V, 16. 'ἔλεγχος = evidence (Hebrews 11:1).

in his book) is that they 'describe true, genuine Christianity, and direct us to the strongest evidence of the Christian doctrine'.[165] This argument that experience can be communicated and provide evidence at second hand obviously has very different implications from the view that experience is private. If the validity of experience can only be attested by the individual who has felt it, then it will inevitably appear enthusiasm to the outsider. But if that experience can be communicated and held up as a model (and though Wesley sometimes asserts the first view, his whole activity as a writer suggests his adherence to the second), then it is essential to distinguish true experience from false enthusiasm.

Wesley uses the term enthusiasm in a number of different though related ways. In one sense it is a common term of abuse, which instantly defines and condemns, and frees the person who uses it from any obligation to analyse his opponent's position. As he says in Part I of *A Farther Appeal*, 'To object "enthusiasm" to any person or doctrine is but a decent method of begging the question. It generally spares the objector the trouble of reasoning, and is a shorter and easier way of carrying his cause.'[166] Wesley often attacks this usage, of which he is a frequent victim, as a cant term directed against experimental religion; in Part III he says the nominal Christians 'have a kind of *cant* word for the whole religion of the heart; they call it "enthusiasm"'.[167] He similarly deplores the nominal Christians' classing of the doctrine of particular providence as enthusiasm; in Wesley's view the attempt to distinguish general from particular providence is both unscriptural and self-contradictory. In Sermon 37, 'The Nature of Enthusiasm' (1750), he asks, 'what is it (except only our own sins) which we are not to ascribe to the providence of God? So that I cannot apprehend there is any room here for the charge of enthusiasm.'[168] However, there is a definition of enthusiasm that both Wesley and his opponents accept, though they disagree utterly in their examples of it. In Part I of *A Farther Appeal* he says, 'I believe thinking men mean by enthusiasm a sort of religious madness, a *false imagination* of being inspired by God; and by an enthusiast one that *fancies* himself under the influence of the Holy Ghost, when in fact he is not.'[169] One of Wesley's objects in the *Appeals* is to clear himself from the charge of being such an enthusiast. In Sermon 37, his most detailed analysis of the subject, he retaliates by charging the nominal Christians with enthusiasm: 'The most common of all the enthusiasts of this kind are those who imagine themselves Christians, and are not.' Because these 'Christians' are in the majority, they believe themselves to be in their right minds. But 'in the sight of God, and his holy angels – yea, and

---

[165] *Works*, ed. Jackson, X, 78–9.   [166] *Appeals*, ed. Cragg, 170.
[167] *Appeals*, ed. Cragg, 268.
[168] *Sermons*, ed. Outler, II, 57. See also no. 67, 'On Divine Providence' (1786), II, 544–8, and *An Estimate of the Manners of the Present Times* (1782), *Works*, ed. Jackson, XI, 159–60.
[169] *Appeals*, ed. Cragg, 170.

all the children of God upon earth – you are mere madmen, mere enthusiasts all.'[170] By means of this usage Wesley is exposing his opponents' abusiveness and at the same time seriously stating his view that they are without religion. But this is an isolated example. Wesley most often uses the term in relation not to his moralist, 'formal' opponents, but to those among his followers and associates who have not understood the full implications of the religion of the heart. Question 34 of the *Large Minutes* reads: 'Why are not we more holy?' The answer is: 'Chiefly because we are enthusiasts; looking for the end, without using the means.'[171] This phrase, which recurs in the correspondence and in 'The Nature of Enthusiasm', means in a specific sense, when applied to the preachers, neglecting study, self-discipline, and rational discourse, and in a more general sense overstressing the experimental or feeling side of religion at the expense of the rational and scriptural. The experience of faith, in the image quoted at the beginning of this section, is the door of religion; holiness is religion itself. True experience can be distinguished from false enthusiasm because it has manifest fruits, so that it can be validated not only by the individual's appeal to his own feeling, but by the observer's appeal to the test of scripture and reason.

Holiness

Wesley was in no doubt that the single most important feature of Methodism was its emphasis on holiness. In his early *Advice to the People called Methodists* (1745) it is this that heads the list of Methodist principles:

There is no other sect of people among us (and, possibly, not in the Christian world) who hold ... all [these principles] in the same degree and connexion; who so strenuously and continually insist on the absolute necessity of universal holiness both in heart and life; of a peaceful, joyous love of God; of a supernatural evidence of things not seen; of an inward witness that we are the children of God; and of the inspiration of the Holy Ghost, in order to any good thought, or word, or work.[172]

In the *Large Minutes* Question 3, 'What may we reasonably believe to be God's design in raising up the Preachers called Methodists?' is answered: 'Not to form any new sect; but to reform the nation, particularly the Church; and to spread scriptural holiness over the land.'[173] In a late letter of 15 September 1790 Wesley comments on full sanctification (one of his synonyms for holiness): 'This doctrine is the grand depositum which God has lodged with the people called Methodists; and for the sake of propagating this chiefly He appeared to have raised us up.'[174] Yet Wesley had great difficulty in defining his doctrine clearly and in defending it from the attacks of his opponents. As with faith, this was a problem partly of the limitations of language and partly

[170] *Sermons*, ed. Outler, II, 51–2.   [171] *Works*, ed. Jackson, VIII, 316.
[172] *Works*, ed. Jackson, VIII, 353.
[173] *Works*, ed. Jackson, VIII, 299.   [174] *Letters*, ed. Telford, VIII, 238.

of the validity of testimony. Wesley defined holiness in a number of ways: by using it interchangeably with certain synonyms, by repeating certain explanatory phrases, by appealing to the interpretation of certain scriptural texts, and by holding up as exemplary models (both to prove the doctrine true and to encourage others) witnesses whom he believed to embody holiness in their lives. His synonyms for holiness are love (sometimes perfect or Christian love), Christian liberty, simplicity, purity, sanctification (sometimes full or entire sanctification), and, most important of these, perfection. For example: 'Perfect love and Christian liberty are the very same thing ... And what is Christian liberty but another word for holiness?' (letter of 5 October 1770); 'The essence of Christian holiness is simplicity and purity' (letter of 14 April 1771);[175] 'Christian perfection ... is only another term for holiness. They are two names for the same thing' (Sermon 40, 'Christian Perfection', 1741);[176] 'This I term sanctification (which is both an instantaneous and a gradual work), or perfection, the being perfected in love, filled with love, which still admits of a thousand degrees. But I have no time to throw away in contending for words' (letter of 28 December 1770).[177]

Certain qualifying adjectives are frequently associated with holiness, and some phrases are used in apposition to or as equivalents for it. The most important of these are 'inward holiness', 'inward or holy temper', 'social holiness', 'holiness of heart and life', 'purity of intention', 'the image of God', and three favourite biblical phrases, 'faith working by love' (from Galatians 5:6),[178] 'the mind that was in Christ' (from Philippians 2:5), and 'walking as Christ walked' (from I John 2:6). An important early statement linking several such phrases (some of which appear to derive from one of the influential works read by the Oxford Methodists in the 1720s, Henry Scougal's *The Life of God in the Soul of Man*, 1677) is the 'new judgement of holiness' given in the *Journal* for 14 October 1738:

He no longer judges it to be an outward thing – to consist either in doing no harm, in doing good, or in using the ordinances of God. He sees it is the life of God in the soul; the image of God fresh stamped on the heart; an entire renewal of the mind in every temper and thought, after the likeness of Him that created it.[179]

Sanctification or holiness is similarly described in the *Journal* for 13 September 1739: 'I believe it to be an inward thing, namely, the life of God in the soul of man; a participation of the divine nature; the mind that was in Christ; or, the

---

[175] *Letters*, ed. Telford, V, 203, 238.   [176] *Sermons*, ed. Outler, II, 104.

[177] *Letters*, ed. Telford, V, 215.

[178] For Wesley's uses of this text see *Sermons*, ed. Outler, I, 139n. Contrast the portrait of the good Dr Greville in Graves's anti-Methodist novel, *The Spiritual Quixote* (1773): 'He had a *Faith*, which worked by *Love*; or, in modern language, his belief of the truths of the Gospel made him consider as an indispensable duty those acts of beneficence which his humanity prompted him to perform' (ed. Tracy (1967), 432).

[179] *Journal*, ed. Curnock, II, 90. See Butler, *Scougal and the Oxford Methodists* (1899), Chapter 8.

renewal of our heart after the image of Him that created us.'[180] That holiness is social is insisted in the Preface to *Hymns and Sacred Poems* (1739), in which the solitary religion of the mystics is repudiated: 'The gospel of Christ knows of no religion, but social; no holiness but social holiness. "Faith working by love" is the length and breadth and depth and height of Christian perfection.'[181] In a letter of 27 June 1769 to 'a pious and sensible woman' who has broken with the Methodists Wesley again links several of his crucial phrases:

By Christian Perfection, I mean (1) loving God with all our heart. Do you object to this? I mean (2) a heart and life all devoted to God. Do you desire less? I mean (3) regaining the whole image of God. What objection to this? I mean (4) having all the mind that was in Christ. Is this going too far? I mean (5) walking uniformly as Christ walked. And this surely no Christian will object to. If any one means anything more, or anything else by perfection, I have no concern with it.[182]

In one of his last sermons, no. 127, 'On the Wedding Garment', published posthumously in 1791, Wesley reiterates the scriptural basis for his account of holiness:

What then is that holiness which is the true wedding garment, the only qualification for glory? 'In Christ Jesus ... neither circumcision availeth anything, nor uncircumcision, but a new creation' [Galatians 6:15], the renewal of the soul 'in the image of God wherein it was created' [Colossians 3:10]. In 'Christ Jesus neither circumcision availeth anything nor uncircumcision', but 'faith which worketh by love' [Galatians 5:6] ... In a word, holiness is the having 'the mind that was in Christ' [Philippians 2:5], and the 'walking as Christ walked' [I John 2:6].[183]

Yet Wesley's difficulties with the definition of his doctrine were perennial. He insisted again and again that it was simple, clear, easily explicated, traditional, obvious to all Christians, and consistent with what he had taught and believed from 1725 (the year in which he first read Jeremy Taylor). And yet it caused offence and distress to both opponents and followers, particularly as he came to use the term perfection, about which he had some hesitations early in his career, more and more frequently as a substitute for holiness and sanctification. It would seem that Wesley was wrong to stress the obviousness and orthodoxy of his doctrine, and his contemporaries were right to be startled. If one accepts at face value Wesley's insistence on the limited and straightforward meaning of his doctrine, then perfection is not the right word for it, and it is odd that he was prepared to do battle at such length for the term. His own defence, of course, was that it is scriptural:

There is scarce any expression in Holy Writ which has given more offence than this. The word 'perfect' is what many cannot bear ... And hence some have advised, wholly to lay aside the use of those expressions, 'because they have given so great offence'. But

---

[180] *Journal*, ed. Curnock, II, 275.   [181] *Works*, ed. Jackson, XIV, 321.
[182] *Journal*, ed. Curnock, V, 324–5; also in *Letters*, ed. Telford, V, 141.
[183] *Sermons*, ed. Outler, IV, 147.

are they not found in the oracles of God? If so, by what authority can any messenger of God lay them aside, even though all men should be offended?

(Sermon 40, 'Christian Perfection', 1741)[184]

But if one sets his definitions alongside his scriptural interpretations and his experimental examples, then it is clear that Wesley arrived at an extraordinarily optimistic view of the capacities of regenerate human nature which completely over-rides his orthodox insistence on the sinfulness of the natural man.

As Wesley used the term, perfection is on the one hand part of a process which begins with justification and ends after death with glorification, so that it is necessarily incomplete and limited by the restrictions of human nature (and hence logically imperfect, though Wesley does not admit this). On the other hand perfection is the fulfilment of all that human nature, aided by grace, can achieve, and it is open to all who have faith. Faith is the essential precondition to holiness: the process of sanctification begins after justification, but they are not the same thing: 'The one implies what God *does for us* through his Son; the other what he *works in us* by his Spirit' (Sermon 5, 'Justification by Faith').[185] The experience of sanctification is distinct from that of justification, as Wesley shows in the *Journal* for 7 June 1763: 'One came to me who believed God had just set her soul at full liberty. She had been clearly justified long before; but said the change she now experienced was extremely different from what she experienced then – as different as the noon-day light from that of day-break; that she now felt her soul all love, and quite swallowed up in God.'[186] Sanctification is the work of God and man together, and it is important that it should be recognised by both the testimony of the Spirit and the fruit of a holy life; Wesley's comment in a letter of 3 April 1766 on one of his preachers who taught that 'there is no such thing in any believer as a *direct, immediate* testimony of the Spirit that he is a child of God, that the Spirit testifies this *only* by the fruits, and consequently that the witness and the fruits are *all one*' was that this was to return to justification by works.[187] Yet the part played by man must not be minimised: in *Thoughts upon Necessity* (1774), he insists that the mistake of all predestinarians, ancient or modern, Manichaean, Stoic, Calvinist, or deist (the contemporaries he aims at are Lord Kames, Jonathan Edwards, and David Hartley), is by denying free will to make man 'a mere machine' incapable of moral choice.[188] In *Predestination Calmly Considered* (1752), Wesley argues that although sanctification is the work of God, man works with God to achieve it:

---

[184] *Sermons*, ed. Outler, II, 99–100.
[185] *Sermons*, ed. Outler, I, 187. Cf. Sermon 43, 'The Scripture Way of Salvation', *Sermons*, ed. Outler, II, 158.
[186] *Journal*, ed. Curnock, V, 16.   [187] *Letters*, ed. Telford, V, 8.
[188] *Works*, ed. Jackson, X, 468–9. Cf. Sermon 62, 'The End of Christ's Coming', *Sermons*, ed. Outler, II, 475.

We allow, it is the work of God alone to justify, to sanctify, and to glorify; which three comprehend the whole of salvation. Yet we cannot allow, that man can only resist, and not in any wise 'work together with God'; or that God is so the whole worker of our salvation, as to exclude man's working at all ... for the Scripture is express, that (having received power from God) we are to 'work out our own salvation' [Philippians 2:12]; and that (after the work of God is begun in our souls) we are 'workers together with Him' [II Corinthians 6:1].[189]

It is through this working together that man achieves perfection, as Wesley explains in Sermon 85, 'On Working out our own Salvation' (1785):

Therefore inasmuch as God works in you, you are now able to work out your own salvation. Since he worketh in you of his own good pleasure, without any merit of yours, both to will and to do [Philippians 2:13], it is possible for you to fulfil all righteousness ... We know indeed that word of his to be absolutely true, 'Without me ye can do nothing' [John 15:5]. But on the other hand we know, every believer can say, 'I can do all things through Christ that strengtheneth me' [Philippians 4:13].[190]

It is this last triumphant claim that the Christian can repeatedly retort to the predestinarian.[191]

Wesley's account of perfection underwent some modifications, but his considered view can be summarised from a number of sources: Sermon 40, 'Christian Perfection' (1741), 76, 'On Perfection' (1785), 83, 'On Patience' (1784); the *Journal*, especially Parts XI to XIV (published 1764–71), the letters, especially those written during the 1760s, and *A Plain Account of Christian Perfection* (1766, last revised edition 1777), in which he reprinted and reaffirmed his previous statements, criticising a few of them, though disregarding his earlier reluctance to use the term. The doctrine is extracted from many passages in the New Testament – in *A Plain Account* he says 'it is the doctrine of St. Paul, the doctrine of St. James, of St. Peter, and St. John'[192] – but three are particularly important: I Corinthians 13 (which Joseph Benson considered to be an exact picture of John Fletcher),[193] I John, and Matthew 5 (the Sermon on the Mount), especially verse 48. Wesley's literal translation of the last is important; he converts the command of the Authorised Version, 'Be ye therefore perfect', into a promise: 'Therefore ye shall be perfect, as your Father who is in heaven is perfect'. In *Explanatory Notes upon the New Testament* (1755), which consists of his revised translation together with doctrinal annotation, part of his note on this verse reads: 'He well knew, how ready our unbelief would be, to cry out, This is impossible! And therefore stakes upon it all the Power, Truth and Faithfulness of Him, to whom all things are possible.'

What does it mean to be perfect? For perfection to be attainable it must not

---

[189] *Works*, ed. Jackson, X, 230–1.   [190] *Sermons*, ed. Outler, III, 207–8.
[191] 'A Thought on Necessity', *Arminian* (1780), *Works*, ed. Jackson, X, 478–9.
[192] *Works*, ed. Jackson, XI, 444.
[193] *Life of Fletcher*, *Works*, ed. Jackson, XI, 354; cf. *Letters*, ed. Telford, V, 268, VII, 120.

be set too high. Here Wesley criticises both his own early confidence in the capacities of the perfect[194] and his brother Charles's conception, which in a letter of 9 July 1766 he objects is beyond any human capacity: '*That perfection* which I believe, I can boldly preach, because I think I see five hundred witnesses of it. Of *that perfection* which you preach, you do not even think you see any witness at all ... Therefore I still think to set perfection *so high* is effectually to renounce it.'[195] What Wesley means by this is summed up in his attack on Thomas Maxfield in the *Journal* for 1 November 1762: 'I dislike your supposing man may be as perfect as an angel; that he can be absolutely perfect; that he can be infallible, or above being tempted; or that the moment he is pure in heart he cannot fall from it.'[196] In Sermon 76 he insists that no man while in the body can attain angelic or Adamic perfection.[197] The perfect are subject to the limitations of their own physical nature: Wesley repeatedly states that they are liable to ignorance, error, infirmities and temptations.[198] On these grounds (and also because the expression is not scriptural) Wesley rejects the phrase 'sinless perfection'.

However, perfection must not be set too low. As he explains in Sermons 40 and 83, in the terms of I John 2:13, perfection is the state not of little children or young men but of fathers.[199] The perfect cannot avoid involuntary transgressions, but these are not sins: sin is defined in *A Plain Account* as 'a voluntary transgression of a known law',[200] and the perfect do not sin, either outwardly or inwardly, as Wesley claims in Sermon 83:

Ye shall then be *perfect*. The Apostle seems to mean by this expression, τέλειοι [James 1:4], ye shall be wholly delivered from every evil work, from every evil word, from every sinful thought; yea, from every evil desire, passion, temper, from all inbred corruption, from all remains of the carnal mind, from the whole body of sin: and ye shall be renewed in the spirit of your mind, in every right temper, after the image of him that created you, in righteousness and true holiness [Ephesians 4:23–4].[201]

The precise definition of the term sin – the distinction between sins and mistakes, and voluntary and involuntary transgressions – involved Wesley in some difficulty with his critics, a difficulty he bypassed (as so often) by turning from the word to the thing, from definition to example. Thus he dismisses the objections of one of his preachers in a letter of 7 June 1761: 'This whole affair is a strife of words. The thing is plain. All in the body are liable to mistakes, practical as well as speculative. Shall we call them sins or no? I answer again and again, Call them just what you please.'[202] In the *Journal* for 18 November

---

194 See *A Plain Account, Works*, ed. Jackson, XI, 378–81.   195 *Letters*, ed. Telford, V, 20.
196 *Journal*, ed. Curnock, IV, 535; also *Letters*, ed. Telford, IV, 192.
197 *Sermons*, ed. Outler, III, 72–3.
198 Sermon 40, *Sermons*, ed. Outler, II, 100–4; *Earnest Appeal, Appeals*, ed. Cragg, 66; *Plain Account, Works*, ed. Jackson, XI, 418–19; Sermon 76, *Sermons*, ed. Outler, III, 73.
199 *Sermons*, ed. Outler, II, 105, III, 175–6.   200 *Works*, ed. Jackson, XI, 396.
201 *Sermons*, ed. Outler, III, 179.
202 *Letters*, ed. Telford, IV, 155.

1763 he gives an account of 'the perfecting of the saints' (Ephesians 4:12): 'After a deep conviction of inbred sin, of their total fall from God, [many persons] have been so filled with faith and love (and generally in a moment) that sin vanished, and they found from that time no pride, anger, desire or unbelief...Now, whether we call this the destruction or suspension of sin, it is a glorious work of God'.[203] In spite of this difficulty with terminology, apparent at several points in *A Plain Account*, Wesley summarised the doctrine towards the end of that work in eleven short and clear propositions (here abbreviated): (1) 'There is such a thing as perfection, for it is again and again mentioned in Scripture.' (2) 'It is not so early as justification'. (3) 'It is not so late as death'. (4) 'It is not absolute'. (5) 'It does not make a man infallible.' (6) 'It is "salvation from sin"' (again, Wesley avoids contending for the term 'sinless'). (7) 'It is "perfect love"' [I John 4:18]. (8) 'It is improvable'. (9) 'It is amissible, capable of being lost'. (10) 'It is constantly both preceded and followed by a gradual work.' (11) It is often but not necessarily instantaneous (this represents a change from Wesley's earlier view that it must be so).[204]

Wesley stresses the attainability of perfection because it is an essential element of his doctrine that it should be consonant with Scripture *and* experience. As he claims in *A Plain Account*, 'by ... comparing it again and again with the word of God on the one hand, and the experience of the children of God on the other, we saw farther into the nature and properties of Christian perfection'.[205] The doctrine is supported by Scripture on the one hand and experience on the other; but if there is no witness to the experience, then the interpretation of Scripture must be wrong. 'If I were convinced that none in England had attained what has been so clearly and strongly preached by such a number of Preachers, in so many places, and for so long a time, I should be clearly convinced that we had all mistaken the meaning of those scriptures'.[206] Hence the problem of identifying the perfect and demonstrating that they are saved from sin is crucial. (It is worth stressing that Wesley never claimed to have achieved this state himself.) The problem is twofold: the individual who thinks he has been sanctified must be able to identify his experience, and he must be able to persuade the observer of the truth of what he claims has happened. Joseph Benson thought Wesley was prone to be taken in by those who told him 'a tale of their being saved from sin and perfected in love'.[207] The letters and *Journal* show how anxious Wesley was to collect and broadcast such evidence. But he believed his methods to be rational: thus in *A Plain Account* he argues that infallible knowledge is

[203] *Journal*, ed. Curnock, V, 41.
[204] *Works*, ed. Jackson, XI, 441–2. Contrast e.g. the account of instantaneous sanctification in the letter to Thomas Olivers of 24 March 1757, *Letters*, ed. Telford, III, 213.
[205] *Works*, ed. Jackson, XI, 385.
[206] *Works*, ed. Jackson, XI, 406; cf. the letter to Charles Wesley of 12 February 1767, *Letters*, ed. Telford, V, 41.
[207] *Letters*, ed. Telford, V, 158.

impossible, but tests can be devised which 'would be sufficient proofs to any reasonable man'. The testimony of the individual should be believed if his past and subsequent behaviour indicates that he is unlikely to lie. If the individual attends carefully to all the 'marks', he is unlikely to be deceived in himself:

> If a man be deeply and fully convinced, after justification, of inbred sin; if he then experience a gradual mortification of sin, and afterwards an entire renewal in the image of God; if to this change, immensely greater than that wrought when he was justified, be added a clear, direct witness of the renewal; I judge it as impossible this man should be deceived herein, as that God should lie. And if one whom I know to be a man of veracity testify these things to me, I ought not, without some sufficient reason, to reject his testimony.[208]

By such a process of 'reasonable proof', in which Scripture, reason, and experience were tested against each other, Wesley satisfied himself of the veracity of his principal doctrine. Perhaps the most confident assertion of the efficacy of this threefold method, though he does not appeal to it specifically here, is in the letter to the Countess of Huntingdon of 19 June 1771 (written in the aftermath of the controversy over the 1770 Minutes),[209] in which Wesley argues that the experimental success of his scriptural interpretation proves its truth: 'the gospel which I now preach God does still confirm by new witnesses in every place ... Now, I argue from glaring, undeniable fact; God cannot bear witness to a lie. The gospel, therefore, which He confirms must be true in substance.'[210]

An essential element of the gospel that Wesley preached is the inevitable conjunction of holiness and happiness. It is a conjunction that is stressed repeatedly in the sermons:[211] 'true religion, or a heart right toward God and man, implies happiness as well as holiness' (Sermon 7, 'The Way to the Kingdom', 1746); 'none but a Christian is happy; none but a real, inward Christian ... he who is not happy is not a Christian; seeing if he was a real Christian he could not but be happy' (Sermon 77, 'Spiritual Worship', 1781).[212] After giving his 'plain, naked portraiture of a Christian' towards the end of his *Letter to Middleton*, Wesley urges his reader to 'look at the substance, – his tempers, his holiness, his happiness', and asks 'Can calm reason conceive either a more amiable or a more desirable character?'[213] This conviction that the true Christian is happy, that misery has no part in the Christian life, and, on the contrary, that it is the ungodly who are miserable now was one that Wesley always held. In an early letter to his mother of 28 May 1725, he objects to the emphasis in the *Imitatio Christi* on human misery:

---

[208] *Works*, ed. Jackson, XI, 398–402.   [209] See above, pp. 212–13.
[210] *Letters*, ed. Telford, V, 259.
[211] This conjunction is frequently noted by Outler; see e.g. *Sermons* I, 35, 185n.
[212] *Sermons*, ed. Outler, I, 223; III, 99–100.
[213] *Works*, ed. Jackson, X, 71.

I can't think that when God sent us into the world he had irreversibly decreed that we should be perpetually miserable in it. If it be so, the very endeavour after happiness in this life is a sin, as it is acting in direct contradiction to the very design of our creation. What are become of all the innocent comforts and pleasures of life, if it is the intent of our creator that we should never taste them? If our taking up the cross implies our bidding adieu to all joy and satisfaction, how is it reconcilable with what Solomon so expressly affirms of religion, that her ways are ways of pleasantness, and all her paths peace [Proverbs 3:17]?[214]

In a sermon published fifty years later, no. 84, 'The Important Question', he insists that 'there cannot be a more false supposition than that a life of religion is a life of misery; seeing true religion, whether considered in its nature or in its fruits, is true and solid happiness', and, dismissing the false assumption that the misery of the Christian now is rewarded by happiness hereafter whereas with the ungodly it is the other way about, he asks his audience to make a fundamental choice: 'Will you be happy here and hereafter – in the world that now is, and in that which is to come? Or will you be miserable here and hereafter, in time and in eternity?'[215] The most striking example of this conviction is in Wesley's treatment of Matthew 5:3–12 in *Explanatory Notes upon the New Testament*. The 'blessed' of the Authorised Version is here rendered 'happy',[216] and Wesley annotates verse 2 as follows:

Knowing that Happiness is our common Aim, and that an innate Instinct continually urges us to the pursuit of it, [Jesus] in the kindest Manner applies to that Instinct, and directs it to its proper Object.

Tho' all Men desire, yet few attain Happiness, because they seek it where it is not to be found. Our Lord therefore begins his Divine Institution, which is the compleat Art of Happiness, by laying down before all that have Ears to hear, the true and only Method of acquiring it.

In this emphasis on the happiness of the Christian life Wesley's debt to the tradition of later seventeenth-century Anglicanism is obvious. Yet it was the development of the same tradition that he attacked from the 1730s onwards as responsible for a widespread belief in salvation by works: the eighteenth-century Church of England, as he saw it, had neglected its own Homilies and Articles and relinquished the true Reformation doctrine of justification by faith.[217] The result was a split between faith and works, to which he attributed the antinomian tendencies he saw in the Revival. Hence his complaint in Sermon 35, 'The Law Established through Faith', I (1750): 'they are the

---

[214] *Letters*, ed. Baker, I, 163.   [215] *Sermons*, ed. Outler, III, 192, 197.

[216] As he says it should be in Sermon 21, the first of thirteen discourses on the Sermon on the Mount, *Sermons*, ed. Outler, I, 475.

[217] See e.g. his attack on Tillotson's sermons on regeneration in his unpreached Sermon 150, 'Hypocrisy in Oxford' (1741, published 1797), *Sermons*, ed. Outler, IV, 396. He is less critical but lukewarm in his comments on Tillotson in *A Christian Library*, XLV (1755); ed. Jackson, XXVII (1826), 3. Whitefield's hostility to Tillotson was notorious; see Tyerman, *Whitefield* (1876), I, 360–1.

Pharisees who make the antinomians. Running into an extreme so palpably contrary to Scripture, they occasion others to run into the opposite one. These, seeking to be justified by works, affright those from allowing any place for them.' And he adds in a very Baxterian tone: 'But the truth lies between both.'[218] Wesley's lifelong aim was to reconcile these extremes, the Reformation, puritan, and nonconformist tradition of faith and experience with the Catholic and seventeenth-century Anglican tradition of works and holiness. From the point of view of his opponents he failed dismally: to Anglican moralists he was an enthusiast, and to Calvinists and 'antinomians' a preacher of the law. His *Christian Library* can be seen as a brave and equally doomed attempt to achieve in a relatively popular and accessible way what Baxter laboured at more systematically and for a more sophisticated audience in *Catholick Theologie*. Wesley's awareness of the strengths and historical limitations of each tradition is explicit in his prefatory comments on the puritan writers he edited and on *The Whole Duty of Man*. Among the faults of the former, he objects that 'they generally give a low and imperfect view of sanctification or holiness'; conversely his list of their strengths concludes: 'the peculiar excellency of these writers seems to be, the building us up in our most holy faith'.[219] *The Whole Duty of Man* is presented as a mid-seventeenth-century antidote to an excessive emphasis on faith at the expense of works: 'Whoever reads the following Treatise, should consider the time wherein it was wrote. Never was there more talk of faith in Christ, of justification by faith, and of the fruits of the Spirit. And scarce ever was there less practice of plain, moral duties, of justice, mercy, and truth.' Wesley is certain that there is nothing in the book inconsistent with the doctrine of justification by faith, and that contemporary readers will not be induced by it 'to seek salvation by their own righteousness'. He trusts that 'many, who have already experienced the free grace of God in Christ Jesus, may hereby be more fully instructed to walk in him, and more thoroughly furnished for every good word and work'.[220] Thus the puritans build up faith but neglect holiness; the *Whole Duty* offers instruction in holiness to those already justified by faith. Wesley is attempting to make works which in their historical context were discontinuous and mutually antagonistic into a complementary whole.

But Wesley's thought represents much more than a middle way between extremes or a reconciliation of opposites. As he conceived it, faith working by love is a process in which grace and reason, faith and works, Scripture and experience, religion and ethics are indissolubly linked in order to produce the holy and happy life, the life of perfection, here on earth. This extraordinarily optimistic and original concept – which Wesley always regarded as the

218 *Sermons*, ed. Outler, II, 27. See Outler's note, I, 593–4. Cf. Chapter 3 above, p. 131.
219 *Christian Library*, ed. Jackson, IV (1819), 106–7. The puritans appeared in Volumes VII to XII (1751); ed. Jackson, IV–VII.
220 *Christian Library*, ed. Jackson, XII (1821), 25–6; originally published in Volume XXI (1753).

traditional teaching of Christianity, true to common experience and expressed in common language – paradoxically can be seen in some respects (but only in some) to belong with the secular ethical enterprise of the contemporary moralists and freethinkers he detested. But the divorce of ethics from religion was inconceivable to Wesley. Only the regenerate man, whose life is a process of recovering in himself the image of God, will be perfect; yet this perfection is possible to all human beings.

Bibliography

This bibliography includes all the works cited, together with some of the works consulted. Books by authors and on subjects relevant to the whole study but treated only tangentially in Volume I (for example Shaftesbury and freethinking) will be found in the bibliography to Volume II. Unless otherwise stated, the place of publication is London.

Primary Sources

[Alleine, Theodosia, *et al.*], *The Life & Death of that Excellent Minister of Christ Mr. Joseph Alleine* (1673).

Allestree, Richard, *Forty Sermons* (Oxford, 1684).

[?Allestree, Richard], *The Practice of Christian Graces. Or the Whole Duty of Man* (1659; 1st pub. 1658).

Ames, William, *The Marrow of Sacred Divinity* (1642).

Arderne, James, *Directions concerning the Matter and Stile of Sermons*, ed. J. Mackay (Oxford, 1952).

Aristotle, *The Nicomachean Ethics*, with trans. by H. Rackham (rev. edn, Cambridge, Mass., 1934).

Politics, with trans. by H. Rackham (Cambridge, Mass., 1932).

The Arminian Magazine, I–XX (1778–97).

Asty, John, 'Memoirs of the Life of John Owen', *A Complete Collection of the Sermons of . . . John Owen* (1721).

Bacon, Francis, *The Advancement of Learning and New Atlantis*, ed. A. Johnston (Oxford, 1974).

Essays, ed. J. Pitcher (Harmondsworth, 1985).

Bacon, Nathaniel, *A Relation of the Fearful Estate of Francis Spira* (1649).

Barrow, Isaac, *The Theological Works of Isaac Barrow, D.D.*, 8 vols. (Oxford, 1830).

The Works of the Learned Isaac Barrow, D.D., ed. J. Tillotson, I (1683).

Baxter, Richard, *Aphorismes of Justification* (1649).

An Extract of Mr. Richard Baxter's Aphorisms of Justification, ed. J. Wesley (Newcastle, 1745).

An Appeal to the Light (1674).

Autobiography, abridged J. M. Lloyd Thomas, ed. N. H. Keeble, rev. edn (1985).

Richard Baxter and Margaret Charlton . . . Being the Breviate of the Life of Margaret Baxter, ed. J. T. Wilkinson (1928).

Richard Baxter's Catholick Theologie (1675).

Rich. Baxter's Confession of his Faith (1655).

How far Holinesse is the Design of Christianity (1671).

254

[Baxter, Richard] *The Judgment of Non-Conformists about the Difference between Grace and Morality* (1676).

Poetical Fragments (2nd edn, 1689).

The Practical Works of the Late Reverend and Pious Mr. Richard Baxter, 4 vols. (1707).

Practical Works of the Rev. Richard Baxter, 23 vols., ed. W. Orme (1830).

Reliquiae Baxterianae (1696).

The Scripture Gospel Defended (1690).

[Bayly, Lewis], *The Practice of Pietie* (1643; 1st pub. c. 1612).

[Bentley, Richard], *The Life and Character of . . . the Late Dr. Edw. Stillingfleet* (1710).

[Bernard, Richard], *The Isle of Man* (9th edn, 1634).

Birch, Thomas, *The Life of the Most Reverend Dr. John Tillotson* (2nd edn, 1753).

Blount, Charles, *Miscellaneous Works*, (New York, 1979; facsimile of 1st edn, 1695).

Boswell, James, *Boswell's Life of Johnson*, ed. G. B. Hill, rev. L. F. Powell, 6 vols. (Oxford, 1934–50).

Browne, Peter, *The Procedure, Extent and Limits of Human Understanding* (New York, 1976; facsimile of 1st edn, 1728).

Bunyan, John, *Grace Abounding to the Chief of Sinners*, ed. R. Sharrock (Oxford, 1962).

The Holy War, ed. R. Sharrock and J. F. Forrest (Oxford, 1980).

The Life and Death of Mr. Badman, ed. J. F. Forrest and R. Sharrock (Oxford, 1988).

The Miscellaneous Works, gen. ed. R. Sharrock, 11 vols. (Oxford, 1976–, in progress).

The Pilgrim's Progress, ed. J. B. Wharey, rev. R. Sharrock (2nd edn, Oxford, 1960).

The Whole Works, ed. G. Offor, 3 vols. (1862).

Burnet, Gilbert, *A Discourse of the Pastoral Care* (3rd edn, 1713; 1st pub. 1692).

An Exposition of the Thirty-Nine Articles of the Church of England (1699).

Bishop Burnet's History of His Own Time, 2 vols. (1724, 1734).

A Sermon Preached at the Funeral of . . . John [Tillotson] . . . *Lord Archbishop of Canterbury* (1694).

Some Passages of the Life and Death of John Earl of Rochester (Menston, Yorks, 1972; facsimile of 1st edn, 1680).

A Supplement to Burnet's History of My Own Time, ed. H. C. Foxcroft (Oxford, 1902).

Calamy, Edmund (the first), *The Godly Mans Ark* (2nd edn, 1658).

Calamy, Edmund (the third), *An Abridgment of Mr. Baxter's History of his Life and Times* (1702).

A Defence of Moderate Non-Conformity, Part II (1704).

An Historical Account of My Own Life, 2 vols. (1829).

Memoirs of the Life of the Late Revd. Mr. John Howe (1724).

The Cambridge Platonists, ed. G. R. Cragg (New York, 1968).

The Cambridge Platonists, ed. C. A. Patrides (1969).

Chillingworth, William, *The Religion of Protestants a Safe Way to Salvation* (Oxford, 1638).

Mr. Chillingworth's Book called The Religion of Protestants a Safe Way to Salvation, made more generally useful [abridged S. Patrick] (1687).

Cicero, Marcus Tullius, *De Re Publica; De Legibus*, with trans. by C. W. Keyes (1952; 1st pub. 1928).

The Speeches, with trans. by N. H. Watts (1964; 1st pub. 1931).

Clarke, Samuel, *A Demonstration of the Being and Attributes of God 1705; A Discourse concerning the Unchangeable Obligations of Natural Religion 1706* (Stuttgart, 1964; facsimile of 1st edns).

[Clifford, Martin], *A Treatise of Humane Reason* (1674).

The Confession of Faith and Catechisms, agreed upon by the Assembly of Divines at Westminster (1650).

The Confession of Faith; The Larger and Shorter Catechisms, with the Scripture Proofs at large (Edinburgh, 1855).

Crisp, Tobias, *Christ Alone Exalted*, ed. S. Crisp (1690).

Cudworth, Ralph, *A Treatise concerning Eternal and Immutable Morality* (1731).

The True Intellectual System of the Universe, ed. T. Birch (2nd edn. 1743; 1st pub. 1678).

Culverwell, Nathaniel, *An Elegant and Learned Discourse of the Light of Nature*, ed. R. A. Greene and H. MacCullum (Toronto, 1971).

A Defence of Natural and Revealed Religion: Being a Collection of the Sermons preached at the Lecture founded by the Honourable Robert Boyle, ed. S. Letsome and J. Nicholl, 3 vols. (1739).

Dell, William, *The Tryal of Spirits* (1653).

Dent, Arthur, *The Plaine Mans Path-way to Heaven* (1601).

Des Maizeaux, Pierre, *An Historical and Critical Account of the Life and Writings of Wm. Chillingworth* (1725).

A Directory for the Publique Worship of God (1644).

Doddridge, Philip, *Calendar of the Correspondence of Philip Doddridge D.D.*, ed. G. F. Nuttall (1979).

The Correspondence and Diary of Philip Doddridge, D.D., ed. J. D. Humphreys, 5 vols. (1829–31).

A Course of Lectures on the Principal Subjects in Pneumatology, Ethics, and Divinity, ed. S. Clark (1763).

Letters to and from the Rev. Philip Doddridge, D.D., ed. T. Stedman (Shrewsbury, 1790).

The Works of the Rev. P. Doddridge, D.D., ed. E. Williams and E. Parsons, 10 vols. (Leeds, 1802–5).

[Eachard, John], *The Grounds and Occasions of the Contempt of the Clergy and Religion enquired into* (1670).

Edwards, Jonathan, *The Great Awakening*, ed. C. C. Goen, Volume IV of *The Works of Jonathan Edwards* (New Haven, Conn., 1972).

Religious Affections, ed. J. E. Smith, Volume II of *The Works of Jonathan Edwards* (New Haven, Conn., 1959).

Erasmus, *The Colloquies*, trans. C. R. Thompson (Chicago, Ill., 1965).

Evelyn, John, *The Diary*, ed. E. S. de Beer, 6 vols. (Oxford, 1955).

Fell, John, *The Life of the Most Learned, Reverend and Pious Dr. H. Hammond* (1661).

Fielding, Henry, *Amelia*, ed. M. C. Battestin (Oxford, 1983).

Fletcher, John, *The Works of the Rev. John Fletcher*, 7 vols. (1825).

Fowler, Edward, *The Design of Christianity* (1671).

[Fowler, Edward?], *Dirt Wip't Off* (1672).

Libertas Evangelica (1680).

[Fowler, Edward], *The Principles and Practices, of Certain Moderate Divines of the Church of England* (1670).

[Fowler, Edward], *The Principles and Practices, of Certain Moderate Divines of the Church of England, abusively called Latitudinarians* (2nd edn, 1671).

Fox, George, *The Journal*, ed. J. L. Nickalls (1975).

Gibbons, Thomas, *Memoirs of the Rev. Isaac Watts, D.D.* (1780).

[Glanvill, Joseph], *An Essay concerning Preaching* (1678).

Glanvill, Joseph, *Essays on Several Important Subjects in Philosophy and Religion* (1676), Vol. VI of *Collected Works*, facsimile edn (Hildesheim, 1979).

[Glanvill, Joseph] *A Seasonable Defence of Preaching* (1678).

Goodwin, Thomas, *Certaine Select Cases Resolved* (1647).

The Works of Thomas Goodwin, D.D., 5 vols. (1681–1704).

[Gough, Strickland], *An Enquiry into the Causes of the Decay of the Dissenting Interest* (2nd edn, 1730).

Graves, Richard, *The Spiritual Quixote*, ed. C. Tracy (1967).

Grotius, Hugo, *The Truth of Christian Religion*, trans. S. Patrick (3rd edn, 1689).

Hammond, Henry, *A Practical Catechisme* (1648; 1st pub. 1644).

Of the Reasonableness of Christian Religion (1650).

Herbert, Edward, *Lord Herbert of Cherbury's De Religione Laici*, ed. and trans. H. R. Hutcheson (New Haven, Conn., 1944).

De Veritate, ed. and trans. M. H. Carré (Bristol, 1937).

[Hill, Richard], *A Review of all the Doctrines taught by the Rev. Mr. John Wesley* (2nd edn, 1772).

Hobbes, Thomas, *Leviathan*, ed. C. B. Macpherson (Harmondsworth, 1968).

Howe, John, *The Whole Works of the Rev. John Howe, M. A.*, ed. J. Hunt, 8 vols. (1822).

Hume, David, *Enquiries concerning Human Understanding and concerning the Principles of Morals*, ed. L. A. Selby-Bigge and P. H. Nidditch (3rd edn rev., Oxford, 1975).

The Natural History of Religion and Dialogues concerning Natural Religion, ed. A. W. Colver and J. V. Price (Oxford, 1976).

Jackson, Thomas, ed., *The Lives of Early Methodist Preachers*, 6 vols. (3rd edn, 1865–6).

Jennings, John, *Two Discourses* (1723).

Keach, Benjamin, *The Progress of Sin* (4th edn, 1707).

[Keach, Benjamin], *The Travels of True Godliness* (3rd edn, 1684).

Keate, George, *An Account of the Pelew Islands, situated in the Western Part of the Pacific Ocean. Composed from the Journals and Communications of Captain Henry Wilson* (2nd edn, 1788).

Law, William, *A Practical Treatise upon Christian Perfection* (1726).

A Serious Call to a Devout and Holy Life (1729).

Leighton, Robert, *The Whole Works of . . . Robert Leighton, D.D., Archbishop of Glasgow*, ed. J. N. Pearson, 4 vols (1825).

Locke, John, *An Essay concerning Human Understanding*, ed. P. H. Nidditch (Oxford, 1975).

Works, 9 vols. (12th edn, 1824).

Luther, Martin, *A Commentarie of Master Doctor Martin Luther upon the Epistle of S. Paul to the Galathians* (1635).

Meade, Matthew, *The Almost Christian Discovered* (1662).

Middleton, Conyers, *A Free Inquiry into the Miraculous Powers, which are supposed to have subsisted in the Christian Church* (1749).

The Minutes of the First Independent Church (now Bunyan Meeting) at Bedford 1656–1766, ed. H. G. Tibbutt (Bedford, 1976).

More, Henry, *A Collection of Several Philosophical Writings*, 2 vols. (New York, 1978; facsimile of 2nd edn, 1662).

Enchiridion Ethicum (New York, 1930; facsimile of *An Account of Virtue: or, Dr. Henry More's Abridgment of Morals, Put into English*, 1690).

An Explanation of the Grand Mystery of Godliness (1660).

A Modest Enquiry into the Mystery of Iniquity, The First Part (1664).

Nelson, Robert , *The Life of Dr. George Bull* (1714).

The New Whole Duty of Man (1741).

Origen, *Contra Celsum*, trans. and ed. H. Chadwick (Cambridge, 1980; 1st pub. 1953).

Owen, John, *The Works*, ed. W. H. Goold, 24 vols. (1850–5).

[Palmer, Samuel], *A Defence of the Dissenters Education in their Private Academies* (1703).

Palmer, Samuel, *A Vindication of the Learning, Loyalty, Morals and Most Christian Behaviour of the Dissenters* (1705).

The Life of the Rev. Isaac Watts, D.D., by the late Dr. Samuel Johnson, with Notes (2nd edn, 1791).

[Parker, Samuel], *A Discourse of Ecclesiastical Politie* (1670).

Patrick, Simon, *The Auto-biography of Symon Patrick, Bishop of Ely* (Oxford, 1839).

P[?], S[?], *A Brief Account of the New Sect of Latitude-Men* ed. T. A. Birrell (Los Angeles, Ca., 1963; facsimile of 1st edn, 1662).

The Works of Symon Patrick, D.D., ed. A. Taylor, 9 vols. (Oxford, 1858).

Penn, William, *No Cross, No Crown* (1669).

P[enn], W[illiam], *The Sandy Foundation Shaken* (1668).

Pope, Walter, *The Life of Seth Lord Bishop of Salisbury*, ed. J. B. Bamborough (Oxford, 1961).

Rowe, Elizabeth, *Devout Exercises of the Heart*, ed. I. Watts (8th edn, 1770; 1st pub. 1737).

The Savoy Declaration of Faith and Order 1658, ed. A. G. Mathews (1959).

[Scougal, Henry], *The Life of God in the Soul of Man*, ed. G. Burnet (1677).

Sherlock, William, *A Discourse concerning the Knowledge of Christ, and our Union and Communion with him* (1674).

Sibbes, Richard, *The Complete Works*, ed. A. B. Grosart, 7 vols. (Edinburgh, 1872).

Smith, John, *Select Discourses*, ed. J. Worthington (1660).

Sprat, Thomas, *History of the Royal Society*, ed. J. I. Cope and H. W. Jones (St Louis, Miss., 1959).

Stillingfleet, Edward, *The Bishop of Worcester's Answer to Mr. Locke's Letter* (1697).

The Bishop of Worcester's Answer to Mr. Locke's Second Letter (1698).

A Discourse in Vindication of the Doctrine of the Trinity (1697).

[Stillingfleet, Edward], *A Letter to a Deist* (1677).

Origines Sacrae, or a Rational Account of the Grounds of Christian Faith (1662).

A Rational Account of the Grounds of Protestant Religion (1665).

The Unreasonableness of Separation (1681).

Taylor, Jeremy, *The Rule and Exercises of Holy Living* (1650).

Taylor, John, *The Scripture-Doctrine of Original Sin Proposed to Free and Candid Examination* (3rd edn, 1750).

Telford, John, *Wesley's Veterans*, 7 vols. (1909–14).

Tillotson, John, *The Works of the Most Reverend Dr. John Tillotson, Lord Archbishop of Canterbury*, ed. R. Barker, 12 vols. (1742–3).

[Tindal, Matthew], *Christianity as Old as the Creation* (1730).

Venn, Henry, *The Complete Duty of Man* (1763).

Warburton, William, *The Doctrine of Grace* (2nd edn, 1763).

Ward, Richard, *The Life of the Learned and Pious Dr. Henry More*, ed. M. F. Howard (1911).

Watson, Richard, ed., *A Collection of Theological Tracts*, 6 vols. (Cambridge, 1785).

Watts, Isaac, *The Works of the Rev. Isaac Watts, D.D.*, ed. E. Parsons, 7 vols. (Leeds, 1800).

ed., *The Assembly's Catechism, with Notes* (4th edn, 1736).

et al., *Faith and Practice Represented in Fifty-four Sermons on the Principal Heads of the Christian Religion*, 2 vols. (2nd edn, 1739).

Webster, John, *Academiarum Examen* (1654).
Wesley, John, *A Christian Library*, 50 vols. (Bristol, 1749–55).
  A Christian Library, ed. T. Jackson, 30 vols. (2nd edn, 1819–27).
  [Wesley, John], *The Complete English Dictionary* (3rd edn, 1777).
  Explanatory Notes upon the New Testament (1755).
  The Journal of the Rev. John Wesley, A.M., ed. N. Curnock, 8 vols. (1909–16).
  The Letters of the Rev. John Wesley, A.M., ed. J. Telford, 8 vols. (1931).
  Wesley's Revision of the Shorter Catechism, ed. J. A. Macdonald (Edinburgh, 1906).
  The Works of the Rev. John Wesley, M.A., 32 vols. (Bristol, 1771–4).
  The Works of the Rev. John Wesley, ed. T. Jackson, 14 vols. (3rd edn, 1831).
  The Works of John Wesley, ed. F. Baker *et al.* (Oxford, 1975–84; Nashville, Tenn.,
    1984–, in progress): Vols. I–IV, *Sermons*, ed. A. C. Outler (Nashville, 1984–7);
    Vol. XI, *The Appeals to Men of Reason and Religion*, ed. G. R. Cragg (Oxford, 1975);
    Vols. XXV–VI, *Letters* I–II, ed. F. Baker (Oxford, 1980–2).
[Wesley, Samuel], *A Letter from a Country Divine to his Friend in London. Concerning the
  Education of the Dissenters in their Private Academies* (2nd edn, 1704).
Wesley, Samuel, *A Defence of a Letter Concerning the Education of Dissenters* (1704).
Whichcote, Benjamin, *Moral and Religious Aphorisms . . . To which are added, Eight Letters*,
  ed. S. Salter (1753).
  Select Sermons, ed. [Lord Shaftesbury] (1698).
  Several Discourses, 4 vols., Vols I–III ed. J. Jeffery, Vol. IV ed. S. Clarke (1701–7).
  Θεοφορουμηνα Δόγματα, *Or, some Select Notions* (1685).
  The Works of the Learned Benjamin Whichcote, D.D., 4 vols. (Aberdeen, 1751).
Whiston, William, *Memoirs of the Life and Writings of Mr. William Whiston* (1749).
Whitefield, George, *Whitfield's Journals*, ed. W. Wale (Gainesville, Fla., 1969; facsimile
  of 1905 edn).
Wilkins, John, *Ecclesiastes, or, A Discourse concerning the Gift of Preaching* (1646); 5th
  impression [1st revised edn] (1669); 6th impression (1675); 7th edn [2nd revised
  edn], ed. J. Williams (1693); 8th edn [3rd revised edn] (1704).
  An Essay towards a Real Character, and a Philosophical Language (1668).
  A Moderate Church-man the best Christian and Subject (1710).
  Of the Principles and Duties of Natural Religion, ed. J. Tillotson (6th edn, 1710; 1st pub.
    1675).
  Sermons Preach'd upon Several Occasions (1677).
  Sermons Preached upon Several Occasions, ed. J. Tillotson (1682).
Williams, Daniel, *Gospel-Truth Stated and Vindicated* (1692).
[Wollaston, William], *The Religion of Nature Delineated* (1722).

Secondary Sources

Allen, Don Cameron, *Doubt's Boundless Sea: Skepticism and Faith in the Renaissance* (Balti-
  more, Md., 1964).
Allen, W.O.B., and McClure, Edmund, *Two Hundred Years: The History of the Society for
  Promoting Christian Knowledge 1698–1898* (1898).
Allison, C.F., *The Rise of Moralism: The Proclamation of the Gospel from Hooker to Baxter*
  (1966).
Armstrong, Brian G., *Calvinism and the Amyraut Heresy: Protestant Scholasticism and
  Humanism in Seventeenth-Century France* (Madison, Wis., 1969).
Ashley Smith, J.W., *The Birth of Modern Education: The Contribution of the Dissenting
  Academies 1660–1800* (1954).

Baker, Eric W., *A Herald of the Evangelical Revival: A Critical Inquiry into the Relation of William Law to John Wesley and the Beginnings of Methodism* (1948).

Baker, Frank, 'A Study of John Wesley's Readings', *LQHR*, CLXVIII (1943), 140–5, 234–41.

A Union Catalogue of the Publications of John and Charles Wesley (Durham, N.C., 1966).

John Wesley and the Church of England (1970).

Barlow, Richard Burgess, *Citizenship and Conscience: A Study in the Theory and Practice of Religious Toleration in England during the Eighteenth Century* (Philadelphia, 1962).

Bebb, E.D., *Nonconformity and Social and Economic Life 1660–1800* (1935).

Bebbington, D.W., *Evangelicalism in Modern Britain: A History from the 1730s to the 1980s* (1989).

Bedford, R.D., *The Defence of Truth: Herbert of Cherbury and the Seventeenth Century* (Manchester, 1979).

Bennett, G.V., and Walsh, J.D., eds., *Essays in Modern English Church History* (1966).

Bogue, David and Bennett, James, *History of Dissenters, from the Revolution in 1688, to the Year 1808*, 4 vols. (1808–10).

Bolam, C.G., *et al.*, *The English Presbyterians: From Elizabethan Puritanism to Modern Unitarianism* (1968).

Bosher, Robert S., *The Making of the Restoration Settlement: The Influence of the Laudians 1649–1662* (1951).

Brown, John, *John Bunyan: His Life, Times and Work*, rev. F. M. Harrison (1928, 1st pub. 1885).

Butler, D., *Henry Scougal and the Oxford Methodists* (Edinburgh, 1899).

Cannon, William Ragsdale, *The Theology of John Wesley, with Special Reference to the Doctrine of Justification* (Nashville, Tenn., 1946).

Carroll, R.T., *The Common-Sense Philosophy of Religion of Bishop Edward Stillingfleet 1635–1699* (The Hague, 1975).

Carruthers, S.W., *Three Centuries of the Westminster Shorter Catechism* (Fredericton, N.B., 1957).

The Westminster Confession of Faith: Being an Account of the Preparation and Printing of its Seven Leading Editions (Manchester, 1937).

Cassirer, Ernst, *The Platonic Renaissance in England*, trans. J.P. Pettegrove (New York, 1970; German edn 1932, trans. 1st pub. 1953).

Christensen, Francis, 'John Wilkins and the Royal Society's Reform of Prose Style', *MLQ*, VI (1946), 179–87, 279–90.

Clarke, W. K. Lowther, *Eighteenth Century Piety* (1944).

A History of the S.P.C.K. (1959).

Clarke, T. E. S., and Foxcroft, H. C., *A Life of Gilbert Burnet, Bishop of Salisbury* (Cambridge, 1907).

Colie, Rosalie L., *Light and Enlightenment: A Study of the Cambridge Platonists and the Dutch Arminians* (Cambridge, 1957).

Colligan, J. Hay, 'The Antinomian Controversy', *TCHS*, VI (1913–15), 389–96.

Coolidge, J. S., *The Pauline Renaissance in England* (1970).

Coomer, Duncan, *English Dissent under the Early Hanoverians* (1946).

Cope, Jackson I., '"The Cupri-Cosmits": Glanvill on Latitudinarian Anti-Enthusiasm', *HLQ*, XVII (1954), 269–86.

Joseph Glanvill: Anglican Apologist (St Louis, Miss., 1956).

Coyle, Martin, *et al.*, eds., *Encyclopaedia of Literature and Criticism* (1990).

Cragg, Gerald R., *Freedom and Authority: A Study of English Thought in the Early Seventeenth Century* (Philadelphia, Penn., 1975).
  From Puritanism to the Age of Reason: A Study of Changes in Religious Thought within the Church of England 1660 to 1700 (Cambridge, 1950).
  Puritanism in the Period of the Great Persecution 1660–1688 (Cambridge, 1957).
  Reason and Authority in the Eighteenth Century (Cambridge, 1964).
Crane, R.S., *The Idea of the Humanities and Other Essays Critical and Historical*, 2 Vols. (Chicago, Ill., 1967).
Cuming, G.J., ed., *Studies in Church History*, Vol. II (1965).
Davie, Donald, *A Gathered Church: The Literature of the English Dissenting Interest 1700–1930* (1978).
Davies, Horton, *The Worship of the English Puritans* (1948).
  Worship and Theology in England, Vol. I, *From Cranmer to Hooker 1534–1603* (Princeton, N.J., 1970); Vol. II, *From Andrewes to Baxter and Fox 1603–1690* (Princeton, N.J., 1975); Vol. III, *From Watts and Wesley to Maurice 1690–1850* (Princeton, N.J., 1961).
Davies, Rupert, and Rupp, Gordon, eds., *A History of the Methodist Church in Great Britain*, Vol. I (1965).
Davis, Arthur Paul, *Isaac Watts: His Life and Works* (1948; 1st pub. 1943).
Deacon, Malcolm, *Philip Doddridge of Northampton* (Northampton, 1980).
De Pauley, W. C., *The Candle of the Lord: Studies in the Cambridge Platonists* (1937).
The Dictionary of National Biography, 2 vols. (compact edn. Oxford, 1975).
Elmen, Paul, 'Richard Allestree and *The Whole Duty of Man*', *The Library*, 5th series, VI (1951), 19–27.
English, John C., 'John Wesley and the Anglican Moderates of the Seventeenth Century', *ATR*, LI (1969), 203–20.
Fiering, Norman, *Jonathan Edwards's Moral Thought and its British Context* (Chapel Hill, N.C., 1981).
  Moral Philosophy at Seventeenth-Century Harvard: A Discipline in Transition (Chapel Hill, N. C., 1981).
Flew, R. Newton, *The Idea of Perfection in Christian Theology: An Historical Study of the Christian Ideal for the Present Life* (1934).
Fox Bourne, H.R., *The Life of John Locke*, 2 vols. (1876).
George, Charles H. and Katherine, *The Protestant Mind of the English Reformation 1570–1640* (Princeton, N.J., 1961).
Golder, Harold, 'Bunyan's Valley of the Shadow', *MP*, XXVII (1929), 55–72.
Gordon, Alexander, *Addresses Biographical and Historical* (1922).
Greaves, Richard, L., *John Bunyan* (Abingdon, 1969).
  'John Bunyan's *Holy War* and London Nonconformity', *BQ*, XXVI (1975), 158–68.
Green, I.M., *The Re-Establishment of the Church of England 1660–1663* (Oxford, 1978).
Green, Richard, *The Works of John and Charles Wesley: A Bibliography* (1896).
Green, V.H.H., *The Young Mr. Wesley: A Study of John Wesley and Oxford* (1961).
Greenall, R.L., ed., *Philip Doddridge, Nonconformity and Northampton* (Leicester, 1981).
Greene, Robert A., 'Whichcote, Wilkins, "Ingenuity", and the Reasonableness of Christianity', *JHI*, XLII (1981), 227–52.
Griffin, Martin I.J. Jr., 'Latitudinarianism in the Seventeenth-Century Church of England' (unpublished Ph.D. thesis, Yale University, 1962).
Griffiths, Olive M., *Religion and Learning: A Study in English Presbyterian Thought from the Bartholomew Ejections (1662) to the Foundation of the Unitarian Movement* (Cambridge, 1935).

Haller, William, *The Rise of Puritanism* (New York, 1957; 1st pub. 1938).

Harris, F. W., 'The Life and Work of Philip Doddridge as Illustrating the Internal and External Relationships of the English Independent Churches during the First Half of the Eighteenth Century' (unpublished B. Litt. thesis, University of Oxford, 1950).

Harrison, A.W., *Arminianism* (1937).

The Beginnings of Arminianism to the Synod of Dort (1926).

'Wesley's Reading in Georgia', *PWHS*, XV (1926), 113–17.

'Wesley's Reading at Oxford', *PWHS*, XV (1926), 161–5.

'Wesley's Reading during the Voyage to Georgia', *PWHS*, XIII (1922), 25–9.

Harth, Phillip, *Contexts of Dryden's Thought* (Chicago, 1968).

Swift and Anglican Rationalism: The Religious Background of A Tale of a Tub (Chicago, Ill., 1961).

Henderson, G.D., *Religious Life in Seventeenth-Century Scotland* (Cambridge, 1937).

Herbert, Thomas Walter, *John Wesley as Editor and Author* (Princeton, 1940).

Hill, Christopher, *The Experience of Defeat: Milton and Some Contemporaries* (1984).

A Turbulent, Seditious and Factious People: John Bunyan and his Church (Oxford, 1988).

The World Turned Upside Down: Radical Ideas during the English Revolution (New York, 1973; 1st pub. 1972).

Hilson, J.C. *et al.*, *Augustan Worlds* (Leicester, 1978).

Hindley, J. Clifford, 'The Philosophy of Enthusiasm: A Study in the Origins of "Experimental Theology"', *LQHR*, CLXXXII (1957), 99–108, 199–210.

Holmes, Geoffrey, *British Politics in the Age of Anne* (1967).

ed., *Britain after the Glorious Revolution 1689–1714* (1969).

Hunt, John, *Religious Thought in England from the Reformation to the End of the last Century*, 3 vols. (1870–3).

Hunter, Michael, *Science and Society in Restoration England* (Cambridge, 1981).

Hughes, H. Trevor, 'Jeremy Taylor and John Wesley', *LQHR*, CLXXIV (1949), 296–304.

Hussey, Maurice, 'John Bunyan and Arthur Dent', *Theology*, LII (1949), 459–63.

Jacob, Margaret C., *The Newtonians and the English Revolution 1689–1720* (Hassocks, Sussex, 1976).

Jones, J.R., ed., *The Restored Monarchy 1660–1688* (1979).

Jones, Richard Foster, *et al.*, *The Seventeenth Century: Studies in the History of English Thought and Literature from Bacon to Pope* (Stanford, 1951).

Jordan, W.K., *The Development of Religious Toleration in England*: Vol. II, *From the Accession of James I to the Convention of the Long Parliament* (1936); Vol. III, *From the Convention of the Long Parliament to the Restoration* (1938); Vol. IV, *Attainment of the Theory and Accommodations in Thought and Institutions* (1940).

Keeble, N.H., 'The Autobiographer as Apologist: *Reliquiae Baxterianae* (1696)', *PS*, IX (1986), 105–19.

Richard Baxter: Puritan Man of Letters (Oxford, 1982).

ed., *John Bunyan: Conventicle and Parnassus* (Oxford, 1988).

The Literary Culture of Nonconformity in Later Seventeenth-Century England (Leicester, 1987).

Kendall, R.T., *Calvin and English Calvinism to 1649* (Oxford, 1979).

Knox, E.A., *Robert Leighton, Archbishop of Glasgow: A Study of his Life, Times and Writings* (1930).

Laird, John, *Philosophical Incursions into English Literature* (Cambridge, 1946).

Lawton, George, *John Wesley's English: A Study of his Literary Style* (1962).
Lessenich, Rolf P., *Elements of Pulpit Oratory in Eighteenth-Century England 1660–1800* (Cologne, 1972).
Lindström, Harold, *Wesley and Sanctification* (Stockholm, 1966).
Lord, H.M., 'John Wilkins: A Bibliography' (unpublished Dip. Lib. bibliography, University of London, 1957).
McAdoo, H.R., *The Spirit of Anglicanism: A Survey of Anglican Theological Method in the Seventeenth Century* (1965).
The Structure of Caroline Moral Theology (1949).
McGee, J. Sears, *The Godly Man in Stuart England: Anglicans, Puritans, and the Two Tables 1620–1670* (New Haven, Conn., 1976).
McLachlan, H., *English Education under the Test Acts: Being the History of the Nonconformist Academies 1662–1820* (Manchester, 1931).
McLachlan, H. John, *Socinianism in Seventeenth-Century England* (1951).
Matthews, A. G., *Calamy Revised: Being a Revision of Edmund Calamy's Account of the Ministers and Others Ejected and Silenced, 1660–2* (Oxford, 1934).
Miller, Perry, *The New England Mind: The Seventeenth Century* (Cambridge, Mass., 1954; 1st pub. 1939).
Milner, Thomas, *The Life, Times and Correspondence of the Rev. Isaac Watts, D.D.* (1845; 1st pub. 1834).
Mintz, Samuel, I., *The Hunting of Leviathan: Seventeenth-Century Reactions to the Materialism and Moral Philosophy of Thomas Hobbes* (Cambridge, 1962).
Mitchell, W. Fraser, *English Pulpit Oratory from Andrewes to Tillotson* (1932).
Monk, Robert C., *John Wesley: His Puritan Heritage* (1966).
Moore, Henry, *The Life of the Rev. John Wesley*, 2 vols. (1825).
Murdock, Kenneth B., *Literature and Theology in Colonial New England* (Cambridge, Mass., 1949).
Neal, Daniel, *The History of the Puritans or Protestant Nonconformists: from the Reformation in 1517 to the Revolution in 1688*, ed. J. Toulmin, 5 vols. (1822; 1st pub. 1732–8).
New, John F. H., *Anglican and Puritan: The Basis of their Opposition 1558–1640* (1964).
Newey, Vincent, ed., *The Pilgrim's Progress: Critical and Historical Views* (Liverpool, 1980).
Newton, John A., *Methodism and the Puritans* (1964).
Susanna Wesley and the Puritan Tradition in Methodism (1968).
Nicolson, Marjorie, 'Christ's College and the Latitude-Men', *MP*, XXVII (1929–30), 35–53.
Nuttall, Geoffrey F., *Richard Baxter* (1965).
Richard Baxter and Philip Doddridge: A Study in a Tradition (1951).
ed., *Philip Doddridge 1702–51: His Contribution to English Religion* (1951).
The Holy Spirit in Puritan Faith and Experience (Oxford, 1946).
'Methodism and the Older Dissent: Some Perspectives', *JURCHS*, II (1981), 259–74.
'The MS of *Reliquiae Baxterianae* (1696)', *JEH*, VI (1955), 73–9.
New College, London and its Library (1977).
'Relations between Presbyterians and Congregationalists in England', in *Studies in the Puritan Tradition: A Joint Supplement of the Congregational and Presbyterian Historical Societies* (1964).
Visible Saints: The Congregational Way, 1640–1660 (Oxford, 1957).
et al., eds., *The Beginnings of Nonconformity* (1964).

and Chadwick, Owen, eds., *From Uniformity to Unity 1662–1962* (1962).

Orcibal, Jean, 'Les spirituels français et espagnols chez John Wesley et ses contemporains', *Revue de l'Histoire des Religions* (1951), 50–109.

Orme, William, *Memoirs of the Life, Writings and Religious Connexions of John Owen, D.D.* (2nd edn, 1826).

Osmond, Percy H., *Isaac Barrow: His Life and Times* (1944).

Outler, Albert C., ed., *John Wesley* (New York, 1964).

Overton, J. H. *The Evangelical Revival in the Eighteenth Century* (1886).

Packer, James I., 'The Redemption and Restoration of Man in the Thought of Richard Baxter: A Study in Puritan Theology' (unpublished D.Phil. thesis, University of Oxford, 1954).

Packer, John W., *The Transformation of Anglicanism 1643–1660, with Special Reference to Henry Hammond* (Manchester, 1969).

Parker, Irene, *Dissenting Academies in England* (Cambridge, 1914).

Passmore, J. A., *Ralph Cudworth: An Interpretation* (Cambridge, 1951).

The Perfectibility of Man (2nd edn, 1972).

Pattison, Mark, *Essays*, ed. H. Nettleship, 2 vols. (Oxford, 1889).

Memoirs (1969; 1st pub. 1885).

Phillimore, Robert, *Memoirs and Correspondence of George, Lord Lyttelton, from 1734 to 1773*, 2 vols. (1845).

Pooley, Roger, 'Language and Loyalty: Plain Style at the Restoration', *LH*, VI (1980), 2–18.

Powicke, Frederick J., *A Life of the Reverend Richard Baxter 1615–1691* (1924).

The Reverend Richard Baxter under the Cross 1662–1691 (1927).

The Cambridge Platonists (1926).

Pratt, Anne Stokeley, *Isaac Watts and his Gifts of Books to Yale College* (New Haven, Conn., 1938).

Rack, Henry D., *Reasonable Enthusiast: John Wesley and the Rise of Methodism* (1989).

Reedy, Gerard, S. J., *The Bible and Reason: Anglicans and Scripture in Late Seventeenth-Century England* (Philadelphia, Penn., 1985).

Reventlow, Henning Graf, *The Authority of the Bible and the Rise of the Modern World*, trans. J. Bowden (1984; 1st pub. 1980).

Rivers, Isabel, *Classical and Christian Ideas in English Renaissance Poetry* (1979).

ed., *Books and their Readers in Eighteenth-Century England* (Leicester, 1982).

Roberts, James Deotis, Sr., *From Puritanism to Platonism in Seventeenth Century England* (The Hague, 1968).

Rogers, Henry, *The Life and Character of John Howe, M.A., with an Analysis of his Writings* (1836).

Rowe, Kenneth E., ed., *The Place of Wesley in the Christian Tradition* (Metucken, N.J., 1976).

Salmon, Vivian, *The Study of Language in 17th-Century England* (Amsterdam, 1979).

Sangster, W. E., *The Path to Perfection: An Examination and Restatement of John Wesley's Doctrine of Christian Perfection* (1957; 1st pub. 1943).

Sasek, Lawrence A., *The Literary Temper of the English Puritans* (Baton Rouge, La., 1961).

Schmidt, Martin, *John Wesley: A Theological Biography*, trans. N. P. Goldhawk, 2 vols. in 3 (1962–73).

Sell, Alan P. F., *The Great Debate: Calvinism, Arminianism and Salvation* (Worthing, 1982).

Semmel, Bernard, *The Methodist Revolution* (1974).

[Seymour, A. C. H.], *The Life and Times of Selina Countess of Huntingdon*, 2 vols. (1844).

Shapiro, Barbara J., *Probability and Certainty in Seventeenth-Century England* (Princeton, N.J., 1983).
John Wilkins 1614–1672: An Intellectual Biography (Berkeley and Los Angeles, Ca., 1969).
Shepherd, T. B., *Methodism and the Literature of the Eighteenth Century* (1947).
Simon, Irène, *Three Restoration Divines: Barrow, South, Tillotson*, 2 vols. (Paris, 1967–76).
'Tillotson's Barrow', *ES*, XLV (1964), 193–211, 273–88.
Simon, John S., *John Wesley and the Religious Societies* (1921).
John Wesley and the Methodist Societies (1923).
John Wesley and the Advance of Methodism (1925).
John Wesley the Master-Builder (1927).
and Harrison, A. W., *John Wesley: The Last Phase* (1934).
Sommerville, John C., *Popular Religion in Restoration England* (Gainesville, Fla., 1977).
Spitzer, Leo, *Classical and Christian Ideas of World Harmony*, ed. A. G. Hatcher (Baltimore, Md., 1963).
Spivey, J. T., Jr., 'Middle Way Men, Edmund Calamy, and the Crises of Moderate Nonconformity (1688–1732)' (unpublished D.Phil. thesis, University of Oxford, 1986).
Sprunger, K. L., *The Learned Doctor William Ames: Dutch Backgrounds of English and American Puritanism* (Urbana, Ill., 1972).
Spurr, John, 'Anglican Apologetic and the Restoration Church' (unpublished D.Phil. thesis, University of Oxford, 1985).
'The Church of England, Comprehension and the Toleration Act of 1689', *EHR*, CIV (1989), 927–46.
'"Latitudinarianism" and the Restoration Church', *HJ*, XXXI (1988), 61–82.
'"Rational Religion" in Restoration England', *JHI*, XLIX (1988), 1–23.
Stephen, Leslie, *History of English Thought in the Eighteenth Century*, 2 vols. (1962; 1st pub. 1876).
Stephenson, William E., 'Isaac Watts and Bishop Wilkins's *Ecclesiastes*', *NQ*, CCXI (1966), 454–5.
Stoeffler, F. Ernest, *German Pietism during the Eighteenth Century* (Leiden, 1973).
The Rise of Evangelical Pietism (Leiden, 1965).
Stranks, C. J., *Anglican Devotion: Studies in the Spiritual Life of the Church of England between the Reformation and the Oxford Movement* (1961).
The Life and Writings of Jeremy Taylor (1952).
Sykes, Norman, *Church and State in England in the XVIIIth Century* (Cambridge, 1934).
Edmund Gibson, Bishop of London 1669–1748 (1926).
'The Sermons of Archbishop Tillotson', *Theology*, LVIII (1955), 297–302.
From Sheldon to Secker: Aspects of English Church History 1660–1768 (Cambridge, 1959).
Talon, Henri, *John Bunyan: The Man and his Works*, trans. B. Wall (1951).
Thomas, Roger, *Daniel Williams 'Presbyterian Bishop'* (1964).
Tindall, William York, *John Bunyan Mechanick Preacher* (New York, 1964; 1st pub. 1934).
Toon, Peter, *The Emergence of Hyper-Calvinism in English Nonconformity 1689–1765* (1967).
God's Statesman: The Life and Work of John Owen (Exeter, 1971).
Toulmin, Joshua, *An Historical View of the State of the Protestant Dissenters in England . . . from the Revolution to the Accession of Queen Anne* (1814).
Towlson, Clifford W., *Moravian and Methodist: Relationships and Influences in the Eighteenth Century* (1957).

Trevor-Roper, Hugh, *Catholics, Anglicans and Puritans: Seventeenth-Century Essays* (1989; 1st pub. 1987).

Tucker, Susie I., *Enthusiasm: A Study in Semantic Change* (Cambridge, 1972).

Tulloch, John, *Rational Theology and Christian Philosophy in England in the Seventeenth Century*, 2 vols. (Edinburgh, 1872).

Tyacke, Nicholas, *Anti-Calvinists: The Rise of English Arminianism c. 1590–1640* (Oxford, 1987).

Tyerman, L., *The Life and Times of the Rev. John Wesley, M.A.*, 3 vols. (3rd edn, 1876).
The Life of the Rev. George Whitefield, B.A., 2 vols. (1876).
Wesley's Designated Successor: The Life, Letters and Literary Labours of the Rev. William Fletcher (1882).

van den Berg, J., and van Dooren, J. P., *Pietismus und Réveil* (Leiden, 1978).

Van Leeuwen, Henry G., *The Problem of Certainty in English Thought 1630–1690* (The Hague, 1963).

Voitle, Robert, *The Third Earl of Shaftesbury 1671–1713* (Baton Rouge, La., 1984).

Wakefield, Gordon Stevens, *Puritan Devotion: Its Place in the Development of Christian Piety* (1957).
ed., *A Dictionary of Christian Spirituality* (1983).

Wallace, Dewey D., Jr., *Puritans and Predestination: Grace in English Protestant Theology, 1525–1695* (Chapel Hill, N.C., 1982).

Watkins, Owen, C., *The Puritan Experience* (1972).

Watts, Michael R., *The Dissenters: From the Reformation to the French Revolution* (Oxford, 1985; 1st pub. 1978).

Westfall, Richard S., *Science and Religion in Seventeenth-Century England* (New Haven, Conn., 1958).

Whiting, C. E., *Studies in English Puritanism from the Restoration to the Revolution, 1660–1688* (1931).

Wilbur, Earl Morse, *A History of Unitarianism: Socinianism and its Antecedents* (Cambridge, Mass., 1946).
A History of Unitarianism in Transylvania, England and America (Cambridge, Mass., 1952).

Williamson, George, *Seventeenth Century Contexts* (1960).

Yolton, John W., *John Locke and the Way of Ideas* (1956).

Index